Pro Access 2007

Martin WP Reid

Apress®

Pro Access 2007

Copyright © 2007 by Martin WP Reid

ISBN-13 (pbk): 978-1-59059-772-9

ISBN-10 (pbk): 1-59059-772-9

Printed and bound in the United States of America 9 8 7 6 5 4 3 2 1

Lead Editor: Jim Sumser
Technical Reviewer: Judith Myerson
Editorial Board: Steve Anglin, Ewan Buckingham, Gary Cornell, Jason Gilmore, Jonathan Gennick, Jonathan Hassell, James Huddleston, Chris Mills, Matthew Moodie, Jeff Pepper, Paul Sarknas, Dominic Shakeshaft, Jim Sumser, Matt Wade
Project Manager: Richard Dal Porto
Copy Edit Manager: Nicole Flores
Copy Editor: Ami Knox
Assistant Production Director: Kari Brooks-Copony
Production Editor: Janet Vail
Compositor: Linda Weidemann, Wolf Creek Press
Proofreader: Lori Bring
Indexer: Carol Burbo
Cover Designer: Kurt Krames
Manufacturing Director: Tom Debolski

Distributed to the book trade worldwide by Springer-Verlag New York, Inc., 233 Spring Street, 6th Floor, New York, NY 10013. Phone 1-800-SPRINGER, fax 201-348-4505, e-mail orders-ny@springer-sbm.com, or visit http://www.springeronline.com.

For information on translations, please contact Apress directly at 2560 Ninth Street, Suite 219, Berkeley, CA 94710. Phone 510-549-5930, fax 510-549-5939, e-mail info@apress.com, or visit http://www.apress.com.

The source code for this book is available to readers at http://www.apress.com in the Source Code/ Download section.

*To my wife, Patricia,
and our children, Aine, Liam, Maeve,
Emer, Roisin, and Eoin*

Contents at a Glance

Contents

About the Author

MARTIN WP REID is an analyst at Queen's University Belfast, where he works in the Training and Assessment Unit. Martin has coauthored two books, *SQL Access to SQL Server* and *Beginning Access 2002 VBA*. He has also written several articles for Microsoft MSDN and other web sites.

Martin is married to Patricia, and together they have six children: Aine, Liam, Maeve, Emer, Roisin, and Eoin. He lives in Belfast, Northern Ireland. He is heavily involved with AccessD, a professional Internet-based Access database support list where he can be found most nights!

About the Technical Reviewer

JUDITH M. MYERSON is a systems architect and engineer. Her areas of interest include middleware technologies, enterprise-wide systems, database technologies, application development, web development, web services, object-oriented engineering, software engineering, network management, servers, security management, information assurance, standards, RFID technologies, and project management. Judith holds a master of science degree in engineering and several certificates, and is a member of the IEEE organization. She has reviewed/edited a number of books, including *Hardening Linux, Creating Client Extranets with SharePoint 2003, Microsoft SharePoint: Building Office 2003 Solutions, Microsoft SQL Server Replication, Microsoft Content Management Server Field Guide, Microsoft Operations Manager 2005 Field Guide, Pro SMS 2003, Pro InfoPath 2007,* and *Windows Vista: Beyond the Manual.*

Acknowledgments

I would like to note the help I received from many individuals on the AccessD list, a group of database developers who give freely of their time and expertise. In particular, I would like to thank John Colby (http://www.colbyconsulting.com), Rocky Smolin (http://www.e-z-mrp.com), Marty Connelly, Drew Wutka, Shamil Salakhetdinov, A. D. Tejpal, Bryan Carbonnell, Gustav Brock, and Robert L Steward. If you are looking for developers, anyone on this list would be an asset to any project.

I would also like to thank Clint Covington at Microsoft for his assistance, information, and opening doors. Clint always responded in a timely and professional manner even when I asked stupid questions.

In addition, the following individuals provided permissions to reference existing works and web sites: Scott Mitchell (http://www.fourguysfromrolla.com) and Brian Goldfarb (http://www.asp.net); both of their sites are more than worth a visit.

I would also like to acknowledge the team at Apress for giving me the opportunity to work on this title, in particular Jim Sumser, who provided support and encouragement for many months; Ami Knox, who got the short end of the stick as my copy editor (Ami did a fantastic job on my poor grammar and spelling); and Judith Myerson, my technical reviewer, for the effort and work.

Thanks go to Ben Saltzer and Jackie Nevelow (http://www.bartracks.com) for permission to steal some code and reference their wonderful product BarTracks, and for their eternal friendship, support, and unique insights into software design.

Finally, a tip of the hat to Patrick Schmid, who provided support, instruction, and a great web site for those starting out with RibbonX. Patrick's site, http://pschmid.net, should be your first port of call when looking at RibbonX.

Introduction

Many people ask, "Why write a book?" Usually, I respond by saying it's an ego trip; it's certainly not for the money, as John Colby recently pointed out. I wrote this book because I had something to say about Access, the most maligned database development environment on the market. In my view and the view of people I consider to be some of the best programmers in the world, this is an attitude based mostly on ignorance of the software and what it can do. I also wrote this book in response to the "Access is dead" argument. Access is a long way from dead, and I believe this book goes some way to showing that. Access is moving forward, perhaps in a direction many developers don't like. It's moving toward the Internet, .NET, and SharePoint. I hope this book helps you accompany it on that journey.

Who This Book Is For

This book is intended for intermediate-to-experienced Microsoft Access developers, but it will also provide value to those just starting out with Access. It also provides a solid grounding in Access 2007 and the new feature set, including coverage on using Windows SharePoint Services as the back-end data store.

How This Book Is Structured

Following is a brief rundown of what each of the chapters in this book covers:

- *Chapter 1, "Access 2007: What's New?"*: This chapter provides a high-level overview of the new features available in Access 2007 and lays the groundwork for the more detailed material in succeeding chapters.

- *Chapter 2, "Text and Templates"*: This chapter begins looking at how you can save Access 2007 objects as text files, which leads into a discussion of the new template tools available in Access 2007. You learn the structure of existing templates and how to create your own.

- *Chapter 3, "Getting Up and Running with RibbonX"*: Here we look at the new navigation system in Access 2007, RibbonX. Following a short introduction to the RibbonX, it's straight into creating your own custom Ribbons and changing existing Ribbons in Access.

- Chapter 4, *"Data Collection Using Microsoft Outlook 2007"*: Starting off with a high-level overview of the new data collection feature, the chapter moves on to look at the structures used to enable this feature, including a section on beginning the process of executing data collection tasks via VBA.

- *Chapter 5, "Introduction to Classes in VBA"*: Here you will get an introduction to class programming and VBA. This chapter provides you with the skills required to take the next steps in your programming with Microsoft Access.

- *Chapter 6, "RAD Development for SQL Server 2000/2005 Express"*: Using SQL Server as the data store and Access 2007 as the front-end application, I discuss some of the issues and problems you will face together with techniques and code examples to resolve many common problems.

- *Chapter 7, "Working with the SQL Server 2005 Express Tool Set"*: Following on from Chapter 6, we take a closer look at working with data held on SQL Server 2005 Express including stored procedures, Access Data Projects, and linked tables.

- *Chapter 8, "DAO, Complex Data Types, and Macros"*: This chapter provides programming techniques and material covering the new data types added to Access 2007.

- *Chapter 9, "Introduction to SharePoint Server"*: One of the major changes in Access is the use of SharePoint as the back-end data store. This chapter introduces you to Windows SharePoint Server and explains how it is structured and introduces how to work with WSS data from Access 2007.

- *Chapter 10, "Access and SharePoint Applications"*: Working with SharePoint as a data store, here we look at the various features within Access and SharePoint, including working with list data offline, caching, and linking to WSS via VBA.

- *Chapter 11, "Access, SharePoint, and SharePoint Designer"*: This chapter gives an overview of using Microsoft SharePoint Designer to work with existing WSS web sites. This chapter introduces you to some of the features of the software used to customize WSS sites.

- *Chapter 12, "Getting Started with .NET Tools"*: Many developers are often asking when Access will work with managed code. In this chapter, we look at two of the .NET tools available when working with Microsoft Access 2007: Visual Basic 2005 Express and Visual Web Developer 2005 Express. While not directly working inside Microsoft Access, the example projects demonstrate the features of managed code.

- *Chapter 13, "Code You Can Steal!"*: Here you'll find examples of real-life DAO and ADO from the AccessD database developers group, the highlight of which is a trip to Area 51 from within Microsoft Access 2007.

- *Appendix, "RibbonX and Custom Add-Ins"*: The appendix is based on materials provided to me by Patrick Schmid, one of the best exponents of RibbonX. This appendix provides you with design guidelines to follow when working with RibbonX, particularly if you are considering designing your own Microsoft Access add-ins.

Prerequisites

For the Windows SharePoint examples, you will need access to Windows SharePoint Services running on Windows Server 2003. Both products can be downloaded freely from http://www. microsoft.com. In the case of Windows Server 2003, a timed-out demo is available. For the web and .NET example applications, you will require Visual Web Developer 2005 Express and Visual Basic 2005 Express.

Downloading the Code

Example code will be available from the Apress site (http://www.apress.com). To download it, click the Source Code/Download link and select the title of this book from the list on the page that appears.

Contacting the Author

Please feel free to contact me at Martireid@gmail.com. It may take a day or two, but I will respond to all e-mails.

CHAPTER 1

■■■

Access 2007: What's New?

It has been a widely held belief that Microsoft Access has been neglected during many of the upgrades to Microsoft Office over the years. However, with the latest release, Microsoft Access 2007, many changes have been made to the interface and the database engine, and integration with Microsoft Outlook 2007 has been added in the form of Collect and Update Data via Email. It is also now possible, by downloading an add-in, to save objects to various formats, such as PDF.

Several new data properties are available, and increased server capability in the shape of Microsoft Office SharePoint Server 2007 has been added to Access—all adding up to a major increase in attention by Microsoft to what is the most widely used desktop database in the world.

Also new in Access 2007 is the increased focus on macros including new error control. While this might surprise many developers, it will meet the needs of many power users who place greater reliance on macros when creating Access applications. The new database templates are macro driven, and while they do contain VBA code, they are developed using embedded macros. Another change, one long called for, is the redevelopment of the Northwind example database traditionally available with Access. The latest version of this example database, Northwind 2007, has been totally redesigned from the ground up and makes extensive use of class modules for data interaction.

Already feeling forgotten by the Access development team, Access developers may not appreciate some of the changes, particularly the shift in focus toward full integration with SharePoint Server, but I hope this book can assist you in moving toward this new storage medium and in familiarizing yourself with this new enhanced version of Access. This chapter provides an overview of the changes facing you when you move to Access 2007. Detailed coverage of the topics I touch on here will appear later in the book. For now, I just give you a taste of some of the changes made to your favorite database application.

The biggest changes in Access 2007 are those that have been made to the JET database engine, which has been referred to as ACE during the beta process by Microsoft. The new engine is a private copy of JET used by the Office 2007 team and has been refined and added to for Access 2007. The default database type is the ACCDB format created using Access 2007, but MDB files are still supported in the new release. Table 1-1 shows some of the differences in behavior when using both the new engine and Access 2007 as opposed to Access 2000/2003 MDB files.

Table 1-1. *Access 2007 and Access 2000/2003 Feature Comparison*

Access 2007	Access 2000/2003
ACCDB file type	Cannot be used
Complex data types	Not available
Attachment data type	Not available
Append-only memo fields	Not available
Offline support for linking to SharePoint	Not available
Linking tables to ACCDB files	Not available
Encrypting with database password	Not available
Linking to SharePoint	Some data types not supported
Rich text support	Not available (will appear as HTML)
Date picker	Not available
Control layouts	Independent controls
Linking to Excel 2007	Not available
Embedded macros	Not available
Control auto-size	Not available
Tabbed Document mode	Not available
Navigation Pane	Database Container
Custom groups in Navigation Pane	Not available
Tables and View mode	Not available
Ribbon	Command bar
Saving imports and exports	Not available
Improvements in filtering and sorting	Not available
Save Database As command	Not available
Sharing database on SharePoint	Not available
Upsizing to SharePoint	Not available
Trust Center	Not available
New sorting and grouping	Not available
Property Sheet Task Pane	Not available
Creating schema in datasheet	Table design only
Office 2007 Options Center	Not available
Editable value lists	Not available
Editing list items for combo and lists	Not available
SharePoint Site Manager	Not available
Form split view	Not available
Search box	Not available
Custom caption for navigation	Not available

The following features are only supported in the new ACCDB database file type:

- Complex data (multivalue data types)

- Attachment data type

- Append-only memo fields

- Compressed image storage for any picture property

- The ability to send an Access file as an e-mail attachment

- Full support for linked tables to SharePoint

- The ability to publish to SharePoint

- The ability to take SharePoint data offline

- The ability to create linked tables to other ACCDB files

- Rich text support

As you can see, there are many differences between this new version of Access and previous versions. Now that you've gotten a brief overview of some of the changes Access 2007 offers, let's take a quick tour of the program, starting with the interface.

Access 2007 Interface

The first thing to hit you when you open Access is the new graphical user interface (GUI), which is used not only by Access, but also by the entire Office 2007 product line. To be honest, although it looks good, at first I preferred the old menu system. It took me some time to find out where all my favorite menu options had gone. Once I got used to the new dynamic menus, I again felt at home with Access. (The appendix at the back of this book maps the old menu system to the new system.)

However, many users will instantly appreciate this new interface. One complaint I always get from Access beginners is that, when the program first starts, they are left looking at a blank database window wondering what to do next. This is no longer the case, as several "getting started" templates come with the application, and many more can be downloaded from Office Online at http://office.microsoft.com/en-gb/access/FX100487571033.aspx. Links to the available template databases are provided within the Access 2007 user interface. At the time of writing, the following templates are planned for Access 2007:

- Assets

- Contacts

- Events

- Issues

- Tasks

- Customer Service

- Projects

- Marketing Projects

- Sales Pipeline Database

- Students

- Faculty

You can access the templates from the Access splash screen on startup or when clicking the Office button and selecting File ➤ New. Links are also provided on the splash screen to training resources, templates, and downloads.

In keeping with the Microsoft view of the world and tying in with the move toward Share-Point Server, these templates are mainly tracking-type applications useful to some users, but the developer and power user community will find them lacking in major functionality. However, it is possible to create custom user templates that focus on your own particular business model. We will be looking at current templates and creating your own in Chapter 2. At some point soon, a new tool will be available from the Access development team to make the template creation process much easier: it will allow developers to avoid having to get to grips manually with the underlying XML file and folder structures.

Templates provide both the developer and the user with a "getting started" opportunity, and this in itself is to be welcomed. Figure 1-1 shows the new-look interface when Northwind 2007 is first opened and you have logged in.

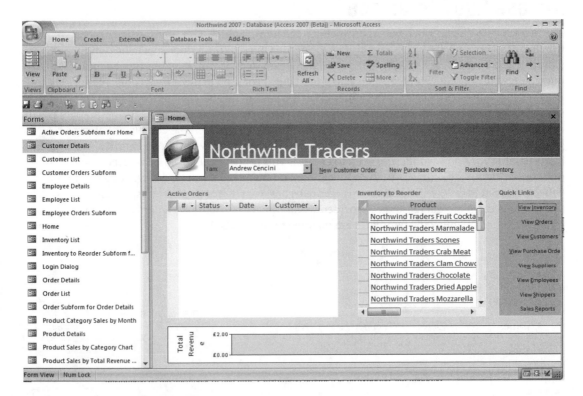

Figure 1-1. *The new Access interface*

■**Note** Templates may also provide a new business opportunity for you. How many times have standard users screwed up a database? Countless consulting projects can arise out of poorly designed applications. There is nothing to stop developers from using the same techniques employed by Microsoft and Access 2007 to create and sell third-party templates for Access 2007. Worth considering?

The user selects the required application template from the interface (or opens an existing database) and follows the instructions for downloading and installing it as a working database. Once you have a database open, the new user interface really takes hold. It uses a dynamic menu system called *Ribbons*. Ribbons and options available change to reflect the task being carried out. A tabbed interface for database objects now makes it possible to have several objects open at once—which can be either a help or a hindrance. Databases created in previous versions open using the standard Access multiple document interface (MDI).

When creating a new database application, Access by default creates a blank table called Table 1. This feature is designed to give the user a starting place when building applications, but developers may find it extremely irritating! The new table determines the appropriate data type as the user enters data, and it can and in all probability should be redesigned as usual in Table Design view.

Navigation Pane Replaces Database Window

The database window is gone, replaced by a new highly customizable Navigation Pane. The Navigation Pane can be organized by Access object, filtered by object types, or totally customized by the developer or end user. Customized groups can be exported to and imported from other databases, all more or less in the same vein as Access 2003. In this case, it is also possible to group related objects together—for example, a table and all its related objects, forms, queries, and reports.

PDF Support Added

PDF support was something long desired by Access developers who in the past relied on third-party tools to provide this flexibility. Now, developers need no longer look to third-party add-ins in order to publish PDF files, as this capability is now available using Office 2007. PDF support must be installed by downloading a particular add-in from http://office.microsoft.com/en-gb/access/HA101675271033.aspx.

■**Note** PDF support is available in all Office 2007 applications; it is not restricted to Access 2007.

Access 2007 Ribbons

The new Office 2007 menu system is comprised of two types of Ribbon-based menu: regular Ribbons, which will always be available, and dynamic task-based Ribbons, which are available when completing a specific task. Many existing users of Access will at first find Ribbons somewhat confusing as they try and work out where all their old favorite commands have gone. One or two older Access menu items are no longer available; for example, the Access Table Wizard has been removed and replaced by a simple Ribbon command used to insert a new table. The following are the new base Ribbon menus available from the main Access menu:

- Home tab

- Create tab

- External Data tab

- Database Tools tab

- Add-ins tab

Of course, many additional Ribbons are available to you depending on the task being carried out. These are referred to as *contextual Ribbons* and are hidden or unhidden as required when the application is running. The appendix at the back of this book contains details on the available Ribbon commands within Access compared to those used in Access 2003.

As you may have gathered from the list of base Ribbon menus, the new menu system consists of a set of tabs. Clicking a tab reveals groups that each contain a set of related commands. For example, the Create tab contains a group providing commands used to insert a new table (the Table group) and a group that gives you the option to add tables using prebuilt table templates (the Table Templates group). Figure 1-2 shows the Table Templates group.

Figure 1-2. *Table Templates group options*

Figure 1-3 shows the Access Create Ribbon. The options are task based and therefore grouped accordingly.

Figure 1-3. *Access Create Ribbon*

If you want to get to the heart of an Office 2007 Ribbon, it's time to learn some XML, because a Ribbon receives its structure from an XML file. We will be looking at Ribbons in much more detail in Chapter 3, including customization. However, it should be said that customizing Ribbons is a little removed from the ability of those who are used to creating custom command bars in the Access interface. Many developers will rely on third-party tools to assist in customization rather than take the leap into XML and .NET languages. This will be useful for developers who have fairly simple needs, for example, turning off menu functions and perhaps creating your own menu options (for instance, a drop-down list presenting a set of reports to the user).

A third-party tool used to customize Ribbons has been developed by one of the Office 2007 beta testers and is available from `http://pschmid.net/blog/category/ribbonx/`. Chapter 3 demonstrates the functionality of Ribbons and the customization features available to you in Access 2007. In the meantime, I strongly suggest you download the add-in. At the time of writing, there is no charge associated with this add-in. However, a developer's version is also available for a small charge. In my opinion, this is well worth the cost.

The new interface also contains a Quick Access Toolbar (QAT), which can be customized with those menu options you use frequently. QAT options are globally available throughout Access rather than as dynamic Ribbon options. This is a useful feature that can help a new user get to grips quickly with the new menu structures. Microsoft recommends that the QAT not be used by developers to position their own commands on the Ribbon. The QAT is designed to permit users to add items they find useful from the existing Ribbon, rather than developers adding their own items to the QAT programmatically. It is also possible that the QAT will change in further releases of Access 2007, and developer changes made to the QAT may not be supported.

■**Tip** You can minimize the Ribbon to save screen space by right-clicking a tab and selecting Minimize Ribbon from the context menu. To maximize the Ribbon, simply click one of the tabs.

Right-clicking a tab item and selecting Customize Quick Access Toolbar (QAT) will open the Access Options dialog box from which any of the available Ribbon commands, controls, or tools can be added or removed. The QAT can be customized for the current database only or all databases opened using Access 2007. Figure 1-4 shows the default QAT before customization.

Figure 1-4. *Quick Access Toolbar*

For applications created in other versions, Office 2007 is backward compatible in as far as your "old" custom menus will still be available. It's well worth noting that there is no object model to permit you to interact with a Ribbon. In addition, little in the way of user customization is available for standard users in terms of creating new Ribbons. For many, it's a case of being stuck with what you've got!

Access Options

The Access Options dialog box provides you with quick access to almost all the configurable options available to you within Access 2007. Each set of options is grouped by a specific category. Some of the options will affect Access only, while others apply to Office 2007 generally. Rather than bore you with the standard options, the following list focuses on those that may be important to you, new in this release, or useful in development.

Popular: Options that are most popular with users. Of course, as this has been decided by Microsoft, it is a little off as the options available, Always use Clear Type, Screen Tip Style, and so on, would not jump out at me as being the most popular options!

Current Database: Options that affect the currently open database, for example, options to add an application title or icon, to turn off Layout view, and one option that will prove useful to many developers, to turn on or off the Navigation Pane. Within the Current Database options, developers can also indicate a custom Ribbon ID to use for this database in place of the built-in Ribbons.

Datasheet: Formatting options for Datasheet view. Using this option, you can select fonts to use, display of grid lines in forms, and default cell effects.

Object Designers: Options that you can set to affect how various design tools are configured for Access. The options are in distinct groups as follows:

- Table Design
- Query Design
- Form Design
- Error Checking

Proofing: Encompasses several options including spell checking, grammar checking, and autocorrection. Many Access developers do not use the autocorrection features available within Access, as they can cause problems with database performance and have been a longtime developer issue. However, it is believed that the performance issues surrounding autocorrection have been resolved with Access 2007.

Advanced: Several options that can be set to deal with how Access interacts with your data and users can interact with an application. The following option groups are available:

- Editing

- Display

- Printing

- General

- Advanced

Customization: Useful to help add or remove Ribbon options from the QAT using the new Access customization dialog box. Users can place frequently used items on the QAT in a similar way to working with command bars in previous versions.

Add-Ins: Listing of all add-ins currently being used by Access. This gives a quick overview of any third-party development tools you happen to be using.

Trust Center: Accesses the Trust Center, one of those areas of Access 2007 you will either love or hate. In all probability, many users will set the trust level to the lowest possible to avoid all the nagging messages that could result when they open a database containing a macro. The recommended approach from Microsoft is to leave the settings at their default: full functionality. Two settings are available in the Trust Center: Show the message bar in all applications when content has been blocked and Never show information about blocked content. On my system, when I am writing, I turn them off. To be honest, I got fed up with getting a nagging message every time I went to do an example for this book and found I had to choose Enable Active Content. Of course, I then realized I could set a folder as a trusted location and resolve the issue that way. That has worked out OK and is a much more sensible approach than turning off everything. Files placed into the Trust Center will not be challenged by the Access security features that block active content. The following locations are marked as trusted when you install Microsoft Office 2007: \Program Files\Microsoft Office\Templates and \Program Files\Microsoft Office\Office12\Startup.

Resources: Contains links to online resources to assist users when working with Access. Links are available to the Office web site, interactive Office 2007 diagnostics, online help and resources, software updates, and a contact Microsoft feature.

As you can see, there are many options, controls, and tools available to you to help with customization of the program and your application without your having to resort to code. However, all options will be available to the end user as well, and in Chapter 3 we will be looking at specific approaches to help close these gaps in customization.

Access 2007 Tables

Tables in Access 2007 remain much as they were in previous versions of the application. There is little that can be done to add or decrease the functionality of a basic table; however, some new data types have been added to complement the ability of Access to deal with other applications (most notably SharePoint Server), and additional table properties have been provided.

The data filtering ability when in Standard view has been greatly improved. The new interface also permits multiple objects to open in either Design or Standard view using a tabbed interface to move between items, for example, multiple forms currently opened. Figure 1-5 shows the new form interface with several form objects open.

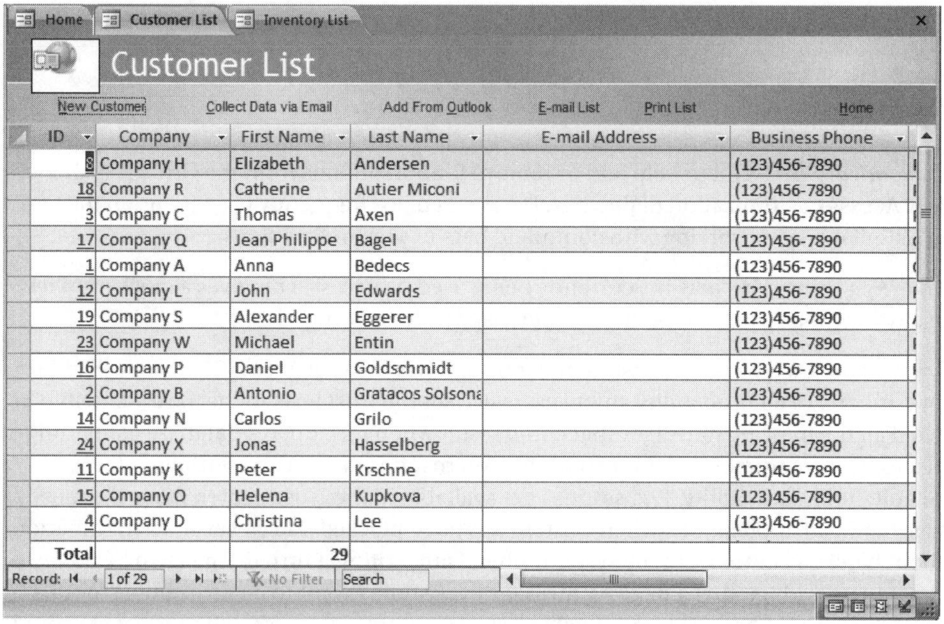

Figure 1-5. *Multitabbed object interface*

Complex Data Types

Developers will notice that a new data type is now available in Access 2007 to support the use of complex data types, for example, documents that have been associated with a database record. This new data type, attachment, permits the user to store many different types of information with a single database record without complex programming by the developer.

A property is also available when using lookup lists, Allow Multiple Values, that does just as it says: it permits a user or developer to associate multiple data values with a single field without having to resolve a many-to-many relationship. One of the main reasons for this is a feature in SharePoint Server lists that allows you to associate multiple values with particular data, for example, multiple developers assigned to a project. Behind such changes is the need to fit Access into the same underlying schema as that used by Share-Point. Another reason is the Microsoft focus on insulating Access users from the finer points of database design, though how they can be expected to take advantage of this feature without knowing what a many-to-many relationship is in the first place escapes me!

To support these new features and, of course, integration with SharePoint, two major changes have taken place in Access 2007—a new data engine (ACE) and extensions to Data Access Objects (DAO) have been added. It should be some consolation to know that under the covers within the data engine a fully normalized relationship is created (that is, the many-to-many relationship is resolved using standard normalization techniques). This relationship is not currently available to you via the user interface. It has been strongly suggested during the beta process that this functionality be provided to developers at the very least. At the time of writing, access to this area is not available.

■**Note** Now before the relational purists jump out of whatever chair they are reading this in, it's real important to say that such changes are intended purely for the world of SharePoint. Now I know that's all fine in theory; we will begin to see hundreds of Access applications using these features, and for many small users this will not be an issue. It will be a real issue in applications that are to be upsized to SQL Server. Such fields will upsize but contain issues that we will need to resolve.

Multivalue Fields

Multivalue fields are not the same text fields in which users are permitted to key in several values (for example, developer names). In this case the data is fully normalized, but within the database engine as opposed to within the table structures. This can be seen especially when it comes to working with these values via DAO and VBA.

This design addition is intended to shield the end user from the classic many-to-many relationship and can be applied to the Lookup property and the attachment data type, introduced earlier. Once the Allow Multiple Values property is enabled, a checklist is available within the field that permits users to select one or more values from the presented list.

Activating the Allow Multiple Values Property

As mentioned previously, Allow Multiple Values is a new property that has been added to the Lookup property, which has long been available in Access. In this case, by setting this property to Yes, it is possible to permit users to select one or more data items to associate with a particular lookup field.

To activate the Allow Multiple Values property, you could, for example, create a new table called Employees with standard fields (fldForeName, fldSurName, and so on) and a second table named Tasks containing a new field named fldAssignedTo. In the field properties for fldAssignedTo, you would click the Lookup tab, change Display As to Combo Box, and set the Allow Multiple Values property to Yes.

Using the Attachment Data Type

The attachment data type permits the storage of multiple file attachments within a single field and is a useful tool when working with documents and other resources. It is no longer necessary to deal with API calls to open File dialog boxes or worse still save such objects within the database file. Internally, the attachment is stored in a binary field, and the underlying relationships are not exposed via the interface. There is no way to see the true nature of the relationship via the GUI. To open an attachment, double-click the file name within the Attachment dialog box.

To illustrate this new data type, I will walk you through a short example.

1. Create a table named tblAttachment.

2. Create a single field with a data type of attachment, and name the field fldMyDocs.

3. Save the table.

4. Open the table in Standard view.

5. Double-click the attachment paper clip icon.

This opens the Attachment dialog box, which can be used to navigate to and select required files.

6. Click Add.

7. Select a file name using the Choose File dialog box.

8. Click Open.

9. Click OK to close the dialog box.

Once finished, note that the field uses a standard attachment icon and shows the number of files referenced.

To view the attachment, you would double-click the field cell containing the attachment to open the Attachment dialog box. Using the dialog box, you can

- Add additional attachments.

- Remove attachments.

- Open an attachment.

- Save an attachment.

- Save the attachment under a new name.

In order to see the real effects of this additional data type, open the relationship window by clicking Database Tools ➤ Relationships. Look at the Attachment table, particularly the Attachments field, and note the additional values: Attachments.FileData, Attachments.FileName, and Attachments.FileType. These are revealed (as shown in Figure 1-6) by clicking the plus symbol beside the Attachment field name. The values are self-descriptive: FileData refers to the file being stored, FileName is just that, the name of the file, and FileType refers to the file extension.

Figure 1-6. *Attachment data type field values*

Let's look at another example, this time using DAO to load an attachment located in C:\AccessAttachments into tblMyDocs. The following code fragment loads a file from the following path, C:\AccessAttachments\test.doc.

Note Remember to change the path and the file name to reflect your own setup before running this example.

```
Public Sub loadfile()
Dim rsttblDocs As DAO.Recordset
Dim rstGetData As DAO.Recordset
Set db = CurrentDb
' Get the parent recordset
Set rsttblDocs = db.OpenRecordset("tblMyDocs")
' Put the parent record into edit mode
rsttblDocs.Edit


' Get the attachment recordset
Set rstGetData = rsttblDocs.Fields("fldMyDocs").Value
' Set first attachment to loaded picture
rstGetData.Edit
rstGetData.Fields("FileData").LoadFromFile ("C:\AccessAttachments\test.doc")
rstGetData.Update
' Update the parent record
rsttblDocs.Update
End Sub
```

Note the use of two recordsets: rsttblDocs to open the main parent recordset and rstGetData to load the "child" recordset to permit access to the attachment field contained within the parent recordset.

Filtering Tables

It has long been possible to filter data directly with an Access table, but this feature has been enhanced in Access 2007. Tables now have a built-in sort-and-filter facility located to the right of each field and indicated by a down arrow. It is possible to sort in ascending and descending order and to filter any of the values being displayed. The filter type is dynamic, changing according to the data type of the field selected. Table 1-2 shows the various filters that you can use at table level according to the data type of the field selected.

Table 1-2. *Access 2007 Table Filters*

Data Type	Filters
Text	Equals, Does Not Equal, Begins With, Does Not Begin With, Contains, Does Not Contain, Ends With, Does Not End With
Date/Time	Equals, Does Not Equal, Before, After, Between, All Dates in a Period
Number/Currency	Equals, Does Not Equal, Smaller Than, Larger Than, Between

Basically the user is creating a standard Access query using the criteria to build up the query. You can open the Query window to view the process by clicking the Data tab and selecting Advanced ➤ Advanced Filter/Sort.

Complex filters can be created directly at the table level by users. The ability to save a complex filter as a stored query is another neat feature of the new filter ability. Once you have filtered a table, select Save As from the File menu and save the filter as a query. The underlying SQL used to filter the table will now be available to you.

The Create Ribbon also provides a new feature in Access, Table Templates, which allows you to choose from a small number of prebuilt table designs. From an Access viewpoint, they can be badly designed. For example, the Task table template includes field names such as % Complete; note the use of the wildcard symbol in the table name and that almost every field contains spaces in field names. The first job therefore for anyone using the templates will be to change most, if not all, the field names to meet proper design standards. Of course, the reason the tables are designed this way is to enable easy integration with SharePoint.

Access 2007 Forms

Wow! Where to start with forms? There are lots of changes as far as forms are concerned, from new properties to a whole new way of designing and working with objects. Some of the new features are useful, some not. You have the ability to work with a form design while viewing data. Through the Create tab, the following menu options are available:

- *Basic Form*: A standard Access form.

- *Split Form*: A new form containing a datasheet at the top and a standard Access form at the bottom. The top of the screen displays multiple records, while the form section shows the detail.

- *Multiple Items*: Standard continuous form.

- *Pivot Chart*: Pivot table–type chart based on the underlying record source.

- *Blank*: A standard blank disconnected form.

- *More Forms*: Pivot table, modal form, and datasheet. Also gives you access to the Form Wizard.

Note When displaying an attachment data type via forms, the attachment is represented by an icon within an object frame. For example, a Word document attachment will be represented using the MS Word icon. Double-click the icon to open the Attachment dialog box. A small floating toolbar is also available to enable you to move through the attachment files.

Form Layouts

You now have three options for how you want to work with forms: Layout view, Design view, and Form view. A layout is used to group like objects together on the form for positioning. Control objects can then be manipulated as a group. Control objects can be detached from their layout group and repositioned elsewhere on the screen. Select an object, right-click, and select Remove From Layout on the context menu. Figure 1-7 shows the Formatting Ribbon, which contains this and other layout options when you are in Layout view.

Figure 1-7. *Layout view and Formatting Ribbon*

Another neat feature added to forms is the ability to add existing fields while in Design view mode (by clicking Add Existing Fields from the Tools group). This feature reminded me of Data Access Pages (DAPs) in which fields are available within a tree view, and you can drag and drop fields from tables onto the form background. Once a field is selected and dragged onto a form, all nonrelated tables are removed from the tree view and the record source of the form is set to a SELECT statement. Figure 1-8 shows the new Field List Pane. In this case, I have clicked the Show all tables link located at the bottom left of the pane. Note this text is dynamic and will change to read Show only fields in the current record source.

Rich text support has also been added within forms, such as the PDF support mentioned earlier, removing the requirement to purchase third-party add-ins for this release. Rich text is available as a field property in the Design view of a table for memo data types only. To activate rich text, select a text field in Table Design view, select Text Format in the field properties, and select Rich Text. Once the property has been set at the table level, you use a small floating toolbar to format the text within the control in Form view. You may also use the formatting options on the main Ribbon. Rich text support is provided using HTML mainly to ensure support when the data is moved to SharePoint Server. Figures 1-9 and 1-10 show the Design and Layout Ribbons and their associated tools.

Figure 1-8. *Inserting existing fields*

Figure 1-9. *Design Ribbon for a form*

Figure 1-10. *Layout Ribbon for a form*

Rich text format is a nice idea; however, at the time of writing, the floating toolbar is difficult to see but fairly easy to use, and personally I always use the main Ribbon. But that's a minor issue compared to the functionality it gives the user and is in keeping with the apparent decision by Microsoft to reduce dependence on third-party tools when working with Access 2007.

New Form Properties

Table 1-3 lists the new form properties available with Access 2007. As you can see, many of these properties are related to the additional ways in which forms can be presented to the user, for example, split-view forms.

Table 1-3. *New Form Properties*

Tab	Property	Comments
Format	Split Form Orientation	Options are On Left, On Right, Top, Bottom.
Format	Split Form Datasheet	Options are Allow Edits, Read Only.
Format	Split Form Splitter Bar	Options are Yes, No.
Format	Save Splitter Bar Position	Options are Yes, No.
Format	Split Form Printing	Options are Form Only, Datasheet Only.
Format	Navigation Caption	Free text caption for navigation buttons.
Data	Filter on Load	Options are Yes, No. (Applies filter on form load.)
Data	Apply OrderBy on Load	Options are Yes, No. (Applies OrderBy to Form start-up.)
Event	After Layout	Options are VBA, Macro for Pivot Table AfterUpdate Event.
Event	Before Render	Options are VBA, Macro for Pivot Table BeforeRender Event.
Event	After Render	Options are VBA, Macro for Pivot Table AfterRender Event.
Event	After Final Render	Options are VBA, Macro for Pivot Table AfterFinalRender Event.
Other	RibbonName Use Default Paper Size Display on SharePoint Site	Loaded Customization Ribbon ID for On Open. Options are Yes, No. Options are Do Not Display, Follow Table Settings.

List Items

A new feature behind lists is the ability to use object properties to open a form, which enables users to edit list items. This works in much the same way as a Not In List event (which is still available); in this case, an object property, List Items Edit Form, is used, which is the form to open if a value entered is not already available in the list. You still need to code the form and repopulate the combo box with the newly added value. Another property, Allow Value List Edits, permits users to add or edit values to an object's value list. A new dialog box, Edit List Items, is opened to allow this.

Reports

Just like Access forms, reports now permit design changes in Data view, filtering in Design view, and interactive grouping. It's also possible to build clickable reports with a drill-down capability using the new report On Click event. An example of this is shown in the Issues template: clicking a contact name in the report opens the contact form in response to the On Click event. The Issues template is available when you create a new database and can be selected in the opening splash screen. Report objects now have the following events available:

- On Click

- On Exit

- On Got Focus

- On Lost Focus

- On Click

- On Dbl Click (Double Click)

- On Mouse Down

- On Mouse Move

- On Mouse Up

- On Key Down

- On Key Up

- On Key Press

Macros

As mentioned earlier, macros have received considerable focus with this release of Access, perhaps on a par with SharePoint and the focus on the power user experience. Several new macro-specific features have been added, and as you may already know, all of the Microsoft template databases contain no VBA in the form control events—they are all macro driven. One of the first areas you might notice the use of macros is in the Command Button Wizard, which, rather than produce VBA, will create an embedded macro. The following is the macro added by the Command Button Wizard to open a form:

```
OpenForm
Assignment List, Form, , , , Normal
```

The use of macros by wizards to create an *embedded macro* (that is, the macro is now saved with the form and can be copied between objects as opposed to appearing in the Navigation Pane and in the event property) is a major departure for Microsoft. One advantage is that such macro-driven functionality will work in a database with code disabled. Oh, and before I forget, I better mention macro error control. Yes, Microsoft has added error trapping to macros! The new OnError feature is much like its equivalent in VBA and allows you to totally ignore the error using the Next action. The Fail action reverts back to no error control, and your execution halts in its tracks, much like the original action of a failed macro. With the Macro Name action, the OnError feature of the macro will pass execution to a named label. However, if your error-handling macro fails, it's back to normal behavior, and the whole show stops working! Another new feature, and one which may prove more useful to developers, is that of temporary variables, or *TempVars*. TempVars are a variant store, and they exist during the lifetime of the application. Many developers avoid the use of variants, as they can add additional overhead to executions, and prefer to explicitly declare variable data types. TempVars have .Value, .Remove, and .RemoveAll properties and could prove useful to store values required elsewhere in code during execution. TempVars provide you with an enumerated collection when you work in VBA and can be used to store data only.

Within a macro, TempVars can be used as local variables to hold values, for example, a form to open or a report to print. They can also be passed between macros and VBA, although many developers will simply use them within macros.

Modules

At long last, developers can use a wheel mouse within the VBA IDE. That's about it for the VBA interface. Other than the mouse wheel, modules remain much as they were in Access 2003.

Working with SharePoint Server

SharePoint is one area where a lot of effort has been made by the Access development team into improving both the user and the developer experience. For users, Access can act as a front-end interface to data held on SharePoint Servers. Chapters 9 through 11 look at using SharePoint in some detail and provide a solid overview of what in my view is a great collaboration and development environment not only for Access, but also for the entire Office suite of applications.

For many Access developers, SharePoint will be something they have read about on MSDN or heard briefly mentioned. It's my own belief that SharePoint may well become the data store of choice for many smaller business groups as well as seeing increasing use in larger organizations. SharePoint is a huge product and offers substantial scope for developers, particularly those who would like to move into the world of .NET. As I have already stated, the tracking application templates provided are designed with SharePoint interaction in mind. Such applications also fit in with the new Office Live service being offered by Microsoft. SharePoint is a free downloadable component for the Windows Server 2003 operating system and provides an Internet development environment based on the .NET Framework 2.0. Windows SharePoint Services Version 3 can be downloaded from the Microsoft web site. Within Access 2007, it is possible to

- Link to a SharePoint list.

- Upsize your Access database to SharePoint.

- Take SharePoint data offline for remote use.

- View document version history and auditing information via SharePoint lists.

■**Note** For the examples later in the book, you will require access to a SharePoint site. For those really keen, this is actually possible using freely downloaded software: Windows Virtual Server 2005, an evaluation copy of Windows Server 2003, and Windows SharePoint Services Version 3. Install the software in a virtual environment and off you go! You will only have a limited amount of time to use the evaluation copy of the Windows Server 2003 OS before it deactivates. The rest of the software is yours to keep.

The ability to work with SharePoint data offline will be very useful to many individuals who already work with SharePoint. Using Access, it's possible to connect to a SharePoint web site, take a list down to Access, disconnect from the SharePoint Server, and when ready reconnect and update your SharePoint list with any changes. Members of staff, for example, could download lists of data and documents into Access, work on the information offline, perhaps at a meeting, and when ready connect and update the central data store.

Given the focus SharePoint has received with this release of Office, I think Access developers would be well advised to start looking at what this product brings to the game in terms of functionality and .NET coding. Chapter 9 looks at SharePoint in some more detail and hopefully will encourage you to take a close look at this software, remembering that Windows SharePoint Services is provided free of charge, and all you need is Windows Server 2003.

Security

The biggest blow to many developers will be the removal of user-level security in the new file type. User-level security is supported for MDB files but not ACCDB files. It would appear to be the Microsoft view that user-level security wasn't actually intended to be used for security but rather for custom navigation! The new file type has had security increased using an encrypted database password, which is no longer stored in the database. Support for user-level security will be maintained for earlier versions of Access.

E-Mail Data Collection

Using Access 2007 and Outlook 2007 (to process the replies), it is now possible to issue an InfoPath form, or HTML form, to users, have them complete the form, reply to the e-mail, and automatically update an Access table with the returned data. Users will need Microsoft InfoPath installed in order to respond if you are using the option to send the request using InfoPath forms; otherwise, standard HTML forms will not be an issue. E-mail data collection and Microsoft InfoPath are discussed in Chapter 4.

Summary

Overall, many new features have been added to Access 2007, some of which will prove useful, and others, as is the nature of things, will make your life as a developer a little bit more complex. The focus of SharePoint Services could fundamentally change the way in which we as developers and power users interact with data, building rich interactive applications. As you progress through this book, I hope you can get a sense of where Access is going and pick up some of the skills necessary to fully enjoy the journey.

CHAPTER 2

■■■

Text and Templates

One of the major changes you will see in Microsoft Access 2007 is the availability of template databases mostly directed at users. Templates are provided with Microsoft Office 2007, and additional templates can be downloaded and installed from the Office Online web site. Templates provide a way for users to get up and running right away with basic applications, whereas before when they opened Access, they were left looking at a blank screen. Many users wondering what to do next simply closed the application, never to return. In this chapter, we will look at the structure of Access database templates before I show you how to create your own.

The use of templates also offers the possibility of opening up a new market for Access developers, creating and selling small template databases for Internet download. For corporate developers, templates may well provide the means to create in-house styles and content for user databases, allowing them to get back some developer control over the applications users are creating (for example, ensuring proper relationship design). In this case, a template structure could be provided, leaving the user to simply populate tables with data, forms, and reports. Of course, you could go the whole way and create a corporate style for use in all applications. One area Access developers in particular should keep an eye on is the use of Windows SharePoint Services (WSS) lists and other data collection objects when thinking about templates. This is an area that may see further development by the Access and WSS development teams in the future. Interestingly, over 1.4 million template downloads took place from the Microsoft web site in 2004, demonstrating how popular templates are with users of Access.

■**Note** The Microsoft Blog site `http://blogs.msdn.com/thirdoffive` and other contacts provided a lot of the background information I supply in this chapter, and I would like to thank them for their assistance and permissions.

XML: A Really Brief Overview!

It is impossible to discuss templates in Access without first referencing XML and the overall way XML is being used to define and work with file formats from the other Microsoft Office system applications. Access templates and their structure are just one part of a large architecture developed as an emerging standard by Microsoft.

It is also difficult to discuss Access templates and XML without a common understanding of what XML is and what it is used for. In this section, I will provide a high-level overview of XML, describing the basic structures and functionality available. It should be pointed out that Microsoft will be making tools available at some point during the release of Office 2007 to make working with XML file formats and templates much easier for the developer and power user.

XML is simply a tool that can be used to describe data and its structure. For example, within Access you can export a table as an XML file (right-click and select Export ➤ XML). You can export the data as shown in Listing 2-1, which shows a single customer record from the Northwind database represented as an XML fragment.

Listing 2-1. *Customer Table As XML*

```
<Company>Company A</Company>
<Last_x0020_Name>Bedecs</Last_x0020_Name>
<First_x0020_Name>Anna</First_x0020_Name>
<Job_x0020_Title>Owner</Job_x0020_Title>
<Business_x0020_Phone>(123)456-7890</Business_x0020_Phone>
<Fax_x0020_Number>(123)456-7890</Fax_x0020_Number>
<Address>123 Any Street</Address>
<City>Any City</City>
<State_x002F_Province>WA</State_x002F_Province>
<ZIP_x002F_Postal_x0020_Code>99999</ZIP_x002F_Postal_x0020_Code>
<Country_x002F_Region>USA</Country_x002F_Region>
</Customers>
```

Or you can export the data and the schema of the table as shown in the schema fragment in Listing 2-2, which is an XSD file created by exporting the schema of the Northwind Customers table.

Listing 2-2. *Customers Table Schema*

```
<xsd:appinfo>
<od:fieldProperty name="ColumnWidth" type="3" value="2295"/>
<od:fieldProperty name="ColumnOrder" type="3" value="0"/>
<od:fieldProperty name="ColumnHidden" type="1" value="0"/>
<od:fieldProperty name="Required" type="1" value="0"/>
<od:fieldProperty name="AllowZeroLength" type="1" value="0"/>
<od:fieldProperty name="DisplayControl" type="3" value="109"/>
<od:fieldProperty name="IMEMode" type="2" value="0"/>
<od:fieldProperty name="IMESentenceMode" type="2" value="0"/>
<od:fieldProperty name="UnicodeCompression" type="1" value="1"/>
<od:fieldProperty name="AggregateType" type="4" value="-1"/>
<od:fieldProperty name="WSSFieldID" type="10" value="JobTitle"/>
<od:fieldProperty name="RowSourceType" type="10" value="Table/Query"/>
<od:fieldProperty name="BoundColumn" type="3" value="1"/>
<od:fieldProperty name="ColumnCount" type="3" value="1"/>
<od:fieldProperty name="ColumnHeads" type="1" value="0"/>
```

```
<od:fieldProperty name="AllowMultipleValues" type="1" value="0"/>
<od:fieldProperty name="AllowValueListEdits" type="1" value="0"/>
<od:fieldProperty name="TextAlign" type="2" value="0"/>
<od:fieldProperty name="ShowOnlyRowSourceValues" type="1" value="0"/>
<od:fieldProperty name="GUID" type="9" value="a1nT7kFvTE+1RamEwGZHkQ=="/>
</xsd:appinfo>
```

In this case, you have two different XML files produced, Customers.xml and Customers.xsd, one for the data and the other for the schema. What's useful about this? Well, you could simply take one or both files and import them into another Access database or SQL Server 2005 Standard, Enterprise, or Express Edition. For example, you could take the preceding XSD file and import it into SQL Server, giving you a copy of the customer table structure.

If you are already familiar with HTML, you will immediately begin to understand the structure of the basic XML file generated. Just like HTML, XML uses opening and closing tags, elements, and attributes to describe the structure and content of the file. Unlike HTML, XML allows you to create your own tags for use with your own data and information. So, for example, if I want a tag called RedDog, no problem, I can create one. As a simple example of an XML file, consider this book. This book has a title, an author, chapter numbers, chapter titles, and a page count. You can represent this information in a simple XML file, structured as shown in Listing 2-3.

Listing 2-3. *Book XML*

```
<?xml version="1.0" encoding="ISO-8859-1"?>
<book>
<title>Professional Access 2007</title>
  <author>M WP Reid</author>
<chapter1>
      <title> What's New</title>
      <pages>30</pages>
</chapter>1
</book>
```

When viewed within Microsoft Internet Explorer, you will get a tree view representation of the data structure. In the preceding file, you have a root element, <book>, followed by several other elements; the <chapter1> element contains two child elements, <title> and <pages>, which have an opening and closing element. Each element in the file will have an opening and closing element. It's worth noting that even this simple example has a defined hierarchy of information. The tree view, or document structure, in the browser is noticeably different from the XML text file: that's because IE is using its own built-in style to display the data. Access can also export via the GUI a style sheet to be used to actually present the data in the browser. Of course, I just made the elements up for this example; as stated earlier, this is one of the advantages of XML—you decide on the elements you require to model your data. An XML document therefore contains the following structure:

1. *Declaration*, `<?xml version="1.0" encoding="UTF-8"?>`, which is the first line in all XML documents and is a required attribute.

2. *Elements*, for example, `<Company>Company A</Company>`, tell you the start and end of a particular bit of information. Here, Company A is the value for the company field in the Northwind Customers table. Elements contain an opening tag, `<Company>`, and a closing tag, `</Company>`. The only difference is the closing tag contains a backward slash (/).

3. *Attributes* provide extra information about an element. For example, in `<book title ="My book">`, `title` would be an attribute of the element `book`.

The ability to import and export XML has been available in Access for some time both via the GUI and using VBA.

Office XML

As you will see in this chapter, XML plays an important role in the structure of both Office files generally and Access templates specifically. Essentially, an Access template file is a single file much like, say, a standard Word document (DOCX, which is the new Microsoft Word 2007 file type), isn't it? Well, actually, it's not—it's really a set of XML files that you can break apart and look at. You can see the XML files by renaming the template file to a .zip extension and opening the file using your favorite compression software. What you have is a ZIP package containing all of the XML and XSD files required to tell Access how to create the database application. This section of the chapter provides a general overview of the Office XML file formats and is not specifically about Access. Access XML files, however, have much in common with the Office XML file formats as the same specification applies to all Office System XML documents.

Open Packaging and OpenXML

Office 2007 file formats are, across all the applications, based on *OpenXML*. The Open Packaging convention provides a specification for taking various XML files and other resources and packaging them into a ZIP file. As mentioned previously, all that is required to actually see the ZIP package is to rename a file with a .zip extension and open it in a compression program. Figure 2-1 shows the structure of such an Access 2007 package once extracted to the hard drive.

Figure 2-1. *Folder structure of Access template package*

If you carry out the rename exercise on, for example, a Microsoft Word DOCX file, you will see the same result, and this applies across all the Office 2007 applications. You can actually import any of the XML files from the package describing table structure into an Access database by using the Ribbon: select External Data ➤ XML and navigate to the required XML table structure file in the extracted package.

Microsoft Office 2007 and Access 2007 XML Structures

In terms of Access, think of the ZIP file package as containing a set of parts. These are the individual pieces that taken together form the database template. The same holds true of other Office documents, such as a standard Word document. The ZIP file is a *container* for these parts and is initially represented as a single binary file—in this case, a standard Access 2007 template file format.

Some "parts" are shared across all the Office applications and file types; for example, image files and metadata and others will be specific to the application being worked in, in this case Access 2007. Parts can contain some or all of the following:

- Relationships with other parts

- Links to external documents (for example, a logo file)

- Parts that serve as a connection between other parts

- Metadata

- Actual data

XML relationships will exist in almost all containers for XML documents, with all parts (or almost all) being referenced by at least one relationship. Relationships are implemented using relationship ID, which allows relationships to be independent of schema specifics. Following is an extract from an Access template XML file, Template.xml. You can see the relationship ID and the relationship target, for example, `target="database/objects/tableCustomers.xsd" Id="tableCustomers"`.

■**Note** A code line that is too long to span the book page but should appear on a single line will be indicated using a code continuation character (➡) where the line breaks. Remember that all such code should be entered on a single line, or you will receive an error.

```
<?xml version="1.0" encoding="UTF-8" standalone="yes"?>
<Relationships Xmlns=➡
"http://schemas.openxmlformats.org/package/2006/relationships">
<Relationship Target="database/databaseProperties.xml"➡
Id="DatabaseProperties" Type="http://schemas.microsoft.com/office/access/2005/04/➡
template/properties"/>
```

```
<Relationship Target="database/objects/tableCustomers.xsd"➡
 Id="tableCustomers" Type="http://schemas.microsoft.com/office/access/2005/➡
04/template/object"/>
<Relationship Target="database/objects/tableEmployeePrivileges.xsd"
Id="tableEmployeePrivileges"
Type="http://schemas.microsoft.com/office/access/2005/04/➡
template/object"/>
<Relationship Target="database/objects/tableEmployees.xsd"➡
Id="tableEmployees" Type="http://schemas.microsoft.com/office/access/2005/04/➡
template/object"/>
```

As I have stated, relationships not only deal with the internal structure of the document or object, but also external links to other objects. For example, when you use the new version of Northwind 2007, there is a company logo in place on the forms; if you check out the XML container for Northwind, you will notice it contains the image file used for the logo, preview.jpeg. This illustrates a feature of the XML package in that it can contain not only resources used to create and populate structures, but also external files for use in the finished database. We look further at Access-specific templates in this chapter, in the section "Built-in Access Templates." But first, you need to have an understanding of Access text formats, discussed next.

Access Text Formats

Before looking at templates, it is worthwhile to look at saving Access objects as text files, as the output from this process shows you the structure of each object. An understanding of this process is useful when we come to look at how the new template files in Access 2007 are structured and created and explore the content of the template XML files.

Saving Objects As Text

Listing 2-4 shows the structure of an Access form when saved as a text file. I have removed a lot of the text simply to save some paper and am only showing the initial part of the file, but you will get the general idea about the structure and nature of the contents. The actual text file runs to several pages in length.

Listing 2-4. *Northwind Customer Form Saved As Text*

```
Version =20
VersionRequired =20
Checksum =1884425071
Begin Form
    RecordSelectors = NotDefault
    AutoCenter = NotDefault
    DividingLines = NotDefault
    AllowDesignChanges = NotDefault
    DefaultView =5
    ScrollBars =0
```

```
TabularCharSet =204
PictureSizeMode =1
DatasheetGridlinesBehavior =3
GridX =24
GridY =24
Width =11055
DatasheetFontHeight =11
ItemSuffix =273
DatasheetGridlinesColor =-2147483632
Tag ="SplitList"
RecSrcDt = Begin
    0x10455ac08d03e340
End
GUID = Begin
    0x4d099361a9a43b4c89b4fce1995f299c
End
```

Note the use of Begin and End to define the form property. Each property will have its own corresponding Begin and End pair used to define each property. For example, the following section defines a form command button:

```
Begin CommandButton
        TextFontCharSet =186
        FontSize =9
        FontWeight =400
        ForeColor =1462991
        FontName ="Arial"
        LeftPadding =30
        TopPadding =30
        RightPadding =30
        BottomPadding =30
        GridlineStyleLeft =0
        GridlineStyleTop =0
        GridlineStyleRight =0
        GridlineStyleBottom =0
        GridlineWidthLeft =1
        GridlineWidthTop =1
        GridlineWidthRight =1
        GridlineWidthBottom =1
    End
```

If you export one of the Northwind 2007 forms, you will also see how the macro "code" is saved with the form definition.

■Note Embedded macros are strictly an Access 2007 deal; they will not work in earlier versions.

How do you get this information about Access objects? You use an undocumented method to copy Access objects as text files. Of course, you can use another undocumented method to load them back in again. The two methods, `Application.SaveAsText` and `Application.LoadFromText`, have been widely used by Access developers to copy database objects to text files for some time. *Undocumented* may be too strong a term, because if you right-click in the Object Browser and select Hidden Members, you will see both methods and their arguments.

First, let's take a closer look at `SaveAsText` as a means of saving Access objects as text files (you will learn more about the other method in the section "Using the LoadFromText Method" later in this chapter).

Using the SaveAsText Method

So although undocumented officially, the `SaveAsText` method is used on a day-to-day basis (as is the `LoadFromText` method). Listing 2-5 shows the procedure used to save the Northwind database forms into distinct text files.

■**Note** If you want to try this out on your own system, remember to change the path used to save the text files into before running the procedure.

Listing 2-5. *Saving Forms As Text Files*

```
Public Sub createtemplate()
    On Error GoTo Err_createtemplate

    Dim db As Database
    Dim doc As Document
    Dim conn As Container
    Dim strPath As String
    Set db = CurrentDb()
    strPath = "C:\forms\"
    Set conn = db.Containers("Forms")

    For Each doc In conn.Documents
        Application.SaveAsText acForm, doc.Name, strPath & "Form_" & doc.Name➡
  & ".txt"
    Next doc

    Set db = Nothing
    Set conn = Nothing

Exit_createtemplate:

    Exit Sub
```

```
Err_createtemplate:
    MsgBox Err.Number & " - " & Err.Description
    Resume Exit_createtemplate

End Sub
```

The procedure in Listing 2-5 can also be modified to actually output the entire database structure as a set of text files. Listing 2-6 demonstrates this approach, and when executed will save queries, forms, reports, tables, and modules to the file system as a set of text files. For this example, the background information on tables and queries will be covered in the section "Saving Tables and Queries" shortly.

Listing 2-6. *Dumping the Entire Database As a Set of Text Files*

```
Public Sub createtemplate()
On Error GoTo Err_createtemplate

    Dim db As Database
    Dim doc As Document
    Dim conn As Container
    Dim strPath As String
    Dim I As Integer
    Set db = CurrentDb()
    strPath = "C:\forms\"
    ' Export the forms
    Set conn = db.Containers("Forms")
    For Each doc In conn.Documents
        Application.SaveAsText acForm, doc.Name, strPath & "Form_"➥
& doc.Name & ".txt "
    Next doc
    ' Export the reports
    Set conn = db.Containers("Reports")
    For Each doc In conn.Documents
        Application.SaveAsText acReport, doc.Name, strPath & "Report_"➥
& doc.Name & ".txt"
    Next doc
    Set conn = db.Containers("Modules")
    For Each doc In conn.Documents
        Application.SaveAsText acModule, doc.Name, strPath & "Module_"➥
 & doc.Name & ".txt"
    Next doc
 For Each td In db.TableDefs ' Tables
        If Left(td.Name, 4) <> "MSys" Then
            DoCmd.TransferText acExportDelim, , td.Name, strPath & "Table_"➥
& td.Name & ".txt", True
        End If
    Next td
```

```
For I = 0 To db.QueryDefs.Count - 1
    Application.SaveAsText acQuery, db.QueryDefs(I).Name, "strPath"➡
& db.QueryDefs(I).Name & ".txt"
Next I

    Set db = Nothing
    Set conn = Nothing
    Set doc = Nothing
Exit_createtemplate:
    Exit Sub

Exit_createtemplate:
On Error Resume Next
    If Not (doc Is Nothing) Then doc.Close: Set doc = Nothing
    If Not (conn Is Nothing) Then conn.Close: Set conn = Nothing
    If Not (db Is Nothing) Then db.Close: Set db = Nothing
Exit Sub
Err_createtemplate:
        MsgBox Err.Description, , "Error in Sub Module1.createtemplate"
        Resume Exit_createtemplate
    Resume 0    '.FOR TROUBLESHOOTING
End Sub
```

In this case, you are exporting queries, forms, tables, reports, and modules. The structure of a report and module text file are shown next. Again, to save space, I have only shown a section of the file contents.

Report Text File Contents

The report text file will contain information on both the structure of a report and any code associated with it.

```
Version =20
VersionRequired =20
Checksum =-785581844
Begin Report
    LayoutForPrint = NotDefault
    AutoCenter = NotDefault
    AllowDesignChanges = NotDefault
    DateGrouping =1
    GrpKeepTogether =1
    PictureAlignment =2
    PicturePages =1
    DatasheetGridlinesBehavior =0
    GridX =24
    GridY =24
    Width =11748
    DatasheetFontHeight =10
```

```
    ItemSuffix =102
    Tag ="Details~Extensions=OnOpen_CancelIfNoFilter"
    RecSrcDt = Begin
        0x7e78f9c78d03e340
    End
    GUID = Begin
        0x33b2547e4d5f014a8c88cd30cccddacf
    End
```

Module Text File Contents

This is a simple text file containing the actual code module exported as a text file:

```
Option Compare Database
Option Explicit
Public Enum InventoryTransactionTypeEnum
    Purchase_TransactionType = 1
    Sold_TransactionType = 2
    Hold_TransactionType = 3
End Enum
Type InventoryTransaction
    ProductID As Long               ' Product being added or removed to inventory
    TransactionType As InventoryTransactionTypeEnum    ' 1=Purchase; 2=Sale;
                                                       ' 3=Hold; 4=Waste;
    Quantity As Long
 ' Quantity specified for purchase, sale, hold, etc.
    QuantityGranted As Long         ' Actual quantity granted;
                                    ' may be less than specified
    InventoryID As Long             ' Inventory Transaction ID returned to the caller
    AllOrNothing As Boolean         ' All or nothing flag for product allocations
    Comments As String
End Type
```

■**Note** Access will only write out objects that have values that differ from their default values, thus helping to keep field sizes small.

Saving Tables and Queries

Saving tables as text files works in a slightly different way than for other objects. With forms, queries, and other database objects, you can walk the database container, returning the definition for each object. For tables, you need to use the TableDef object and transfer each table out of the application as a text file. This is a historical problem, as SaveAsText and LoadFromText text are not meant to carry out day-to-day work, but rather to be used by Access wizards to create objects. However, the process is much the same as before, only on this occasion, you have to loop through the TableDefs, selecting each table for output.

Of course, you also need to ignore the system tables, as you don't actually need them at this point. Listing 2-7 demonstrates this approach.

Listing 2-7. *Walking the TableDef Object*

```
For Each td In db.TableDefs ' Tables
        If Left(td.Name, 4) <> "MSys" Then
            DoCmd.TransferText acExportDelim, , td.Name, strPath & "Table_"➥
& td.Name & ".txt", True
        End If
    Next td
```

> **Note** The If statement excludes all system tables from the export routine. You also concatenate the pre-fix "Table" to each text field generated, as this will be required later on when you reload the definitions into another database.

Queries are very similar; they require you use the QueryDef object with the SaveAsText procedure used earlier. Listing 2-8 outlines this approach.

Listing 2-8. *Exporting Queries As Text*

```
For i = 0 To db.QueryDefs.Count - 1
    Application.SaveAsText acQuery, db.QueryDefs(I).Name, "strPath" &
 db.QueryDefs(I).Name & ".txt"
Next i
```

Listing 2-8 again uses a loop to cycle through the QueryDefs and outputs each individual query as a standard text file. Again you concatenate the text "Query" to the file name to help you reimport the files to a database later. Listing 2-6, shown earlier, puts it all together and provides a generic procedure that can be used to export all database objects to the file system as text files.

In my case, I executed the procedure in the Northwind database, exporting tables, queries, forms, reports, and modules into C:\Forms. This also included linked SharePoint tables.

> **Note** Have a look at some of the text files created to get an idea about the structure of the files and the objects they represent. You will be using this information shortly.

Using the LoadFromText Method

Once you have saved an object as a text file, you will of course want to get it back into a database. The example in Listing 2-9 takes one of the text files output by Listing 2-6 and loads it into a new blank database using the LoadFromText method.

Listing 2-9. *Loading Exported Files into Access*

```
Public Sub ImpFromText()
Dim strTemp As String
Dim path As String

path = "c:\temp\test\Form*.*"
strTemp = Dir(path)
Do While strTemp <> ""
Dim test
test = Mid(strTemp, InStr(1, strTemp, "_", vbTextCompare) + 1)
Dim test2
test2 = Left(test, InStr(1, test, ".", vbTextCompare) - 1)
    Application.LoadFromText acForm, test2, "C:\temp\test\" & strTemp
    strTemp = Dir
Loop
End Sub
```

At this point, what have you got? Well, you have an entire copy of the database structured in text files. Could you have just performed a copy and paste of the MDB file? Of course! What I am doing here is trying to lay the groundwork for how the new templates in Access 2007 work.

Built-in Access Templates

As stated earlier, Access comes with several templates built into the software. A quick-and-easy way to ensure that your users all have the same database style is to follow the upcoming instructions.

In many organizations, one of the complaints about Access user–created databases is that they are often poorly designed and unprofessional. The ability to create templates that your users can use to get up and running is greatly enhanced with this version of Access. I used the SaveAsText and LoadFromText discussions to introduce you to the structure of Access objects. Hopefully, you have tried out the examples and checked out the files produced, as this will be useful in the "Template Structure" section later in this chapter. However, outside some complex programming, there is a very simple way to make template databases available to your users. All you need to do is to create a new database called blank.accdb and save it in \Program Files\Microsoft Office\Templates\1033\Access.

When a user clicks Blank Database in the Getting Started screen, a copy is made of your blank.accdb file, and the user is almost up and running. Your blank template file can contain any Access object you choose to create, including

- Library code
- References
- Database properties
- Ribbon XML and the loader
- Default forms and reports
- Other configuration settings

You user database will be created with the objects required already in place. To try this out, create a new Access 2007 database named blank.accdb. Within the database, create a set of standard tables; for example, I created a set of tables called tblStudent, tblSchool, tblModule. In addition, I created a standard form set, for example, a data maintenance form that contains the command buttons Add, Edit, Delete, and View, and some standard queries and reports. I added a small logo and set a standard design color for each form. For the student form, I added in a customized RibbonX menu to provide quick access to standard activities for the user.

■**Note** Don't forget, for this to work, the database must be named blank.accdb and saved to \Program Files\ Microsoft Office\Templates\1033\Access.

This gives you a powerful and easy-to-use tool that can be used to distribute partially complete applications to end users. Once complete, simply save the changes and close the database. To test it out, create a new database by choosing Blank Database from the Getting Started screen, save it to a local folder, and click Create. Note that all of the objects contained within the template file will also be contained in the new database file. The main issue with this approach is the location the blank database must be saved to. In this case, it's a local folder on the user's PC. This is fine for those organizations where the installation of a common desktop and applications is the norm, but what about those systems that will not allow you to do this? One way to deal with this issue would be to use typical deployment scripts, pushing the template out to the user's desktop, much like standard software.

Template Structure

As mentioned previously, in order to see how an Access template is put together, you must first rename one with a .zip extension. On my PC, templates are located in \Program Files\ Microsoft Office\Templates\1033\Access. For the examples that follow, I have renamed the Northwind.accdt file Northwind.zip. Once the file has been renamed, right-click, select Open with, and choose your compression program, for example, Win Zip. Figure 2-2 shows the folder structure inside my new zipped archive. Access templates are not actually database files but a set of related XML and metadata files describing the database structure, objects and content, and any relationships that exist between the various XML files. To view the various files, including the metadata files, simply open one of the template folders or subfolders.

The archive contains the following folder structure:

- _rels

- docProps

- template

The template folder contains two subfolders, _rels and database. It also contains the Northwind logo image and a single XML file, template.xml. For the moment, we will concentrate on the database subfolder, as it contains the main items of interest to Access developers.

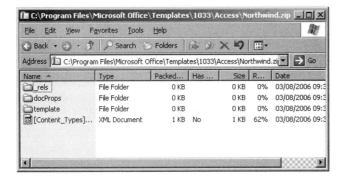

Figure 2-2. *Northwind ZIP archive*

Database Subfolder

The database folder contains a single subfolder, Objects, and several XML files, as listed here:

- *databaseProperties.xml* contains a set of XML files related to each Access object. For example, the file formCustomerDetails_Metadata.xml maintains metadata about the Customers form. This file contains the following XML, which details the type, in this case a form, and the name of the object, Customer Details.

```
<?xml version="1.0" encoding="UTF-8" standalone="yes"?>
<AccessObject xmlns="http://schemas.microsoft.com/office/access/2005/04/template/➥
    object-metadata">
    <Type>Form</Type>
    <Name>Customer Details</Name>
    </AccessObject>
```

You will find one such file for every Access object, table, query, form, report, macro, and module. Each file contains the same metadata, type of object and name of object.

- *navpane.xml* contains the initial objects and structure for the Access Navigation Pane. It contains the contents for the Navigation Pane system tables: MSysNavPaneGroup Categories, MSysNavPaneGroups, MSysNavPaneGroupToObjects, and MSysNavPaneObjectIDs. The following example XML shows the objects that will be placed into the Navigation Pane:

```
<MSysNavPaneObjectIDs>
<Id>-2147483470</Id>
<Name>Top Ten Orders by Sales Amount</Name>
<Type>5</Type>
</MSysNavPaneObjectIDs>
<MSysNavPaneObjectIDs>
<Id>-2147483469</Id>
<Name>CustomerOnOrders</Name>
<Type>8</Type>
</MSysNavPaneObjectIDs>
```

```
<MSysNavPaneObjectIDs>
<Id>-2147483468</Id>
<Name>EmployeePrivilegesforEmployees</Name>
<Type>8</Type>
</MSysNavPaneObjectIDs>
<MSysNavPaneObjectIDs>
<Id>-2147483467</Id>
<Name>EmployeePrivilegesLookup</Name>
<Type>8</Type>
```

- *relationships.xml* contains the contents of the MSysRelationships system table.

- *vbareferences.xml* contains external VBA references.

Tables and Database Objects

Remember that earlier in the chapter we looked at LoadFromText and SaveAsText. Well, you will see why now. Again, all objects are defined using the same structure as previously shown except tables, each of which are defined in two files of format XSD and XML. The XSD file contains the schema for a table, while the XML file contains the actual data to be used for the table.

WHAT IS AN XSD FILE?

An *XSD file* describes the schema or structure of an XML document. In this case, it describes the schema of a database table, for example, the Customers table in Northwind. The Customers XSD file is very large, and I have not included it in full in this chapter. Following is a small section defining the Company column:

```
<xsd:element name="Company" minOccurs="0" od:jetType="text"
od:sqlSType="nvarchar">
<xsd:annotation>
<xsd:appinfo>
<od:fieldProperty name="ColumnWidth" type="3" value="-1"/>
<od:fieldProperty name="ColumnOrder" type="3" value="0"/>
<od:fieldProperty name="ColumnHidden" type="1" value="0"/>
<od:fieldProperty name="Required" type="1" value="0"/>
<od:fieldProperty name="AllowZeroLength" type="1" value="0"/>
<od:fieldProperty name="DisplayControl" type="3" value="109"/>
<od:fieldProperty name="IMEMode" type="2" value="0"/>
<od:fieldProperty name="IMESentenceMode" type="2" value="0"/>
<od:fieldProperty name="UnicodeCompression" type="1" value="1"/>
<od:fieldProperty name="TextAlign" type="2" value="0"/>
<od:fieldProperty name="AggregateType" type="4" value="-1"/>
<od:fieldProperty name="WSSFieldID" type="10" value="Company"/>
<od:fieldProperty name="GUID" type="9" value="6NxONm/dAOupv734KdgMSg==
```

This section of the XSD file defines the Access field and sets the field properties; for example, Company is defined in line 1 as text for JET, the required field property is set to "No", and AllowZeroLength is set to "No". In addition to the XSD schema file, you will also find for each table object a standard XML file containing the data. Indeed, if you import the Customers table's XML from the subfolder, you will find that it creates an exact copy of the existing Customers table in Northwind.

Note The following web site contains links to several articles on Access 2003 and XML, many of which apply to Access 2007: http://www.officezealot.com/office2003zone/access.aspx.

Forms, reports, queries, and other objects retain the format we looked at earlier in this chapter. Again, using the Customers table from Northwind, here is a short section that defines some of the fields of this table:

```
<xsd:sequence>
<xsd:element name="ID" minOccurs="1" od:jetType="autonumber"➥
 od:sqlSType="int" od:autoUnique="yes" od:nonNullable="yes"➥
 type="xsd:int"/>
<xsd:element name="Company" minOccurs="0" od:jetType="text" od:sqlSType="nvarchar">
<xsd:simpleType>
<xsd:restriction base="xsd:string">
<xsd:maxLength value="50"/>
<xsd:restriction>
</xsd:simpleType>
</xsd:element>
<xsd:element name="Company_x0020_Furigana" minOccurs="0"➥
 od:jetType="text" od:sqlSType="nvarchar">
<xsd:simpleType>
<xsd:restriction base="xsd:string">
xsd:maxLength value="50"/>
</xsd:restriction>
</xsd:simpleType>
```

Almost all of the template files made available use embedded macros as opposed to VBA for processing. In this case, the macros are also part of the form definition file. The next example shows the OnClick embedded macro in the customers form XML file, much the same as for SaveAsText shown earlier.

```
OnClickEmMacro = Begin
                    Version =196611
                    ColumnsShown =10
                    Begin
                        Action ="OnError"
                        Argument ="0"
                    End
                    Begin
                        Action ="SendObject"
                        Argument ="-1"
                        Argument =""
                        Argument =""
                        Argument ="=[E-mail Address] & IIf(Nz([E-mail ➥
Address])<>\"\",\" [\" & [E-mail Address] & \"]\")"
```

```
                    Argument =""
                    Argument =""
                    Argument =""
                    Argument =""
                    Argument ="-1"
                End
                Begin
                    Condition ="[MacroError].[Number]<>0"
                    Action ="MsgBox"
                    Argument ="=[MacroError].[Description]"
                    Argument ="-1"
                    Argument ="0"
                End
            End
```

So for the new Access templates, rather than saving and persisting to text files, you are doing more or less the same thing, but persisting the objects to XML and XSD files. However, the real interesting feature here is, in addition to allowing you to create corporate templates or even set up a small Internet template business, the possibility to use templates to export and import data and its structures to and from Microsoft Office SharePoint Services.

A neat example of this is the ability to create a new Access database based on an existing Windows SharePoint site. In this case, WSS could be considered a template for the new application.

In addition, when working with one of the available Access templates, it is possible to create the database and link it to Windows SharePoint Services. In this way, Access creates an application linked to a set of SharePoint lists already created on the server. In essence, what you also have available are web application templates.

WSS Templates

We have already looked at the templates available for Access, but there are also some templates available for Windows SharePoint Services located in Program Files\Microsoft Office\Templates\1033\Access\WSS, which contains the following Access/WSS template files:

105: This is an Access template for the Windows SharePoint Services Contact list. For example, if you create a new Access-linked application from WSS, the linking process will use this template to provide additional functionality and objects in the resulting Access database file—for example, forms and reports based on the template definitions.

107: This creates a new database based on a Windows SharePoint Services Task list. Just like the Contacts database, this template also contains useful Task-based objects, forms, and reports.

1100: This creates a new issue-tracking application. This is one of the most extensive WSS-based templates and contains an almost complete out-of-the-box WSS experience.

■**Note** It's important to remember that you need to check the Create and Link Your Database to a Windows SharePoint Services Site check box when creating the database from the templates provided via the Access Ribbon. If you don't, you end up with a standard Access database file.

It is expected that Microsoft will in the near future release a wizard-driven development tool that will make the creation of templates very straightforward. This new tool, which may be available as part of the Access Developers Extensions, will take an existing database and create the XML structures required to allow you to save it as a template. This opens up great opportunities to permit professional applications to be distributed as templates in a corporate environment. It also, as I have already said, opens up a new market for Access developers, selling professional templates for specific business purposes.

From the WSS side, it may also be possible to save a WSS site as an Access template. You can develop additional features either on the SharePoint server or in the Access back-end database. I would expect this development to take place in the near future.

Summary

For the end user, templates provide a way to get up and running with Access quickly. Granted, the templates provided by Microsoft are basic and have a focus toward Windows SharePoint Services. Until Microsoft releases its template creation tools, it's likely that almost all developers will remain on the sidelines when it comes to creating these objects. Once the template software is released, it could be we will begin to see professional Access applications offered as templates on the Web. Within the corporate environment, it's likely that templates could be widely used to ensure that at least the basic structure of applications has been created by Access professionals.

CHAPTER 3

■ ■ ■

Getting Up and Running with RibbonX

In this chapter, we will be looking at the new menu interface in Access 2007, RibbonX. The goal with this chapter is to get you started creating your own menu system. The Ribbon will be the single most visible change to many developers and power users new to Access 2007, and by the end of this chapter, you will have gained experience that will provide a solid grounding in helping you to customize the menu system in Access 2007.

Being completely up front about this chapter, Ribbons were completely new to me, just as they are to you. Like you, I had to wait on Microsoft examples to get started exploring this new technology and try it out. Probably unlike you, however, I do have contacts within the beta group to whom I can direct questions, and many questions have been asked.

This chapter is partially based on the RibbonX examples provided by Microsoft, as this is the basis for my own understanding of RibbonX. I also had a great coach in the form of Patrick Schmid, who has moved into the RibbonX code and done more with it than anyone else up to this point. His help has been crucial to speeding up my own learning in terms of Ribbons. So this chapter is a primer on RibbonX, but it is also a record of my personal experience playing with RibbonX and XML, and I hope that it is of value to you.

Note Patrick has released an add-in that allows you to customize the Ribbons in Office 2007, and it is available free of charge from his web site at `http://pschmid.net`. It will be worthwhile to check out Patrick's site every so often, as it is Patrick's intention to develop tools that will remove the need for developers and users to actually hand-code changes to the Ribbon interface.

Perhaps the best way to get started with the new menu system in Access 2007 is to dive into some examples. The first example will create a totally blank menu system to which you will add several different features as you progress through the remaining examples. Your new Ribbon will be visible on the main Access Ribbon as a new tab. During the process, I will define and explain each of the features you will be using. So without further ado, let's get started working with Access 2007 Ribbons. For all the examples in this chapter, you will need to set a reference to the Microsoft Access Office 12 Object Library.

■**Note** Command bars and custom toolbars from previous versions should work as is with Access 2007. However, they will appear on an additional tab called Add-Ins. Also, given the fact that most Access developers and power users are not familiar with C# and other .NET languages, we will not be looking at using these languages to create Ribbons.

RibbonX code is basically XML. XML is a means to both describe and store data. If you are new to XML, you might want to try the tutorial available at http://www.w3schools.com/xml/ before working through the examples in this chapter. Also, in order to work with the XML files required for the examples (and your own development projects), you need to be using a free Microsoft XML editor, Custom UI Editor, available at http://openxmldeveloper.org/articles/ CustomUIeditor.aspx, that is designed for use with RibbonX. One of the really good things about the Custom UI Editor is that it will generate all the callback code stubs for you. Callback functions simply execute and pass control back to the Ribbon. They can then be pasted into the VBA IDE, and you are almost ready to go (of course, you still need to add the specific functionality for the callback code). Figure 3-1 shows the editor screen for the partially complete Ribbon you will be creating in this chapter. The XML editor will also ensure that your XML is indeed valid. Figure 3-2 shows the generated code stubs created for this Ribbon.

Figure 3-1. *Custom UI Editor*

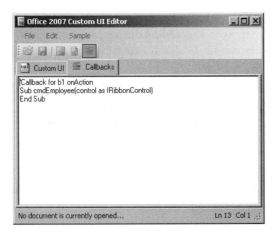

Figure 3-2. *Callback code stub generation*

■**Tip** Error reporting is crucial when starting out with RibbonX. In Access, if your XML Ribbon code fails, you will not get an error message. It just will not appear. However, in the Access Options dialog box, make sure you turn on the Show Add in User Interface Errors option located in the Advanced group. In order to code for the Ribbon, you will need to set a reference to the Microsoft Access Office 12 Object Library.

Creating Your First Ribbon

In order to view some of the Ribbon features, you will need some data to work with. Create a new database and then create a table called tblEmployee containing several fields. Table 3-1 shows the structure of the employee table for this example.

■**Note** You can run the following examples in any database you choose; just change the table and field names as appropriate.

Table 3-1. *Employee Example Table*

Field Name	Data Type
fldEmpID	AutoNumber
fldSurName	Text
FldForeName	Text
fldAddress1	Text
fldAddress2	Text
fldTown	Text
fldZip/PostCode	Text

Populate the table with some appropriate data to be used for the examples that follow.

You can start creating a Ribbon from scratch in Access by adding the following structures to the new database, closing and opening the database file to view the new Ribbon, in this case a blank Ribbon. Here are the steps:

1. Create a new table called USysRibbons. This is a hidden system table used to store the RibbonX. When Access opens a database, it immediately looks for this table and will load any Ribbon defined in it. You will need to have hidden objects exposed in the database if you want to work directly with this system table.

2. Add two fields, RibbonName (Text) and RibbonXML (Memo), to the table.

3. Create a new record and name it as you like. (In the steps to come, I've used MyRibbon, but you can use the Ribbon name of your choice.) Add the following XML to the RibbonXML field:

```
<customUI xmlns="http://schemas.microsoft.com/office/2006/01/customui">
<ribbon startFromScratch="true">
<tabs>
  <Ribbon Code>
</tabs>
</ribbon>
</customUI>
```

■Note All your Ribbon XML should be in lowercase. The majority of mistakes I encountered with Ribbon code were related to spelling, initial capitals, and other typos. XML attributes and elements are case sensitive, as are idMSOs (IDs for Microsoft-provided controls).

---

4. Click the Office Button and select Access Options. Click the current database. In the Toolbars option, set the custom Ribbon ID to MyRibbon (or whatever name you used in step 3).

5. Restart the database.

Figure 3-3 shows the Access interface with the default Ribbons removed. Because you have not as yet defined a replacement Ribbon, the Ribbon is blank.

Turning off the display of the default Ribbon is achieved using the XML file you have added to the table. The XML line startFromScratch="true" hides the default Ribbon and any add-in tabs. Several options will also be removed from the Microsoft Office button. If this attribute is not used and you had set startFromScratch to false as in the following code snippet, your new Ribbon would blend into the existing Access Ribbon, showing up on the Add-Ins tab on the main Access Ribbon.

```
<customUI Xmlns="http://schemas.microsoft.com/office/2006/01/customui">
<ribbon startFromScratch="false">
</ribbon>
</customUI>
```

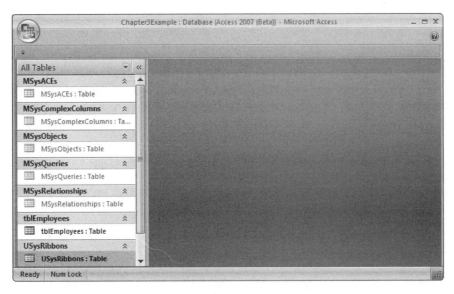

Figure 3-3. *Access 2007 without a Ribbon*

Table 3-2 shows the commonly used XML elements and attributes you will initially use when working with Ribbons.

Table 3-2. *Common Ribbon XML Elements and Attributes*

Element/Attribute	Comment
customUI	The top-level element for a custom Ribbon.
ribbon	Element that defines the Ribbon.
tab	Element that creates a tab in the Ribbon.
group	Element that creates a group in the Ribbon. You use groups to logically group related items.
id	Unique name of a control in the Ribbon.
label	Static text displayed within a control.
button	Similar to a command button. Use the onAction attribute to specify the name of a callback function in the database, which will be called when you click the button.
dropDown	Element that creates a drop-down list that cannot be updated. To type text in a drop-down list, you use a combo box control instead.
imageMso	Name of a built-in control in Office that you can use to add an icon to your Ribbon.
getImage	Path to an image file to load.

USING DAO TO LOAD A RIBBON

It is also possible to load a ribbon using a DAP recordset as described in the MSDN article located at `http://msdn2.microsoft.com/en-us/library/bb187398.aspx`. This article covers Ribbon customization in great detail and is well worth a read. The DAO required to load the Ribbon is shown here for information. The Ribbon table, of course, has the same structure as the Ribbon system table.

```
Function LoadRibbons()
Dim db As DAO.Database
Dim rstRibbon as DAO.Recordset
Set db = Application.CurrentDb
Set  rstRibbon =db.Openrecordset("YourRibbonTable")
Do Until  rstRibbon.EOF
Application.LoadCustomUI rstRibbon("RibbonName").Value, ➥
rstRibbon("RibbonXml").Value
rstRibbon.MoveNext
Loop
rstRibbon.Close
Set rstRibbon = Nothing
db.Close
Set db = Nothing
End Function
```

The function is then called from an AutoExec macro when the application starts. If you are changing the Ribbon in an Access Data Project, you must use the `LoadUI` method to load your custom Ribbon.

Adding Functionality to the Ribbon

In RibbonX, a tab contains a group (or groups) that contains one or more buttons. Each button displays a single icon and carries out a specific action when it is clicked. You can use groups to combine similar functionality into a common interface object. Therefore, the general idea with RibbonX is to create or amend a tab, define a group, and then add the associated buttons and code for the functionality of each button click. Of course, all of this (other than the code events) is written in XML and loaded into the Access interface when the application opens or can be executed on an object-by-object basis (for example, attaching specific Ribbon functionality to an Access form). The following XML elements will create a single Ribbon tab called Employees.

```
<customUI xmlns="http://schemas.microsoft.com/office/2006/01/customui">
<ribbon>
<tabs>
<tab id="EmpTab" label="Employees">
</tab>
</tabs>
</ribbon>
</customUI>
```

Additional tabs are created within the opening (`<tabs>`) and closing (`</tabs>`) elements. As you can see in the preceding example, each tab is opened with an opening `<tab>` element and closed with a corresponding closing `</tab>` element. If you are one of those who work with HTML, this should be very familiar.

Once you have created the tab itself, you can then start to add in the group, which will contain the buttons for this item. The following XML fragment will create a group:

```
<group id ="empGroup" label="emplist">
</group>
```

Placing buttons onto the Ribbon is a straightforward process. `imageMso` points at an existing Office icon, and `button id` creates the button on the Ribbon. The following fragment will add a button to the group just created:

```
<button id ="mybutton" imageMso="image file name"?>
```

Just like with HTML, there are additional attributes you can add to the button XML to extend the element. For example:

```
<button id ="mybutton" imageMso="image file name"➡
size = "small" label ="Employee List"  onaction ="run code" ?>
```

In this case, you are indicating that you would like a small button (as opposed to a large one) and are assigning a label to the button. The `onAction` attribute executes the function containing the actions you would like the button to carry out.

So now that you have an understanding of the XML elements you need to construct the parts of a ribbon, you'll next put what you have together, create the XML file, and add it to Access to see the effect on the Ribbon interface.

Putting Together a Simple Tab

The initial shell of the XML document you are adding to the Employee database is shown in Listing 3-1. Over the next few pages, you will add features to the basic Ribbon and see what happens. I will walk you through this example in several stages, each time adding XML elements and features to the XML file in the Ribbon table. The first step is to create the following XML file in the XML editor. Once created, you simply copy and paste the content into the RibbonXML field of USysRibbons.

■**Note** When creating Ribbons, you will need to close and restart Access each time you make a change to the Ribbon XML.

Listing 3-1. *Creating Your First Ribbon*

```
<customUI xmlns="http://schemas.microsoft.com/office/2006/01/customui">
<ribbon startFromScratch="false">
<tabs>
<tab idMso="TabAddIns">
<group id="EmpGroup" label="Employees">
<button id="btnEmp" imageMso="AddOrRemoveAttendees"➡
size="large" label="Employee Menu" onAction="cmdEmployee"/>
</group>
</tab>
</tabs>
</ribbon>
</customUI>
```

Listing 3-1 creates a new tab, called Add-Ins, on the existing Ribbon. This new tab contains a single group, EmpGroup, which is labeled Employees. You then create a single button in the group named Employee Menu with an onAction of cmdEmployee. Of course, at the moment, if you click this button, an error message will result. onAction can be equated to the On Click event of a standard Access button, and later you will see how the code associated with this action is created using VBA. Figure 3-4 shows the new Add-Ins tab and the Employee Menu button.

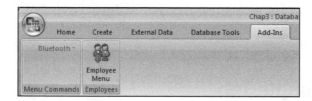

Figure 3-4. *The Add-Ins tab and Employee Menu button*

So now you have created your own tab containing a single group and a single button. Adding additional buttons is as simple as creating a block of XML as follows:

```
<button id="b1" imageMso="HappyFace"➡
size="large" label="Employee Menu" onAction="Code to execute"/>
```

and placing it into the appropriate group element. So now you will add a new button, which in time will be used to open an employee form. Insert the following XML elements into the XML shown in Listing 3-1 between the opening and closing <Group> tags.

```
<button id="frmbt" imageMso="HappyFace"➡
size="small" label="Employee Form" onAction="OpenEmpfrm"/>
```

In keeping with the approach just presented, add several additional buttons and features to this group. Listing 3-2 show the full listing for EmpGroup. In this case, you simply use an assortment of available Office graphics as indicated by the imageMso attribute.

Listing 3-2. *EmpGroup RibbonX*

```
<customUI xmlns="http://schemas.microsoft.com/office/2006/01/customui">
<ribbon startFromScratch="false">
<tabs>
<tab idMso="TabAddIns">
<group id="EmpGroup" label="Employees">
<button id="btEmp" imageMso="AddOrRemoveAttendees"➥
size="large" label="Employee Menu" onAction="cmdEmployee"/>
<button id="frmbt" imageMso="RecordsAddFromOutlook"➥
size="large" label="Employee Form" onAction="OpenEmpfrm"/>
<button id="frmAddbt" imageMso="MeetingsWorkspace"➥
size="large" label="Add Employee" onAction="AddEmpfrm"/>
<button id="frmVwbt" imageMso="FileManageMenu"➥
size="large" label="View Employees " onAction="VwEmpfrm"/>
</group>
</tab>
</tabs>
</ribbon>
</customUI>
```

Figure 3-5 shows the completed EmpGroup in the Add-Ins tab.

Figure 3-5. *EmpGroup custom group*

■**Note** If you need to save screen real estate, you can choose to hide the label of a button or buttons by adding in the XML element showlabel="false" immediately after the imageMso element.

Now that you have created a simple group and a few buttons, let's look at actually doing something useful with them—for example, opening an employee form. To do so, however, you will need to use VBA with RibbonX. So next, I give you some background and information on VBA so you can move to the next step.

Adding VBA Callback Functions

IRibbonControl exposes the following properties for use in your code:

Context Object: Read-only. Returns an object that represents the window where the Ribbon is about to be displayed.

Id String: Read-only. Returns a string that represents the id attribute for the control.

Tag String: Read-only. Returns a string that represents the tag attribute for the control. This could be the name of a form or a report you would like to pass to the onAction command.

You also need to create the employee form: click the table in the Navigation Pane, click the Create tab, and finally click Form. This generates a basic form that you can use for the following example.

Looking at the button XML, repeated here, you can see that the onAction element contains a reference to a callback function, OpenEmpfrm. OpenEmpForm will be the VBA callback function that opens the employee form you just created.

```
<button id="frmbt" imageMso="HappyFace"➥
size="large" label="Employee Form" onAction="OpenEmpfrm"/>
```

To enable the callback function, create a new module called basRibbons and add the following procedure:

```
Sub OpenEmpfrm(ByVal control As IRibbonControl)
   DoCmd.OpenForm "frmEmployees"
End Sub
```

Note the use of ByVal to pass the control ID of the button into the procedure. A simple DoCmd statement to open the required form is all that is needed in this case. Try it out by clicking the button on the menu to see the results of adding in the callback. A more generic procedure can be created by associating the form name with the tag element of the Ribbon XML. This procedure is demonstrated in the Microsoft MSDN example code and in the Northwind 2007 demonstration database. For example:

```
<button id ="mybutton" label="MyLabel" imageMso="ImageName"➥
Size="large" onAction="MyAction" tag="myformName" />
```

A VBA callback is then created with the control ID and the form name passed to the onAction procedure, for example, DoCmd.OpenForm control.tag.

The final bit of customization you will do is to add a tooltip to the button that opens the employee form. Change the button element for the open employee form feature as follows, adding in the supertip element shown in bold:

```
<button id="frmbt" imageMso="RecordsAddFromOutlook" size="large"➥
label="Employee Form" supertip ="Open the Employees form to add,➥
edit and review records" onAction="OpenEmpfrm"/>
```

■Note Remember that every time you make a change to the code, you will need to close and reopen the database file so that your changes take effect.

To view the tooltip, just hover the cursor over the button icon. To open the form, simply click the appropriate button in the EmpGroup group. Of course, using DoCmd, you could open the form in any available mode: Edit, Add, Read-Only. For example, Listing 3-3 shows a new VBA callback function that has been added to basRibbons and is used by the Add Employee button to open the employee form in Add mode.

Listing 3-3. *Opening a Form in Add Mode*

```
Public Function AddEmpfrm()
On Error GoTo Err_AddEmpfrm
DoCmd.OpenForm "frmEmployees", acNormal, , acFormAdd
Exit_AddEmpfrm:
Exit Function
Err_AddEmpfrm:
        MsgBox Err.Description, , "Error in Function basribbons.AddEmpfrm"
        Resume Exit_AddEmpfrm
    Resume 0     '.FOR TROUBLESHOOTING
End Function
```

Continuing on with EmpGroup, you will now add a drop-down list to the group by amending the elements used to create the button labeled View Employees. This is a little more complex than the previous steps, as you will be populating the drop-down list from the database table. First off, let's look at the XML elements used to create the actual drop-down list, which you are going to use in place of the following definition:

```
<button id="frmVwbt" imageMso="HappyFace"➥
size="large" label="View Employees " onAction="VwEmpfrm"/>
```

Listing 3-4 shows these elements.

Listing 3-4. *Creating a Drop-Down List*

```
<dropDown id="empDropdown" label="Emp List" supertip="See list of employees"➥
 imageMso="HappyFace" onAction="text"></dropDown>
```

Not that much different from the elements used to create a button. However, you still have a few items to add to the listing. At the moment, if you add the fragment in Listing 3-4 to your XML file, you will get an empty drop-down list added to the EmpGroup group. Figure 3-6 shows the Ribbon at this point in the process. Notice also the Ribbon groups could use a little tidying up. You can do so by placing a vertical separator between the button items; just add the following XML line to the code: the separator is used to provide distance if required between the items within the same Ribbon group.

```
<separator id="sep3"/>
```

Here, sep3 is simply a separator ID. You would include a series of such IDs (e.g., sep1, sep2, and so on) to give a unique value to each separator.

Figure 3-6. *Initial drop-down list in EmpGroup*

You can also use menuSeparator id to actually place some text between menu items. For example:

```
<menuSeparator id="YourMenuSplit" title="New Menu Items"/>
```

To continue with the process, you now need to create a couple of callback functions to provide information to the interface—specifically, how many items you will be displaying in the list and, of course, the items themselves. You use the getItemCount and getItemLabel elements to provide this information to the Ribbon. To continue, add the following elements in bold to the definition shown previously in Listing 3-4:

```
<dropDown id="empDropdown" label="Emp List" supertip="See list of employees"➥
getItemCount="" getItemLabel=""  imageMso="HappyFace"➥
onAction="text"></dropDown>
```

Now you have to actually write up the VBA callbacks to be executed and provide the required information to the drop-down list. The population of the drop-down list is achieved using callback functions. First you need to tell Access how many items are actually in the callback. Access will then execute the callback once for every item, giving you an ID (0-based) as the parameter. The ID is used as an index into the internal object array that contains the values for the drop-down list.

The onAction callback for the drop-down list will give you two values that can be used: selectedId is the actual string the user selected in the drop-down list, and selectedIndex is the same ID used earlier to populate the list. So it should be identical to the index of the internal array.

■**Note** A combo box returns only the text the user chose or entered. An index value is not returned in this case.

Listing 3-5 shows the first callback, ItemLabel, which improves slightly on that used in the Microsoft beta documentation. In this case, you use a single DLookup to get the values required for display in the list. Listing 3-6 returns the count of the number of objects to be displayed.

Listing 3-5. *Callback Function to Populate Drop-Down Labels*

```
Public Function ItemLabel(control As IRibbonControl, ➥
index As Integer, ByRef label)
Dim stFirstLastName As String
 stFirstLastName = Trim(Nz(DLookup("nz(FirstName,'') &  ' ' & ➥
nz(LastName,'')", "tblEmployees", "ID = " & index + 1), ""))
 label = stFirstLastName
End Function
```

Listing 3-6. *Callback Function to Get Record Count for Drop-Down List*

```
Public Function CountEmp(control As IRibbonControl, ByRef count)
 count = Nz(DCount("*", "tblEmployees"), 0)
End Function
```

Listing 3-7 shows another approach, this time using a recordset to populate the drop-down list. The basic process is the same. The only difference is on this occasion you build up your sting to pass to the callback label using a recordset. In this case, you also pass in Index +1 (because it's a zero-based array) as the WHERE clause to ensure you get the correct records listed.

Listing 3-7. *Using VBA to Populate Drop-Down Lists*

```
Public Function LogLabelempdata(control As IRibbonControl,➥
 Index As Integer, ByRef label)
Dim strData As String
Dim rstEmp As Recordset
Dim lngindex As Integer
Dim db As Database
Set db = CurrentDb
Set rstEmp = db.OpenRecordset("SELECT FirstName,LastName,➥
Company FROM tblemployees Where EmployeeID = " & Index + 1)
strData = rstEmp!FirstName & " " & rstEmp!LastName & " " & Company
label = strData
End Sub
```

The procedure illustrates the point that virtually anything you can do within VBA you can use within your RibbonX code calls. You will be reusing and completing the code you have created so far.

Creating Split Buttons

Figure 3-7 shows another approach to button design, this time using a *split button design*. A split button provides a nice interface to group several related objects together and combines the functionality of a button and a menu—for example, you can create a single button to display forms or reports; when the button is clicked, a drop-down menu appears listing the objects, as opposed to using a drop-down list, which is text based. For me, a drop-down split button containing relevant icons is a much improved experienced for the user. The main difference between a split button and a regular button is the use of the MENU attribute to create the drop-down menu portion of the button.

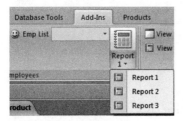

Figure 3-7. *Split button*

In this case, related reports are grouped together in a "drop-down menu" approach. Clicking the visible button on the Ribbon drops down a number of choices. Just like all other buttons, split buttons are created using XML. Listing 3-8 shows the XML structure required to create a split button.

Listing 3-8. *Creating a Split Button Drop-Down Menu*

```
<splitButton id = "mysplitbutton" size ="large">
<menu id ="Reports" imageMso="PasteDuplicate" >
<button id = "button1" label="Report 1" imageMso ="CreateReport"➥
onAction="vba or macro to execute" />
<button id = "button2" label="Report 2" imageMso ="CreateReport"➥
onAction="vba or macro to execute" />
<button id = "button3" label="Report 3" imageMso ="CreateReport"➥
onAction="vba or macro to execute" />
</menu>
</splitButton>
```

The XML button elements are then repeated for each individual button required on the drop-down menu. In this case, note that you use another XML tag, <menu>, to create the menu structure for the split button. Listing 3-9 shows the full RibbonX code you have added at this point.

Listing 3-9. *Custom RibbonX*

```
<customUI xmlns="http://schemas.microsoft.com/office/2006/01/customui">
<ribbon startFromScratch="false">
<tabs>
<tab idMso="TabAddIns">
 <group id="EmpGroup" label="Employees">
 <button id="btEmp" imageMso="AddOrRemoveAttendees"➥
size="large" label="Employee Menu" onAction="cmdEmployee"/>
```

```
<button id="frmbt" imageMso="RecordsAddFromOutlook"➥
 size="large" label="Employee Form" supertip ="Open the Employees form to ➥
add, edit and review records"➥
onAction="OpenEmpfrm"/><button id="frmAddbt" imageMso="MeetingsWorkspace"➥
size="large" label=" Add Employee" onAction="AddEmpfrm"/>
<dropDown id="empDropdown" label="Emp List" supertip="See list of employees"➥
getItemCount="CountEmp" getItemLabel="LogLabel"  imageMso="HappyFace"➥
onAction="text"></dropDown>
<splitButton id = "mysplitbutton" size ="large">
<menu id ="Reports" imageMso="PasteDuplicate" >
<button id = "button1" label="Report 1" imageMso ="CreateReport"➥
onAction="vba or macro to execute" />
<button id = "button2" label="Report 2" imageMso ="CreateReport"➥
onAction="vba or macro to execute" />
<button id = "button3" label="Report 3" imageMso ="CreateReport"➥
onAction="vba or macro to execute" />
</menu>
</splitButton>
</group>
</tab>
</tabs>
</ribbon>
</customUI>
```

Adding Custom Images

Up until this point, you have been using the images available as part of Office, simply including them as required for the customized Ribbons. However, you can of course use your own custom images in place of these built-in objects. Not being very graphically minded (that is, hands like feet), I have not provided images for this example but rather will outline the approach, assuming that you have images available. In order to use your own images, you will use another new Ribbon XML attribute, getImage. In addition, of course, you will need to create a simple VBA function to which you will pass the control ID of the button and use a CASE statement within your VBA procedure load up the required image file. You will also be using the LoadPicture function to actually load the picture to the Ribbon. Listing 3-10 shows the RibbonX code to begin the process, and Listing 3-10 shows the VBA procedure that is called to provide the image file. The function uses a basic CASE statement to ensure that the correct button image file is loaded based on the control ID being passed in.

I have shown the initial SELECT CASE statement. The rest of the statement is just the same, with a CASE statement for each image you would like to use.

Listing 3-10. *Loading Custom Images*

```
Function GetImage(control As IRibbonControl, ByRef image)
    Dim controlName As String
    controlName = control.ID
  Select Case controlName
    Case "Products":
        Set image = LoadPicture("c:\images\Product.bmp")
    Case "Customers"
        Set image = LoadPicture("c:\images\Customers.bmp")
    End Select
End Function
```

Adding Additional Groups

You can use the <group> tag to create additional function groups on your Ribbon. As you may have picked up already, you must always have an opening tag, in this case an opening <group> tag, and a closing tag, in this case </group>. Other XML elements specific to this tag group go into the opening and closing tags. So, for example, on your existing Add-Ins tab, you could add another group—for example, a group showing employees working in a specific department. The notation that follows should be familiar to you if you have worked with HTML in that there is a main tag (<group>) and then attributes that refine and define the behavior of the tag. In this case, you give it an id and a label, which is displayed in the user interface. For example:

```
<group id="TrainingEmp" label ="Training Staff">
```

As before, you then need to define the buttons for the Ribbon and provide them with functionality. The full code for the new group listing is shown in Listing 3-11.

Listing 3-11. *Creating the TrainingEmp Group*

```
<group id="TrainingEmp" label ="Training Staff">
<button id ="btnViewrecord"  label = "View My Record"➥
 imageMso="ThesaurusRR" onAction="ViewTrRecord" />
</group>
```

Figure 3-8 shows the new group added to the Add-Ins tab. You will create the VBA callback in a moment. It is also possible to provide a pseudo drop-down menu listing displaying, for example, database objects. The techniques to do this are similar to those you have seen before and are again built around a callback that populates the list with, for example, user forms in your database. Just for a moment, think about how you would provide a list of the database forms in a "normal" access application. In my case, I would use the MSysObjects table to get a listing of all forms in the database, and in the example for the Ribbon callback I will do just that.

Figure 3-8. *Training Staff group*

Now let's have a look at how you could add this feature to a Ribbon button. Again, you first define the Ribbon object and then add the code for the object into your new group. This is a drop-down list, and the XML is similar to that used earlier. Listing 3-12 shows the XML snippet to create the drop-down list displaying user forms in the database.

Listing 3-12. *Creating the Drop-Down List*

```
<dropDown id="FormList" label="View forms" ➥
imageMso="CreateReport" getItemCount=➥
"GetFormCount" getItemLabel="GetFormNames">
</dropDown>
```

Listings 3-13 and 3-14 show the callback functions used to populate the drop-down list with form names and provide a count of forms back to the Ribbon code.

Listing 3-13. *Getting a Form Count*

```
Function GetFormCount(control As IRibbonControl, ByRef count)
    Dim FormNames As String
 FormNames = "SELECT Name FROM MSysObjects ➥
WHERE  (((MSysObjects.Type)=-32768)) ➥
ORDER BY Name;"
    Set rstForms = CurrentDb.OpenRecordset(FormNames)
    count = rstForms.RecordCount
End Function
```

One of the advantages of this approach is that if you wanted to populate the drop-down menu with a list of other system objects, all that is required is changing the WHERE clause to reflect the object type needed: reports, queries, macros, and so on. Once you can populate the drop-down menu with the names of the required forms, you then need to provide an ID for the form. Listing 3-14 returns the ID for the form on each execution of the callback function.

Listing 3-14. *Callback That Returns the Form Names*

```
Function GetFormNames(control As IRibbonControl, index As Integer, ByRef ID)
    rsForms.MoveFirst
    rsForms.Move index
    ID = rsForms("Name").Value
End Function
```

Of course, you then need to provide a means for the information to be returned, in this case the label that you would like to display. The easiest way to do this is by using the already opened recordset and retrieving the form names. Listing 3-15 will return the labels used by the list.

Listing 3-15. *Returning the Drop-Down Form Label*

```
Function GetFormLabel(control As IRibbonControl, index As Integer, ByRef label)
rstForms.MoveFirst
rstForms.Move index
label = rstForms("Name").Value
End Function
```

Removing the Built-in Ribbon Items

In addition to creating your own options in the Ribbon, it is also possible to remove the main Ribbon items already available. You need to be careful here, as "remove" is actually the wrong word to use. All you can really do is set the visible property of an object to false. This is a useful feature that many Access developers currently employ to turn off options they do not want to have available to the user. Again, like everything else Ribbon related, you use XML and XML attributes to turn off the Ribbon items. The following code fragment will turn off some of the options in the File menu:

```
<fileMenu>
          <button idMso="OpenDatabase" visible="false"/>
          <button idMso="NewDatabase" visible="false"/>
          <splitButton idMso="AccessSaveAsMenu" visible="false"/>
  </fileMenu>
```

All that we require to know beforehand is the idMso of the menu choice you want to remove. A full listing of control IDs can be downloaded from the Microsoft web site. Just search for "2007 Office System Document: Lists of Control IDs." As mentioned previously, the idMso indicates that this is a Microsoft-provided item as opposed to one that you have created yourself. The idMso is also available as a tooltip if you go to the main Access customization screen. Hover the mouse over a menu option, and in the tooltip the idMso appears as text in brackets. So, for example, if you did not want your users to be able to view the properties for your application, you could remove the appropriate tab item from the main Access Ribbon. The View Database Properties option is on the File menu, its idMso is DatabaseProperties, and it can be turned off as follows:

```
<fileMenu>
<button idMso="DatabaseProperties" Visible = "false"/>
</fileMenu>
```

You can also change and remove items from the Office menu button itself. For example, to turn off the Office menu New database item, you could run the following Ribbon XML:

```
<officeMenu>
<button idMso="FileNewDatabase" visible="false"/>
</officeMenu>
```

If you need to change the position of menu options on the Office menu button, this can also be achieved using XML to manipulate the Ribbon. The following fragment shows the technique you can use to achieve this:

```
<button idMso="Menu Item to appear" insertBeforeMso ="FileCloseDatabase" />
```

```
The insertBeforeMSO and insertAfterMSO attributes allow you to control where your
commands appear in respect to the placement of other command buttons (that is,
before or after a specific named command).
```

Using Contextual Ribbons

In addition to creating generic Ribbons for use by the entire application, it is also possible to create Ribbons associated with particular forms (that is, contextual). You can see examples of contextual Ribbons using the Office applications, as Ribbons change depending on the task at hand. Each form and report has a hidden contextual Ribbon that will remain hidden unless it has content in it to display. You shall see in the next example how you can insert your own commands into this hidden Ribbon, thus causing it to be displayed. However, in order to discuss some additional important Ribbon elements, you will start off by creating a totally new Ribbon from the first example.

Here you will need to create a basic product form (or a form based on the table of your choice). You will then add a Ribbon with options specific to that form. If you look at the forms properties, you will notice a new property has been added. Clicking the Other tab in the form property sheet reveals a Custom Ribbon ID property. This can be set to the Ribbon associated with the specific form. Creation of the Ribbon is identical to the process already outlined. In this case, you add the new Ribbon into USysRibbons as a new record. Do not add the Ribbon code to the existing Ribbon record. Listing 3-6 shows the new Ribbon code for the form frmProducts. This gives you the ability to build very sophisticated dynamic menu systems.

This time I have added several layers of complexity, and we will look at each in turn including viewing and running reports and reusing some of the existing Access groups and commands. So let's look at the functionality you might need for a Product Ribbon:

- *Group*: Data Maintenance

- *Group*: General Access Menu Items

You will also remove several standard Access Ribbon commands that are not required by users or that you explicitly would like to remove, for example, database backup, SQL Server-related items, and the ability to use some of the items on the External data tab. The ideas and code discussed can be applied to any Ribbon you would like to change. So the outline for your Ribbon will be

Tab

Group1: Data maintenance including opening form for editing, adding, deleting

Group2: Product report listing

Group3: Mixture of Access Ribbon items

Group4: Removal of Access Ribbon items

End Tab

So the basic outline the Ribbon translates to is shown in the Ribbon XML Shell in Listing 3-16.

Listing 3-16. *Ribbon XML Shell*

```
<customUI xmlns="http://schemas.microsoft.com/office/2006/01/customui">
    <ribbon startFromScratch="false">
        <tabs>
            <tab id="tabProducts" label="Products">
                <group id="grpHome" label="Home">
                </group>
                <group id="group1" label="Products">
                </group>
                        <group id="group2" label="Products">
                </group>
<group id="group3" label="Products">
</Group>


            </tab>
        </tabs>
    </ribbon>
</customUI>
```

Group4 will simply be turning off some of the Microsoft Ribbon groups. This is a useful Ribbon feature if you want to restrict user ability within an application. Listing 3-17 creates a new tab for the group.

Listing 3-17. *frmProducts Ribbon Code*

```
<customUI xmlns="http://schemas.microsoft.com/office/2006/01/customui">
    <ribbon startFromScratch="false">
        <tabs>
            <tab id="tabProducts" label="Products">

            </tab>
        </tabs>
    </ribbon>
</customUI>
```

You have already worked on creating tabs, groups, and buttons. Listing 3-17, however, includes some new features. Figure 3-9 shows the new tab and your new Ribbon opened with the product form. At this point in the process, the Ribbon is blank.

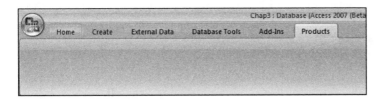

Figure 3-9. *Blank Products Ribbon tab*

As I have said, Group1 will provide access to the product data, including adding new records, viewing existing records, and running some product reports. The Ribbon code required is shown in Listing 3-18.

Listing 3-18. *Product Group: Group1*

```
<customUI xmlns="http://schemas.microsoft.com/office/2006/01/customui">
<ribbon startFromScratch="false">
<tabs>
<tab id="tabProducts" label="Products">
<group id = "ProdMain" label ="Product Menu">
<button id="ProdList" label="Product Listing" size="large" ➥
onAction="OpenProdList" getImage="GetImage"/>
<button id ="ProdForms" label="Product Forms" size="large" ➥
onAction="OpenProdForm" getImage="GetImage"/>
</group>

<group id="frmdrop" label ="Object Drop Downs">
<dropDown id="cboForms" label="Show Forms" onAction="OpenForm" ➥
getItemCount="GetFormCount" getItemID="GetFormName" />
<dropDown id="cbogetreports" label="Show Reports" onAction="OpenReports" ➥
getItemCount="GetReportCount" getItemID="GetReportName" />

</group>
          </tab>
       </tabs>
    </ribbon>
</customUI>
```

Figure 3-10 shows the Ribbon groups at this point.

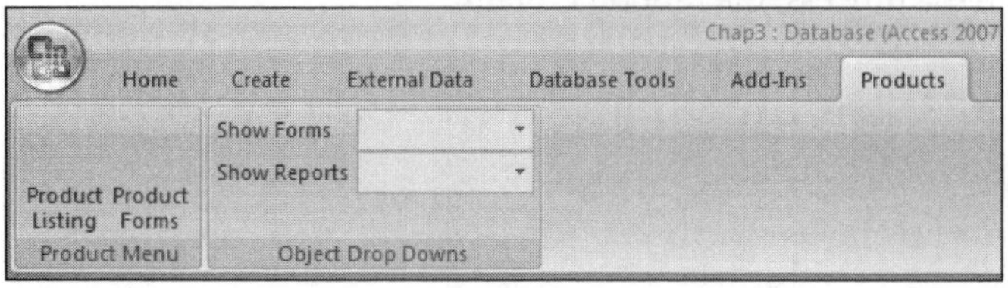

Figure 3-10. *Group1 Product Ribbon*

Note that there are no icons, as you have not yet added the getImage attribute to the XML file. Nor indeed have you written the VBA callbacks required. Add an additional Dim statement to the module as follows:

Dim rstReports as Recordset

The report drop-down callback functions are almost identical to those used to populate the list with form objects and can be changed as shown in Listings 3-19 and 3-20.

Listing 3-19. *Getting the Report Count*

```
Function GetReportCount(control As IRibbonControl, ByRef count)
    Dim ReportNames As String
    ReportNames = "SELECT Name FROM MSysObjects ➥
    WHERE  (((MSysObjects.Type)=-32768)) ➥
    ORDER BY Name;"
    Set rstReport = CurrentDb.OpenRecordset(ReportNames)
    count = rsReports.RecordCount
End Function
```

Listing 3-20. *Getting the Report Names*

```
Function GetReportName(control As IRibbonControl, index As Integer, ByRef ID)
    rsReports.MoveFirst
    rsReports.Move index
    ID = rsReports("Name").Value
End Function
```

Defining the onAction attribute for the form and report drop-downs is next in the list. Of course, if you wished, you could complete the Ribbon creation and then complete the XML. The onAction VBA callback for the reports is again fairly straightforward, but it demonstrates the technique required to open the report based on the value chosen in the list. As you have already seen, the Ribbon drop-down list can pass its selectedID to the callback to ensure the chosen report is opened. Listing 3-21 shows the basic function used to open a report based on a choice from the drop-down list.

Listing 3-21. *Opening a Report*

```
Function OpenReports(control As IRibbonControl, selectedId As String, ➥
selectedIndex As Integer)
DoCmd.OpenReport selectedId, acViewReport
End Function
```

■**Note** I have found it is almost always better from a debugging point of view to create the Ribbon and individual groups, then create the callbacks for each group, and then create the onAction function or procedure for each of the buttons. In this way, if something goes wrong with the XML, you are simply debugging one group at a time rather than a lengthy XML script.

Manipulating Existing Groups and Controls

It is also possible, as I have stated, to remove built-in groups from the Ribbons. To illustrate this process, the code in Listing 3-22 leaves the Create tab in place but removes all of the group items. The required XML is shown in bold. This code could be used with the final grouping for the custom menu for the product form.

Listing 3-22. *Removing the Create Groups*

```
<customUI xmlns="http://schemas.microsoft.com/office/2006/01/customui">
    <ribbon startFromScratch="false">
        <tabs>
  <tab idMso="TabCreate" visible="true">
<group idMso="GroupCreateTable" visible="false" />
<group idMso="GroupCreateForm" visible="false" />
<group idMso="GroupCreateReport" visible="false" />
<group idMso="GroupCreateAdvanced" visible="false" />
</tab>
<tab id="tabProducts" label="Products">
<group id = "ProdMain" label ="Product Menu">
<button id="ProdList" label="Product Listing" size="large" ➥
onAction="OpenProdList" getImage="GetImage"/>
<button id ="ProdForms" label="Product Forms" size="large" ➥
onAction="OpenProdForm" getImage="GetImage"/>
</group>
<group id="frmdrop" label ="Object Drop Downs">
<dropDown id="cboForms" label="Show Forms" onAction="OpenForm" ➥
getItemCount="GetFormCount"  getItemLabel="GetFormLabel"/>
        <dropDown id="cboReports" onAction="OpenReport" ➥
getItemCount="GetReportCount" getItemID="GetReportName" ➥
getItemLabel="GetReportCaption"/>
```

```
    </group>
            </tab>
        </tabs>
    </ribbon>
</customUI>
```

First of all, you specify the tab you would like to work with, in this case the Create tab, `<tab idMso="TabCreate" visible="true">`. You want to keep the tab visible to demonstrate the changes the code in Listing 3-22 brings about. The Create tab contains the following four groups:

- GroupCreateTable

- GroupCreateForm

- GroupCreateReport

- GroupCreateAdvanced

Turning the groups off is simply a matter of setting their visibility to false (that is, `<group idMso="GroupCreateReport" visible="false" />`). It's unlikely that you will want to remove all the groups and all their individual controls from a tab, but this shows how easy it is and the fact that you can actually do it. It is more likely that you would want to remove particular items from an individual group or groups. The bad news is that you can't. Nice and easy that one. You cannot remove or disable individual items from the Microsoft group controls in any way other than remove them as shown.

Adding Other Group Controls

Most of the controls you have used so far have been fairly standard controls used on a day-to-day basis by many Access developers. However, RibbonX allows you to make use of additional objects and techniques when creating menu systems.

Check Box

Listing 3-23 shows the XML used to create a check box group and controls. In this case, I am using the check box group to ask a couple of questions of the user. The input from the user could then be inserted into a questionnaire table, for example.

Listing 3-23. *Creating a Check Box Group*

```
<group id="StaffGroup" label="Quick Question">
<checkBox id="Q1" label="Staff Pension" onAction="chkPension"/>
<checkBox id="Q2" label="Overtime" onAction="chkOvertime"/>
<checkBox id="Q3" label="Flexi" onAction="chkFlexi"/>
</group>
```

The XML in Listing 3-23 can be added to your existing RibbonX XML as a new group item, and it will appear as so on the Products tab. Figure 3-11 shows the Products tab with this new group added.

Figure 3-11. *Adding a check box group*

In this example, you could use a simple SELECT CASE statement to carry out an action based on the check box ID returned. For example, you could run an update statement incrementing a question table field for that option by 1 or open a data collection form for more information concerning the chosen topic.

Toggle Buttons

Toggle buttons simply stay down when clicked. Other than that, there are no major differences between a toggle button and a standard Ribbon button. The XML to create the toggle button is also very similar:

```
<toggleButton id="btntoggle" imageMso="Image to display"➽
    size="large" label="Label for image" onAction="Callback to execute"/>
```

Summary

As you may be beginning to see, RibbonX gives you a fairly dynamic and flexible way to build custom menu systems for your applications. The actual XML coding of the Ribbon is nothing complex and is made reasonably easy using the free tools supplied by Microsoft. Over time, it is highly likely that many third-party developers will develop graphical tools for amending existing menus and creating your own without the need to get up to your elbows in RibbonX XML.

In this chapter, we only looked at creating Ribbons and some VBA callbacks; we did not look at the issue of developing add-ins using other software such as Visual Studio. This was a deliberate choice on my part, as many Access developers and power users will not have access to such tools; indeed they might not even wish to get involved in this side of the development process, and truthfully, I don't want to either. All I require is the ability to create my own menu items and remove those that could pose a danger to the application. RibbonX and a good XML editor meet these requirements for me without the need to begin developing custom solutions using .NET. At the start of this chapter, I was open and up front about my own experience with XML and Ribbons, and I hope by this stage in the chapter you too have started the journey into Ribbons and customizing Access 2007. For further information on Ribbons, the appendix at the back of this book discusses some issues and recommendations about actual Ribbon design as opposed to the mechanics of Ribbon creation.

CHAPTER 4

■■■

Data Collection Using Microsoft Outlook 2007

In this chapter, we look at another new feature of Microsoft Access 2007: the ability to automatically collect information by using a combination of Access 2007 and Microsoft Outlook 2007. This is mostly an interface-driven process at the moment, but even so it offers another useful tool for developers and power users who have a need to collect data within an organization. When I learned this feature had been added, I immediately began thinking about surveys for users of our services. Here was a nice, simple, almost automatic approach to this issue. Of course, you could still create a web-based form and have that input directly fed into a database table, but this approach is another option available to you.

You can use a table or a query as the basis for the data collection process and can indeed use a multiple table query if you require data to be added or updated in more than one table. Two types of forms are available to you for e-mail data collection: standard HTML and Microsoft InfoPath. InfoPath will allow you to create highly interactive collection forms, but with the restriction that the user must have InfoPath installed in order to use the form for data collection. When building your own data collection model as you will do shortly, you follow three main steps:

1. Create the data collection action inside Access.

2. Register the data collection action with Outlook.

3. Create and send the e-mail.

We'll take a closer look at how this is done next.

■Note I would like to thank Shamil Salakhetdinov, Gustav Brock, and Marty Connelly, talented members of AccessD (Access developers list at http://www.databaseadvisors.com), for the advice, testing, and specific functions they provided when I was writing this chapter.

■**Note** As collecting data using Access and Outlook is a wizard-driven process, there are lots of screens to complete. I have decided not to include all the screen shots, rather only those that may require some additional configuration by you during the process. Also be aware that this chapter was written using Beta 2 TR2 software and based on beta documentation, so some of the XML information and instructions may be subject to change, as is the nature of beta software.

Getting Started with HTML Forms

The examples that follow use the Northwind demonstration database available with Access 2007. I have also added my own e-mail address to the Customers table for demonstration purposes.

To see the principles involved, you will start off by using the Customers table to begin the process:

1. Select the Customers table in the Navigation Pane.

2. Right-click and select Collect and Update Data via Email.

This starts the Collect Data Through Email Wizard, which will offer you several options during the process.

3. Click Next.

You can collect data using either an HTML or InfoPath form. Initially, you will use an HTML form to collect your responses.

4. Select HTML Form.

5. Click Next.

6. Select Collect new information only. The next screen offers you two options:

    • *Collect new information only*: Using this option enables you to select existing e-mail addresses or enter new e-mail addresses in Outlook, to which the request is issued. Data returned via the HTML form will be appended to the database table.

    • *Update existing information*: If you choose this option, all e-mail addresses used must exist in the database.

7. Click Next.

8. Select the fields for which you would like to collect data. Any field with a required property set to yes will be preselected by the wizard. The wizard does not support the following data types—AutoNumber, OLE, attachment, or multivalued fields—so these fields cannot be used in the collection process.

Once you have selected the fields, you can then choose whether you would like Access to automatically process the replies or process them manually yourself. If you choose automatic processing, you must have the database open in shared mode for it to work.

9. Check the Automatically process replies option.

10. Click Next.

11. Select Enter the email addresses in Microsoft Office Outlook.

12. Click Next.

13. You may if you like customize the message in the next screen and then click Next.

14. Click Create.

Outlook 2007 will open, requesting you to enter the required e-mail address. Figure 4-1 shows the generated HTML form in the e-mail message.

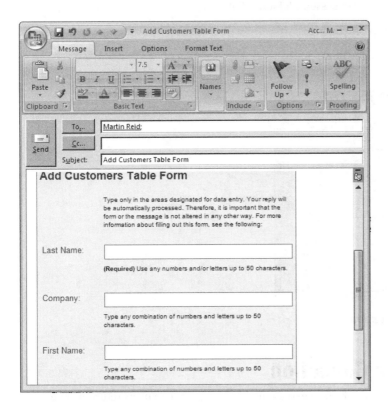

Figure 4-1. *Access HTML e-mail form*

15. Enter an e-mail address and click Send.

Nothing much to this really. On receipt, the user simply completes the form and sends it back. Outlook will keep a copy of the e-mail returned in a folder named Access Data Collection Replies. The wizard allows you to select a folder of your choice for replies. Click Access Data Collection Replies on the Process Email page of the wizard. On the same wizard screen, you can also set some of the properties for automatically processing replies. Clicking set properties to control the automatic processing of replies opens a new dialog box where you can set the following options:

- Automatically process replies and add to database

- Discard replies from those to whom you did not send the e-mail

- Accept multiple replies from each recipient

- Allow multiple rows per reply

- Only allow updates to existing data

- Number of replies to be processed (default is 25)

- Date and time to stop processing

Figure 4-2 shows this dialog box.

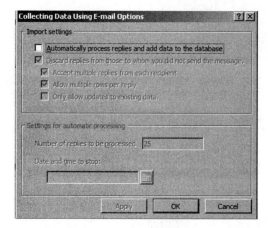

Figure 4-2. *Data collection options*

Processing the Collection

If you have specified that replies be processed automatically, the data users return will be added to the table for you. However, there is also the option to manually process the data in e-mail replies. Figure 4-3 shows the Manage Data Collection Messages dialog box, available on the External Data tab by clicking Managing Replies in the Collect Data group.

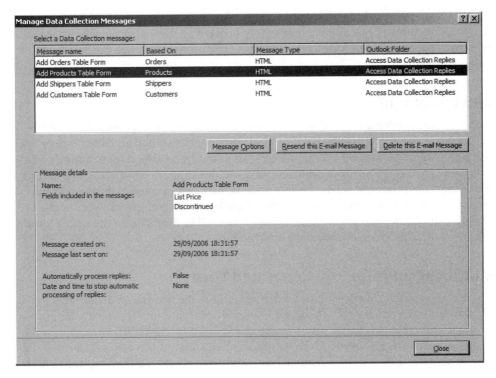

Figure 4-3. *Manage Data Collection Messages dialog box*

Using this dialog box, you can perform the following actions:

- Change the data collection options discussed earlier.

- Re-send a particular message. If you choose to use this option, Access will ensure that the original tables and queries still exist.

- Delete a message or messages.

- View general information about the message.

In addition to using a table, it is also possible to use a query as the source of a data collection e-mail. This is essential if you would like to use this process to work with more than one table, because a SELECT query is the only way to pass data to more than one table. In this case, the process is just the same as if you where using a table.

Collecting Data Using an InfoPath Form

InfoPath, which has been available for some time, gives you more control over how users can interact with your collection form. With the HTML form, what you see is generally what you get. InfoPath allows some customization of your form above what the HTML form supplies, provided of course you actually have InfoPath installed. The end user will also need InfoPath installed in order to respond to the e-mail. Another point to consider is that the InfoPath form is sent as an attachment with the collection e-mail and must be opened locally, filled in, and reattached before the user can respond. However, you may find there are instances when the customization opportunities InfoPath gives you over HTML forms outweigh the drawbacks of using InfoPath forms.

What Is InfoPath?

InfoPath is a form development tool that supports XML. It allows you to create dynamic, interactive forms and may be useful if you require additional validation and other interactive options when running a data collection process—for example, creating a list of options via a drop-down list to enable some user selection. As usual, due to space constraints, I cannot go into every aspect of this software, but I will provide an overview of some of the more useful things you can do. Once Access has created the InfoPath attachment, you can open and edit it using InfoPath. Changes made can then be saved and will be available for the e-mail form when it is issued, as they are saved into the attachment.

Customizing an InfoPath-Generated Form

Take for example the Job Title field of the Customers table in the Northwind database. By default, the data collection form you generate from this table will contain a corresponding text field. What if you wanted to change this to a drop-down list? With the HTML form, this would not be possible, but using InfoPath it is straightforward, providing again you actually have the software. To edit the form before you actually issue the data collection e-mail, run the Collect Data Through Email Wizard, select the Customers table, and choose InfoPath for the e-mail. Once you click the Create button, Outlook will open and you will then have access to the InfoPath attachment. To continue:

1. Right-click the attachment.

2. Select Open to open the file in InfoPath.

3. In InfoPath, select Tools ➤ Design This Form.

4. Click the Job Title field to select it.

5. Right-click and select Change to from the context menu.

6. Select Drop-Down List.

7. Double-click the new drop-down list to open the Drop-Down List Box Properties dialog box shown in Figure 4-4.

8. Select Enter list box entries manually.

9. Click Add.

10. Enter each job title required, clicking Add after each entry.

11. Click OK to close the dialog box.

12. Select File Save to save the changes and close the form.

13. Exit InfoPath.

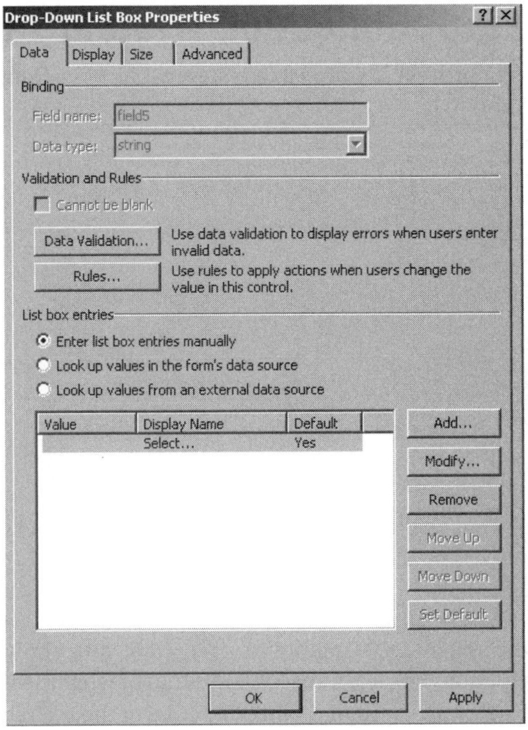

Figure 4-4. *Drop-Down List Box Properties dialog box*

The changes made to the form will be reflected in the e-mail attachment, which can now be sent to users. Following are other features InfoPath lets you include in your forms:

- Placeholder text (for example, an instruction to the user about what to actually enter into a text box)

- Validation on each form object

- Conditional formatting

- Linking to a data source (for example, Access or SQL Server complex rule building to populate one form field based on the input from another)

InfoPath is a powerful interactive form development environment with its own programming model. Using a combination of this software, Outlook 2007 and Access 2007 developers can create highly efficient and interactive e-mail data collection forms. Outside the data collection area, InfoPath also provides you with a tool that lets you link directly to an Access table or query data for similar data collection purposes. An overview of using Access and InfoPath together can be found at http://office.microsoft.com/en-us/assistance/ha011032471033.aspx.

Up to this point, we have been looking at how the interface is used to both begin and process the e-mail data collection process. As is standard with Access, the functionality is provided by data help within one of the Access system tables, which you will learn about next.

Overview of the MSysDataCollection System Table

Information relating to the data collection process is stored in a system table, MSysDataCollection, that is structured as shown in Table 4-1.

Table 4-1. *MSysDataCollection Table Structure*

Field	Type
Active	Yes/No
BasedOnType	Number
CreatedDate	Date/Time
ExternalID	Number (PK)
FormName	Memo
InfoPathForm	Yes/No
Mapping	Memo
OutlookFolder	Memo
DateSent	Date/Time

As you can guess from Table 4-1, the system table maintains a record of your choices when running the Collect Data Through Email Wizard, a sort of audit trail of what the wizard carried out on your behalf. It does not maintain the actual e-mail address of the recipient, but of course this information can be retrieved from Outlook 2007. This system table is created the first time you run the wizard, but as you will see later in the section "Populating MSysDataCollection Manually," you can also work with the table manually. The following list gives a bit more detail on each field:

Active: This field is not actually used, but it should always be set to true.

BasedOnType: This stores the source of the data collection (that is, a table or a query). The data reflects the ACE database engine object types, 1 for a table, 4 for a linked SQL Server table, 5 for a query, and 6 for a linked Windows SharePoint Services list.

CreatedDate: This is the date the data collection activity was created.

ExternalID: This is the primary key of the table and contains a GUID; for example, {C6EBA1EA-948E-495B-B101-05319D3E7362} is the GUID from an e-mail data collection record.

FormName: This is the default value in the subject line of the e-mail issued. If you are using an InfoPath form, this is the InfoPath file name.

InfoPathForm: Set this to true if you are using an InfoPath form and false if you are using HTML.

Mapping: This is XML data that contains the instructions for the data collection action. Listing 4-1 shows the XML data for a data collection task. (I will discuss the actual XML shortly in the next section.) As you can see from the listing, this XML data contains all of the instructions I passed to the wizard while executing the data collection activity.

Listing 4-1. *Data Collection Mapping XML Data*

```
<mapping>
<formProperties>
<automateDataCollection>true</automateDataCollection>
<enableDataCollection>true</enableDataCollection>
<maxReplies>25</maxReplies>
<numReplies>0</numReplies>
<allowMultipleReplies>true</allowMultipleReplies>
<allowMultipleRows>true</allowMultipleRows>
<onlyUpdates>false</onlyUpdates>
<stopDateTime>0</stopDateTime>
<onlySentTo>true</onlySentTo>
</formProperties>
<tables>
<table name="table1" accessTable="Customers" collectionType="insert">
<iterate root="/AccessInfoPathForm/dcip:inlinedata/dcip:row">
<mapitem IsPrimaryKey="1" formNode="dcip:PrimaryKey" tableCell="ID"/>
<mapitem formNode="table1:field1" tableCell="Company" caption="Company" ➡
readOnly="false" required="false" type="x:string"/>
<mapitem formNode="table1:field2" tableCell="Last Name" caption="Last Name" ➡
readOnly="false" required="false" type="x:string"/>
<mapitem formNode="table1:field3" tableCell="First Name" caption="First Name" ➡
readOnly="false" required="false" type="x:string"/>
</iterate>
</table>
</tables>
</mapping>
```

OutlookFolder: This is the EntryID for the Outlook folder to which replies will be sent.

DateSent: This is the last time an e-mail was issued for this data collection event. This date is updated each time an e-mail is issued using the Manage Data Collection Messages dialog box.

Breaking Down the Data Collection Mapping XML File

The XML file shown in Listing 4-1 contains items specific to data collection. For example, `<formProperties>` contains information on the automatic processing of replies. The listing consists of several elements and attributes as follows:

`automateDataCollection`: Set this to true if you have selected to automatically process replies. Of course, if the process is to be manual, this property will be set to false.

`enableDataCollection`: This is in fact not used and is always set to true.

`maxReplies`: This is the maximum number of replies that will be processed automatically. Once this limit is reached, you must process the rest of the replies manually.

`numReplies`: This keeps a record of the number of replies received after each export to Access. When `numReplies` is greater than `maxReplies`, automatic e-mail processing stops.

allowMultipleReplies: If true, the user receiving the e-mail can reply several times. If false, the replies are limited to one.

onlyUpdates: If true, replies can only update existing table data. If false, the replies can actually add new data to the table and update existing records.

stopDateTime: This is the date and time to stop automatic processing of replies. This is a useful feature when you require date/time-dependent responses. Replies received after this date will not be processed.

onlySentTo: This is a useful element as well. Only those to whom the e-mail was originally sent will have their replies processed automatically. If set to false, anyone can reply and have his or her reply processed.

Listing 4-2 shows the properties from an e-mail data collection file demonstrating the configuration information; for example, note that maxReplies has been set to 25, nunReplies has been set to 0, and automateDataCollection has been set to true. All are items that are selected when working through the Collect Data Through Email Wizard.

Listing 4-2. *Form Properties XML Section*

```
<formProperties>
<automateDataCollection>true</automateDataCollection>
<enableDataCollection>true</enableDataCollection>
<maxReplies>25</maxReplies>
<numReplies>0</numReplies>
<allowMultipleReplies>true</allowMultipleReplies>
<allowMultipleRows>true</allowMultipleRows>
<onlyUpdates>false</onlyUpdates>
<stopDateTime>0</stopDateTime>
<onlySentTo>true</onlySentTo>
</formProperties>
```

The next major section in the XML data deals with the Access tables. The table section shows the mapping between table or query. Listing 4-3 shows just the tables section from Listing 4-1.

Listing 4-3. *Table XML Section*

```
<tables>
<table name="table1" accessTable="Customers" collectionType="insert">
<iterate root="/AccessInfoPathForm/dcip:inlinedata/dcip:row">
<mapitem IsPrimaryKey="1" formNode="dcip:PrimaryKey" tableCell="ID"/>
<mapitem formNode="table1:field1" tableCell="Company" caption="Company" ➥
readOnly="false" required="false" type="x:string"/>
<mapitem formNode="table1:field2" tableCell="Last Name" caption="Last Name" ➥
readOnly="false" required="false" type="x:string"/>
<mapitem formNode="table1:field3" tableCell="First Name" caption="First Name" ➥
readOnly="false" required="false" type="x:string"/>
</iterate>
</table>
```

`tables`: This is the name of the table or query the data is being processed into. There is only one single tag with no attributes.

`name`: Always set this to table1. This is used internally for data collection purposes.

`accessTable`: This is the name of the Access table or query data is being collected into. In Listing 4-3, you can see that this data collection is designed for the Customers table.

`collectionType`: This specifies an update or insert depending on the data collection operation taking place. In Listing 4-3, you can see that this is an INSERT operation.

`Iterate root`: This contains the location inside the e-mail of the data to be stored.

■Note `root` refers to the XPath to the XML used internally to actually process the e-mail. For a full overview of XPath, which is used to address XML files, please see `http://www.w3.org/TR/xpath`. The entry in this element depends on the type of form you want to send. For a standard HTML form, you enter AccessInfoPathForm/inlinedata/row; for an InfoPath form, the entry is AccessInfoPathForm/dcip:inlinedata/dcip:row.

`mapItem`: This maps each column in the table or query to the data on the form. There will be one item for each item in your data collection form plus one additional item for the primary key even if you have not selected it.

`IsPrimaryKey`: If set to true, the column will be the primary key of the collection table.

`formNode`: This is the internal name for the field. Fields will be named in the order they appear on the form, not the table, field1, field2, and so on.

`tableCell`: This is the column name of the field in Access.

`Caption`: This is the name displayed on the form for the chosen field and can be customized when creating the data collection e-mail.

`Type`: This is the type of field using XSD data types. XSD defines an XML document in terms of structure, elements, and attributes you can use and the types of data they can contain. Table 4-2 shows some of the Access data types and their XSD equivalents.

Table 4-2. *Access Data Types and XSD*

Access	XSD
Text, memo	x:string
Byte, integer, long integer	x:integer
Currency, decimal, float	x:double
Date/Time	x:dateTime
Yes/No	x:Boolean
Hyperlink	x:anyURI

Replication ID, AutoNumber, and binary are not supported.

Breaking Down the Recipients Section of the XML File

The recipients section of the XML file is handled by Outlook and contains information about who the e-mail was sent to. It is completed when the e-mail is actually sent out. Listing 4-4 shows the structure. It is mainly used to enforce automatic processing rules.

Listing 4-4. *Recipients XML Section*

```
<recipients>
<recipient email="" responded="">
<primaryKey value=""/>
</recipient>
</recipients>
```

The following list describes the elements and attributes of this section of the XML file:

recipient: This adds the name of each user who received the e-mail.

email: This is the e-mail address of each user who will receive a copy of the data collection.

responded: This will show true if the user has responded to the e-mail; otherwise it will show false.

primaryKey: When your e-mail deals with updating existing data, each user will be associated with a specific set of primary keys marking the data as his or hers. This is used to keep track of which rows have been sent to each user and makes sure users cannot update rows that are not theirs.

Value: This is the value of the primary key sent to the user.

Processing the Replies

Replies can be processed automatically by selecting the appropriate option in the Collect Data Through Email Wizard. They can also be processed manually using the Access interface. Manual processing gives you a little more control over the process, and speaking for myself, makes me feel a little better when I can see what is happening within the database.

Populating MSysDataCollection Manually

So now that you know all this data is required, what can you do about it? Well, from DAO using standard VBA, you can create an insert procedure to add the records to the system table for you. However, the documentation and system hooks for this are incomplete, especially in terms of the XML mapping at this stage, so this section will provide a theoretical overview. I have included code where it may help you out once the documentation and the hooks into this process are made public.

The first thing you may need to do if populating the table manually from code is to actually create the system table MSysDataCollection using DAO. This table is created automatically the first time you run the wizard and may already exist.

Once the information discussed earlier has been added to the system table, the data collection information will then appear in the Manage Data Collection Messages dialog box. The only tricky parts about the table are the GUID primary key and the XML field, which you will need to populate. Listing 4-5 shows the code used to generate a GUID for the ExternalID PK field. I would like to thank Gustav Brock, a longtime member of the AccessD list, for supplying the GUID functions.

Listing 4-5. *Creating a GUID*

```
Public Type GUID
  Data1         As Long
  Data2         As Integer
  Data3         As Integer
  Data4(0 To 7) As Byte
End Type

Private Declare Function CoCreateGuid Lib "ole32.dll" ( _
  ByRef pguid As GUID) As Long

Private Declare Function StringFromGUID2 Lib "ole32.dll" ( _
  ByRef rguid As Any, _
  ByVal lpstrClsId As Long, _
  ByVal cbMax As Long) As Long

Public Function GetGUIDString() As String
' Create a GUID and return its string representation.
'' 2002-12-15. Cactus Data ApS, CPH.
  ' Length of GUID string per definition.
  Const clngGUID    As Long = 38
  ' Length of buffer with added space for zero terminator.
  Const clngBuffer  As Long = clngGUID + 1

  Dim udtGuid       As GUID
  Dim strGUID       As String * clngGUID
  Dim abytGUID()    As Byte

  ' Dim byte array.
  abytGUID() = String(clngBuffer, vbNullChar)
  ' Create GUID.
  If CoCreateGuid(udtGuid) = 0 Then
    ' GUID was successfully created.
    If StringFromGUID2(udtGuid, VarPtr(abytGUID(0)), clngBuffer) = clngBuffer Then
      ' GUID was successfully copied into byte array abytGUID in Unicode.
      ' Convert byte array to Ansi GUID string stripping zero terminator.
      strGUID = abytGUID
    End If
  End If

  GetGUIDString = strGUID
End Function
```

The next tricky part is the XML field data. This is the area that restricts what you can actually do via code at the moment. The documentation at Beta 2 TR2 is still incomplete, and some hooks into the code are not yet available. I have found the easiest way to do this is to simply create the XML field and its data in an XML editor and cut and paste it into the table. However, you could use VBA to create a concatenated string and pass the variables into the procedure.

For this section, I am breaking the XML field down into its various elements and attributes. The shell of the XML file format is shown in Listing 4-6.

Listing 4-6. *XML File Structure*

```
<mapping>
<formProperties>

</formProperties>

<tables>
<table name=
<iterate root="">

</iterate>

</table>
</tables>

</mapping>
```

Each XML file created will have this same basic shell structure. For this example, you will collect data for the Orders table of the Northwind database. Table 4-3 shows the XML tags and their meaning in the context of this collection process. I have left out the structure tags and some of the table tags, but this gives a general idea of what's going on in this process. You can refer back to the full example shown in Listing 4-1 for reference.

Table 4-3. *XML Data Collection File*

XML	Comments
`<automateDataCollection>true </automateDataCollection>`	Data will be processed automatically.
`<maxReplies>25</maxReplies>`	A maximum of 25 replies will be processed manually.
`<allowMultipleReplies>true </allowMultipleReplies>`	The user will be able to submit multiple e-mail replies.
`<numReplies>0</numReplies>`	This is the default value, which will be incremented.
`<allowMultipleRows>true </allowMultipleRows>`	The user may submit multiple rows for the Orders table.
`<onlyUpdates>false</onlyUpdates>`	The user can update and insert new rows.
`<stopDateTime>0</stopDateTime>`	This is the date and time to stop processing. Date and time is stored as a double (38990.00069444444).

XML	Comments
<onlySentTo>true</onlySentTo>	Only the individual the e-mail was issued to can have responses automatically processed.
<tables>	This tag set refers to the table and fields that will be used for the collection process.

The actual VBA procedure to carry out the insert to the system table is straightforward and is shown in Listing 4-7. I have created the XML mapping field data as a distinct XML file, and I will pass this to the record once the VBA code has executed.

Listing 4-7. *Adding a Record to MSysDataCollection*

```
Public Sub addEmail()
On Error GoTo Err_addEmail
' Manually add a record to MSysDataCollection

Dim rstsysObj As DAO.Recordset
Dim strsql As String
Dim db As Database
Set db = CurrentDb

Set rstsysObj = db.OpenRecordset("MSysDataCollection")

With rstsysObj
.AddNew
!Active = "-1"
!BasedOnType = 1
!CreatedDate = Now()
!ExternalID = GetGUIDString()
!FormName = "My Data Collection Form"
InfoPathForm = "0"

.Update

End With

Exit_addEmail:
On Error Resume Next
    If Not (rstsysObj Is Nothing) Then rstsysObj.Close: Set rstsysObj = Nothing
    If Not (db Is Nothing) Then db.Close: Set db = Nothing
Exit Sub
Err_addEmail:
        MsgBox Err.Description, , "Error in Sub basEmailDC.addEmail"
        Resume Exit_addEmail
    Resume 0    '.FOR TROUBLESHOOTING
End Sub
```

As I said earlier, data collection is a two-part process, and the second part involves working with Outlook 2007 and letting Outlook know that you are going to start using e-mail data collection. Let's now turn our attention to this process.

Working in Outlook

Outlook contains a COM add-in that enables e-mail data collection and processing. When working with the wizard, this add-in is turned on for you. By default, it is disabled within Outlook. This COM add-in examines e-mails as they arrive, and if they are data collection e-mails, they are processed according to the instructions issued from the Access side of things. Once again, XML is used to tell Outlook about the e-mails and their data collection properties. You learned earlier that the primary key from the MSysDataCollection table contains a GUID that uniquely identifies each e-mail collection process. To manually enable the data collection COM add-in, follow these steps:

1. Click Tools.

2. Click Customize.

3. Click the Commands tab.

4. Scroll to the bottom of the command listing.

5. Select COM Add-Ins.

6. Drag and drop the COM Add-Ins button onto the Outlook toolbar.

Figure 4-5 shows the COM Add-Ins button in Outlook with the dialog box open. Notice that I have enabled all the COM add-ins, and Outlook 2007 will now be ready to process data collection. As shown in Figure 4-5, you may have additional COM add-ins installed in Microsoft Outlook 2007 e-mail, among other things.

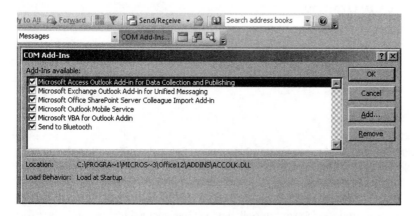

Figure 4-5. *Enabling Outlook 2007 COM add-ins via the interface*

To find out whether the COM add-ins are loaded in Outlook, you can execute the VBA procedure shown in Listing 4-8 from within Access. This is a useful routine if you need to actually create the collection process via VBA code.

Listing 4-8. *Checking Outlook COM Add-Ins*

```
Public Sub GetCom()
On Error GoTo Err_GetCom
Dim OutObj As Object
Dim myAddIn As Office.COMAddIn
Set OutObj = CreateObject("Outlook.Application")
    For Each myAddIn In OutObj.Application.COMAddIns
       With myAddIn
          Debug.Print "Connected = " & .Connect;
          Debug.Print " , ProgId = " & .ProgId & " - ";
          Debug.Print .Description
       End With
    Next myAddIn

Exit_GetCom:
On Error Resume Next
    If Not (OutObj Is Nothing) Then OutObj.Close: Set OutObj = Nothing
Exit Sub
Err_GetCom:
       MsgBox Err.Description, , "Error in Sub basEmailDC.GetCom"
       Resume Exit_GetCom
    Resume 0    '.FOR TROUBLESHOOTING
End Sub
```

This will output all the Outlook COM add-ins to the Intermediate window as shown here. Note the first add-in is the data collection add-in, which in this case is active.

```
Connected = True , ProgId = AccessAddin.DC - Microsoft Access Outlook ➥
Add-in for Data Collection and Publishing
Connected = True , ProgId = BtOfficeAddin.BtOfficeIntegration.1 - Send to Bluetooth
Connected = True , ProgId = ColleagueImport.ColleagueImportAddin - Microsoft ➥
Office SharePoint Server Colleague Import Add-in
Connected = True , ProgId = Microsoft.OMSAddin - Microsoft Outlook Mobile Service
Connected = True , ProgId = Microsoft.VbaAddinForOutlook.1 - Microsoft VBA for ➥
Outlook Addin
Connected = True , ProgId = UmOutlookAddin.FormRegionAddin - Microsoft Exchange ➥
Outlook Add-in for Unified Messaging
```

This result also gives you the ProgID, which can then be used to start the required COM add-in. To start the add-in, you can replace the For statement in Listing 4-8 with the fragment shown in listing 4-9; in fact, the code in Listing 4-9 is all that is required.

Listing 4-9. *Starting the Data Collection COM Add-In*

```
For Each myAddIn In OutObj.Application.COMAddIns
          With myAddIn
          If .ProgId = "AccessAddin.DC" Then
          .Connect = True
          Exit For
      End If
    End With
  Next myAddIn
```

This will enable the data collection COM add-in within Outlook 2007. However, the COM add-in should not be enabled until you have added the Outlook configuration e-mail discussed next.

When you first run the Collect Data Through Email Wizard from within Access 2007, it will also create two Outlook folders: a Data Collection Search folder, Access Data Collection Replies, which makes it easy for Outlook to find the collection e-mail, and a default Data Collection Replies folder, to store the replies upon receipt. Using the wizard, you can override this default folder and redirect collection e-mails into a folder of your choice. In order to get the COM add-in to recognize data collection e-mails, you must also have an XML configuration file that contains the details of the data collection. When you are using the wizard, the configuration file is generated for you. If you are trying this using code, you have to create the file yourself. The XML configuration has the following format:

```
<ActionConfigFile>
<outlookFolders>
<defaultFolder/>
<searchFolder />
</outlookFolders>
<mdbMap />
</ActionConfigFile>
```

Listing 4-10 shows the structure and data contained in an example file. Some of the XML structure and information should already be familiar to you from reading through the earlier sections of this chapter.

Listing 4-10. *AccessDCActionFile.XML*

```
<ActionConfigFile>
<outlookFolders>
<defaultFolder>00000000DED792DDC981714FBC3➡
FD0EB94D7AB9382820000</defaultFolder>
<searchFolder>00000000DED792DDC981714FBC➡
3FD0EB94D7AB93E3000800</searchFolder>
</outlookFolders>
<mdbMap><form id="{5CD85176-C249-44D2-9009-38E8C6863478}" ➡
moveToFolder="00000000DED792DDC981714FBC3FD0EB94D7AB9382820000"➡
FormType="HTML">
```

```
<path>C:\AccessBook\Chapter4\Northwind2007.accdb</path>
<userReply>false</userReply>
<formProperties>
<automateDataCollection>true</automateDataCollection>
<enableDataCollection>true</enableDataCollection>
<maxReplies>25</maxReplies>
<numReplies>0</numReplies>
<allowMultipleReplies>true</allowMultipleReplies>
<allowMultipleRows>true</allowMultipleRows>
<onlyUpdates>false</onlyUpdates>
<stopDateTime>0</stopDateTime>
<onlySentTo>true</onlySentTo>
</formProperties>
</form>
```

Note the section `<mdbMap>` in bold. Each data collection action created in Access will get an entry in this section. Also note the form properties, which are the same as in the Access system table (that is, these are the instructions given to the wizard if it has been run, otherwise they are whatever instructions you have coded). The following tags will be new to you:

`defaultFolder`: This is the default folder for the e-mail responses. Each additional e-mail collection can override this folder if required and be sent to a new folder. This is useful, for example, if you were sending out the same e-mail but to users in different business functions. Note that the Outlook EntryID is used instead of the folder name.

`searchFolder`: This is the search folder, which again would be created by the wizard. Just as with the `defaultFolder`, the EntryID is used to identify this folder.

Both of these folders will be populated by Access even if you are not using the wizard to run the data collection.

Each individual data collection carried out will, however, require an entry under the `<mdbMap>` tag. This section of the XML file is shown in Listing 4-11.

Listing 4-11. *<mdbMap> Tag Structure*

```
<mdbMap>
<form id="" moveToFolder="" FormType="">
<path />
<userReply />
<formProperties />
</form>
</mdbMap>
```

Following is a brief rundown of the elements and attributes of this section:

`form`: This is the root tag for each action that gets added. There can be an unlimited number of these tags, one per data collection action.

`id`: This is the unique GUID that identifies the form. This value should match the ExternalID field in the MSysDataCollection table. There should only be one form entry for each ID.

moveToFolder: This is the EntryID for the folder that you will move the replies to.

FormType: This is set to InfoPath or HTML, depending on the type of e-mail form you are using.

path: This is the fully-qualified path to the database that you'll be collecting data into.

userReply: This tag tracks whether or not the original sender of the data collection form has replied to it himself or herself. False means that the original sender has not, and true means that the sender has. This is used to handle moving e-mails to the moveToFolder and will be updated by Outlook as needed. It should default to false.

formProperties: This is an exact copy of the formProperties in the mapping column in the system table inside Access.

Once the Access system table has been populated, the Outlook COM add-in activated, and the AccessDCActionFile.XML file created, Outlook will be data collection aware and can begin listening for collection activities. To actually send a data collection e-mail, the recommended approach is to use the Access interface Collect Data Through Email Wizard as opposed to using code for this action.

Summary

Data collection via e-mail is another useful tool available to Access users. How useful it will be to developers remains to be seen. The XML and coding required to automate this process using VBA is somewhat confusing, but that may just be because the software is still at beta stage and documentation is not as yet complete. Personally, I can see a use for it even now, but using the wizard-driven interface as opposed to writing my own code to duplicate the process. Hopefully, this will change once more information and system hooks into the process become available. I have tried in this chapter to open up the data collection process and explain some of what goes on behind the scenes. While still incomplete, this information does provide you with a start in looking at running this process via VBA.

CHAPTER 5

■ ■ ■

Introduction to Classes in VBA

If you have installed Northwind 2007, you may notice that almost all the VBA used in the application is based on VBA classes. This is a major departure from previous versions and so will be new to many Access 2007 users and developers. In this chapter, we will look at getting started with class programming in Access. Hopefully, it will set you on the path to more advanced VBA class programming, extending Microsoft Access 2007 even further than before.

This chapter is not designed to teach you class programming, but to introduce the concepts and lay the groundwork for further study. Classes are one of those areas in coding that you look at and say, "So what?" But once you begin to explore them, all of a sudden the light will come on, and you will wonder how you ever got along without them. So I encourage you to take this chapter as a springboard to investigating the power of VBA class modules and Microsoft Access 2007.

Note A good friend of mine, John Colby, has published an entire set of VBA class and framework tutorials at http://www.colbyconsulting.com. John is an Access expert and is one of the leading proponents of class and framework programming. His lectures on classes and WithEvents is well worth looking at, downloading, and trying out. You are guaranteed to learn something. While on John's site, have a look at some of his other demos, which push Access programming to its limits. I would also like to thank Drew "Code Boy" Wutka for his help and patience with this chapter, and for giving permission for his examples to be used. So thank you, John and Drew, for your help and patience over the years.

Some Definitions

Before looking at classes in VBA, you need to understand some useful terms related to object-oriented programming (OOP). But first, a quote:

> *More important, VBA class modules offer concrete benefits to you, the developer, so what difference does it make if VBA is not completely object oriented?*

> *Access 2002 Developers Handbook,*
> Ken Getz, Mike Gunderloy, and Paul Litwin (Sybex, 2001)

Classes in Access are not fully OOP, but as Getz and co. say, who cares? They offer you many benefits when working in development and should not be overlooked in your learning. So on to the definitions you will need:

Abstraction: When you use a recordset in VBA, you have no idea how the actual recordset object is put together, nor should you care, to be honest. All you know is that here is an object you can use; you know you can open the object, close the object, and use MoveNext and MovePrevious procedures to navigate the recordset. This is the idea of abstraction: you don't need to know the finer details of how something works, you only need to know what you can pass to it and what it will pass back. You can therefore use its object and methods to make it work. These "tools" you can use collectively are called the *interface* of the object. It's via the interface that you can work with the objects and methods of the object.

Encapsulation: Class objects should contain within them everything they need to let them do what they are designed to do. They contain their own methods, properties, and data and do not need to rely on anything external in order to do their job.

Polymorphism: Objects can have the same properties and methods but they can implement them in different ways.

Inheritance: This is the ability of one class to inherit the features of another. For example, a basic printer class could provide the core objects and methods to enable printing. From this call, a specific printer class would inherit the core features and then build on them to create specific functionality. Access does not support inheritance using VBA. Interestingly, though, .NET does.

Now with these important terms defined, let's turn our attention to what makes for a class in VBA.

What Is a Class?

Basically a *class* is a module that contains all the code to describe and allow you to interact with an *object*. An object can be something as simple as an order or as complex as a registration process. It important that each class models a single object; for example, a Student class would not contain all of the objects required to model a student. You might have a class for student registration, student module marks, and student attendance, but you would not use a single class for all three. You would in this case have several classes, each modeling a specific object and containing all the methods required for that object. You can maybe see how confusing it would be if everything was in the same class—a maintenance nightmare!

So if you have a class that modeled a student, this class would have properties describing the student, his or her name, address, contact details, and so forth—all of the *properties* that make up a student. The class, however, doesn't actually describe anything until you actually load it up with data. Once you set the properties with data, you have a class instance that describes a specific student. In order to describe multiple students, you would load up multiple instances of the Student class. However, not every class needs to be opened multiple times. Classes can also be opened once to perform a specific function—for example, loading up system global variables.

One interesting feature about Access is that if you are already programming Access VBA in forms, you are already using classes. Each form has a class module associated with it. How many times have you coded ME.SomeValue = Some Value? ME in this case is actually manipulating the instance of the form class to refer to a property of the form itself. See, you are already a class programmer, and you maybe didn't even know it!

However, one of the drawbacks to class programming in forms is that the class is not only the form's class, but it is also the class for every object on the form. Let's have a look at an example of some standard code and some of the issues that may arise. The procedures in Listing 5-1 simply change the background color of a form's text boxes as you tab through them.

Listing 5-1. *Using a Class to Change Background Color*

```
Private Const mclngBackColor As Long = 16777088        ' A pretty blue color to set
                                                       ' the text box back color to

Private mlngBackColorOrigFName As Long
Private mlngBackColorOrigLName

Private Sub txtFName_Enter()
mlngBackColorOrigFName = txtFName.BackColor  ' When you enter the text box, save
                                             ' the original back color
txtFName.BackColor = mclngBackColor      ' Set the back color to your favorite color
End Sub

Private Sub txtFName_Exit(Cancel As Integer)
txtFName.BackColor = mlngBackColorOrigFName      ' Set the back color to the original
                                                 ' color
End Sub

Private Sub txtLName_Enter()
mlngBackColorOrigLName = txtLName.BackColor  ' When you enter the text box, save
                                             ' the original back color
txtLName.BackColor = mclngBackColor      ' Set the back color to your favorite color
End Sub

Private Sub txtLName_Exit(Cancel As Integer)
txtLName.BackColor = mlngBackColorOrigLName      ' Set the back color to the original
                                                 ' color
End Sub
```

The code uses the OnEnter and OnExit events to change the background color of the text box. At the top of the procedure is a variable to hold the original color of the text box. So if you have, say, 40 text boxes, you would need 40 different variables to hold the original values. Not only that, but you would also need to set the OnExit and OnEnter events for each of the controls. This could lead to a whole lot of code needing to be written.

Now this is where a class can come in handy. You can create a class that will model a control, in this case, a text box. This example may be a little complicated if you are just starting out, but bear with me. I would also advise entering the code yourself rather than cutting and pasting from the example database. You will learn much more if you do this the hard way. Listing 5-2 presents the bones for the class to achieve what we are after.

Listing 5-2. *Your First Class Module*

```
Option Compare Database
Option Explicit
' Dimension a text box WithEvents
Private WithEvents mtxt As TextBox
Private Const mstrEventProcedure = "[Event Procedure]"
Private Const mclngBackColor As Long = 16777088
Private mlngBackColorOrig As Long

' The init function of every class "initializes" the class.
' Pass in a pointer to a specific control.

Function Init(ltxt As TextBox)
Set mtxt = ltxt
mlngBackColorOrig = mtxt.BackColor   ' When you enter the text box, save the
                                     ' original back color
mtxt.OnEnter = mstrEventProcedure
mtxt.OnExit = mstrEventProcedure
End Function

Function Term()
 Set mtxt = Nothing                  ' Set the pointer to the control to nothing
End Function
```

To create the class, follow these steps:

1. Press Alt+F11 to open the VBA IDE.

2. Select Insert ➤ Class Module.

3. Name the class clstextboxs.

4. Enter the code shown in Listing 5-2 into the new class module.

■**Note** If the Properties window is not visible, select View ➤ Properties Browser from the main menu. You can change the name property to the required value in the browser.

You will also need to create an Access form containing four text boxes. The text boxes on the form should be named as follows for this example:

- txtFName

- txtLName

- txtAddr1

- txtAddr2

In Listing 5-2, you have a single variable to hold the new background color, and I introduce a new item, WithEvents. This lets the class know you will be sinking events for this class. See the sidebar titled "WithEvents" for more details. Next, you have an init function where you pass in a pointer to a specific text box. You save this pointer to the text box to your private variable in the class header. You also set the OnEnter and OnExit properties of that control to the string [Event Procedure]. Setting any form or control property to [Event Procedure] will cause the form or control to broadcast an event for that particular event. The reverse is also true in that if you remove the [Event Procedure], you turn off this event broadcasting. Setting this property in your class results in the event broadcast being made, and the class can then sink to the event.

Function is used to clean up the pointer to the text box once you have finished with it. The final bit of coding you have to do is to create the OnEnter and OnExit events to deal with the form's controls, as shown in the following fragments.

```
Private Sub mtxt_Enter()
mtxt.BackColor = mclngBackColor    ' Set the background color to your
                                   ' favorite color
End Sub


Private Sub mtxt_Exit(Cancel As Integer)
 mtxt.BackColor = mlngBackColorOrig
End Sub
```

WITHEVENTS

WithEvents allows you to handle events within any class outside the form. The example we are looking at here changes the background color of a text box. Using WithEvents, you could handle this for any text box within your applications. In normal use, you could, for example, dim mytext as a text box using WithEvents as in Private WithEvents mtxt As TextBox. This is saying that the text box can source events and that you will be sinking those events inside the class. It is worth noting that if you define WithEvents inside a standard module in Access, you will get a compile error, as it can only be used inside class modules. You let the class know which text box is sinking the event inside the Init function—for example, Set mtxt = ltxt. You must of course then actually handle the particular event being sunk.

So why is this so powerful? Well, you can now sink form or control events outside the form's code module within class modules. So if you want to change the background color of all of your form, you would simply sink to events in your change background color class, which would be held separately from the form. If you need to change the particular color being used, it would simply be a matter of changing the color within the class module, and there you go, all done. For a quick example of using WithEvents, try out the following:

1. Open Northwind 2007.

2. Create a new class module.

3. Enter the following code:

   ```
   Dim WithEvents MyCombo As ComboBox
   Public Function init(lcbo As ComboBox)
       Set MyCombo = lcbo
       MyCombo.AfterUpdate = "[Event Procedure]"
   End Function
   ```

4. Open the Northwind 2007 Product Details form in Design view.

5. Enter the following into the `AfterUpdateEvent` of the Supplier combo box.

   ```
   MsgBox "Handled by WithEvents"
   ```

6. At the top of the form module, enter the following:

   ```
   Dim mywitheventtest as cbodemo
   ```

As you can see, `WithEvents` opens up a whole new world in Access when you can sink events virtually anywhere, resulting in very powerful, centrally managed applications.

Returning to the form example, Listing 5-3 shows the code behind the form.

Listing 5-3. *Code Behind Your Form*

```
Option Compare Database
Option Explicit

Private fdclsCtlTextBoxFName As dclsCtlTextBox
Private fdclsCtlTextBoxLName As dclsCtlTextBox
Private fdclsCtlTextBoxAddr1 As dclsCtlTextBox
Private fdclsCtlTextBoxAddr2 As dclsCtlTextBox

Private Sub Form_Close()
    fdclsCtlTextBoxFName.Term
    Set fdclsCtlTextBoxFName = Nothing

    fdclsCtlTextBoxLName.Term
    Set fdclsCtlTextBoxLName = Nothing

    fdclsCtlTextBoxAddr1.Term
    Set fdclsCtlTextBoxAddr1 = Nothing
```

```
    fdclsCtlTextBoxAddr2.Term
    Set fdclsCtlTextBoxAddr2 = Nothing
End Sub

Private Sub Form_Open(Cancel As Integer)
    Set fdclsCtlTextBoxFName = New dclsCtlTextBox
    fdclsCtlTextBoxFName.Init txtFName

    Set fdclsCtlTextBoxLName = New dclsCtlTextBox
    fdclsCtlTextBoxLName.Init txtLName

    Set fdclsCtlTextBoxAddr1 = New dclsCtlTextBox
    fdclsCtlTextBoxAddr1.Init txtAddr1

    Set fdclsCtlTextBoxAddr2 = New dclsCtlTextBox
    fdclsCtlTextBoxAddr2.Init txtAddr2
End Sub
```

Initially, you dimension the class four times, once for each of the text boxes on the form, and each class instance is initialized by the form's open event. As you move into each text box, the background color will change.

Up to this point, there is still a considerable amount of coding required. However, there are a few other things to classes that you can use, including class factories and collections, that will decrease the amount of code you will have to write. Let's have a look at these now.

Class Factories

A *class factory* is a function that returns a class based on the parameters passed into it. The function dims the class, gets the new class and initializes it, and returns a pointer to the class instance. In the majority of cases, the parameter is the data passed into the class. A class factory is also useful when you cannot directly reference a class—for example, if the class is held in a library database (MDA file).

Listing 5-4 outlines a class factory function.

Listing 5-4. *Class Factory*

```
Function ClassFactory(txt As TextBox) as dclsCtlTextBox
Dim ldclsCtlTextBox as new dclsCtlTextBox
    Set ldclsCtlTextBox = New dclsCtlTextBox
    ldclsCtlTextBox.Init txt
    set ClassFactory = ldclsCtlTextBox......' Returns the pointer to the new class
                                            ' instance
End Function
Function ClsDestroy(ldclsCtlTextBox As dclsCtlTextBox)
    ldclsCtlTextBox.Term
    Set ldclsCtlTextBox = Nothing
End Function
```

Collections

An excellent example of a situation that calls for a collection is when you want to keep track of what classes are actually loaded and keep a check that when you are finished with them they are unloaded. This is a problem in Access; loading a class and failing to unload it when you are finished using it can cause memory leaks in Access and Windows. You can maintain a collection of loaded class names and check that the class name is removed from the collection once you are done using the class instance.

■**Caution** It is important to realize that classes do not truly unload from memory until the last pointer to the class is set to nothing. Thus, if you instantiate a class, store a pointer in this collection, and include a variable in a form header, for example, the class will not unload until you delete the pointer in the collection *and* in the form.

Listing 5-5 demonstrates the approach of creating a collection and adding and removing the class names as required. This code declares the variables mlngObjCounter to maintain the actual count and mcolObjNames to store the actual class name.

Listing 5-5. *Counting Class Instances*

```
Private mlngObjCounter As Long
Public mcolObjNames As Collection
Public Sub IncObjCounter(strObjName As String)
    mlngObjCounter = mlngObjCounter + 1
    mcolObjNames.Add strObjName
End sub
```

The public subroutine in Listing 5-5 simply increments and adds the class name.

Listing 5-6 is used to remove the class name from the collection and decrease the count of loaded classes.

Listing 5-6. *Removing a Class Instance*

```
Public Sub DecObjCounter(strObjName As String)
    mlngObjCounter = mlngObjCounter - 1
    mcolObjNames.Remove strObjName
End sub
```

You can use a simple public function to read out the class names from the collection. Listing 5-7 shows the function used.

Listing 5-7. *Public Function to Read Class Strings*

```
Public Function ObjNames() As String
On Error GoTo Err_ObjNames
Dim strName As Variant
Dim str
    For Each strName In mcolObjNames
        If Len(str) > 0 Then
            str = str & "; " & vbCrLf & strName
        Else
            str = strName
        End If
    Next strName
    ObjNames = str
end function
```

Working with Data

In this next example, I show you how to create a set of classes that will allow you to actually manipulate some data. For this example, two classes will be required: People and Persons. To begin the process, create a new blank database containing a single table, tblPeople. Define the following fields in the table:

- PersonID (AutoNumber type, primary key)

- FirstName (text type)

- LastName (text type)

■**Note** It is preferable to use a naming convention in which classes that hold data about one item are named in the singular. ClsPerson is a class where each instance holds information about one person. ClsPeople is a class where each instance may hold information about more than one person (a collection of clsPerson, for example).

Next you will create your first class module.

1. From the main Access menu, click Create.

2. Click Macro.

3. Select Class Module from the drop-down list.

4. Change the name of the module from Class1 to Person.

5. Add the following properties to the class:

```
Public ID As Long
Public FirstName As String
Public LastName As String
```

In addition, you are going to create a fourth property, FullName. This will be a concatenation of the first and last name fields from tblPerson. Listing 5-8 shows the procedure to add to the class.

Listing 5-8. *Creating a FullName Property*

```
Property Get FullName() As String
FullName = FirstName & " " & LastName
End Property
```

This will be a read-only property, as indicated by the Property Get statement. If you had wanted the property to be writable, you would need to use a Property Let statement instead.

You have now created a simple class to represent a person within the database. You will now create a second class that will contain collections of persons in your database.

1. Create a new class module and call it People. You are creating collections of people, one sorted by first name the other by last name.

2. Add in the statements in Listing 5-9 just below Option Explicit at the top of the People class module.

Listing 5-9. *Dimming the Vars*

```
Dim PeopleByFirst As Collection
Dim PeopleByLast As Collection
```

Next up you need to create a procedure that will be used to fill the collections. Listing 5-10 shows the procedure required.

Listing 5-10. *Populating the Collections*

```
Private Sub GetPeople()
Dim rs As ADODB.Recordset
Dim strSQL As String
Dim ps As Person
Dim i As Long
Set PeopleByFirst = New Collection
Set PeopleByLast = New Collection
Set rs = New ADODB.Recordset
strSQL = "SELECT PersonID, FirstName, LastName FROM tblPeople ORDER BY FirstName"
rs.Open strSQL, CurrentProject.Connection, adOpenKeyset, adLockReadOnly
```

```
If rs.EOF = False Then rs.MoveFirst
i = 1
Do Until rs.EOF = True
    Set ps = New Person
    ps.ID = rs.Fields(0).Value
    ps.FirstName = rs.Fields(1).Value
    ps.LastName = rs.Fields(2).Value
    ps.FirstSortOrder = i
    PeopleByFirst.Add ps, "ID:" & ps.ID
    Set ps = Nothing
    rs.MoveNext
    i = i + 1
Loop
rs.Close
Set rs = Nothing
Set rs = New ADODB.Recordset
strSQL = "SELECT PersonID, LastName FROM tblPeople ORDER BY LastName"
rs.Open strSQL, CurrentProject.Connection, adOpenKeyset, adLockReadOnly
If rs.EOF = False Then rs.MoveFirst
i = 1
Do Until rs.EOF = True
    Set ps = PeopleByFirst("ID:" & rs.Fields(0).Value)
    ps.LastSortOrder = i
    PeopleByLast.Add ps, "ID:" & ps.ID
    Set ps = Nothing
    rs.MoveNext
    i = i + 1
Loop
rs.Close
Set rs = Nothing
End Sub
```

Within the procedure, you initialize the collections you have dimensioned in the class header; the recordset is ordered first by first name and then added to the collection in the order provided by the recordset. When you add the data to the collection, you use the PS object and include a second argument, a custom ID. Collections can be recalled by the order in the collection (for example, PeopleByFirst(1) would give you the first person in the collection) or by the custom (unique) ID that you give it, which you do in the second loop (PeopleByFirst("ID:" & rs.fields(0).value)).

In the second loop, you are again letting ADO/JET sort things for you, but you aren't creating any more Person objects. A collection is really a set of pointers to objects, so you can have one object in several different collections. The advantage to this is that if you change an object that is in multiple collections, referencing it from any of those collections will show the change. For example, if you change "Bob Smith" to "Bobby Smith," both collections (sorted by first and last name) will reference the new "Bobby Smith" object. A pointer is simply a long integer, so if you were dealing with larger class objects, you wouldn't suffer from having duplicate objects in memory.

Next step in the process is to initialize the class. To do this, add the procedure shown in Listing 5-11 to the class.

Listing 5-11. *Initializing the Class*

```
Private Sub Class_Initialize()
GetPeople
End Sub
```

Now you are almost done. You will need to add several records to tblPeople and create an unbound form. The form should contain the following items:

- A label named lblRecordDisplayed

- A frame/option group, called SortOrder

- Two radio buttons: FirstName with an option value of 1, and LastName with an option value of 2

- Three text boxes: txtFirstName, txtLastName, txtFullName

- Two command buttons: cmdNextRecord and cmdPreviousRecord

The GetPerson procedure created ensures that each Person class knows its own sort order. What is now required is a process to get the person out of the People class, and you also need to know how many people there actually are. Listings 5-12 through 5-14 will do this for you.

Listing 5-12. *Getting the First Name*

```
Property Get PersonByFirstName(intOrder As Long) As Person
Set PersonByFirstName = PeopleByFirst(intOrder)
End Property
```

Listing 5-13. *Getting the Last Name*

```
Property Get PersonByLastName(intOrder As Long) As Person
Set PersonByLastName = PeopleByLast(intOrder)
End Property
```

Listing 5-14. *Getting a Count*

```
Property Get PeopleCount() As Long
PeopleCount = PeopleByFirst.Count
End Property
```

At this point, you can close and save the class module, as you will be working now with the form, frmPeople. Open frmPeople in Design view and add the information in the upcoming listing to the form's code module. In the code module, you need to dimension a variable for the collection of people and a variable to let you know who the current person is. Listing 5-15 shows the declarations.

Listing 5-15. *Dimensioning Variables*

```
Dim PeopleClass As People
Dim CurrentPerson As Person
```

Listing 5-16 is added to the form's OnLoad event.

Listing 5-16. *Form OnLoad Event*

```
Private Sub Form_Load()
Set PeopleClass = New People
Set CurrentPerson = PeopleClass.PersonByFirstName(1)
DisplayPerson
End Sub
```

Next you need to actually create the DisplayPerson function, which is used to actually display the record to the user. Listing 5-17 shows the required function.

Listing 5-17. *DisplayPerson Function*

```
Private Sub DisplayPerson()
Me.txtFirstName = CurrentPerson.FirstName
Me.txtLastName = CurrentPerson.LastName
Me.txtFullName = CurrentPerson.FullName
Select Case Me.SortOrder.Value
    Case 1 ' Sorted by first name
        Me.lblRecordDisplayed.Caption = "Record " &
CurrentPerson.FirstSortOrder & _
        " of " & PeopleClass.PeopleCount
        If CurrentPerson.FirstSortOrder = 1 Then
            Me.cmdNextRecord.SetFocus
            Me.cmdPreviousRecord.Enabled = False
        Else

            Me.cmdPreviousRecord.Enabled = True
        End If
        If CurrentPerson.FirstSortOrder = PeopleClass.PeopleCount Then
            Me.cmdPreviousRecord.SetFocus
            Me.cmdNextRecord.Enabled = False
        Else
            Me.cmdNextRecord.Enabled = True
        End If
    Case 2 ' Sorted by last name
        Me.lblRecordDisplayed.Caption = "Record " & ➥
CurrentPerson.LastSortOrder & ➥
        " of " & PeopleClass.PeopleCount
```

```
            If CurrentPerson.LastSortOrder = 1 Then
                Me.cmdNextRecord.SetFocus
                Me.cmdPreviousRecord.Enabled = False
            Else
                Me.cmdPreviousRecord.Enabled = True
            End If
            If CurrentPerson.LastSortOrder = PeopleClass.PeopleCount Then
                Me.cmdPreviousRecord.SetFocus
                Me.cmdNextRecord.Enabled = False
            Else
                Me.cmdNextRecord.Enabled = True
            End If
End Select
End Sub
```

With all the changes saved both to the classes and the form, try it out. Open frmPeople to see the class at work. As you will see, the command buttons do not yet work. Listings 5-18 through 5-20 provide this functionality. Add the code in these listings into the form's code module.

Listing 5-18. *Dealing with Sort Order*

```
Private Sub SortOrder_Click()
DisplayPerson
End Sub
```

Listing 5-19. *MoveNext Procedure*

```
Private Sub cmdNextRecord_Click()
Select Case Me.SortOrder.Value
    Case 1
        Set CurrentPerson =➥
PeopleClass.PersonByFirstName(CurrentPerson.FirstSortOrder + 1)
    Case 2
        Set CurrentPerson =➥
PeopleClass.PersonByLastName(CurrentPerson.LastSortOrder + 1)
End Select
DisplayPerson
End Sub
```

Listing 5-20. *MovePrevious Procedure*

```
Private Sub cmdPreviousRecord_Click()
Select Case Me.SortOrder.Value
    Case 1
        Set CurrentPerson =➥
PeopleClass.PersonByFirstName(CurrentPerson.FirstSortOrder - 1)
```

```
    Case 2
        Set CurrentPerson =➡
PeopleClass.PersonByLastName(CurrentPerson.LastSortOrder - 1)
End Select
DisplayPerson
End Sub
```

With these listings added to the form, try it out again. Now you should have a fully functional form—well, almost!

■Note Clicking the Next button (because the Previous button should be disabled by the DisplayPerson routine) will let you click your way through your list of people. The label displays which record you are in at any given time. Once you reach the end, the Next button is disabled. Now if you switch the sort order, none of the data changes, but the Record x of y label should show you a new position in the recordset, and moving back and forth in the recordset will go by the new sort order. All of the displaying and controlling functions are in DisplayPerson, and the controls that are moving things around are triggering that function once they do their initial jobs. That is, in the Next and Previous buttons, you are setting the CurrentPerson object to a new person (based on the current sort order and the position the old reference is currently in). For the changing of the sort order, the applicable value is already changed, so you just run the DisplayPerson function. To me, this is a wonderful process that demonstrates the simplicity of using classes!

Adding Functionality

Next you need to add additional functionality to the form—for example, the ability to create a new person, delete an existing person, and edit a person's info. The best place to do this would be in the Person class itself. It already has all of the appropriate code but will require some modification. The ID is set as a simple property (Public ID As Long). You need to change this. The ID field is the unique identifier, so getting the value is going to require a straightforward Property Get; however, when this value is set, you may want the class to fill itself out, or you may not. So you are going to create a StorageOnly property, a simple Boolean variable that you will set to false when the class initializes. In your People class, you will change the GetPeople procedure to set that property to true, before it sets the ID value.

At the moment, the class has properties but cannot actually do anything on its own; for example, if it initializes itself, all the property values will be blank. In the next examples, you will change that so that you can call a particular person simply by setting the ID value. As you know, the People class fills its collections with the Person class, and it has to set the ID property. You could let each instance of Person get its own data based on ID; however, you would be opening and closing a lot of recordsets to do that. It's faster and more efficient to let the "group" class pull up the whole recordset and just fill in the data. To do this, you use the StorageOnly property as a switch to override the independence of the Person class.

You also are going to create a Save routine, and for it you will want to determine whether the record currently being worked on is an existing one or new. This can be accomplished in several ways. You could initialize the intID variable with a value of 0. In this particular case, this would work pretty well, as the 0 won't show up as a value in an AutoNumber field for quite sometime. However, there is a foolproof method that isn't much more difficult. You create another module-level Boolean variable, blNew. When the class is initialized, you set it to true, and when the ID is set (regardless of StorageOnly), you set it to false (because it is then an existing Person instance). Listing 5-21 shows the new Person class required to achieve these results.

Listing 5-21. *New Person Class*

```
Public FirstName As String
Public LastName As String
Public FirstSortOrder As Long
Public LastSortOrder As Long
Public StorageOnly As Boolean
Dim intID As Long
dim blNew as Boolean
Property Get FullName() As String
FullName = FirstName & " " & LastName
End Property
Property Get ID() As Long ID = intID
End Property

Property Let ID(intEnter As Long)
intID = intEnter
blNew=False
If Not StorageOnly Then
    Dim rs As ADODB.Recordset
    Dim strSQL As String
    strSQL = "SELECT FirstName, LastName FROM tblPeople WHERE PersonID=" &➥
ID
    Set rs = New ADODB.Recordset
    rs.Open strSQL, CurrentProject.Connection, adOpenKeyset, adLockReadOnly
    If rs.EOF = False Then
        rs.MoveFirst
        FirstName = rs.Fields(0).Value
        LastName = rs.Fields(1).Value
    End If
    rs.Close
    Set rs = Nothing
End If
End Property
Private Sub Class_Initialize()
StorageOnly = False
blNew=True
End Sub
```

In the preceding code, you add the StorageOnly property in the declarations. You also set that property when the class is initialized. Get and Let statements have been created to allow the ID property to be read/write. When the ID property is set now, if StorageOnly is still false, it gets the FirstName and LastName properties based on the ID set. You must also make a change to the GetPeople function created earlier. The third line in bold in the following fragment shows the change required to the function.

```
Do Until rs.EOF = True
    Set ps = New Person
    ps.StorageOnly = True
    ps.ID = rs.Fields(0).Value
    ps.FirstName = rs.Fields(1).Value
    ps.LastName = rs.Fields(2).Value
    ps.FirstSortOrder = i
    PeopleByFirst.Add ps, "ID:" & ps.ID
    Set ps = Nothing
    rs.MoveNext
    i = i + 1
Loop
```

■**Note** You only create a new Person instance in the first loop (because the second loop is using existing instances), so you just need to set that value right after you create the new instance.

You need to make one other addition at this point to the Person class. You need to create a Property Let statement for FirstName. Listing 5-22 shows the statement you need to use. Go ahead and add it to the Person class.

Listing 5-22. *Property Let Statement for the Person Class FirstName*

```
Property Let FullName(strEnter As String) Dim strArray() As String strArray➥
= Split(strEnter, " ") FirstName = strArray(0) LastName = strArray(1)
End Property
```

Now, as discussed previously, you want the Person class to be able to save its own record; however, you need to check whether you are actually adding a new record or changing an existing one. This is achieved using the btNew variable you added to the module earlier in the process. Listing 5-23 shows the new Save function that will be added to the Person class.

Listing 5-23. *Save Function Added to the Person Class*

```
Friend Function Save()
Dim rs As ADODB.Recordset
Dim strSQL As String
Set rs=new ADODB.Recordset
```

```
If blNew Then
    rs.Open "tblPeople", CurrentProject.Connection, adOpenKeyset,➥
adLockOptimistic, adCmdTableDirect
    rs.AddNew
Else
    strSQL = "SELECT PersonID, FirstName, LastName FROM tblPeople WHERE➥
PersonID=" & ID
    rs.Open strSQL, CurrentProject.Connection, adOpenKeyset,➥
adLockOptimistic
    If rs.EOF = False Then rs.MoveFirst
End If
rs.Fields("FirstName").Value = FirstName
rs.Fields("LastName").Value = LastName
rs.Update
If blNew Then
    intID = rs.Fields("PersonID").Value
    blNew = False
End If
rs.Close
Set rs = Nothing
End Function
```

Similarly, Listing 5-24 shows the new Delete function added to the Person class.

Listing 5-24. *Delete Function in the Person Class*

```
Friend Function Delete()
Dim strSQL As String
strSQL = "DELETE * FROM tblPeople WHERE PersonID=" & ID
If blNew = False Then CurrentProject.Connection.Execute strSQL
End Function
```

■**Note** Adding Friend before Function makes this function visible inside your project but not outside it.

You now need to return to frmPeople and add in the AfterUpdate commands shown in Listings 5-25 through 5-27.

Listing 5-25. *txtFirstName AfterUpdate*

```
Private Sub txtFirstName_AfterUpdate()
CurrentPerson.FirstName = Me.txtFirstName
DisplayPerson
End Sub
```

Listing 5-26. *txtFullName AfterUpdate*

```
Private Sub txtFullName_AfterUpdate()
CurrentPerson.FullName = Me.txtFullName
DisplayPerson
End Sub
```

Listing 5-27. *txtLastName AfterUpdate*

```
Private Sub txtLastName_AfterUpdate()
CurrentPerson.LastName = Me.txtLastName
DisplayPerson
End Sub
```

You will then need to add three additional controls to frmPeople. Listings 5-28 and 5-29 show the click event code for the command buttons.

Listing 5-28. *Delete Command*

```
Private Sub cmdDelete_Click()
Dim intPos As Long
Select Case Me.SortOrder.Value
    Case 1
        intPos = CurrentPerson.FirstSortOrder
    Case 2
        intPos = CurrentPerson.LastSortOrder
End Select
CurrentPerson.Delete
Set CurrentPerson = Nothing
Set PeopleClass = Nothing
Set PeopleClass = New People
If intPos > PeopleClass.PeopleCount Then intPos = PeopleClass.PeopleCount
Select Case Me.SortOrder.Value
    Case 1
        Set CurrentPerson = PeopleClass.PersonByFirstName(intPos)
    Case 2
        Set CurrentPerson = PeopleClass.PersonByLastName(intPos)
End Select
DisplayPerson
End Sub
```

Listing 5-29. *New Command*

```
Private Sub cmdNew_Click()
Set CurrentPerson = New Person
DisplayPerson
Me.txtFirstName.SetFocus
Me.cmdNew.Enabled = False
End Sub
```

The Save command is slightly different because if you are adding a new record, you need to insert it into the existing records while remaining on the current record. Listing 5-30 shows the new property you need to add to the People class.

Listing 5-30. *New Property for the People Class*

```
Property Get PersonByID(intID As Long) As Person
Set PersonByID = PeopleByFirst("ID:" & intID)
End Property
```

You can then create the Save routine shown in Listing 5-31.

Listing 5-31. *Save Command*

```
Private Sub cmdSave_Click()
Dim intID As Long
CurrentPerson.Save
intID = CurrentPerson.ID
Me.cmdNew.Enabled = True
Set PeopleClass = Nothing
Set PeopleClass = New People
Set CurrentPerson = PeopleClass.PersonByID(intID)
DisplayPerson
End Sub
```

Full Code Listings for Class Examples

For easy reference and double-checking your work, I have included the fully working code examples in this section. I present the listings in the order you might tackle creating a similar application: Listing 5-32 shows the entire Person class for this example, Listing 5-33 shows the People class, and Listing 5-34 shows the code behind frmPeople. The listings work—I know because I typed every last one of them into Access. Provided you follow the instructions in creating frmPeople and name each of your objects as instructed, you will have no problems with this code. Play, experiment, and enjoy. I know I plan on doing that with VBA classes and Access 2007.

Listing 5-32. *People Class*

```
Option Compare Database
Dim PeopleByFirst As Collection
Dim PeopleByLast As Collection
Property Get PersonByID(intID As Long) As Person
Set PersonByID = PeopleByFirst("ID:" & intID)
End Property
Property Get PeopleCount() As Long
PeopleCount = PeopleByFirst.Count
End Property
```

```vba
Property Get PersonByFirstName(intOrder As Long) As Person
Set PersonByFirstName = PeopleByFirst(intOrder)
End Property
Property Get PersonByLastName(intOrder As Long) As Person
Set PersonByLastName = PeopleByLast(intOrder)
End Property
Private Sub GetPeople()
Dim rs As ADODB.Recordset
Dim strSQL As String
Dim ps As Person
Dim i As Long
Set PeopleByFirst = New Collection
Set PeopleByLast = New Collection
Set rs = New ADODB.Recordset
strSQL = "SELECT PersonID, FirstName, LastName FROM tblPeople ORDER BY FirstName"
rs.Open strSQL, CurrentProject.Connection, adOpenKeyset, adLockReadOnly
If rs.EOF = False Then rs.MoveFirst
i = 1
Do Until rs.EOF = True
    Set ps = New Person
    ps.StorageOnly = True
    ps.ID = rs.Fields(0).Value
    ps.FirstName = rs.Fields(1).Value
    ps.LastName = rs.Fields(2).Value
    ps.FirstSortOrder = i
    PeopleByFirst.Add ps, "ID:" & ps.ID
    Set ps = Nothing
    rs.MoveNext
    i = i + 1
Loop
rs.Close
Set rs = Nothing
Set rs = New ADODB.Recordset
strSQL = "SELECT PersonID, LastName FROM tblPeople ORDER BY LastName"
rs.Open strSQL, CurrentProject.Connection, adOpenKeyset, adLockReadOnly
If rs.EOF = False Then rs.MoveFirst
i = 1
Do Until rs.EOF = True
    Set ps = PeopleByFirst("ID:" & rs.Fields(0).Value)
    ps.LastSortOrder = i
    PeopleByLast.Add ps, "ID:" & ps.ID
    Set ps = Nothing
    rs.MoveNext
    i = i + 1
```

```
Loop
rs.Close
Set rs = Nothing
End Sub
Private Sub Class_Initialize()
GetPeople
End Sub
```

Listing 5-33. *Person Class*

```
Option Compare Database
Public FirstName As String
Public LastName As String
Public FirstSortOrder As Long
Public LastSortOrder As Long
Public StorageOnly As Boolean
Dim intID As Long
Dim blNew As Boolean

Property Get FullName() As String
FullName = FirstName & " " & LastName
End Property

Property Let FullName(strEnter As String)
Dim strArray() As String
strArray = Split(strEnter, " ")
FirstName = strArray(0)
LastName = strArray(1)
End Property

Property Get ID() As Long
ID = intID
End Property
Property Let ID(intEnter As Long)
intID = intEnter
blNew = False
If Not StorageOnly Then
    Dim rs As ADODB.Recordset
    Dim strSQL As String
    strSQL = "SELECT FirstName, LastName FROM tblPeople WHERE PersonID=" & ID
    Set rs = New ADODB.Recordset
    rs.Open strSQL, CurrentProject.Connection, adOpenKeyset, adLockReadOnly
    If rs.EOF = False Then
        rs.MoveFirst
        FirstName = rs.Fields(0).Value
        LastName = rs.Fields(1).Value
    End If
```

```
    rs.Close
    Set rs = Nothing
End If
End Property


Private Sub Class_Initialize()
StorageOnly = False
blNew = True
End Sub


Friend Function Delete()
Dim strSQL As String
strSQL = "DELETE * FROM tblPeople WHERE PersonID=" & ID
If blNew = False Then CurrentProject.Connection.Execute strSQL
End Function


Friend Function Save()
Dim rs As ADODB.Recordset
Dim strSQL As String
Set rs = New ADODB.Recordset
If blNew Then
    rs.Open "tblPeople", CurrentProject.Connection, adOpenKeyset, ➡
adLockOptimistic, adCmdTableDirect
    rs.AddNew
Else
    strSQL = "SELECT PersonID, FirstName, LastName FROM tblPeople WHERE ➡
PersonID=" & ID
    rs.Open strSQL, CurrentProject.Connection, adOpenKeyset, adLockOptimistic
    If rs.EOF = False Then rs.MoveFirst
End If
rs.Fields("FirstName").Value = FirstName
rs.Fields("LastName").Value = LastName
rs.Update
If blNew Then
    intID = rs.Fields("PersonID").Value
    blNew = False
End If
rs.Close
Set rs = Nothing
End Function
```

Listing 5-34. *frmPeople VBA Module*

```
Private Sub cmdSave_Click()
Dim intID As Long
CurrentPerson.Save
intID = CurrentPerson.ID
```

```vba
Me.cmdNew.Enabled = True
Set PeopleClass = Nothing
Set PeopleClass = New People
Set CurrentPerson = PeopleClass.PersonByID(intID)
DisplayPerson
End Sub
Private Sub Form_Load()
Set PeopleClass = New People
Set CurrentPerson = PeopleClass.PersonByFirstName(1)
DisplayPerson
End Sub
Private Sub DisplayPerson()
Me.txtFirstName = CurrentPerson.FirstName
Me.txtLastName = CurrentPerson.LastName
Me.txtFullName = CurrentPerson.FullName
Select Case Me.SortOrder.Value
    Case 1 ' Sorted by first name
        Me.lblRecordDisplayed.Caption = "Record " & ➥
CurrentPerson.FirstSortOrder & " of " & PeopleClass.PeopleCount
        If CurrentPerson.FirstSortOrder = 1 Then
            Me.cmdNextRecord.SetFocus
            Me.cmdPreviousRecord.Enabled = False
        Else
            Me.cmdPreviousRecord.Enabled = True
        End If
        If CurrentPerson.FirstSortOrder = PeopleClass.PeopleCount Then
            Me.cmdPreviousRecord.SetFocus
            Me.cmdNextRecord.Enabled = False
        Else
            Me.cmdNextRecord.Enabled = True
        End If
    Case 2 ' Sorted by last name
        Me.lblRecordDisplayed.Caption = "Record " & ➥
CurrentPerson.LastSortOrder & " of " & PeopleClass.PeopleCount
        If CurrentPerson.LastSortOrder = 1 Then
            Me.cmdNextRecord.SetFocus
            Me.cmdPreviousRecord.Enabled = False
        Else
            Me.cmdPreviousRecord.Enabled = True
        End If
        If CurrentPerson.LastSortOrder = PeopleClass.PeopleCount Then
            Me.cmdPreviousRecord.SetFocus
            Me.cmdNextRecord.Enabled = False
        Else
            Me.cmdNextRecord.Enabled = True
        End If
End Select
```

```
End Sub
Private Sub SortOrder_Click()
DisplayPerson
End Sub
Private Sub txtFirstName_AfterUpdate()
CurrentPerson.FirstName = Me.txtFirstName
DisplayPerson
End Sub
Private Sub txtFullName_AfterUpdate()
CurrentPerson.FullName = Me.txtFullName
DisplayPerson
End Sub
Private Sub txtLastName_AfterUpdate()
CurrentPerson.LastName = Me.txtLastName
DisplayPerson
End Sub
```

Summary

In this chapter, I introduced you to VBA classes. I hope what you have found in this chapter gets you started on the road to VBA classes. I can tell you a great place to begin learning about classes is the AccessD database developers community, where developers at the cutting edge of Access programming like John Colby and Drew Wutka hang out, giving of their time and skill on a daily basis.

CHAPTER 6

■■■■

RAD Development for SQL Server 2000/2005 Express

One of the major advantages of Microsoft Access for developers and power users has long been the ability of Access to act as a Rapid Application Development (RAD) environment when working with SQL Server. This chapter looks at working with SQL Server as the back-end data store. We will look at upsizing to SQL Server 2000 or SQL Server 2005 Express Edition and have a look at some of the other features available as part of the SQL Server 2005 Express product including Reporting Services. Chapter 7 looks at working with SQL Server 2005 Express in more detail.

■Note The Chapter6 database (available as part of the downloads for this book at http://www.apress. com) contains all the examples from this chapter.

As this is a single chapter, it's difficult to cover everything on the topic at hand, but it does provide an overall flavor of what's involved in upsizing to SQL Server. Also, given the removal of support for Microsoft SQL Server Desktop Engine (MSDE) in Vista by Microsoft, it is important that if you do need to move your databases from MSDE, you have at least a basic understanding of MSDE's replacement.

As an aside, the vast majority of Access database applications *do not* require upsizing to SQL Server of any flavor. Some may require a rewrite, some may require a complete redesign, but the databases that actually require an upsize are few. Databases that have become widely used and provide a core business function are prime candidates for an upsize, but only if justified in terms of business provision and cost.

Access 2007 has one major change when moving to SQL Server. The focus is on using ODBC-linked tables as opposed to creating an Access Data Project (ADP). ADPs are still available as a second-choice option, and in my opinion they offer a superb feature set when working with SQL Server 2000/2005. (Most of this chapter also applies to upsizing to SQL Server 2005 Express.)

■Note When working with a linked application, I often use an ADP in order to take advantage of the ADP RAD GUI tools used to create stored procedures and other objects.

For server-side data, there is also the option of using SharePoint Server as the data store. This has limits, and for a heavy-duty data-driven business application, it may not be suitable. In the majority of cases, developers will use one of two back-end databases, SQL Server 2000 or increasingly SQL Server 2005 Express Edition. SQL Server 2005 Express is becoming the database engine of choice for Access developers who need a little more guts in their data application. In addition, as I discovered recently, if you need a quick-and-dirty web application, it's hard to beat the development time achieved using Access 2007 and Visual Web Developer 2005 Express. Chapter 12 looks at using Access 2007 as the back-end data store for a small application created using Visual Web Developer 2005 Express. This will be a real application, small and unsophisticated, but one which demonstrates the ease of use of the Visual Web Developer Express tools.

There are many reasons to upsize your database to SQL Server. For example, you may find you have increased users, and the application may be slowing down as a result. Or, increased security may be required due to legal changes; for example, in the UK the Data Protection Act requires appropriate security be taken with personal information, and in the US, Sarbanes-Oxley financial control requirements are now standard. The following are some of the main reasons many developers find they have to upsize MS Access databases:

- Increased database capacity

- Improved backup and recovery

- Integration with Microsoft Windows Authentication

- Interaction with a back end using .NET or Internet-based applications

- Broadened development base

- Improved network performance

■Note The fifth bullet point is increasingly becoming one of the main reasons to upsize. More and more organizations are being required to reduce the number of smaller satellite data stores in use and to centrally pool data. In this way, organizations can be more flexible in how they access such data via the Internet, SharePoint, or Access. Of course, there is also a long-term cost saving associated with having data held centrally.

Another reason to upsize is the continual pressure placed on Access developers from system administrators and IT managers to move data onto "real" database back ends. In my own field, I have noticed that this pressure is increasing as more and more applications are pulled into the center for various reasons, including decreasing maintenance budgets, central management of systems, and control of data. In many industries, Access is simply used as a data store that is populated overnight using SQL Server Data Transformation Services (DTS) to download updated data files or indeed complete tables for users to work with.

Options When Working with SQL Server

There are three main choices available to Access developers who need to use SQL Server:

- Transfer your existing Access tables to SQL Server, retaining the Access front-end.

- Link to an existing SQL Server database using Access as the front end.

- Create an Access Data Project, moving almost totally into the world of SQL Server.

■**Note** If you expect to move your application to SQL Server, it is advisable to think of this at the design stage and plan accordingly. For example, do not use spaces in table names, and if you want to be able to edit and insert data, make sure each and every Access table has a unique index, or else it will be read-only when moved to SQL Server.

Which option you choose depends on what it is you want to do, and for the majority of applications, linking to the SQL Server table from Access is adequate. ADPs can be used, but this moves you out of the pure Access world into full-blown SQL Server development environments. However, you will have the advantage of working within an application development optimized for SQL Server, while at the same time using familiar objects such as forms and reports and VBA to build your application. On the other hand, working with linked tables keeps your feet firmly in the Access world of queries and other familiar Access objects. One other major advantage to working in a linked application is that there are no restrictions on what you can link to. An ADP, on the other hand, is a pure Microsoft SQL Server solution.

SQL Server DTS is also a great tool that can be used to bring your data into SQL Server 2000. One of its chief benefits is that it permits you to manipulate the data on the way into the server (for example, changing field sizes and altering data types yourself). You can import entire tables or use queries in a wizard-driven interface to restrict the data being imported. The DTS Wizard will not import your relationships, and they will need to be re-created on SQL Server, but this is a small price to pay for the flexibility offered by this tool. Running the DTS Wizard is discussed later in this chapter in the section "Importing Data with Data Transformation Services." For SQL Server 2005 Express, DTS has been replaced with SQL Server Integration Services; however, you will find that DTS still plays a major role in the new services.

DOWNLOADING DTS FOR SQL SERVER 2005 EXPRESS

DTS is not available with the initial installation of SQL Server 2005 Express. However, you can download the DTS runtime. The runtime allows you to run existing DTS packages with SQL Server 2005 Express. The runtime is part of the feature pack for Express 2005 and can be downloaded from http://www.microsoft.com/downloads/details.aspx?familyid=d09c1d60-a13c-4479-9b91-9e8b9d835cdc&displaylang=en.

Comparing Access and SQL Server

SQL Server 2000 is still widely used in many corporations, and the majority of Access developers will find it available. However, we will also be looking at the structure of SQL Server 2005 Express here, as it is expected that this option, which is freely available from Microsoft, will be increasingly used for upsizing projects.

SQL Server offers Access developers a somewhat familiar development environment, and you will find many features similar to, but more complex than, those in Access; for example, the relationship designer, query builders, tables, columns, and relationships all work in much the same way as they do in Access. There are many differences, of course, some minor and some major. In this section, I will highlight some of the similarities and differences you will find between Access and the versions of SQL Server this chapter focuses on.

SQL Server 2005 Express Edition is the replacement for MSDE, the free version of the SQL Server data engine long made available by Microsoft. However, unlike previous versions, the performance of SQL Server 2005 Express is not restricted. Microsoft has also provided a free management interface that is similar in many ways to the Enterprise Manager used by the full version of SQL Server.

Note SQL Server 2005 (commercial version) is covered only in minor detail here, as many Access developers may not have access to this professional version.

SQL Server 2005 Express is a major improvement over MSDE. SQL Server 2005 Express has its own management interface, similar in many ways to the Enterprise Manager, available with the full version of SQL Server. The Express Management tool can also be used with SQL Server 2000 and MSDE 2000. Access developers using SQL Server 2005 Express can now manage the database directly via the GUI rather than fight with command-line arguments. SQL Server 2005 Express is also not restricted in any way, unlike MSDE, which has a restriction when more than five threads were executing at any one time. There are still practical limitations to SQL Server 2005 Express, but it does provide a free and improved database engine for Access developers. It is therefore another tool that can be added to the arsenal of every developer.

Table 6-1 shows some of the features of SQL Server 2005 Express compared to MS Access. SQL Server 2005 Express can be downloaded from http://msdn.microsoft.com/vstudio/express/sql/.

Table 6-1. *SQL Server 2005 Express Feature Set*

Feature	Access	SQL Server 2005 Express
Automated tuning	No	Yes
GUI manager	Yes	Yes
Stored procedures	No	Yes
Triggers	No	Yes
User-defined functions	No	Yes
.NET CLR Support	No	Yes, but must be turned on
Full text search	No	Yes
Reporting Services	No	Yes
Code access security	No	Yes
Windows Authentication	No	Yes
Free	No	Yes
DB size	2GB	4GB
Integration with VS 2005	No	Yes

One of the features that may attract Access developers to SQL Server 2005 Express is the ability to code stored procedures in one of the .NET languages, as Express can integrate with the common language runtime (CLR) hosted within the database software.

CLR SUPPORT

SQL Server 2005 supports the creation of database objects such as stored procedures using any of the .NET languages. I will not be providing coverage on CLR integration with SQL Server 2005 Express because, like many of the readers of this book, I am also just starting out on the path to writing managed code in SQL Server. I should also say that many SQL Server 2005 DBAs do not support the use of managed code inside the database for performance, design, and scalability. From the Access developer's point of view, I think that moving to SQL Server 2005 Express is a big enough headache without having to learn C# and Visual Studio 2005 as well. For those of you who would like to get started on this road there is a good basic tutorial available at `http://www.aspfree.com/c/a/MS-SQL-Server/NET-CLR-Programming-with-SQL-Server-2005-Made-Simple/1/`.

Let's take a closer look at specific areas of difference between Access and SQL Server, starting with data types.

Data Type Differences

A table is a table is a table, right? Wrong—well, sort of. In Access, a table is used to store data, and the same is true of a table in SQL Server 2000. However, some things are different, for example, data types. SQL Server provides a more comprehensive range of data types than

Access, and it is important to know which ones to use and which ones equate to a similar data type in Access. This is particularly true when you run the Microsoft Access Upsizing Wizard, which converts data types automatically. Table 6-2 shows the differences in data types between the programs.

Table 6-2. *Access Data Types When Upsized to SQL Server 2000*

Access 2007 Data Types	SQL Server 2000 Upsized Data Type
Text	char, nchar, varchar, nvarchar
Memo	text, ntext
Integer	smallint
Long integer	integer
Single	real
Double	float
Replication ID	uniqueidentifier
Decimal	decimal
Date/Time	smalldate, datetime, timestamp
Currency	smallmoney, money
AutoNumber	int
Yes/No	bit (yes =1 and no =0)
OleObject	image
Hyperlink	N/A
None	binary, varbinary
Attachment	N/A

It's also worth noting that SQL Server offers you much more choice when using certain data types; for example, SQL Server offers several alternatives to the single Access text data type: char, nvarchar, varchar, and nchar. Note also that timestamp is not a true date/time data type, as it is used to record data changes. It's useful to have a timestamp column in SQL Server tables. This saves Access scanning every column for changes when doing updates. Instead, it can check the timestamp column.

In addition, SQL Server 2005 Express also contains the new data types available with the full versions of SQL Server 2005. These data types are generally designed to store large amounts of blog data such as images (data type varbinary(max)). Also, there is a new XML data type that allows you to store complete XML documents within the database.

Delimiters

One of the main gotchas for Access developers who turn to SQL Server is the differences in delimiters. Table 6-3 shows the various delimiters used by SQL Server. In the case of mathematical operators, they are the same in Access and SQL Server 2000/2005.

Table 6-3. *Delimiters in SQL Server*

Delimiter	Example
Date delimiter	'
String delimiter	'
Concatenation	+ (Access developers sometimes use this.)
Char wildcard	%
Not equal	!=, <>
Not less than	!<, >=
Not greater than	!>, <+

■**Note** The use of the % (percentage sign) is a major reason for query failure when a database has been upsized. Before you upsize, it's useful to check out all VBA code doing a simple find and replace of both the * and & characters used by Access with % and +. This saves some work later on.

System Tables

As you know, Access contains it own system tables. SQL Server does the same, plus a little bit more. As well as your database, SQL Server also contains its own system databases, each of which performs a specific role in the system:

Master database: The master database contains information on all databases on the system. This includes information on security (for example, user logins, server configuration, data file locations, and system procedures).

Model database: This is the template database for all new databases created on the server. Each database created on SQL Server will inherit the features contained within the model database. The model database can be changed to include specific features you may require in all new databases. It's worth backing up before you make any changes, just in case something goes wrong.

Tempdb: Tempdb exists when the server is started and removed when shut down. Tempdb is used to hold temporary tables and stored procedures.

MSDB: This database stores information on backups and restores. It also maintains information used by SQL Server Agent (for example, job scheduling).

Security

Access security is poor when compared to the security features available using SQL Server 2000/2005. Basically, there are three levels to SQL Server security: logins to the server, permissions on database objects, and permissions on individual objects. In practice, a user is granted access to the server and then granted permissions to use one or more databases. The user can have permissions assigned directly or can be added to an SQL Server group to which permissions have already been assigned.

■Tip It is much easier to manager users and permissions by using groups. Permissions assigned to a group are inherited by all members of the group. In the same way, permissions can be revoked from the group and hence the individuals. Much easier to manage than working with 1000 individual user accounts.

SQL Server login accounts can work in Windows Authentication mode (that is, the user's Windows Account details are used by SQL to check permissions for login). For example, an Active Directory group could be assigned login permission to SQL Server. All members of the group thus inherit the permissions. SQL Server also supports Mixed Mode security (that is, using Windows Authentication security together with SQL Server's own security system). If using SQL Server security, users will be prompted for a username and password before they can log in.

It is also possible to manipulate logins via the Access interface using SQL Distributed Management Objects (SQLDMO). The Chapter6 database contains an example form, frmLogin, that requests a username and password from the user. Basically, all that is required is for you to create a connection dynamically using VBA and execute the code to connect. The frmLogin command button does just that. Figure 6-1 shows the final form required to log in.

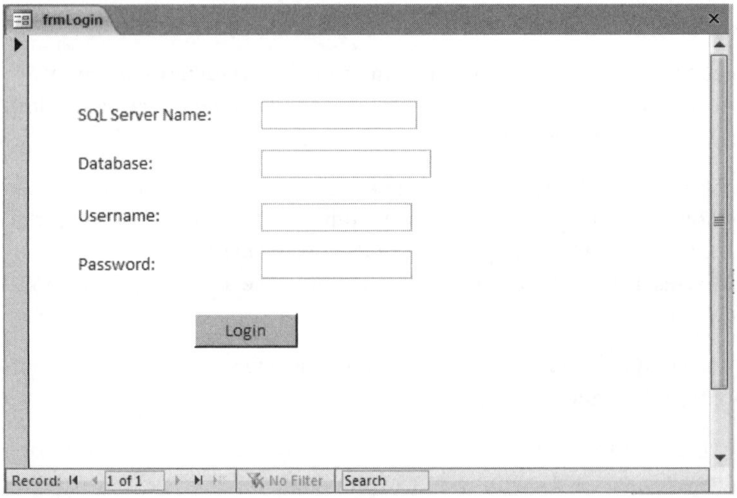

Figure 6-1. *Using a form to log in to SQL Server*

Error control has not been added to keep the procedure clear—many examples show the use of the sa password or even a blank password. Do not take either of these approaches. Create a new account on SQL Server with the appropriate permissions to carry out the upsizing task.

Before looking more closely at frmLogin, let's examine the connection string SQL Server is expecting.

There are several forms that can be used to create and pass the connection information to SQL Server, depending on the method used for the connection and the security context being used. The following connection strings are based around ODBC, and which one you choose will depend on the security model being used to log in to the server.

Standard security (no DSN):

```
Conn.Open "Driver={SQL Server};" & ➥
          "Server=Your SQL Server Name;" & ➥
          "Database=Your Database Name;" & ➥
          "Uid=UserName;" & ➥
          "Pwd=Your Password"
```

Windows Authentication (trusted connection—no DSN):

```
Conn.Open "Driver={SQL Server};" & ➥
          "Server=Your SQL Server Name;" & ➥
          "Database=Your Database Name;" & ➥
          "Trusted_Connection=yes"
```

Using a DSN:

```
Conn.Open "DSN=Your System DSN Name;" & ➥
          "Uid=Your Username;" & ➥
          "Pwd=Your Password"
```

Listing 6-1 uses a DNS-less connection and Mixed Mode SQL Server security. Completing the connection string is simply a matter of passing the appropriate values to the VBA function via Access text boxes to create the connection string. The code to create this is shown in the listing and is executed via command button.

Listing 6-1. *Creating a Connection String*

```
Dim strSQLServer As String, strDatabase As String,
strUsername As String, strPassword As String
Dim strConnect As String

strSQLServer = Me!txtserver
strDatabase = Me!txtdatabase
strUsername = Me!txtuser
strPassword = Me!txtpass

strConnect = "ODBC={SQL Server)" ➥
                & ";SERVER=" & strSQLServer ➥
                & ";DATABASE=" & strDatbase ➥
                & ";UID=" & strUsername ➥
                & ";PWD=" & strPassword & ";"
```

Running a Debug.Print statement to the Intermediate window shows the connection string created (based on my input, of course):

```
ODBC=(SQL Server);
SERVER=MARTIN\BARTRACKS;
DATABASE=Pubs;
UID=mwpreid;
PWD=mwpreid;
```

One drawback to this example is that users must enter the SQL Server name and then the database name. It's unlikely that your users will have this information, nor in fact should they be expected to have it. There are a couple of ways to resolve this issue, but generally you can hard-code the server and database names into the code, as in frmLoggin2. The Chapter6 database contains the code and form example to achieve this. In this case, both the database and the server details are already created as default values within the form.

For completeness and to illustrate some of SQLDMO's features, Listing 5-2 in the next section demonstrates how you can use SQLDMO to enumerate both an SQL Server and the objects on the server. In this way, you can present such information to the user as required.

Tip You will need a reference set to the Microsoft SQLDMO Object Library for the following examples. SQLDMO is the object model used to interact with many of the features made available using Enterprise Manager. Enterprise Manager is the GUI tool used to manage SQL Server 2000 databases. For SQL Server 2005, SQLDMO has been replaced with SQL Management Objects (SMO), and for management you will download the SQL Server Management Studio Express.

Using SQLDMO

SQL Data Management Objects provide you with an object model with which to manipulate the management of an SQL Server.

Using SQLDMO it is a fairly straightforward process to return the SQL Server names (we will briefly look at SMO, its replacement, in the sidebar "Enumerating SQL Server Database Names"). Listing 6-2 will retrieve a list of all available servers on the system and add the server names to an Access list box. The list box row source property must be set to the value list for this to work. lstServers is the name of an Access list box placed onto a form.

Listing 6-2. *Enumerating SQL Server Names*

```
        Dim oApp As SQLDMO.Application
        Dim oNames As SQLDMO.NameList
        Dim oName As Variant

        Set oApp = New SQLDMO.Application
        Set oNames = oApp.ListAvailableSQLServers()
For Each oName In oNames
lstServers.AddItem oName
        Next
```

ENUMERATING SQL SERVER DATABASE NAMES

The following code will list all the database names on the stated server to the Intermediate window:

```
Dim server As SQLDMO.SQLServer
Dim dbnames As SQLDMO.Database

Set server = New SQLDMO.SQLServer
With server
.LoginSecure = True
.Connect "MARTIN\BARTRACKS"
End With

For Each dbnames In server.Databases
    Debug.Print dbnames.Name
Next dbnames
```

You could have bypassed the ODBC connection string and went for a pure SQLDMO solution, passing the server name, username, and password to the Connect method of SQLDMO. However, I wanted to demonstrate the features of creating a generic connection string, as this will prove useful when working with Access and other engines.

SMO is the replacement for SQLDMO and is used by SQL Server 2005. SMO provides many of the same features as SQLDMO and should be backwards compatible. SMO is actually a .NET assembly and therefore has many features in common with other .NET object models including framework integration. SMO is the preferred method when working with SQL Server 2005.

Putting It All Together to Create a Mixed Mode Login Form

Listing 6-3 outlines an example that permits a user to enter a username and password and log in to an SQL Server 2000 application. Both the server and the database names are hard-coded into the open event of the form for simplicity. Figure 6-2 shows the resulting form.

Listing 6-3. *Creating a Login Form Procedure*

```
Dim strSQLServer As String, strDatabase As String,
strUsername As String, strPassword   As String
Dim strConnect As String

If IsNull(Me!txtuser) Then
strError = "Enter Your Username."
MsgBox strError, vbCritical, "Username Required"
Me!txtuser.SetFocus
Me.txtuser.BackColor = 255 'RED
```

```
    ElseIf IsNull(Me!txtpass) Then
        strError = "Enter Your Password."
        MsgBox strError, vbCritical, "Password Required"
        Me!txtpass.SetFocus
        Me!txtpass.BackColor = 255

Else

strSQLServer = Me!txtserver
strDatabase = Me!txtdatabase
strUsername = Me!txtuser
strPassword = Me!txtpass
' Create the connection string

strConnect = "ODBC DRIVER ={SQL Server)" ➥
                & ";SERVER=" & strSQLServer ➥
                & ";DATABASE=" & strDatabase ➥
                & ";UID=" & strUsername ➥
                & ";PWD=" & strPassword & ";"

End If
```

When the form opens, you set the values for the SQL Server and the database to be used to the respective values. All the user must do is enter the correct username and password.

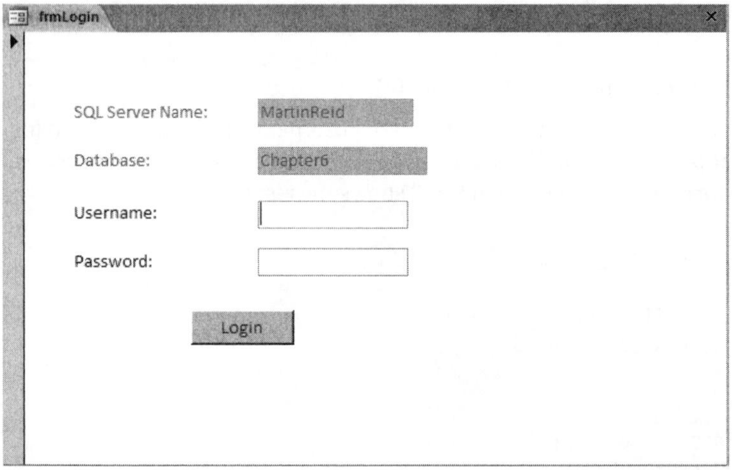

Figure 6-2. *Logging in to SQL Server*

The code behind the login command button is basic and straightforward. You ensure that the user enters a username and password. Failure to enter the required data is checked using the ISNULL function, which returns an error if no data is entered and turns the text box red (as a visual clue); the user can then enter the correct information.

■**Tip** Remember, you will need to change the server and database names to reflect those on your own system.

Upsizing to SQL Server 2000

Access 2007, in common with all recent versions of Access, includes the Upsizing Wizard, which will take your existing database and convert its tables to SQL Server 2000 and SQL Server 2005 (both Express and Enterprise Editions). Once the wizard is finished, you will be left with an unchanged Access front end containing new tables linked to the SQL Server database. The majority of all other objects will remain unchanged, functioning as before. The wizard will also leave your existing tables in place suffixed with the text _local.

For this example, I am going to use a real-world application for the upsizing process. BarTracks (http://www.bartracks.com) is an asset management application developed in Access 2003 and widely used by customers worldwide. The main reason I do this is because many books use Northwind or some other fictional database to describe this process. I want to use a real-world application and thus uncover real-world issues and problems. The Bar-Tracks application is comprised of a large number of unbound forms populated using DAO recordsets. In order to protect the commercial code, I will be rewriting procedures as required, so you will not be looking at "real" code. However, the table structures and design will be the real-world examples. In case you are the suspicious sort, understand that the database has not been adjusted in any way for this process. The only change is that an early version will be used.

■**Note** BarTracks uses a number of hand-held scanners as part of its application, but you will not be looking at this area. At this point, all we are interested in is the database structure and any issues that may arise during that process. Please note that any commercially sensitive information has been removed. When an issue is discovered, it will be resolved and demonstrated using the Chapter6 database.

Creating a new linked application is a multistage process, and as usual it is now my standard practice to run SSW Upsizing Pro, a tool that checks your database before you upsize it (available at http://www.ssw.com.au), on the MDB file to be upsized. Even if mainly done as a time-saving or peace-of-mind action, this is always worthwhile in my opinion. Of course, you can download various VBA procedures from the Web to do this or indeed write your own.

■**Tip** If a table has no primary key, it will be read-only to SQL Server. So it pays to check (unless, of course, you want a table to be read-only).

Given this is a professionally designed application, Upsizing Pro returns two common errors: zero length and missing unique index. The actual error messages returned are detailed here:

```
Warning: Field tblXXX!fldUserXXX is a text field and 'Allow Zero Length' set to➡
NO The Microsoft Upsizing Wizard SHOULD upsize this to an nvarchar(varchar) ➡
column    with 'Allow Zero Length' = NO However it incorrectly will upsize ➡
this to a nvarchar(varchar) column with 'Allow Zero Length' = YES More: ➡
http://www.ssw.com.au/ssw/kb/KB.asp?KBID=q711400

Warning: Table tblXXX does not have a unique index. It will be upsized but will ➡
be read-only from Access unless a unique index or primary key is added (optional)
```

This particular database will upsize with little additional work on my behalf, as far as the table structures are concerned. However, this is not always the case. For comparison, I tried running Upsizing Pro against Northwind.mdb. In the case of the Northwind database, I received 32 warning messages. In addition to the warnings, as earlier, some tables where found to include spaces in the table names. SQL Server does not permit spaces in table names, so avoid this naming convention. Many of the example databases provided with Access 2007 contain field names including spaces, and these should be changed if you are moving them to SQL Server.

The key to reducing errors is obvious: taking time to design an Access application and applying professional development techniques from the start of the project. Many SQL Server and Oracle developers view Access as a "toy" database because in many cases the applications they see are not written by developers. Generally, they are poorly designed applications written to solve a simple problem (for example, a company mailing label database). Almost all Access developers I work with apply the same techniques to their Access databases as they do to SQL Server systems: no spaces in table names, a proper naming convention for Access objects, choosing the right data types for the job, and applying Access Referential Integrity when building relationships. But perhaps the most important factor is planning from the start for future growth and perhaps the future use of SQL Server.

In my previous coauthored book, *SQL: Access to SQL Server* (Apress, 2002), I stated that ADPs were the way to go with upsizing projects (we will look at ADPs later in this chapter and again in Chapter 7). ADPs are almost fully functional with SQL Server 2005 (both Enterprise and Express versions). The main proviso is that they will work as before, provided you have not used any of the new SQL Server data types.

■**Note** Always bear in mind the upsizing tools in Access are there to deal with data. Everything else is for you to do, and there is no substitute for good planning.

Now that you have checked the MDB file and, of course, fixed any issues, you can go ahead and run the Access Upsizing Wizard, which you'll do next. The preceding errors can be fixed manually once the database has been upsized using the SQL Server design tools.

Running the Upsizing Wizard

For this example, I am using Windows Authentication and have logged on the system using an Administrator account. SQL Server provides two modes of security, its own and Windows Authentication.

To run the Upsizing Wizard, follow these steps:

1. Click the Database Tools tab.

2. Click the SQL Server icon.

3. Accept the default on the first Wizard screen—Create New Database.

4. Click Next.

5. Select the name of the SQL Server you would like to use from the drop-down list.

6. Enter a name for the soon-to-be-upsized SQL Server database.

7. Click Next. The wizard will change the name of your database if it already exists on SQL Server.

8. Select the tables to upsize to SQL Server.

■**Note** Tables with a suffix of _local will be ignored by the wizard.

---

9. Click Next.

Figure 6-3 shows the next screen in the wizard-driven process. In this screen, you can choose which objects you would like to upsize in addition to the actual table.

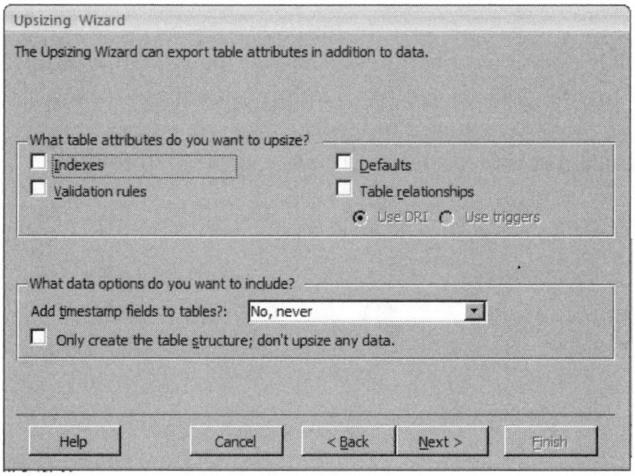

Figure 6-3. *Upsizing objects*

The objects you can upsize are indexes, validation rules, and table relationships, and we'll look at each in more detail next.

Indexes

Table 6-4 shows how Access indexes will be upsized.

Table 6-4. *Index Upsizing*

Access Index	SQL Server 2000 Index	SQL Server 2005 Express Index
None	None	None
Yes (duplicates)	Nonclustered	No change
Yes (no duplicates)	Unique nonclustered	No change
Primary key	Primary key nonclustered, unique nonclustered	No change

You must manually make the nonclustered primary key a clustered key within SQL Server using either T-SQL or Enterprise Manager. The following SQL statement will create a single table with an incrementing (AutoNumber) primary key and a clustered index. The following T-SQL statement will alter the same table and create a clustered index. Note that first you must delete or drop the existing index before creating the new clustered index. The DROP Index statement takes the following form:

```
DROP Index tblStudent.Student_PK
```

Once the index has been removed, you can create a new clustered index by executing the following SQL statement:

```
ALTER TABLE [dbo].[tblStudent] ADD  CONSTRAINT [Student_PK] PRIMARY KEY CLUSTERED
([StudentRef] ASC)
```

Validation Rules

Validation rules will be exported to SQL Server as constraints. For example, the following is reported by the wizard for a DateTime field with a table validation rule set as >=Now(). sp_addextendedproperty is an SQL Server system stored procedure that will add an extended property to the table. Listing 6-4 shows a validation rule re-created from the Access table constraint.

Listing 6-4. *Upsizing a Validation Rule*

```
ALTER TABLE [tblProps] ADD CONSTRAINT
[CK tblProps fldDateofBirth] CHECK
(fldDateofBirth>=getdate())
EXEC sp_addextendedproperty
N'MS_ConstraintText', N'Must be greater
than today', N'user', N'dbo', N'table',
N'tblProps', N'constraint', N'CK tblProps
```

Now() is replaced with an SQL function, GetDate(), which is functionally equivalent.

Table Relationships

Relationships will be created as they exist in Access and copied across to the SQL Server database.

You will also be asked to include a timestamp field with each table and offered an option to only upsize the tables, ignoring any data content. The timestamp is useful, as it records the last change to a row of data and can help with reducing overheads in query execution, updates, and inserts.

Issues Before, During, and After Upsizing

Creating a new SQL Server database and linking to it is a fairly straightforward process, especially if you are working from a blank canvas. Existing databases should be comprehensively checked out before you begin the upsizing process. As I mentioned earlier, a good tool for this is Upsizing Pro. Upsizing Pro will examine your Access database and report on any issues that may inhibit the process. This allows you to fix any issues before starting the task. Some of the main areas you should be looking at are as follows:

Spaces in field names: This is important with this release of Access, as Microsoft is emphasizing ease of use and compatibility with SharePoint. Thus users may be encouraged to use spaces in field names to fit in with the SharePoint model.

Dates: The date range used by Access is different from that used by SQL Server. It is important that all tables be checked for dates outside the SQL Server–supported ranges of 1 Jan 1793 to 31 December 9999.

Indexing: SQL Server offers much more flexibility in terms of indexing than Access. There are two index types available: clustered and nonclustered. Each table can have a single clustered index and multiple nonclustered indexes. You will have to set the index manually once the tables are upsized.

Primary keys: Make sure all your Access tables have a primary key defined. If not, they will be read-only when upsized.

Access indexes: One issue that has been around for some time is the issue of Access adding an index to any field ending with the text "ID." Any field in a table—for example, filenameID—will automatically be added to the Access index. While this may not be a major issue, it is worth looking at if it is a substantial database and you take a performance hit.

dbOpenDynaset, dbSeeChanges: Once a system has been upsized, you will find you have to use dbOpenDynaset, dbSeeChanges for every VBA recordset that is working with a linked table containing an IDENTITY column. Many developers use this notation "just in case" upsizing may be required at some future point. Access will prompt you with a message about using these terms with recordsets.

Reserved words: When creating an Access table, it is still possible to enter a reserved word as a field name—for example, Date. Access will warn you that you are using a reserved word and then continue to save the design changes in the table. Do not use reserved words when creating database structures.

■**Tip** The new data type attachment and the new property Allow Multiple Values do not upsize correctly. Both will upsize as text and be shown in the Access interface as memo data types. If an Access database is dependent on using these new features, it is conceivable that SQL Server 2000/2005 is not the appropriate data store, and Windows SharePoint Services may be more appropriate. Don't worry—I will be covering Windows SharePoint Services in Chapters 9 and 10.

Many developers have found that upsizing large applications does not in fact improve performance, but may actually degrade it. This is mainly due to the way in which Access tables are linked using ODBC together with DAO, which is geared more toward working with local MDB files (JET) rather than a large-scale client server database like SQL Server. In such a case, a rewrite of much of the application using ActiveX Data Objects (ADO) may be required. Another issue is that Access developers often use VBA- and Access-specific functions. In a linked application, SQL Server knows nothing about such functions. All data is passed to the client for processing. This can result in huge network traffic depending on the size of the tables, of course.

■**Note** There are no equivalent objects in SQL Server (any version) that match Access forms or reports. Conversely, as you will see, there are multiple SQL Server objects with no Access equivalent.

Upsizing to SQL Server 2005 Express

When working with SQL Server 2005 Express, the upsizing process is identical to that in SQL Server 2000, including using the wizard interface to upsize tables. Figure 6-4 shows the results within SQL Server Management Studio Express of upsizing the Issues template database to SQL Server 2005 Express.

At the time of writing, some errors are reported in this process, but overall the upsizing works well, in terms of tables at least. Just like in SQL Server 2000, the Access interface will show the linked tables while maintaining a copy of the original table suffixed with _local—for example, tablename_local. You will, however, lose the new features for complex data types, and fields with attachments will no longer function as before. (The attachment data type will be upsized as text.)

In my opinion, if you require the functionality of such fields (that is, the ability to show multiple items within a field), you will need to revert back to the "old fashioned" way of design using many-to-many relationships. The word "show" is used in this context because this is a visual effect made possible using the new Access database file type. Behind the scenes, a fully relational structure is maintained. See Chapter 1 for more information on the new complex data types.

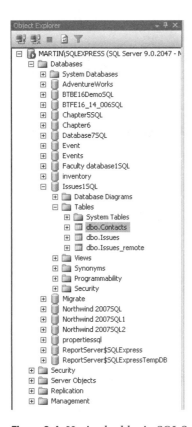

Figure 6-4. *Upsized tables in SQL Server 2005 Express*

Complex data types could become a major issue in the future, as users of Office 2007 may want to see the same functionality in upsized applications. This depends, of course, on how often such features are implemented. For instance, take the ability to permit multiple values in lookups. When a table with the Allow Multiple Value property set is upsized, the result is a comma-separated list within the field (that is, value1,value2,value3), hardly meeting with relational requirements. You will manually have to sort this out by adding the data to the appropriate table. Listing 6-5 uses the `split` function to retrieve the values of a field storing multiple values. In this listing, multiple developers' names have been associated with a project. The `split` function is used to parse the multiple values using the semicolon as the delimiter to create a string array of the required values.

Listing 6-5. *Using split to Sort Out Multivalue Fields*

```
While not rs.EOF
strDevelopers() = split(rs!DeveloperNames,";")
For lngLoop =  0 to UBound(strDevelopers)
```

```
strSQL = "Insert into tblDevelopers (Project,Developer) Values ➥
(" & rs!Project  & ",'" & strDevelopers(lngLoop) & "')"
' Write new record using the SQL string
Next
rs.movenext
Wend
```

Table 6-5 compares Access and SQL Server 2005 Express data types after a table has been upsized.

Table 6-5. *Comparing Data Types Following Upsizing*

Access 2007	SQL Server 2005 Express
AutoNumber PK	int PK nonclustered
Date/Time	datetime
Hyperlink	ntext
Currency	money
Memo	ntext
Yes/No	bit
Attachment	ntext

As mentioned previously, the new data type attachment is upsized, but with a loss of the Access interface function. Any data held within the field will be upsized to a comma-separated multivalue field list. In addition to the data types show in Table 6-5, SQL Server 2005 Express provides the standard SQL Server data types plus several types that will be new to many Access developers, in particular the XML data type.

Impact of Upsizing on Access Forms and Data

Upsizing is mainly concerned with getting table structures into SQL Server. To the Upsizing Wizard, everything else is secondary to this function. Many of the issues you will face concern common features many developers build into Access front ends. A linked application will not result in many form issues; however, an Access Data Project that results in all data processing passing to SQL Server may require a lot of rewriting of such things as queries and dealing with issues around passing form parameters to what were once Access queries that have become stored procedures or user-defined functions (UDFs).

In an ADP, all queries will be translated to equivalent SQL Server stored procedures or UDFs. As they become server-side objects once upsizing is complete, they are no longer aware of such things as form parameters or Access VBA functions and will thus fail. As an example, the following query will fail to function if the database is moved totally to SQL Server and your queries are converted to SQL Server stored procedures:

```
SELECT fldCompanyName,fldTown,fldCounty FROM
tblCompany
WHERE
tblCompany.City like forms!formcompany!txtcity
```

In a linked application, this will work as before, but in an ADP application, the parameter will fail, as SQL Server does not recognize a parameter passed to the procedure via a form using the preceding syntax. In this case, the form's reference will be replaced by passing a parameter to a stored procedure either using a pass-through query or via ADO parameters.

In order to repair such objects, knowledge of stored procedures will be invaluable, so I will give you an overview on stored procedures next that discusses some of the major features. (A full reference can be found in SQL Server Books Online if you want to know more about stored procedures.)

A Short Introduction to Stored Procedures

SQL Server uses a version of SQL referred to as *T-SQL*, which works similarly in many ways to Access queries but with some huge differences. Just like an Access query, a stored procedure can accept input parameters, but it can also return output parameters. Stored procedures can insert, update, and delete records, and they can contain conditional logic using `Begin`, `End`, and `Case` statements. Stored procedures can be manipulated using VBA, DAO via pass-through queries, and ADO from within Access. ADO will give you much more flexible control over a stored procedure than any of the other methods. This is particularly true when working with ADPs.

There are several advantages to using stored procedures including the following:

- Network traffic is reduced, as only an `execute` statement (and parameters) is passed to the server.

- Execution plans can be reusable.

- Stored procedures can be shared between applications (such as Access and web applications).

- Users can be granted permissions to work with data via stored procedures without access to tables.

- Each user uses the same stored procedure.

- Stored procedures can contain conditional logic

The execution of a stored procedure is very simple. Listing 6-6 uses ADO to execute two procedures, `usp_CreatePeople` and `usp_InsertData` (the "usp" prefix indicates a user stored procedure). The first procedure creates a table on the server, and the second will insert some sample data.

Listing 6-6. *Executing Stored Procedures*

```
Private sub cmdSQLData_Click()
Dim Conn as ADODB.Connection
Set conn = CurrentProjectAccessConnection
Conn.execute "usp_CreatePeople"
Conn.execute "usp_InsertData"
Set Conn=Nothing
End Sub
```

■**Note** The `AccessConnection` property is available within an ADP and provides the same functionality as a standard connection property.

The stored procedures themselves can contain basic SQL statements, such as SELECT or INSERT statements, or complex procedural code written using T-SQL.

Listing 6-7 shows a stored procedure containing a basic SELECT statement.

Listing 6-7. *A Basic Stored Procedure*

```
Create Procedure usp_CreatePeople as
SELECT [ID], [fldEmpname],
[fldComments], [fldMemo],
[fldDriver], [fldYesNo],
 FROM [Chapter6].[dbo].[tblEmployee]
```

You can execute the procedure from within Access and assign the results to a recordset. Using ADO, this is a straightforward task. Listing 6-8 executes a stored procedure, uspGetStudents, returning the records into an ADO recordset and assigning them to a form. In this case, a stored procedure and an ADO command object are used to execute the procedure (frmExecuteStoredProc in the Chapter6 database demonstrates this).

Listing 6-8. *Executing a Stored Procedure Using ADO and Assigning It to a Recordset*

```
Private Sub Form_Open(Cancel As Integer)
Dim rstStudent As ADODB.Recordset
Dim cmd As ADODB.Command
Dim conn As ADODB.Connection
Set conn = New ADODB.Connection
Set rstStudent = New ADODB.Recordset
Set cmd = New ADODB.Command
conn.ConnectionString = ➥
    "Provider = SQLOLEDB.1;" & ➥
    "Data Source =MARTIN\BARTRACKS;Initial Catalog=LinkedStudent;" & ➥
    "User ID=martinreid;Password=martinreid"
conn.Open
cmd.ActiveConnection = conn
cmd.CommandText = "uspGetStudents"
Set rstStudent = cmd.Execute
Me.txtforename = rstStudent!fldStudentForeName
End Sub
```

■**Note** The connection string in this example is built into the code. It would be better to take the string generated in the earlier example and hold it centrally, creating a global connection object that can be reused. This is discussed in Chapter 7.

Passing Parameters

Passing parameters is something that you will do on a constant basis. SQL Server stored procedures can accept parameters and pass parameters back to the user interface. The example shown later in this chapter (in Listing 6-12) uses a parameter, `@ModuleCode`, that is passed into the procedure. As you will see, multiple parameters can be passed. Using the tblStudent table contained in the Chapter6 database, you can add parameters to a stored procedure as shown in Listing 6-9.

Listing 6-9. *Declaring Parameters in a Stored Procedure*

```
Create Procedure Inst_Student
        @StudentName varchar(20)
        @StudentRef int
AS
INSERT INTO tblStudent
VALUES
@StudentName
@StudentRef
```

In addition, you must also declare the parameter data type. Here, both parameters are passed to the stored procedure via ADO using its parameter object and Access.

A simple approach to executing stored procedures using DAO is to create a pass-through query that executes the procedure. Using the Access main Ribbon, click the Insert tab and select Query. In the Design view of the query, right-click and choose SQL Specific ➤ Pass-Through. Enter the following text into the blank query document:

```
Execute Your Stored Procedure Name
```

Close and save the pass-through. You may at this point be prompted for a DSN connection.

It is also possible to execute a stored procedure via DAO by executing the pass-through query and thus the procedure. In order to do this, you can use a standard `QueryDef` object and pass the results into a DAO recordset. For example:

```
Set db=CurrentDb
Set qdf =db.QueryDefs("Pass-Through Query Name")
Set rstStudent = qdf.OpenRecordset
```

You can also amend VBA shown to accept a parameter using the `Parameters` collection of the `Command` object. When passing a parameter to a command, you must also set its appropriate data type. An example should help clarify this. The following fragment creates a stored procedure, `usp_AddStudent`, which is will be used to carry out an insert operation to a table, tblStudent.

```
CREATE Procedure usp_AddStudent
@StudentForename nvarchar (25),
@StudentSurName nvarchar (25)
AS
INSERT INTO tblStudent
(fldStudentForeName,fldStudentSurName)
VALUES
(@StudentForename,@StudentSurName)
```

Listing 6-10 shows the procedure that will insert a single record into tblStudent. In this case, you are using ADO, as it is a more appropriate programming language for SQL Server stored procedure manipulation.

Listing 6-10. *Passing Parameters to Stored Procedures*

```
Sub PassParam()

Dim conn As ADODB.Connection
Dim cmd As ADODB.Command
Dim prm As ADODB.Parameter
Set conn = New ADODB.Connection
conn.Open "Provider=sqloledb;" & ➥
          "Data Source=MARTIN\BARTRACKS;" & ➥
          "Initial Catalog=LinkedStudent;" & ➥
          "Integrated Security=SSPI"
Set cmd = New ADODB.Command
cmd.ActiveConnection = conn
cmd.CommandText = "usp_AddStudent"
cmd.CommandType = adCmdStoredProc
Set prm = cmd.CreateParameter("StudentForeName", adVarWChar, adParamInput, 25,➥
 "William ")
        cmd.Parameters.Append prm
    Set prm = cmd.CreateParameter("StudentSurname", adVarWChar, adParamInput, ➥
25, "Reid ")
        cmd.Parameters.Append prm
    cmd.Execute
Set prm = Nothing
Set cmd = Nothing
Set conn = Nothing
End Sub
```

Using Conditional Expressions

SQL Server stored procedures can also contain conditional logic. One of the common uses of such logic is the replacement of the Access IIF function with a T-SQL CASE statement when it is necessary to evaluate several values. Listing 6-11 illustrates the use of the CASE statement to produce a summary query based on the Northwind database. (Well, no good Access book would be complete without one!) To complete the procedure, the CASE statement, shown in bold, is copied for each date range required.

Listing 6-11. *Using a CASE Statement*

```
CREATE Procedure usp_Orders
AS
SELECT Customers.CustomerID,
 Customers.CompanyName,
Sum(CASE When Orders,OrderDate Between 101-Jan-2000'
And '31-12-2001' THEN UnitPrice ELSE 0 END)
AS [2001],
Sum(CASE When Orders,OrderDate Between '01-Jan-2001'
And '31-12-2002' THEN UnitProce ELSE 0 END)
AS [2002]
GROUP BY Customers.CustomerID,
Customers.CompanyName
ORDERBY Customers.CustomerID
```

The CASE statement works with the Sum function to return the total unit sales for each period.

Another example uses a conditional IF statement to branch processing within the stored procedure to alternative SQL. In Listing 6-12, a parameter of the Student module is passed into the procedure using the form @ModuleCode.

Listing 6-12. *Using Multiple Parameters*

```
IF (@ModuleCode < (SELECT ModuleCode
FROM Modules
WHERE MODULECODE = @Code))
BEGIN
UPDATE Student
SET ModuleCode = @ModuleCode
END
ELSE
BEGIN
DELETE Student Where ModuleCode = @ModuleCode
END
```

SQL Server 2000 provides several ways in which to work with stored procedures, but perhaps the easiest way to start off is to duplicate your linked application with an Access Data Project. In the ADP, you can take advantage of the graphical tools that allow you to work with such things as stored procedures, user-defined functions, and table design in the familiar Access interface. ADPs can be used with SQL Server as powerful design tools for your system, even if the solution is not going to be implemented

Populating Forms and Other Objects

As with any standard Access application, you can go the bound or unbound route when creating forms. Having recently been working on a large unbound application, I have slowly moved to the dark side of unbound forms. This is mainly for the control they can give, and in the case of SQL Server, the way in which you can restrict the number of records you take down from the server at any one point. Binding a form to a table returns all records to the application as opposed to restricting the amount of data transferred.

Note A good friend of mind, Arthur Fuller, has a nice phrase for populating forms one record at a time: he refers to it as "opening the kimono slowly."

Listing 6-13 populates a short form in Access with records from tblStudent in the Chapter6 database using DAO. Note the use of dbSeeChanges as discussed earlier. Without this, Access will return an error message actually requesting that you include dbSeeChanges. Note that the recordset is dimmed outside the procedure, as this permits its manipulation outside the initial procedure.

Listing 6-13. *Populating Unbound Forms*

```
Set db = CurrentDb
Set rstStudent = db.OpenRecordset("Select * FROM tblStudent",➥
 dbOpenDynaset, dbSeeChanges)
' Assign the recordset fields to the form text boxes.
With rstStudent
txtStudentForeName = !fldStudentForeName
txtStudentSurName = !fldStudentSurName
txtStudentEmail = !fldStudentEmail
txtStudentAddr2 = !fldStudentAddr2
End With
End Sub
```

Because the form is now unbound, you then have to code all the other procedures and commands that Access normally does for you: move to the next record, move to the previous record, delete, save, and so forth. For example, to move to the next record, you call the recordset's MoveNext using DAO (for example, rstStudent.MoveNext). What, you tried that and nothing happened? Welcome to the world of unbound Access forms. You do it all yourself. In addition to calling MoveNext, you need to repopulate the form text boxes with the next record. To do this, a new function, getStudent, needs to be added. This function repopulates the form with the next record. The procedure getStudent is called immediately following the MoveNext statement attached to a command button.

```
rstStudent.MoveNext
call getStudent
```

Listing 6-14 shows the getStudent function.

Listing 6-14. *Another Approach to Populating a Record*

```
Private Sub getStudent()
With rstStudent
txtStudentForeName = !fldStudentForeName
txtStudentSurName = !fldStudentSurName
txtStudentEmail = !fldStudentEmail
txtStudentAddr2 = !fldStudentAddr2
End With
 End Sub
```

The getStudent procedure can also now be used to replace the initial code in the form open event used to populate the text boxes. But what happens if the user has changed the record before moving on? Well, again, you need to cover that possibility by checking the recordset for changes. As may be apparent, there are many things you must take care of yourself if you use unbound forms in your applications. The Chapter6 database contains a fully functioning example of this approach.

When working with a combo box, a recent approach used by Rocky Smolin (http:// www.e-z-mrp.com), a member of the AccessD developers list and a good friend of mine, was to store the combo records locally, thus reducing the overhead of connecting to the server and retrieving all the records. For data that does not change a great deal, this is a reasonable approach to take. Of course, a facility to update the local records should also be provided to ensure they remain up to date. Listing 6-15 shows a more sophisticated example using this approach.

Listing 6-15. *Public Subroutine for Filling Combo Boxes from Local Tables*

```
Public Sub gSetComboBoxValues(argForm As String)
'****************************
' Initial Course Combo Source
'****************************
    gstrcboCourse = "SELECT tblCourse.CourseRef, tblCourse.fldCourseName" ➥
    & "FROM tblLocalCourse;"
    Forms(argForm)!cboCourse.RowSource = gstrcboCourse
   '****************************
' Initial Student Row Source
'****************************
    gstrcboStudent = "SELECT tblStudent.StudentRef, tblStudent.fldStudentSurName" ➥
    & "FROM tblLocalStudent;"
    Forms(argForm)!cboStudent.RowSource = gstrcboStudent
End Sub
```

A public function is created that accepts the name of the calling form, argform, and passes back the appropriate row set for the named combo box. In this way, you can store all the combo population code and SQL statements in one place, making application maintenance much easier. In this case, this makes sense, as each combo box will be used on multiple forms, and there is no sense creating the same recordset on a form-by-form basis when it can be done in one place one time.

The neat idea behind this process is that the public function can be called from anywhere you are using the combo box simply by passing in the form name (frmComboExample in the Chapter6 database demonstrates this approach). Within the public subroutine is a set of SQL statements used to populate each of the combo boxes required by the application. A public variable declared as a string is also created for each of the combos to be populated. frmComboExample contains two combo boxes to illustrate this technique, cboStudent and cboCourse. The following global variables have been declared in the module:

```
Public gstrcboStudent as String
Public gstrcboCourse as String
```

The form name calling the procedure is passed into the argument argForm. As you can see in Listing 6-15, this is a very basic procedure in terms of coding requirements, but it releases endless possibilities for the populations of combo boxes without hitting the server time. The SELECT statements have been changed to reflect the local tables being used rather than pulling data down the network from SQL Server. Of course, this is also a useful technique for non–SQL-Server-based applications.

The public subroutine is called in the open event of the required form as shown here:

```
Call gSetComboBoxValue (Me.Name)
```

It's also worth noting that the same technique can be used for any other object that makes use of static data within the application other than combo boxes.

ANOTHER APPROACH TO FILLING COMBO BOXES

Another way to fill combo boxes would be to simply execute a local query from the form open event and requery the combo box rowsource. The effect would be the same, but not as flexible as that shown previously. In addition, you are storing the SQL statements in global variables for reuse in other areas of the application. The approach outlined previously does, I believe, give you the best of both worlds: the use of local tables for static data and ease of code management.

Storing and Retrieving Local Records

Storing records locally in tables can also be a useful tool when working with server-side data, and the process is straightforward. In this case, a local table will be populated with records from SQL Server. What's the advantage? Well, you can reduce the number of connections to SQL Server and at the same time improve the speed of response by not hauling static records across networks. Static records may not change a great deal or in fact never change; for example, in the UK a postcode is 100% set in stone. That being the case, why bother connecting to a server every time you are required to populate a postcode or ZIP code combo box list? Repopulation of the local tables can range from the simple execution of an update query to get a data refresh to the creation of a VBA solution for those so inclined. Listing 6-16 contains the SQL statement required to repopulate a local table. In future calls to this data, the local table is used to retrieve the data, thus saving a server connection.

Listing 6-16. *SQL to Repopulate a Local Table*

```
INSERT INTO tblLocalStudent ( fldStudentForeName,➡
fldStudentSurName, fldStudentEmail, flsStudentAddr1,➡
fldStudentAddr2, fldStudentAddr3, fldTown,➡
fldPostCode, fldStudentDOB, [Date] )
SELECT tblStudent.fldStudentForeName,
tblStudent.fldStudentSurName,
tblStudent.fldStudentEmail, tblStudent.flsStudentAddr1,
tblStudent.fldStudentAddr2, tblStudent.fldStudentAddr3,
tblStudent.fldTown, tblStudent.fldPostCode,
tblStudent.fldStudentDOB, tblStudent.Date
FROM tblStudent;
```

Even getting the local table is easy. When you upsize Access tables, the wizard leaves a copy in the database for you. All that is required is to remove the AutoNumber primary key field and replace it with a number field. Execute the SQL INSERT statement shown previously, and you are good to go.

Of course, you will then need some form of interface to permit users to repopulate the tables on occasion. Again, this process should be standard. Create a form permitting the user to select which tables to repopulate or set the default to repopulate all tables. Attach some code to a command button, and you're done. The Chapter6 database contains a working example of this approach. The code, using a standard DoCmd statement to execute SQL, is shown in Listing 6-17.

Listing 6-17. *Repopulating Local Tables*

```
DoCmd SetWarnings false
DoCmd.RunSQL "DELETE * FROM LOCALTABLENAME"
DoCmd.RunSQL "DELETE * FROM LOCALTABLENAME"
DoCmd.RunSQL "DELETE * FROM LOCALTABLENAME"
DoCmd.SetWarnings True
Set qdf =db.QueryDefs ("QUERYNAME")
    qdf.Execute
```

As shown in the last two lines of Listing 6-17, you can use a QueryDef to execute your INSERT query to repopulate the table.

The code could also be executed when the application opens, ensuring that your local tables are always updated directly from the server. This means perhaps taking a one-time hit at the start of the application in return for the speed of local processing. The other issue that may arise is that of the Not In List event. When using local tables, what do you do when you need to add a value? Using the Not In List event, you can execute code to write directly back to the server and repopulate the combo box by executing your repopulation code and doing a requery of the combo box record source per standard practice.

Importing Data with Data Transformation Services

Many of the issues surrounding upsizing an Access database are issues with data as discussed previously. DTS allows you to import data to SQL Server and manipulate that data during the import process. At the time of writing, DTS is not available for those using SQL Server 2005 Express. In SQL Server 2005, DTS has been replaced by Integration Services, which is a complete redesign of DTS from SQL Server 2000. SQL Server 2000 provides a wizard-driven interface when you work with DTS. The DTS Wizard can import single or multiple tables, or you can create queries within the process to return data meeting set criteria. DTS in SQL Server 2000 provides a very flexible means of importing large amounts of data. Many developers moving to SQL Server use the Upsizing Wizard to move the tables to SQL Server and then use DTS Wizard to import the data to the newly upsized tables. One of the reasons for doing this is that the data can be manipulated during the import using the DTS Wizard to change data types to more suitable SQL Server types, for example. You can also create queries during the import itself to reduce the amount of data you want to bring into SQL Server 2000, for example.

Access Data Projects

Access Data Projects—what can I say about them? ADPs are one of those features you will either love or hate. Some developers swear by them, while others have never used the technology. Perhaps that is one of the reasons they have taken a back seat in the design of Access 2007, and linking to SQL Server is the preferred method of connection and application building. Given the focus that SharePoint Server is receiving in this release, this is no surprise; however, considerable work has been done by the Microsoft development team to ensure that ADPs are still a viable option with SQL Server 2005.

Initially, many experts predicted the death of ADPs with any new release of SQL Server. That's definitely not the case, and they still provide another option for the developer. The graphical tools that can be used to design SQL Server objects are still available and can be used with the new version of SQL Server, and they function in much the same way as in previous versions.

One of the limitations of ADPs (and one of the reasons linking is now the preferred method) is that, unlike linking, you cannot use multiple data stores, and in particular you cannot link to SharePoint list data. However, you can get around this limitation by using SQL Server linked servers to connect to other data stores and then in turn use the linked servers from within Access.

ADPs move you totally into the world of SQL Server. All data is held on the server, with Access providing a container for user objects, forms, reports, and VBA modules. In theory, all data processing is also carried out by SQL Server using stored procedures, user-defined functions, and views. As already stated, ADPs give you access to a graphical tool set with which to build such objects, lessening the development time involved. Graphical tools are available for everything from table design and manipulation to creating basic stored procedures and are a great learning device for those who are just starting out with this technology. ADPs are discussed in more detail in Chapter 7.

Upsizing to SQL Server Reporting Services

When speaking about SQL Server 2005 Express, so far we have looked at the basic version. There are actually several versions available for download as follows:

- SQL Server 2005 Express Edition

- SQL Server 2005 Express Edition with Advanced Services

- SQL Server 2005 Express Edition Toolkit

Both Advanced Services and the Toolkit versions include Reporting Services and all are available for free! The example presented in this section will walk you through the process of taking an Access report and converting it to Reporting Services. The free availability of Reporting Services, either with an Express Edition or as part of a licensed install of SQL Server 2005, offers you the opportunity to take advantage of a server-based reporting tool. For the first time using Reporting Services, it is possible to not only upsize an Access database, but also upsize Access reports as well. I wonder how long it will be before someone develops something to assist in upsizing Access forms to Windows Forms.

Just like upsizing MDB files, reports will have problems of their own when upsized to Reporting Services, and some manual work is usually required by the developer. I should also say that Reporting Services and its design tools are a lot more sophisticated than Access reports and are fully covered in SQL Server 2005 Books Online, which contains several tutorials and walkthroughs in their use and programming. Figure 6-5 shows the blank report designer in Visual Studio.

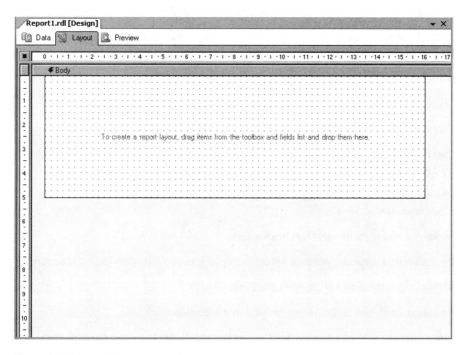

Figure 6-5. *Report designer*

In order to run Reporting Services, you will also need to install the SQL Server Express Toolkit, also available from Microsoft. Business Intelligence Development Studio (BIDS), available as part of the download, is required to develop reports using Reporting Services. The following walkthrough is based on using Visual Studio 2005, SQL Server 5000 Express with Advanced Services, and the SQL Server Express Toolkit. Initially, you will use the wizard interface to build a new report, and then you will look at importing and amending some existing reports.

■**Note** Reports are written using Report Definition Language (RDL), which is an XML-based language that contains all the details about the report (for example, connection, design layout, properties, and content). Reports created this way are viewed via web browser, further expanding the platform and reachability of your data. Given this is a short section, we will only look at creating reports via the interface, providing you with the mechanics of getting started with these tools. There are many resources available to further your learning in this area; SQL Server 2005 Books Online is a good place to start, as it contains many examples and tutorials.

Creating a Basic Report Using the Report Server Project Wizard

In this walkthrough, you will create a new report using Visual Studio and SQL Server 2005 Express via the Report Server Project Wizard.

1. With Visual Studio open, select File ➤ New Project ➤ Business Intelligence Projects.

2. From the Templates group, select Report Server Project Wizard. Enter a name for the project and select a location to save the project files into.

3. Click OK.

4. If the project already exists, you will be prompted to overwrite the solution.

5. The Report Server Project Wizard will start up. Once it does, click Next.

6. The next screen deals with naming and connection. Enter a name for the data source. In my case, I used dsStudentReport.

7. There are several different connection types available using the drop-down list. Specify a type of SQL Server.

8. To create the connection, start by clicking Edit.

9. In the screen that appears, enter or select the appropriate values for the connection.

10. Click Test Connection to ensure all is working.

11. When you are finished setting the connection properties, click OK.

Before moving on with the Report Server Project Wizard dialog box, you must set the security credentials for this connection. In my case, I am using Windows Authentication. If you are not using the same security mechanism, click Credentials to enter a username and password to be used for this connection. You can also have the user prompted for the username and password. That's the first step in the report process. You have named the report solution and created a connection to the database. Next, you will provide the data source for the report.

The next stage in the wizard allows you to either enter an SQL statement directly into the query builder or change it into a graphical query tool. To change to GUI query building, follow these steps:

1. Click Query Builder. The query builder text editor will open.

2. Click the Generic Query Builder icon located at the top left of the query builder window.

3. Right-click in the GUI and select Add Table.

4. Select the table to add (in my case, I chose tblStudent) and close the Add Table dialog box.

5. Click the * to select all fields form the table.

6. Execute the query by clicking the Execute icon to ensure it returns the data you require.

7. Click OK.

8. Click Next on the Design Query dialog box.

9. Select Tabular as the report layout type.

10. Click Next on the Select Report Layout dialog box.

11. Click Next as you are not adding any grouping to this report.

12. Select a Table style.

13. Click Next to move to the next screen in the wizard and accept the default location for the reports server. Accept the default for the deployment folder.

14. Click Next.

15. Enter a name for the report (I called mine rptStudent).

16. Click Finish.

Nothing to it. You are taken to the report designer window where you can add the finishing touches to the report. As you will see, this is very similar to the Report Designer in Access. Unlike in Access reports, notice how each field within the report designer is defined: =Fields!Forename.Value. Of course, you are no longer in the world of Access, and the terminology will be different. In Reporting Services, this is termed an *expression*. The expression builder available will appear very familiar to many Access developers, as it looks and works in a similar way to the Access query builder. Just like in Access reports, you can use expressions to add some of the features commonly seen in Access reports. For example, to concatenate fields together, simply join them in a report text box:

```
=fields!Surname.value +" "+fields!Forename.value
```

You need to precede an expression with an equals sign. Calculations are created in a similar way. For example, using the Sum function:

```
=Sum(Fields!CourseRef.Value)
```

While the wizard gets you up and running, it's almost as easy to create your own report. Once again, the first step is naming it and creating a connection. The SQL scripts to create the example SQL Server 2005 Express database can be downloaded from the Apress Source Code/Downloads web page.

Creating a Report Manually

In this section, you will see how to use Visual Studio and SQL Server 2005 Express to create a new report manually. With a project open, follow the instructions in the preceding section to create a data connection to the Chapter6 example SQL Server 2005 Express database and a query to select all values from tblCourse. This query will be used to provide the dataset for the report. Name the dataset dsCourse. Once you have done this, you are ready to create the report:

1. Click the toolbox.

2. Click and drag a table onto the blank design grid.

3. Click within the table to activate it.

4. Click dsCourse to view the columns.

5. On the table within the design page, click the button icon containing three solid vertical lines to activate the detail section.

6. Drag each field you would like to appear in the report into the detail cells (one field per cell).

7. The last row in the table is called the Total Row. In the first cell of the last row, enter the text Total Number of Courses.

8. In the second cell, enter the following text:

   ```
   =count(fields!fldCourseName.value)
   ```

   This returns a simple record count for the report.

Figure 6-6 shows the designer at this stage in the process.
You can tidy up the report count by creating a new expression in the first cell of the last row.

9. Add the following expression to the cell, replacing the text Total Number of Courses:

   ```
   ="Total Number of Courses: " & count(fields!fldCourseName.value)
   ```

10. Click Preview to view the report. Figure 6-7 shows how the report looks in the report designer if you click the Preview tab.

Report1.rdl [Design]*
Data
Layout
Preview
Body
Course Ref
fld Course
fld Course
fld Course
=Fields!CourseRef.Value
=Fields!fldCours
=Fields!fldCours
=Fields!fldCours
Total Number of Courses
=Count(fields!flc

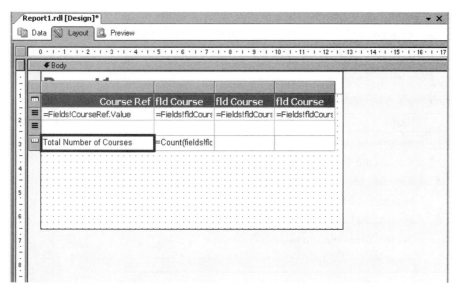

Figure 6-6. *The report designer at the current stage of building your report*

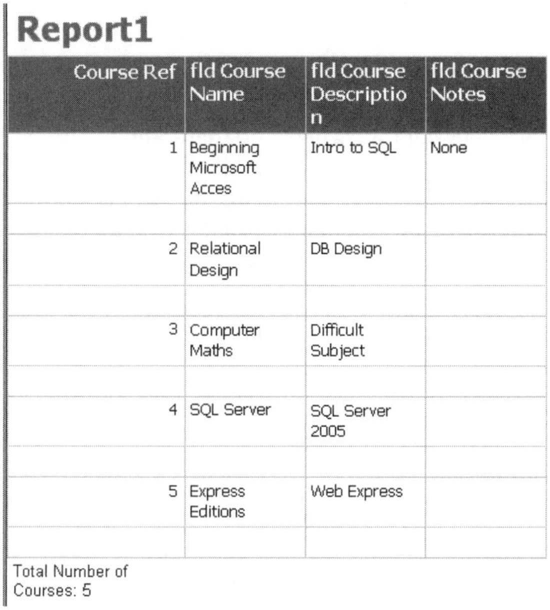

Report1
Course Ref
fld Course Name
fld Course Descriptio n
fld Course Notes
1
Beginning Microsoft Acces
Intro to SQL
None
2
Relational Design
DB Design
3
Computer Maths
Difficult Subject
4
SQL Server
SQL Server 2005
5
Express Editions
Web Express
Total Number of Courses: 5

Figure 6-7. *Previewing the report in the report designer*

Table 6-6 shows the aggregate functions available to you in the report designer, together with an example of usage. Each function accepts a single parameter scope, which can apply to a dataset or a grouping of data; that being the case, the value changes on break of a group or can be applied to a data region.

Table 6-6. *Reporting Service Aggregrate Functions*

Function	Usage
Sum	Returns the summation of a range of values
AVG	Returns the average of a range of values
CountDistinct	Returns a count of distinct rows ignoring duplicated values
First	Returns the first value in the dataset
Last	Returns the last value in the dataset
Min	Returns the minimum value in the dataset
Max	Returns the maximum value from the dataset

SQL Server Books Online provides comprehensive coverage of all the functions available to you within Reporting Services.

Upsizing Existing Reports

When it comes to upsizing existing reports, a walkthrough using the Northwind database wouldn't be very practical: you could import every report from the Northwind database into a Reporting Services project, change a few minor things here and there, and they will all work. Complex reports in the real world are another story. For this discussion, we will look at the results of my using the Import Reports tool in SQL Server to import real-world reports from the BarTracks application into Reporting Services. I did not expect this to achieve great success, because the reports in this particular application are very sophisticated, as they are highly configurable by the user.

■**Note** You cannot select individual reports to import. This is an all-or-nothing event. You must import all the reports in a specific database and then remove those not required. Depending on the number of reports, this can be a time-consuming process, so be patient.

Following the import, I received 38 errors and 16 warnings, as expected. Out of a substantial number of reports, I only managed to import four working copies. In the majority of cases, the reports failed to import due to the widespread use of Access VBA and various report events (that is, the reports are very code-heavy, relying on VBA modules both in the reports and within the application to function). For this particular application, it would be just as "easy" to write the reports entirely in the report designer. The four reports that actually upsized were basic reports with single table data, but no VBA code behind the reports.

So, in my opinion, for simple listing-type reports and reports that do not have a great deal of VBA code associated with them, the Import Reports tool is a useful choice. For reports that are driven by VBA or that receive user options, this tool may not prove worth while.

Interestingly, overlapping items on reports result in report import failure. In my case, almost all the reports contain overlapping labels and text boxes that are turned on and off via VBA. So it was not a successful experiment for this real-world application. In addition, any particular VBA functions used will also have to be rewritten or replaced with their Report Definition Language equivalents.

One of the main reasons several reports failed to upsize was the use of the On No Data event. This in fact is one of the easiest errors to fix, as the detail list has a No Rows property, which serves the same purpose (that is, it indicates what to do if the report has no data to show). In this case, you would simply add an expression into the No Rows property of the region, for example:

```
= "No Data For This Report"
```

It has to be said that the reporting environment in SQL Express Advanced is powerful and flexible and for experienced Access developers the learning curve is short. My advice is to jump straight in and try it out.

Passing Parameters to Reports

One of the reasons many reports were not upsized when I tried importing the BarTracks application into Reporting Services was the use of parameters. In almost every case, parameters are passed to the report VBA using report query forms. Although this gives the user a more flexible experience and is common in Access applications, it again means that it would be just as easy to rewrite the reporting module in .NET, as the number of changes to code would be immense. However, reports can also be configured to accept parameters within the report designer.

For this example, first create a basic stored procedure that accepts a single parameter, the `CourseCode` of the course you would like to report on. The stored procedure is outlined in Listing 6-18.

Listing 6-18. *Report Stored Procedure*

```
CREATE PROCEDURE usp_Course
(@courseref int)
AS SELECT      tblStudent.fldStudentForeName,➡
 .tblStudent.fldStudentSurName,  tblCourse.fldCourseName,   tblCourse.CourseRef
FROM   tblStudent
INNER JOIN
tblStudentCourse ON
tblStudent.StudentRef =
tblStudentCourse.fldStudRef INNER JOIN
tblCourse ON  tblStudentCourse.fldCourseRef
= tblCourse.CourseRef
WHERE    ( .tblCourse.CourseRef = @courseref)
ORDER BY  .tblStudent.fldStudentSurName
```

Within Visual Studio, create a new Business Intelligence project called ClassProject and add in a shared connection to the SQL Server database LinkedStudent. (The script for this is included with the reference material for this chapter.) Figure 6-8 shows the report once you have finished. It's particularly important to note the inclusion of the parameter entry text box located at the top of the report screen. Parameters are fed to the reports in this way during the design process.

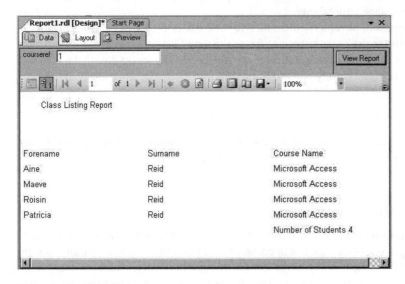

Figure 6-8. *Finished report*

In this next example, you will create a report, ClassListing, that accepts a single parameter. The report is based on uspCourse, a stored procedure to which the parameter is provided.

1. With an existing project open, right-click the Reports folder and select Add New Item. Do not run the Report Server Project Wizard!

2. Select Report.

3. On the screen that appears, enter ClassListing as the report name.

4. Click Add.

5. Click the Data tab and select New Dataset from the Dataset combo box.

6. Enter dsClassReport in the Name field.

7. Select your data source.

If you have created a totally new project, you will need to create a new data source.

8. Select Stored Procedure as the command type.

9. Click OK.

10. Select the stored procedure, uspCourse, from the Stored Procedure combo box. Click the execution icon to run the procedure.

11. Enter a value of 1 as the parameter value in the Define Query Parameters dialog box.

12. Click OK.

The stored procedure will execute, populating the dataset with the returned records, so you know the stored procedure runs and accepts the parameter entered.

Now its time to build the report itself:

13. Click the Layout tab.

14. Click the Toolbox tab.

15. Select the Table item and drag it onto the report designer.

16. Click the Datasets table.

17. Expand the dataset dsClassReport available by clicking the Datasets tab.

18. Drag each field into a detail cell on the report designer.

Next you will add a simple count into the footer of the report:

19. Click in the far-right footer cell and enter the following expression:

```
="Number of Students " & count(fields!fldCourseName.Value)
```

20. Click Preview to view what you have to date.

21. At the top of the screen, you will see a parameter entry box. Enter a value and click View report.

Your report should now open and return a subset of records.

When your query and procedure return no data, you should pass a sensible message back to the interface as follows:

22. Select the table by clicking the top-left square above the detail section.

23. In the properties for the tab, scroll down until you see the No Rows property located in the Data category.

24. Enter the following text for the No Rows property:

```
"No Course Records Found"
```

25. Click Preview.

26. Enter a value of 12 into the Parameter text box.

27. Click View report.

The text entered as the No Rows property should now be displayed.

Now via the reporting interface you have a report that is based on a stored procedure, accepts a parameter, and has a No Data event triggered. All achieved without too much "rocket science" involved.

Summary

When I started this chapter, I wanted to give you a flavor of what's involved in upsizing your Access database to both SQL Server 2000 and SQL Server 2005 Express. I hope I have achieved that. It's difficult, if not impossible, in a single chapter to cover a subject so broad, but at the end of the day, SQL Server should not be a product outside the reach of almost all Access developers—developers who are more than used to making software jump through hoops to meet the needs of their clients. At the end of the chapter, I touched on Reporting Services as another tool available freely to Access developers. There are many tutorials and notes available in the SQL Express Books Online, and I encourage you to take the basics introduced here and try it out. It's a powerful, flexible tool whose popularity can only grow.

■ ■ ■

Working with the SQL Server 2005 Express Tool Set

In this chapter, we look at working with SQL Server 2005 Express using Access Data Projects (ADPs) and linked tables. In Chapter 12, I move on to discussing working with two of the other tools in the SQL Server 2005 Express product set, Visual Web Developer Express and VB Express, in terms of using Access to build quick, efficient applications.

During the course of the beta testing of Access 2007, many developers asked the question, "What about ADPs?" The question also surfaced on many web sites, as those who had invested in this technology began to wonder if ADPs would be supported in the new version. The answer to that question, as we now know, is "Yes!" In this chapter, many of the example functions, triggers, and stored procedures will be created either in an ADP front end or on the server itself. It is really worthwhile when working with SQL Server to create an ADP, even if you are going to go with a linked table application. This way, you can take advantage of the graphical tools of Access to build many server-side objects.

In Chapter 6, we looked at the Access Upsizing Wizard; in this chapter, we will be looking at a recent Microsoft development, the SQL Server 2005 Migration Assistant for Access, which should be available by the time this book hits the shelves. For those working with SQL Server 2000, the Upsizing Wizard and third-party tools are likely the way to go. However, you could always use the Migration Assistant as a simple error reporting tool for a move to SQL Server 2000, because many of the issues you face will be the same irrespective of which version of SQL Server you are migrating to.

For those working with SQL Server 2005, this new application should be the tool of choice. This application is in a whole different league from the built-in features of the Upsizing Wizard. You can guess from its name what it does, and it does it very well. However, it's a pure SQL Server 2005 solution to upsizing and therefore cannot be used with earlier versions of SQL Server.

▌Note When talking about SQL Server or SQL Server Express in this chapter, I am specifically referring to SQL Server 2005 Express Edition, unless otherwise noted.

■**Note** In the Management Studio, it is really worthwhile looking at the templates provided for things like stored procedures, functions, and views. SQL Server 2005 Express comes with a couple hundred "getting started" T-SQL templates.

This chapter provides you with an overview of many of the features available to you in SQL Server Express, from table design to triggers and stored procedures; migration issues are covered in the section "SQL Server Migration Assistant for Access." At the end of this chapter, you should have enough information to continue exploring on your own the features of this free database back-end server and management environment.

SQL Server Express 2005 Overview

SQL Server Express will be a new environment to many Access developers and indeed many power users who wish to make use of this technology. Figure 7-1 shows the SQL Server Management Studio Express environment, which will be a huge advance for developers who have been using MSDE, which did not have a graphical management interface.

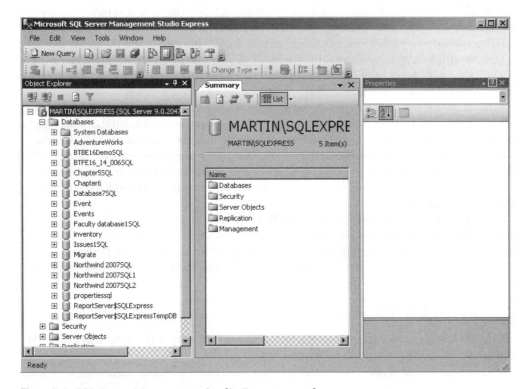

Figure 7-1. *SQL Server Management Studio Express console*

As you can see, this environment is a little bit more complex than that of Access, and it closely resembles the environment of the full version of SQL Server 2005.

I think it is safe to assume that you can figure out the download and install instructions without help from me. The only suggestion I have is that you download and install the Express Edition Toolkit, which contains everything you will ever need (at this stage) for working with SQL Server Express, including the reporting development tools for .NET Reporting Services. For your information, when perusing the examples in this chapter, my own setup is Windows Server 2003, SQL Server Express Toolkit, Visual Studio 2005, and Office 2007.

Table 7-1 shows the differences between SQL Server Express and MSDE, with which you may already be familiar.

Table 7-1. *SQL Server Express vs. MSDE*

Item	SQL Server Express	MSDE
Database size	4GB	2GB
Workload governor	No	Yes
RAM	1GB	2GB
SMP	1	2
GUI tools	Yes	No

This new database and management environment, SQL Server Express together with Management Studio Express, contains many features to assist the Access developer and is in itself a development environment. It is worth remembering that SQL Server Express is not an application front end in the same way as Access. It's a database engine, but there is no application interface. All it does is manage your data and other server-side objects. The interface to these objects is provided by developers using either Access, as in our case, or another development environment to build the front-end interface. One of the nice features of Management Studio Express and one you may use a great deal is the Query Editor.

Query Editor

The Query Editor can be used to work with many types of server-side objects (for example, stored procedures, functions, views, and triggers). Results from query execution can be displayed directly in a grid, or passed to a text file or a report file for later use. A useful feature is the ability to change from text editor view to a graphical query builder much like that in Access. Ctrl+Shift+Q will open the Query Editor for those who prefer the graphical approach. Within the Query Editor, several tools are available to assist you in developing queries (for example, fast access to SQL Server execution plans and client statistics). Figure 7-2 shows the execution plan for a standard query. To add the execution plan to the results, right-click within the Query Designer window and select the appropriate option from the context menu. Several options may be added at any one time.

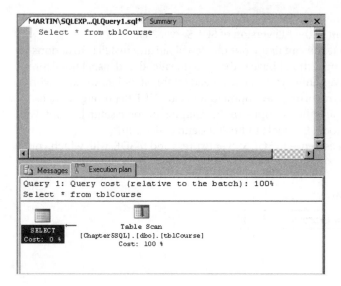

Figure 7-2. *Execution plan in query builder*

The execution plan will show you how SQL Server will optimize (or not) the statements being executed. You can view the proposed execution plan before the statements are actually executed or the actual plan used upon execution. This is a great learning tool you can use to speed up poorly performing statements—for example, statements that make full table scans can indicate that better use of indexes may be required.

SQL Server Schemas and Other Objects

When migrating to SQL Server 2005, you will encounter a number of terms that may seem unfamiliar. SQL Server describes a database in terms of a *schema*; a single database can consist of a number of logical schemas. The examples in this chapter will feature a small SQL Server database that contains data about students and modules (the scripts for these examples are available for download from the Apress web site at http://www.apress.com).

Management Studio Express's Object Explorer provides a tree view of the objects available to you on the server, and while I cannot go into great detail about all of them, I will provide a general introduction to the features you will use daily in your development. Figure 7-3 shows Management Studio Express with the database folder open.

Figure 7-3. *Management Studio Express Object Explorer*

Databases and System Objects

Of course, expanding the database node will reveal the databases on the server; both user and system databases are available to you. Chapter 6 briefly discussed the system databases, but in SQL Server Express, you will have additional nodes under each of the system databases and some items that we have not looked at yet. Here we will be looking at those nodes you will need to understand in order to get up and running with the software. Each database folder contains a similar set of subfolders, the contents of which are described here:

Database Diagrams: This folder contains interactive relationship diagrams that provide more functionality than their Access counterpart. For example, you can work with table properties and add and amend tables and columns.

Tables: Here you will find all user and system tables for the specific database.

Views: Database-specific views are stored in this folder.

Synonyms: As you can guess, this folder contains synonyms, which are basically names for other objects, for example, an alias to another SQL Server, a table in the same database, or a stored procedure or function. It is import to realize that SQL Server does not check for existence of objects at the time the synonyms are created, only when they are executed.

Programmability: This subfolder groups the programmability objects together. Each database on the server will contain the same sort of substructure for these objects. Here you will find everything related to programming and code, for example, stored procedures, user-defined functions, database triggers, assemblies, types, rules, and defaults.

Of the objects in the Programmability folder, what will be new to Access developers and power users will be *assemblies* and *triggers*. Assemblies are .NET code that has been taken into SQL Server to perform a specific task. Triggers warrant a bit more discussion, so we'll take a longer look at them next.

Creating Triggers

A trigger is a block of code that can be fired when a database event takes place. For example, if you want to track user inserts to a table, the trigger shown in Listing 7-1 will do this for you. In this case, you simply get the table name, username, and the date the insert action took place. However, this example shows the possibilities for triggers. Before creating the trigger, you create a logging table, tblLogg, to store the results when the trigger is fired. Execute the following SQL statement by first clicking New Query in SQL Server Management Studio Express. Remember to change the database name in line 1 to reflect your database, if you are not using the Chapter7 example.

Listing 7-1. *Creating the Table Template*

```
USE [Chapter7]
GO
/****** Object:  Table [dbo].[tblLogg]    Script Date: 06/04/2006 15:39:19 ******/
SET ANSI_NULLS ON
GO
SET QUOTED_IDENTIFIER ON
GO
CREATE TABLE [dbo].[tblLogg](
 [logID] [int] IDENTITY(1,1) NOT NULL,
 [LogTable] [nvarchar](50) COLLATE Latin1_General_CS_AI NULL,
 [LogDate] [datetime] NULL,
 [logUser] [nvarchar](50) COLLATE Latin1_General_CS_AI NULL,
 CONSTRAINT [PK_tblLogg] PRIMARY KEY CLUSTERED
(
 [logID] ASC
)WITH (PAD_INDEX  = OFF, IGNORE_DUP_KEY = OFF) ON [PRIMARY]
) ON [PRIMARY]
```

Execute the statement in Listing 7-1 to create the table. Once the table is created, you can then follow the steps here create the new trigger.

■Tip It's important when working in the Query Designer window of Management Studio Express that you ensure you are working in the correct database. A drop-down list is available that allows you to choose a database for the procedure being written—*use it*!

---

1. Open Management Studio Express if it is not already open.

2. Open the database of interest. In this case, I have opened the Chapter7 example database.

3. Expand the Trigger folder for the database selected.

4. Right-click the Trigger folder and select New Trigger.

The structure of new trigger will be created for you. Listing 7-2 shows the trigger template.

Listing 7-2. *Trigger Template*

```
SET ANSI_NULLS ON
GO
SET QUOTED_IDENTIFIER ON
GO
-- =============================================
-- Author:<Author,,Name>
-- Create date: <Create Date,,>
-- Description: <Description,,>
-- =============================================
CREATE TRIGGER <Schema_Name, sysname, Schema_Name>.<Trigger_Name, ➥
sysname, Trigger_Name>
   ON  <Schema_Name, sysname, Schema_Name>.<Table_Name, sysname, Table_Name>
   AFTER <Data_Modification_Statements, , INSERT,DELETE,UPDATE>
AS
BEGIN
-- SET NOCOUNT ON added to prevent extra result sets from
-- interfering with SELECT statements.
SET NOCOUNT ON;

    -- Insert statements for trigger here

END
GO
```

The trigger template gets you started with the syntax and is useful until you become more comfortable with how these things are written. The trigger you will create will be attached to tblLogg and fired in response to an INSERT statement. Once an insert takes place, tblLogg will be updated. Replace everything after the CREATE statement with the trigger shown in Listing 7-3.

Listing 7-3. *Log Trigger*

```
CREATE TRIGGER tr_addLog  ON dbo.tblLogg
FOR INSERT
AS
INSERT INTO tblLogg
(LogTable,LogDate,logUser)
VALUES
('tblStudent',getdate(),user_name())
```

Note that the actual trigger in this case is much simpler than the outline proposed by the template. In the trigger body, you use two built-in SQL Server functions: getdate(), which returns the current date, and user_name(), which returns the name of the user doing the insert. If you want to capture the Windows username of the account, you can also use

SUSER_SNAME. For example, to get my own Windows username, I can execute the following SQL within the Query Designer window:

```
SELECT SUSER_SNAME()
```

The preceding trigger could be changed to also reflect updates and deletes by changing the FOR INSERT line to read FOR INSERT, UPDATE, DELETE. In such cases, the trigger will fire if any of the three named events take place. You may need to refresh tblLogg in order to see the effect. The trigger will fire in response to a data event, but what if you also want to log and audit a database schema event (for example, a user adding a column or, even worse, dropping a table)? Triggers can also be fired in response to SQL Data Definition Language events. Rather than the trigger being attached to a table, it can also be attached to fire with the ON DATABASE statement. For example, if an attempt were made to drop or alter a table, the following trigger could execute:

```
CREATE Trigger DontDrop
ON DATABASE
FOR DROP, ALTER
AS
"Text for Message"
ROLLBACK;
```

SQL Server Express contains an excellent overview on both data-level triggers and database-level triggers, and they are well worth exploring, particularly if you need to log either table-level or database-level events. Of course, it goes without saying that the trigger is fired when adding data to the table from Access. You can see this if you create and link to tblLogg in the previous example. Within SQL Server, you can view information on triggers by writing a SELECT statement against one of the system views, sys.triggers, as follows:

```
SELECT * FROM sys.triggers
```

Triggers are a useful approach for jobs like audit trails, but for general data manipulation you will work with stored procedures in some shape or form.

Stored Procedures

Stored procedures, briefly mentioned in Chapter 6, will be the mainstay of your development effort in SQL Server Express. Graphical tools are available to assist you in this regard when working in an ADP. For this example, you will create a stored procedure that can be called to populate a record from an unbound form. The fairly basic form is based on two tables, tblStudent and tblModule. Of course, you will also need some user input. Thus your procedure must also accept parameters. Parameters within stored procedures are declared as

```
Declare Variable name Datatype
```

For example:

```
@CustomerName Nvarchar(250)
```

Parameters can also have a default value assigned, and you can declare your own variables to hold the results of processing. You will see an example of this a little later in the section "Error Trapping in Stored Procedures."

You will be creating the procedure in Management Studio Express by turning on the Query Designer (select View ➤ Toolbars ➤ Query Designer). Creating a query in the Query Designer is very similar to creating a standard Access query. The main difference, as you shall see, is how stored procedures are executed from code using ADO. Enter Listing 7-4, the code for this example, into the Query Designer window and execute it to create the procedure. You can test the results by typing Exec Usp_FindStudent into the Query Designer window and executing it. The actual procedure can also be created via the Access ADP interface using graphical tools. If you do so, you may only see the SQL SELECT statement as opposed to the full stored procedure definition shown in Listing 7-4.

Listing 7-4. *Creating a Parameter in a Stored Procedure*

```
CREATE Procedure usp_FindStudent
(@StudentRef int)
AS SELECT
dbo.tblStudent.StudForeName, dbo.tblStudent.StudSurName,
dbo.tblStudent.StudAdd1, dbo.tblStudent.StudAdd2,
dbo.tblStudent.StudTown, dbo.tblModule.ModName
FROM
dbo.tblModule INNER JOIN
dbo.tblStudent ON dbo.tblModule.ModStudent
= dbo.tblStudent.StudRef
WHERE
dbo.tblStudent.StudRef = @StudentRef
```

The procedure accepts a single parameter, StudentRef, which in this case will be passed using ADO. Let's add a few refinements to the procedure: a default value and a line to deal with null values. In this case, if the value is null, you want all the student records to be returned. The procedure can be passed the StudentRef parameter or indeed a null value, and it will return records to the caller. Listing 7-5 shows the stored procedure rewritten to deal with the possibility of a null variable.

Listing 7-5. *Dealing with Nulls*

```
CREATE Procedure usp_FindStudent
(@StudentRef int = null)
AS
IF @StudentRef is null
BEGIN
SELECT * FROM dbo.tblStudent
END
Else
BEGIN
SELECT
dbo.tblStudent.StudForeName, dbo.tblStudent.StudSurName,
dbo.tblStudent.StudAdd1, dbo.tblStudent.StudAdd2,
dbo.tblStudent.StudTown, dbo.tblModule.ModName
```

```
FROM
dbo.tblModule INNER JOIN
dbo.tblStudent ON dbo.tblModule.ModStudent
= dbo.tblStudent.StudRef
WHERE
dbo.tblStudent.StudRef= @StudentRef
END
```

The changed version includes some conditional branching. @StudentRef has been given a default value, in this case null; @StudentRef is tested for a null value, and if true, processing is carried out by the first BEGIN/END statement, in this case a simple SELECT * statement. If @StudentRef does contain a value, the second set of SQL statements is executed. Within an ADP, you can execute the procedure in Listing 7-5 and pass Access form values to it as parameters. ADO parameters were introduced in Chapter 6 and offer you a quick method to feed values from Access ADPs to stored procedures. Within Access, if you need to pass a parameter to a procedure from a form, you can use the Input Parameter property. Input parameters are discussed later in this chapter in the section "Passing Parameters to Stored Procedures."

In the preceding example, you could also have captured and halted the passing of the null value from within the Access interface, and this is often viewed as the best way to deal with such issues by building rules into the application. However, if you need to move the interface to the Web, for example, you would need to rebuild the "smarts" into the front end all over again. In the preceding case, the "smarts" are part of the procedure and are thus independent of the application accessing it.

It is also possible to execute a stored procedure via DAO by using a QueryDef and a pass-through query. Listing 7-6 shows how this is achieved.

Listing 7-6. *Executing a Pass-Through Using DAO*

```
Public Sub PtSPs()
On Error GoTo Err_PtSPs
Dim db As DAO.Database
Dim qdf As QueryDef
Dim rstlog As DAO.Recordset

Set db = CurrentDb
Set qdf = db.QueryDefs("pt_GetDbRoles")
Set rstlog = qdf.OpenRecordset()

Do While Not rstlog.EOF
    Debug.Print rstlog!DbFixedRole
    rstlog.MoveNext
Loop
```

```
Exit_PtSPs:
On Error Resume Next
    If Not (rstlog Is Nothing) Then rstlog.Close: Set rstlog = Nothing
    If Not (qdf Is Nothing) Then qdf.Close: Set qdf = Nothing
    If Not (db Is Nothing) Then db.Close: Set db = Nothing
Exit Sub
Err_PtSPs:
        MsgBox Err.Description, , "Error in Sub Module2.PtSPs"
        Resume Exit_PtSPs
    Resume 0    '.FOR TROUBLESHOOTING
End Sub
```

Error Trapping in Stored Procedures

So far, the examples are basic to illustrate the procedure. If you can create an INSERT procedure and use it to add two values using VBA and ADO, for example, or directly in the Management Studio Express interface, the move to insert 200 records should not prove to be that difficult. So, before moving on, let's look at how SQL Server Express deals with error control. For this example, you will be looking at adding error management into the INSERT procedure used to add a record into the module table, tblModule. I should say straight away that error handling in stored procedures is poor to say the least. You have already seen a simple example of procedure control when testing for a NULL parameter. Using IF @parameter Is NULL, you can execute an alternative statement, or if you use the RETURN keyword, you can kill execution of the procedure before it hits your code. For example:

```
IF @ModuleRef Is Null
RETURN
```

The only problem with this is that you will not receive any notification from the SQL Server side that your procedure has been terminated.

On many occasions, you may want to catch and validate errors on the client, but placing error control into the stored procedure itself can give you a much more flexible back end. Listing 7-7 shows the approach. The following procedure is taken from SQL Server Books Online and demonstrates the new features for error control with SQL Server 2005.

Listing 7-7. *Using TRY/CATCH*

```
CREATE PROCEDURE usp_GetErrorInfo
AS
    SELECT
        ERROR_NUMBER() AS ErrorNumber,
        ERROR_SEVERITY() AS ErrorSeverity,
        ERROR_STATE() as ErrorState,
        ERROR_PROCEDURE() as ErrorProcedure,
        ERROR_LINE() as ErrorLine,
        ERROR_MESSAGE() as ErrorMessage;
GO
```

```
BEGIN TRY
    -- Generate divide-by-zero error.
    SELECT 1/0;
END TRY
BEGIN CATCH
    -- Execute the error retrieval routine.
    EXECUTE usp_GetErrorInfo;
END CATCH;
```

The actual procedure is easy enough, but it contains much more sophisticated error control than was previously available with SQL Server. The bones of this error control come from standard .NET programming language C# and involve the use of a TRY/CATCH block. What happens is that your code will be contained within the TRY block. If an error occurs, control of the program flow is passed into the CATCH block for processing. Processing then continues at the first SQL statement following the end of the CATCH block. Each TRY block is associated with at most one CATCH block.

As can be seen in the preceding example, several functions have been declared in the procedure. Table 7-2 shows their use.

Table 7-2. *Try/Catch Error Functions*

Function	Comment
ERROR_NUMBER()	Returns the error number
ERROR_MESSAGE()	Returns the complete text of the error message
ERROR_SEVERITY()	Returns the error severity
ERROR_STATE()	Returns the error state number
ERROR_LINE()	Returns the line number inside the routine that caused the error
ERROR_PROCEDURE()	Returns the name of the stored procedure or trigger

With SQL Server, an error is associated with a severity level that may kill the code or disable your connection. SQL Server Books Online contains a great section with examples on error control.

Passing Parameters to Stored Procedures

When working with stored procedures and other server-side objects, you will often need to pass one or more parameters to the objects using ADO and the parameters' arguments to the Command object and its execute method. The basic idea is to append the parameters to the ADO Command object. The basic premise for passing a parameter is as follows:

```
Set parameter = command.CreateParameter("StudRef",adInteger,adParamInput)
Command.Parameters.Append Parameter
```

Each parameter must be in the same position as in the stored procedure. For this example, the parameters will be passed to the procedure from a form that contains two text boxes, Student ForeName and Student SurName. The code will be attached to the On Click event and the values within the text boxes passed into the procedure. The code will execute the stored procedure, inserting the values into the SQL Server student table. Listing 7-8 shows the click event for the insert. I have omitted the cleanup code from this procedure.

Listing 7-8. *Passing Parameters to Stored Procedures*

```
Private Sub Command5_Click()
On Error GoTo Err_Command5_Click
Dim cmd As ADODB.Command
Dim prmForeName As ADODB.Parameter
Dim prmSurName  As ADODB.Parameter
Dim rstStudent As ADODB.Recordset
Dim conn As ADODB.Connection
Set conn = CurrentProject.AccessConnection
Set cmd = New ADODB.Command
cmd.ActiveConnection = conn
cmd.CommandType = adCmdStoredProc
cmd.CommandText = "usp_InsertStudent"

Set prmForeName = cmd.CreateParameter("@ForeName", adVarChar, adParamInput, 10)
Set prmSurName = cmd.CreateParameter("@SurName", adVarChar, adParamInput, 10)

cmd.Parameters.Append prmForeName
prmForeName.Value = Me.txtforename
cmd.Parameters.Append prmSurName
prmSurName.Value = Me.txtsurname

cmd.Execute


 Exit_Command5_Click:
On Error Resume Next

Exit Sub
Err_Command5_Click:
      MsgBox Err.Description, , "Error in Sub Form_Form1.Command5_Click"
      Resume Exit_Command5_Click
   Resume 0    '.FOR TROUBLESHOOTING
End Sub
```

The number of CreateParameter statements depends on the number of parameters being passed to the event and can grow substantially given the size of the typical form. Note that there is no visual indication within the interface that you have actually added the record, even though the insert actually does work. What you need to do is amend the procedure to indicate that a record has been added. One way to do this is to return the new record's primary key using a built-in SQL Server function, @@Identity.

Returning to the CreateParameter statement, there are several parts to the syntax:

CreateParameter(name,type,direction,sizevalue)

name is the name of the parameter, type refers to the data type of the value, direction refers to input or output value, and sizevalue relates to the maximum size of the value being passed in. The size stated is usually related to the size of the column value being used. Type is one area where new users of parameters can make some basic errors equating the parameter type to the data type of the value. The data type used by the parameter is different from that of your database. http://www.activeserverpages.ru/ADO/daprop06_4.htm contains a listing of all the ADO types available, and their definitions are well worth a look.

Stored Procedures and Access Forms

When working with stored procedures and Access 2007, you can bind a form directly to a procedure. Simply select the procedure, click Create ➤ Form, and you have a fully updatable recordset created by Access behind the scenes. An updatable snapshot is used by default for forms based on stored procedures. However, this can give rise to issues when working with a master detail form, as only the many side of a relationship can be updated. The Chapter7 example database contains a small example of working with an unbound form, frmStudent, which displays student data. (The form is deliberately simplified to illustrate the point.) This example is also unbound—that is, the data is provided to the form via VBA and a stored procedure. Before creating this form, you will create an unbound form to allow a user to enter and edit student data. The form will be populated using a number of stored procedures, which are shown in Listings 7-9 through 7-11. Each procedure is created within the Access interface. The INSERT procedure is simply a fuller example of the parameter example shown previously.

Listing 7-9. *Basic Stored Procedure to Populate frmModule*

```
CREATE PROCEDURE [dbo].[usp_GetStudentData]
AS
SELECT
StudForeName, StudSurName,
StudAdd1, StudAdd2, StudTown
FROM
dbo.tblStudent
```

Listing 7-10. *Stored Procedure to Insert a New Student*

```
CREATE PROCEDURE usp_InsertStudent
    (
@StudentFName nchar(10),
@StudentSName nchar(10),
@StudentAddr1 nchar(10),
@StudentAddr2 nchar(10),
@StudentTown nchar(10)
```

```
)
AS
INSERT INTO dbo.tblStudent(StudForeName,
StudSurName, StudAdd1, StudAdd2, StudTown)
    VALUES
            (@StudentFName,
            @StudentSName,
            @StudentAddr1,
            @StudentAddr2,
            @StudentTown)
```

Listing 7-11. *Stored Procedure to Delete a Module*

```
CREATE PROCEDURE dbo.usp_deletemodule
(@StudRef int)
AS DELETE FROM dbo.tblStudent
WHERE     (StudRef = @StudRef)
```

It is also possible to script the procedures with Management Studio Express. Right-click a table name and select Script Table As. You will then be presented with several scripting choices:

- CREATE

- ALTER

- DROP

- INSERT

- UPDATE

- DELETE

Choosing an option will create a new SQL statement that requires modification to change it into a stored procedure. Of course, you can use the statement as is. Listing 7-12 shows an INSERT statement generated for tblModule.

Listing 7-12. *Generated INSERT Statement*

```
INSERT INTO [Chapter7].[dbo].[tblModule]
            ([ModName]
            ,[ModStudent])
    VALUES
            (<ModName, nvarchar(50),>
            ,<ModStudent, nchar(10),>)
```

Note the placeholders indicated by the angle brackets (< >); these can be automatically populated by selecting Query ➤ Specify Values for Template Parameters from the main menu. Simply provide a parameter value in the Specify Parameter dialog box to have all placeholders populated for you.

These procedures, even if basic, illustrate several of the principles involved when manipulating data via stored procedures. The stored procedures themselves contain basic SQL statements. Note the use of the prefix before each object name. In this case, the prefix is dbo. When using SQL Server objects, they are created and prefixed with the name of the owner who created them. In this case, dbo is the system admin, which I am logged in as. From VBA, there are several ways in which you could make use of the procedure and indeed execute it.

Returning to the example in Listing 7-12, you now have three stored procedures: one returns all records, one inserts a record, and one deletes a record. Again, the approach is not complicated, but it is designed to illustrate the process of how this can work. (And always bear in mind that there is more than one way to skin a cat!) One tip I picked up relates to populating form text boxes using code. In form design, if the text boxes are named exactly the same as the column names in the table, a simple FOR LOOP can be used to populate the data. This technique is demonstrated in the MoveNext event for information. In Chapter 5, you explicitly set the value of each text box to a particular field.

```
For Each fld in rst.Fields
    Me(fld.Name).Value = fld.value
Next
```

This simply looks over the values returned from your statement in VBA and populates each matching text box on the form. The form's On Open event is shown in Listing 7-13, and the associated events for filing the recordset are shown in Listing 7-14. Listings 7-15 and 7-16 show the techniques used for the MoveNext and MovePrevious commands.

Listing 7-13. *Form Open Event*

```
Private Sub Form_Open(Cancel As Integer)
Dim cmd As ADODB.Command
Dim conn As ADODB.Connection

Set conn = CurrentProject.Connection
Set cmd = New ADODB.Command

Set rststudent = New ADODB.Recordset
Set cmd.ActiveConnection = conn
cmd.CommandText = "usp_getStudentData"
cmd.CommandType = adCmdStoredProc

rststudent.Open cmd, , adOpenKeyset, adLockOptimistic, adCmdStoredProc

Call fillform
End Sub
```

Listing 7-14. *Providing Data for the Form*

```
Public Sub fillform()
On Error GoTo Err_fillform
Me.StudForeName = rststudent!StudForeName
Me.StudSurName = rststudent!StudSurName
Me.StudAdd1 = rststudent!StudAdd1
Me.StudAdd2 = rststudent!StudAdd2
Me.StudTown = rststudetn!StudTown
Exit_fillform:
Exit Sub
Err_fillform:
        MsgBox Err.Description, , "Error in Sub Form_frmClearListbox.fillform"
        Resume Exit_fillform
    Resume 0    '.FOR TROUBLESHOOTING
End Sub
```

Listing 7-15. *MoveNext*

```
Private Sub cmdnext_Click()
On Error GoTo Err_cmdnext_Click
rststudent.MoveNext
If Not rststudent.EOF Then
For Each fld In rststudent.Fields
     Me(fld.Name).Value = fld.Value
Next
End If
Exit_cmdnext_Click:
Exit Sub
Err_cmdnext_Click:
     MsgBox Err.Description, , "Error in Sub Form_frmClearListbox.cmdnext_Click"
     Resume Exit_cmdnext_Click
    Resume 0    '.FOR TROUBLESHOOTING
End Sub
```

Listing 7-16. *MovePrevious*

```
Private Sub cmdPrevious_Click()
On Error GoTo Err_cmdPrevious_Click
rststudent.MovePrevious
If Not rststudent.EOF Then
For Each fld In rststudent.Fields
     Me(fld.Name).Value = fld.Value
Next
End If
Exit_cmdPrevious_Click:
Exit Sub
```

```
Err_cmdPrevious_Click:
        MsgBox Err.Description, , "Error in Sub ➥
Form_frmChapter7SPExample.cmdPrevious_Click"
        Resume Exit_cmdPrevious_Click
    Resume 0    '.FOR TROUBLESHOOTING
End Sub
```

In this example, you use a Command object in the form open event and the stored procedure directly in the recordset open event; note you must include the option adcmdStoredProc, which indicates that this is a stored procedure. An SQL statement would be identified as adcmdText. As in Chapter 5, because this is an unbound recordset, you need to take care of the MoveNext and MovePrevious commands yourself. Listing 7-17 shows the code behind a New Record button. The first thing it does is clear each of the form's text boxes. The next step is to enable a Save button, which has had its enabled property set to false.

■**Note** I am keeping each operation separate to show how the techniques work as opposed to setting a value, for example, a Mode variable that can hold a value for testing of Add, Edit, or Delete. For example, if Mode equals Add, add a new record, and if Mode equals Edit, edit the existing record.

Listing 7-17. *Clearing Text Boxes*

```
Me.StudForeName = ""
Me.StudSurName = ""
Me.StudAdd1 = ""
Me.StudAdd2 = ""
Me.StudTown = ""
```

Once the form is cleared, the user can then enter a new record. Finally, you need to validate the data entered by the user (for example, leaving a text box null). This is tested in the ValData routine attached to the click event of cmdSave.

Inserting a New Record

In this case, when inserting a new record, you will call your INSERT procedure, passing in the required parameters. The procedure being called is that shown earlier in usp_InsertStudent. Missing data errors are trapped within the front-end application. CmdSave checks the data and executes the stored procedure to carry out the actual insert of the record. Listing 7-18 shows the code to achieve this.

Listing 7-18. *Inserting a Record Using a Stored Procedure*

```
Private Sub cmdSave_Click()
On Error GoTo Err_cmdSave_Click
Call valData
Dim cmd As ADODB.Command
Dim prmForeName As ADODB.Parameter
Dim prmSurName  As ADODB.Parameter
Dim prmAddr1 As ADODB.Parameter
Dim prmAdd2 As ADODB.Parameter
Dim prmTown As ADODB.Parameter
Dim rststudent As ADODB.Recordset
Dim conn As ADODB.Connection
Set conn = CurrentProject.AccessConnection
Set cmd = New ADODB.Command
   cmd.ActiveConnection = conn
   cmd.CommandType = adCmdStoredProc
   cmd.CommandText = "usp_InsertStudent"

   Set prmForeName = cmd.CreateParameter("@ForeName", adVarChar, adParamInput, 10)
   Set prmSurName = cmd.CreateParameter("@SurName", adVarChar, adParamInput, 10)
   Set prmAddr1 = cmd.CreateParameter("@StudentAddr1", adVarChar, adParamInput, 10)
   Set prmAdd2 = cmd.CreateParameter("@StudentAddr2", adVarChar, adParamInput, 10)
   Set prmTown = cmd.CreateParameter("@StudentTown", adVarChar, adParamInput, 10)
      cmd.Parameters.Append prmForeName
   prmForeName.Value = Me.StudForeName
   cmd.Parameters.Append prmSurName
   prmSurName.Value = Me.StudSurName
   cmd.Parameters.Append prmAddr1
   prmAddr1.Value = Me.StudAdd1
   cmd.Parameters.Append prmAdd2
   prmAdd2.Value = Me.StudAdd2
   cmd.Parameters.Append prmTown
   prmTown.Value = Me.StudTown
   cmd.Execute
 Exit_cmdSave_Click:
On Error Resume Next
    If Not (prmTown Is Nothing) Then prmTown.Close: Set prmTown = Nothing
    If Not (prmAdd2 Is Nothing) Then prmAdd2.Close: Set prmAdd2 = Nothing
    If Not (prmAddr1 Is Nothing) Then prmAddr1.Close: Set prmAddr1 = Nothing
    If Not (prmForeName Is Nothing) Then prmForeName.Close: ➥
Set prmForeName = Nothing
    If Not (cmd Is Nothing) Then cmd.Close: Set cmd = Nothing
    If Not (conn Is Nothing) Then conn.Close: Set conn = Nothing
Exit Sub
```

```
Err_cmdSave_Click:
        MsgBox Err.Description, , ➥
"Error in Sub Form_frmChapter7SPExample.cmdSave_Click"
        Resume Exit_cmdSave_Click
    Resume 0    '.FOR TROUBLESHOOTING
End Sub
```

Deleting a Record

All that is required for this example is to pass to the DELETE procedure the ID of the record
you would like to delete. In this case, you delete a single student record, passing in the
StudRef of the required record. On this occasion, you will add in a TRY/CATCH example to
roll back any changes should an error occur. The entire operation has also been wrapped
into a transaction. Listing 7-19 shows the amended procedure. (Yes, I know there's mostly
error collection code in this procedure!)

Listing 7-19. *Amended Delete Procedure*

```
set ANSI_NULLS ON
set QUOTED_IDENTIFIER ON
GO
ALTER PROCEDURE [dbo].[usp_deletemodule](@modRef int)
AS
BEGIN TRANSACTION;

BEGIN TRY
DELETE FROM dbo.tblModule
WHERE       (ModRef = @modRef)
END TRY
BEGIN CATCH
    SELECT
        ERROR_NUMBER() AS ErrorNumber,
        ERROR_SEVERITY() AS ErrorSeverity,
        ERROR_STATE() as ErrorState,
        ERROR_PROCEDURE() as ErrorProcedure,
        ERROR_LINE() as ErrorLine,
        ERROR_MESSAGE() as ErrorMessage;

    IF @@TRANCOUNT > 0
        ROLLBACK TRANSACTION;
END CATCH;

IF @@TRANCOUNT > 0
    COMMIT TRANSACTION;
```

Deleting the actual record is a matter of passing the module reference primary key value
to the procedure. This is demonstrated in the Chapter7 example ADP file, which deletes a single module using the preceding procedure.

User-Defined Functions

Again, as briefly mentioned in Chapter 6, user-defined functions are a useful tool when working with SQL Server Express and indeed SQL Server 2000. A UDF itself is much like a stored procedure in that it contains a set of SQL statements that carry out a specific task or tasks. The big thing about them is that in addition to returning single values, they can in fact return a table. The table returned can also be used in a standard JOIN statement, and you can also write SQL, including WHERE clauses, against the function. Take the function fnStudentNames, shown in Listing 7-20.

Listing 7-20. *User-Defined Function fnStudentNames*

```
CREATE FUNCTION dbo.fnStudentNames
()
RETURNS TABLE
AS
RETURN ( SELECT StudForeName + ' ,' + StudSurName AS Name,Studref➡
FROM    dbo.tblStudent )
```

For this example, you will use the Access interface within the Chapter7 example ADP file. To create the function, follow these steps:

1. Click Create.

2. Click Query Wizard.

3. Select Design In Line Function.

4. Click tblStudent and click Add.

5. Click Close to close the Add Table dialog box.

6. Enter StudForeName + ',' + StudSurName in the column field.

7. Enter Name into the Alias field.

8. Click Run.

9. Click OK to save the changes.

So what use is this? Well, first off, any time you need the student name (or other concatenated data), it's available for use. Listing 7-21 shows the function being used within a stored procedure and in a JOIN statement.

Listing 7-21. *Using a UDF*

```
CREATE PROCEDURE dbo.uspFunctionJoin
AS
SELECT
fnStudentNames.Name, dbo.tblModule.ModName
FROM
dbo..tblModule INNER JOIN
dbo.fnStudentNames() fnStudentNames ON
dbo.tblModule.ModStudent = fnStudentNames.StudRef
```

In this case, you are simply treating the function as if it were a table, and you don't have to worry about entering the concatenation statements again. In addition, your new function can also accept parameters; for example, changing one line in Listing 7-21 enables you to pass values to the function. Enter the statement in Listing 7-22 into a new Query Designer window in Management Studio Express. Note the change of keyword to ALTER used to change a function or stored procedure definition. In this case, you are amending the definition of the function to include a new column and a parameter, studref.

Listing 7-22. *Adding a Parameter to a Function*

```
ALTER PROCEDURE dbo.uspFunctionJoin
(@studref int)
AS
SELECT
fnStudentNames.Name, dbo.tblModule.ModName,
dbo.tblModule.ModStudent, fnStudentNames.StudRef
FROM
dbo.tblModule INNER JOIN
dbo.fnStudentNames() fnStudentNames
ON dbo.tblModule.ModStudent = fnStudentNames.StudRef
WHERE
(fnStudentNames.StudRef = @studref)
```

If the function is executed with Access, you will be prompted for a parameter value. If the value is null (that is, you don't enter anything), zero records will be returned.

No discussion of UDFs would be complete without a look at scalar and table-valued functions. A *scalar function* is a function that takes a single value, carries out an operation, and returns a single value, for example, the Access Len and DateDiff functions. Listing 7-23 shows a short scalar function that concatenates StudForeName and StudSurName based on the StudentRef number passed in. Note this function was created directly in the Query Editor of SQL Server Express as opposed to Access.

Listing 7-23. *Scalar Function*

```
CREATE FUNCTION dbo. udf_GetStudent
(@StudentRef As int)
RETURNS nvarchar(40)
BEGIN
DECLARE @Name As nvarchar(40)
SELECT @Name =  StudForeName+ ' ' + StudSurName
FROM tblStudent
WHERE StudRef = @StudentRef
RETURN (@Name)
END
```

Following is the SELECT statement that calls the function, passing in a value of 2:

```
SELECT [Chapter7].[dbo].[udf_GetStudent] (2)
```

A *table-valued function*, on the other hand, returns a table of results instead of a single value. Inline functions are interesting animals, as they return a table that can then be used within a SELECT statement. Listing 7-24 shows the syntax for a standard UDF template created in the Access interface and is used as a building block for the function in Listing 7-25, which accepts a StudentRef number and returns a table of student data. The SELECT statement that follows passes the StudentRef number to the function.

Listing 7-24. *UDF Syntax*

```
CREATE FUNCTION "Function1"
 (
/*
@parameter1 datatype = default value,
@parameter2 datatype
*/
)
RETURNS TABLE
AS
RETURN ( /* sql select statement */ )
```

Listing 7-25. *Example User-Defined Function*

```
Create FUNCTION dbo.udf_GetStudent
(@StudentRef int)
RETURNS TABLE
AS
RETURN ( SELECT      StudentRef, StudentSurname, StudentForename
FROM          dbo.tblStudent
WHERE      (StudentRef = @StudentRef) )
```

Access permits you to create a user-defined function either graphically in the Query Designer or directly within the SQL pane of the query builder.

Using the function is as easy as this:

```
SELECT * FROM udf_GetStudent (2)
```

The ability to use functions as if they were tables is a major improvement over the standard Access query types.

Views

SQL Server views are very handy objects for the developer and work much like saved queries in Access. Views can serve a number of purposes in an ADP; for example, they hide complex SQL statements and restrict the columns a user can see, and they can also be indexed, thereby increasing performance. Views are also useful from a security standpoint: as with stored procedures, a user can be given access to a particular view only, thereby adding another level of security to your application without too much effort on your behalf. You can use a view within a linked application, or with an ADP as if it were a physical table. Of course, in an unbound application, you can also use the view as a virtual table.

Creating a view is straightforward, whatever the means you are using to do so. Within an ADP, you can create a view using the graphical query builder, which is a handy way to go and is another reason I advise building an ADP even if you are going with linked tables.

1. Click Create on the Ribbon.

2. Select Query Wizard.

3. Select Design View.

4. Click OK.

5. Within the Query Designer window, select the table or tables for the view. In my case, I am adding tblStudent and tblModule.

6. Select the required fields from the tables.

7. Close and save the view (I used the name vwStsudentModule).

To execute the resulting view, double-click the view name within the Query category of the Navigation Pane. Listing 7-26 shows the statement created within the view definition.

Listing 7-26. *View SQL*

```
CREATE VIEW [dbo].[vw_studentModule]
AS
SELECT
dbo.tblStudent.StudRef, dbo.tblStudent.StudForeName,
dbo.tblStudent.StudSurName, dbo.tblStudent.StudAdd1,
 dbo.tblStudent.StudAdd2, dbo.tblStudent.StudTown,
 dbo.tblModule.ModName
FROM
dbo.tblModule INNER JOIN
dbo.tblStudent ON dbo.tblModule.ModStudent
 = dbo.tblStudent.StudRef
```

Within an Access ADP, you can base a form on a view simply by clicking the view name in the Navigation Pane, and then clicking Create ➤ Form. Access will generate a form for you based on the view selected. If you want to actually use the view to add records, you must change one of the View properties. To do this, follow these steps:

1. Execute the view.

2. Change to Design view.

3. Right-click and select Properties.

4. Check Update Using View Rules.

5. Close the dialog box.

6. Close and save the changes to the view definition.

7. Create a new form based on the view.

It is also possible to create a view directly via ADO when working with an ADP. Listing 7-27 shows a short procedure used to create a simple view. Note the simplicity of this statement; as opposed to one containing command objects, procedures, and so forth, this just executes the appropriate SQL string. This will also work in a linked application or indeed anything using SQL Server.

Listing 7-27. *Creating a View Using ADO and ADPs*

```
Public Sub createadoview()
Dim strSQL As String
Dim conn As ADODB.Connection
Set conn = CurrentProject.Connection
  strSQL = "CREATE VIEW VwModules " & ➥
  "AS SELECT * FROM tblModule"
conn.Execute strSQL
conn.Close
End Sub
```

Figure 7-4 shows the resulting view created within Management Studio Express. It is worth noting that in Access all you will see are the SQL statements used to create the view. In Management Studio Express, the full syntax of the view is visible, and you also get a graphical builder similar to that in Access.

Figure 7-4. *New view within Management Studio Express*

The resulting view can be used anywhere you would normally place a table recordset, for example, a form's record source, a combo box, or indeed a list box. You can also run SQL statements directly against the view, again simplifying the SQL requirements of applications. In a linked application, you can link to a view much like you would to a normal table.

Views are a useful tool for read-only recordsets; for example, they provide a great way to populate reports with static recordsets, particularly if the SQL is complex. Using a view, Joins can be performed on the server and a simple WHERE clause executed on the Access side to prepare data for a report. In fact, this is a good technique to follow whenever you can: shift as much of the complex processing to the server as possible and filter the returning records from Access.

Note Some time ago I coauthored an article on using SELECT Top 100 percent to add an ORDER BY to a view. By its nature, a view cannot be created using ORDER BY. It is worth noting that this workaround is ignored by SQL Server 2005 Express. You do not get an error message from the Access 2007 ADP designers, but the ORDER BY is ignored. From a pure SQL viewpoint, it is better to leave the ORDER BY to the statements querying the view as opposed to the view creation statement.

SQL Server Express Security

In SQL Server Express, security is defined in terms of principles. A *principle* is anything that requires access to your database such as a Windows user, a Windows user group, or, if using Mixed Mode security, an SQL Server login. Generally, you will require access to the server itself and then permissions to work with a specific database or databases. In addition to login access, SQL Server Express contains a number of prebuilt server and database *roles*. By default, each user is a member of the built-in public role. Next in line, you have *securables*, items the database engine can control access to. Securables are objects like tables, stored procedures, functions, and views, and they exist within a schema, which exists within a database. The database itself resides upon an SQL Server instance, which resides upon a physical operating system. Phew! To make this a bit easier to comprehend, think of a table as a securable object, the user as a principle, and the database objects as the schema. Note that the database itself is not the schema, rather it is a container for the schema!

Database Roles

Just like SQL Server 2000, SQL Server Express has a number of built-in database roles to which users can be assigned. Table 7-3 outlines each of the built-in roles available to you.

Table 7-3. *SQL Server Express Database Roles*

Role Name	Comment
db_accessadmin	Permission to add and remove logins
db_backupoperator	Permission to perform a database backup
db_datareader	Permission to read data
db_datawriter	Permission to write data
db_ddladmin	Permission to run DDL commands
db_denydatareader	No permission to read data
db_denydatawriter	No permission to write data
db_owner	Permission on all objects within the database
db_securityadmin	Permission to administrate security on the database

To view the database roles from within Access 2007, create a pass-through query containing the following command:

```
exec sp_helpdbfixedrole
```

`sp_helpdbfixedrole` is a system stored procedure that will display the database roles available. In addition to the built-in role, the neat thing is you can create your own. The interface to create roles for those used to doing this via MSDE is superb. Creating your own database roles can be a useful tool that will help cut down on the administrative overheads in managing security for your server database. Once created, users can then be added to a role and immediately receive the same permissions as the role.

Server Roles

Server roles are specific to the server as a whole. Just like the built-in database roles, SQL Server Express comes with some server-wide roles already created for you. Table 7-4 shows the roles available.

Table 7-4. *SQL Server Express Server Roles*

Role Name	Comment
bulkadmin	Permission to run bulk `INSERT` statements
dbcreator	Permission to create, alter, restore, and drop a database
diskadmin	Permission to manage disk files
processadmin	Permission to kill processes running on the server
securityadmin	Permission to manage server security
serveradmin	Permission to change server properties and shut down the server
setupadmin	Permission to add and remove linked servers
sysadmin	Permission to perform any action on the server

Logins

Before you can do anything on the server, you need to decide which security model you will use: either Windows Authentication or SQL Server Mixed Mode. You can, of course, change this in the server properties. Windows security allows you to map a user's Windows account into SQL Server, but you cannot then use SQL Server's own built-in security system in Mixed Mode. Mixed Mode permits you to use either Windows Accounts or SQL Server's own security system. The interface and some of the details are slightly different using Management Studio Express than was the case in SQL Server 2000, but the basics remain the same. The login simply provides permissions for an individual or group to access the server. It is generally accepted that where possible Windows Authentication should be used, as it is more secure.

To create the login within Management Studio Express, follow these steps:

1. Expand the Security folder.

2. Right-click the Login folder and select New Login. This brings up the Login – New dialog box shown in Figure 7-5.

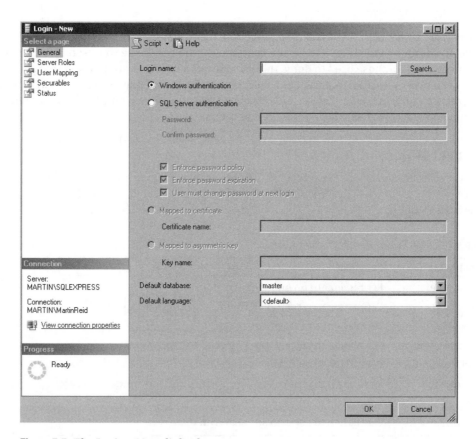

Figure 7-5. *The Login – New dialog box*

This dialog box presents several categories and options depending on which security model you are using.

Windows Authentication

If you are using Windows Authentication, follow these steps in the Login – New dialog box:

1. Click Search.

2. Click Advanced.

■**Note** The Advanced dialog box lets you search all users and groups to which you have access (for example, Active Directory).

---

3. Click Find Now.

4. Select the name of a user or group and click OK.

5. Specify a default database from the drop-down list on the Login – New dialog box. This is the database this user or group will be defaulted to on login.

6. If this user or group has to be assigned a server role, click the Server Roles category to view the built-in server roles (as discussed previously) and then check the appropriate role or roles.

7. Click OK to save the changes for the login.

■**Note** The User Mapping category allows you to assign the login to a particular database or databases and at the same time add the user or users to a database role.

SQL Server Authentication

Before using SQL Server authentication, you have to change the properties of the server if it's already been set up for Windows Authentication. To do this, right-click the server name, and select Properties ➤ Security ➤ SQL Server and Windows Authentication. The process to create the login and permissions is almost identical with the exception of the following steps:

1. Change the login to SQL Server authentication by clicking the appropriate radio button in the Login – New dialog box.

2. Enter a login name.

3. Enter a password (a strong password, please!).

4. Assign the user to a database or databases using User Mappings and assign that user to a database role using either a built-in role or a new role created for this purpose.

Once you complete the change of security method, check that your user has access to the required database by expanding the database folder, select and expand Users, and ensure you can see the new user listed. One thing that may not be visible is the way in which SQL Express has named the tables. In a linked application, the tables are prefixed dbo, while in an ADP application, the tables are suffixed dbo.

Working with Functions, Views, and Other Objects with Access 2007

Access provides you with a graphical interface to allow you to create stored procedures when using an ADP that is similar in nature to the standard query builder or da Vinci tool set. Access 2007 contains two new Ribbon icon shortcuts, Stored Procedures and Views. Figure 7-6 shows the Stored Procedure icon on the Create ribbon in an ADP.

Figure 7-6. *The Create Ribbon in an ADP*

Note the graphical options to create main server-side objects, stored procedures, functions, and views. This feature is very useful for helping you get to grips with the syntax of these objects.

Table 7-5 shows the options now available in the Query Wizard while working inside an ADP. In a linked application, you will simply see the standard Access Ribbon.

Table 7-5. *Query Wizard in ADPs*

Option	Purpose
Design In Line Function	Create a table-valued function.
Design View	Create an SQL Server view.
Design Stored Procedure	Graphically create an SQL Server procedure.
Create Text Stored Procedure	Create a stored procedure using a simple text editor.
Create Text Scalar Function	Create a scalar function using the text editor.
Create Text Table Valued Function	Create a table-valued function using the text editor.

As you can see, it's possible to graphically create a number of SQL Server objects directly via the GUI. Now let's turn our attention to a detailed look at how ADPs interact with SQL Server Express.

ADPs and SQL Server 2005 Express

Access Data Projects are an excellent technology for working with SQL Server 2000 and now SQL Server 2005. They appear to have fallen from grace with Microsoft because they are a pure SQL Server technology and don't fit neatly into the world of "access data anywhere." In my view, for those working with SQL Server, ADPs still offer one of the fastest ways to build a front-end application than almost anything else available. They are restricted in that they can only be used for SQL Server, and if you need to access data in other systems (for example, Oracle), you will need to build up a linked server from within SQL Server itself. In order to use ADPs, you must first understand some of the objects on the server side. In Chapter 6, we looked at some of the major objects in SQL Server of interest to developers. In this chapter, we will look again at some of those options and explore how you can use these features within your user interface.

So what exactly is an ADP? Simply put, it's an Access front end to a pure SQL Server data store. All data is held on SQL Server, and the Access front end contains only Access objects, forms, reports, and VBA. All data processing takes place on the server (when possible) via stored procedures, user-defined functions, and views. The ability to create an ADP has also been "hidden" in Access 2007 and is available by clicking the folder icon when entering a new database name. So it is not an obvious option in this release.

ADPs also provide a rapid development tool and teaching aid when working with a linked solution using SQL Server. Working with an ADP at the same time as building your linked table application permits you to take advantage of the graphical tools to create many SQL Server objects. The resulting code can then be pasted into SQL Server using Enterprise Manager or Query Analyzer.

So are there any problems with ADPs? Just like any technology, there are issues; with an ADP, you are working in the world of SQL Server, and many of the techniques you are familiar with will not be suitable. Queries will be a thing of the past as you move to stored procedures. DAO can still be used, but ADO may be more appropriate for server data manipulation. You will need to learn new skills when working with SQL Server (for example, you need an understanding of server-side security, SQL Server management, and creating views and other server objects), but personally, I believe none of the issues are an obstacle to Access developers.

Access 2007 provides a couple of ways to create ADPs: you can create a new ADP and an SQL Server database, or create the SQL Server database and then the ADP telling Access which server database you would like to use during the creation process. As mentioned previously, this process is slightly hidden in Access 2007.

The following example walks you through the process of creating an ADP:

1. Click the Office button.

2. Enter a file name for the new application.

3. Click the folder icon.

4. Select Microsoft Office Access Project in the Save As Type drop-down list.

5. Click OK.

6. Click Create. You will then be prompted to connect to an existing server database or create a new one.

7. Click No to create a new server database.

8. Select the server required.

9. Select the security method to be used.

10. Click Next.

11. Click Finish to create the server database and the ADP.

As this is a new database, you can use the ADP interface to work with server-side objects.

In this next example, you will create a new table within the ADP to illustrate the difference in table structure and features when working with SQL Server. To begin:

1. Click Create on the main Ribbon.

2. Click Table Design.

Note the differences in the Table Design window. Columns equate to fields in Access. Also note the multiple data types available to you now that your table is being created in SQL Server. One of the major differences you will find is when you click the table Properties sheet when in Table Design view (located on the Design tab). The properties of a table on the server will be markedly different from those of an Access table, as described in Table 7-6. There are several tabs available on the properties, each of which details a different element.

Table 7-6. *SQL Server Table Properties*

Tab	Property	Comment
Tables		This tab allows you to view properties of specific tables.
	Selected Table	Drop-down list used to select a table to view and work with its properties. Will default to the currently selected table.
	Owner	System owner of the table. This option will be grayed out.
	Table Identity Column	A column that equates in a way to an AutoNumber data type.
	Table ROWGUIDID	ID Used during replication.
	Table FileGroup	Table storage area.
	Text FileGroup	Storage area for text data types.
	Description	
Relationships		This tab allows you to view existing relationships and create new ones.
	Check existing data on creation.	
	Enforce relationships for replication.	
	Enforce relationship for inserts and updates.	

Tab	Property	Comment
Indexes/Keys		This tab lets you delete or add a new index to table
	Create Unique	Create a constraint or an index.
	Create as Clustered	Create a new clustered index.
Check Constraints		Use this tab to create new constraints for the table data.

Let's take a closer look at some of these options. You will have little choice in Access about the type of index you get. SQL Server, on the other hand, is different. Each table can have a single clustered index, meaning that the rows on the data pages are sorted in index order. A nonclustered index stores the keys and a pointer to the actual data. You can have multiple nonclustered indexes per table.

Constraints work much like Access table validation rules and follow the same format. They will return either true or false based on the data. You need to be careful when using constraints to check values, as they ignore nulls and will not cause an error. For example, the following CREATE TABLE SQL statement contains a check constraint to ensure the student number is between 1 and 9999.

```
CREATE TABLE tblStudent
(
StudentID Int PRIMARY KEY,
StudentForename varchar(25),
StudentSurname varchat (25),
StudentAddress1 varchat (35),
StudentNumber int
CONSTRAINT check_SID(StudentNumber Between 1 AND 9999) )
```

In Chapter 6, I briefly discussed the ability to control program flow within a stored procedure. Control of flow is very similar to controlling logic within VBA. For example, the following fragment shows the general CASE syntax to control behavior of code.

```
CASE expression

  WHEN value1 THEN result1

  WHEN value2 THEN result2

    (

  ELSE elseDifferentResult

  )

END
```

SQL Server Migration Assistant for Access

Still in beta at the time of writing, the SQL Server 2005 Migration Assistant for Access is designed to assist you in moving your Access database to SQL Server 2005 and creating a linked application as opposed to an ADP. It can be used with SQL Server Express and the full version of SQL Server 2005. As for Access, this tool currently doesn't support the new ACCDB file type, only the MDB file type, so you can use it only with Access 97 to Access 2003. Hopefully, a release for Access 2007 should be available once the product is embedded in the market. So why have I included this discussion here? In a lot of cases, many developers will still be working with MDB file types, which may require moving to SQL Server Express. That being the case, this free software will aid you in that process. In a few months, as the new Access 2007 file types see more usage, this software will again become invaluable when working with SQL Server 2005. The Migration Assistant will function in the same way as described here once the development team catches up with the Access file type ACCDB.

Table 7-7 outlines some of the issues you may face moving to SQL Server 2005. It's worth noting that many are similar to those you face moving to SQL Server 2000. In almost all cases, the Migration Assistant will warn you about the issue. In fact, via some of its options, it will help you to avoid some of the more common problems.

Table 7-7. *Access Issues That Can Affect Migration to SQL Server 2005*

Issue	Comment
Access tables do not have unique indexes.	Table cannot be changed once migrated.
Access tables use replication columns.	Replication will not function after migration.
Access tables include null unique indexes.	Migration for such tables will fail.
Date values are out of SQL Server range.	Migration will fail with an error report.
Index is over 900 characters.	Migration may fail.
SQL Server reserved words have been used.	Migration will be successful if the words are enclosed in quotes or brackets.
Foreign keys appear on different data types.	These keys will not be created on SQL Server.
Relationships have been created on tables without a primary key or unique index	These relationships will need to be re-created once the tables are repaired.
Hyperlinks are included.	There is no support for hyperlinks.
Access or VBA functions are included.	There is no support for these functions.

As you can see, many of the issues you will face are just like those you will see when moving to SQL Server 2000 as opposed to 2005. In almost all cases, proper preparation of the database is required before running the Migration Assistant for Access. Well, that's not strictly the case. Migration Assistant will load your Access database into its project workspace, check it for errors (for example, conflicting date formats), and provide a very comprehensive fix report. It's then a case of fixing the issues and reloading the files into the project.

When it comes to converting your SQL and queries, Migration Assistant will make a better job of it than the Upsizing Wizard and offer you a lot more control over the process. The focus of Migration Assistant is to create linked applications, and it will be of little use to those moving to ADPs. Perhaps this signifies the future of ADPs as a viable development technology? We will have to wait and see! At the moment, you will work with what's there and what's available;

currently ADPs still work with SQL Server 2005 and therefore can still be used. Table 7-7 can help you in sorting out some of the major problems before you begin. Following are the requirements for this tool:

- Windows XP SP 2 or Windows Server SP 1

- Microsoft Windows Installer 3.1 or later

- .NET Version 2 Framework, free download (Most users should have this from the SQL Server Express install.)

- J# 2 redistributable package, free download

Overview: Migrating an Access MDB File to SQL Server 2005

Unlike the built-in Upsizing Wizard, the Migration Assistant gives you the developer much more control over what's going on when migrating data to SQL Server 2005. The best way to see this is to walk through a migration. In this case, the Northwind database will be migrated to SQL Server Express. The database being moved is not important to this example; what I want to do is demonstrate the features of the software and how it can help you avoid migration issues. Of course, as discussed in Chapter 6, there is no substitute for advance planning no matter what tool you will use to carry out the migration.

Before moving the actual tables, let's take a quick look at the Migration Assistant interface. Figure 7-7 shows a blank interface to Migration Assistant. This tool is not limited to a single Access file; multiple files can be added to a single project and treated individually or en masse. In addition, it is also possible to scan a network share for any MDB files that may exist and "pull" them into Migration Assistant.

■**Caution** This section is based on the latest beta build of the SQL Server 2005 Migration Assistant available at the time of writing, which was an incomplete build in terms of query migration.

Following are the general steps for the migration process, with details on the various steps to come:

1. Create a new project file.

2. Add one or more Access databases.

3. Prepare your Access database for migration.

4. Connect to SQL Server.

5. If required, change the default schema for mapping.

6. Convert your Access objects to SQL Server Objects.

7. Move the objects into SQL Server using Migration Assistant.

8. Move your data to SQL Server.

9. Link the tables from SQL Server to your Access application.

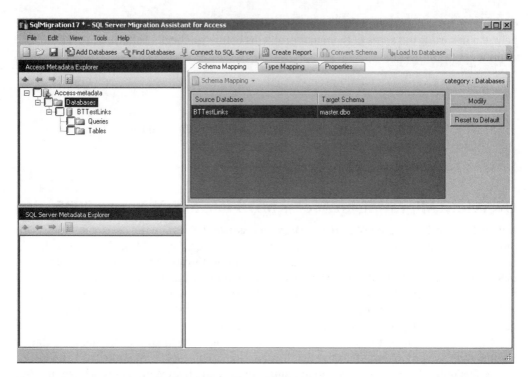

Figure 7-7. *SQL Server Migration Assistant for Access*

Creating a New Project File

The first step in the process is to create a new migration project. To do so, follow these steps:

1. From the main menu, select File ➤ New Project.

2. Enter a name for the project (for example, NorthWindMigrate).

3. Select a location to save the project files.

4. Click OK.

Note that a tree view is added into the project interface in which you can see the Access Meta Data node and a database folder. As your project is populated, objects from Access databases will be added to the folders, as you'll see in the next step.

Adding MDB Files

The next step in the process is to add some MDB files to your project. A really cool feature of Migration Assistant is its ability to actually scan your local disk or a network and discover all the Access files available to you. This will be a useful feature to help discover how many Access databases are in, for example, small work groups. We will come back to this feature shortly.

To add a database or databases to the project, follow these steps:

1. Click Add Files.

2. In the Open dialog box, navigate to the MDB file you would like to add to the project. (In my case, I selected Northwind.mdb.) Note that multiple database files can be added to the project at any given time.

3. Expand the project database folder.

4. Expand the Northwind database or the database you are working on; for this example, I have abbreviated the database name to Nwind.

The Tables and Queries folders within the Northwind database will now be available. In addition, you can also view indexes and keys for each table. Figure 7-8 shows the Northwind database with Tables expanded.

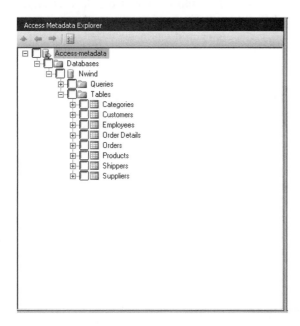

Figure 7-8. *Expanded Access metabase showing Northwind*

At this point, let's pause and look at some of the configuration settings available to you. Settings should be explored and set before you begin your migration project but can also be set/unset on a case-by-case basis. There are several settings you can apply to an individual project or globally to all projects created. Configuration options are available from the Tools menu, and we'll look at some of these in the next section. Global options allow you to define when and where the error reports are made. I have found it useful to run the error logging options within the interface. You can set up the log files to be used and make several minor error settings.

Preparing Your Database for Migration

This section describes some of the project settings you can make to prepare for migrating your database. You can also generate reports that provide you with comprehensive information on issues and problems that may need attention before migrating. Data type mapping can be changed, default date replacement values can also be added, but mostly tables usually migrate with little trouble. Also, it is wise to ensure each table has a primary key by adding one either automatically in Migration Assistant (by setting the appropriate option in the Project Settings dialog box) or manually in the MDB before migration.

Specifying Project Settings

Selecting Tools ➤ Project Settings opens the dialog box shown in Figure 7-9. The default settings are different depending on which mode the software is being operated in. Full mode is perhaps the best option, but Migration Assistant for Access will take control of the process. Of course, you can also change the setting within each of the three modes: Optimistic, Default, and Full. A fourth option, Custom, is also available that will allow you to fully configure the conversion options to your personal preferences. The project settings available fall into three areas: Global, Project, and Default.

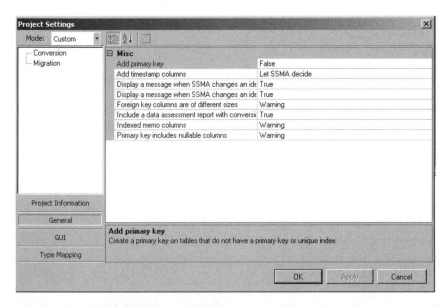

Figure 7-9. *Project setting options in Migration Assistant*

Let's take a closer look at the various areas of this dialog box.

Project Information

Settings in the Project Information area affect the individual project you are working on and basically indicate the name and location for the project.

Conversion

Options in the Conversion area will save an awful lot of time and help reduce errors in the conversion to SQL Server Express. The settings mostly involve the level of error messaging within the project, but one or two settings are very useful in terms of fixing problems:

Add primary key: If true, Migration Assistant for Access will add a primary key to any table identified as not having one from the Access side. The key, of course, is added to the SQL Server 2005 database once the migration is complete.

Add timestamp columns: Migration Assistant will add a timestamp column as required.

Foreign key columns are of different sizes: This allows you to set the level of error as Warning, No Message, or simply Error.

Indexed memo columns: Here you specify the type of message Migration Assistant issues when it finds an index on a memo column.

Migration

The Migration area contains the options that are going to save you a lot of trouble when moving to SQL Server. Again, the default settings change depending on the mode, and the following options are available:

Check constraints: Here you tell SQL Server whether you would like check constraints carried out when inserting data into the tables.

Fire triggers: This fires any associated insert triggers during data inserts.

Keep identity: This lets you specify whether identity values in the Access table should be preserved when moved to SQL Server.

Keep nulls: This option lets you retain null values, ignoring any defaults in the table being migrated.

Table locks: This option lets you retain a full *table* lock on the table or use row-level locking when migrating.

Date correction: One of the major problems you face when migrating is the different date range used by SQL Server. This option allows you to correct any Access dates earlier than the SQL Server date range of 01 January 1753. You can also edit the date field, adding your own default date, which will be used in the migration to replace any problem dates.

Type Mapping

Type Mapping is one of the most useful areas in the Project Settings dialog box. This deals with the way Access maps its data types to SQL Server data types. Table 7-8 shows the default mappings.

Table 7-8. *Access to SQL Server 2005 Data Type Mappings*

Access Data Type	SQL Server Data Type
Binary	varbinary
Boolean	bit
Byte	tinyint
Currency	money
Date/Time	datetime
Double	float
GUID	uniqueidentifier
Integer	int
Memo	nvarchar(max)
Memo (Access 97)	varchar(max)
Single	real
Text	nvarchar
Text (Access 97)	varchar

Each mapping can also be removed and edited; for example, Access text data types can have their length edited within the dialog box. Mappings can be set at either the project level or customized at the database level. This ability to use either defaults or custom mapping at the database level gives you a very flexible tool when moving tables to SQL Server 2005. To set mapping for the entire project, select Tools ➤ Project Settings ➤ Type Mapping.

At the database level, select a database and in the right pane click the Type Mapping tab. To add a new mapping, click Add, and to edit an existing type, click Edit. Individual types can also be double-clicked to open the Edit dialog box. I am sure most developers will agree that this is a huge improvement over the Upsizing Wizard in regards to the level of control you now have when moving to SQL Server 2005. Figure 7-10 shows the Type Mapping tab for the Northwind project created earlier.

Notice that there are two other tabs available to you, Schema and Properties. You need to be real careful with the schema tab, as this indicates where on SQL Server and to which database your project is to be moved. In order to edit this property, you must first connect to SQL Server.

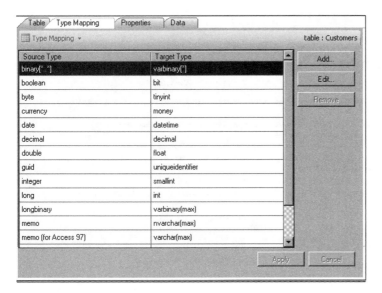

Figure 7-10. *Northwind type mapping tab*

Viewing Access Tables

With a database open, you can then view the structure of the table and its index. Simply click on a table, and the structure will be available in the right-hand pane of Migration Assistant. For each table, the following information is viewable:

- Columns

- Data type

- Validation rules

- Auto increment

- Defaults

- Nullable

- Zero length allowed

- Hyperlink

Right-clicking a table name allows you to run a quick report that will highlight any potential problems and also show suggested fixes. Figure 7-11 shows the report for the Northwind Categories table. The report produced is highly interactive and uses a tree view to allow you to expand and contract tables, indexes, and keys.

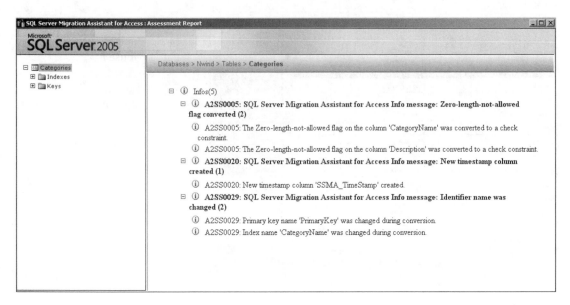

Figure 7-11. *Running a single table report*

The same report can be executed for all tables within the database by selecting the database name, right-clicking, and selecting Create Report. Such a report is shown in Figure 7-12.

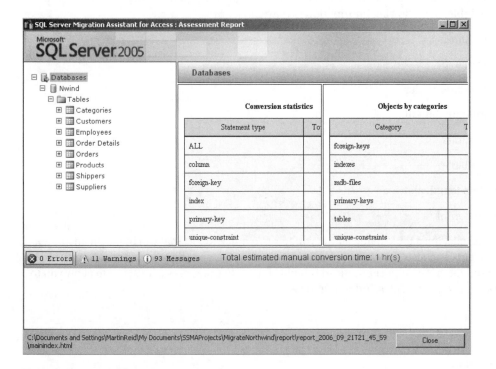

Figure 7-12. *Database report*

Clicking a table name and expanding the tree will reveal a summary report of issues with the selected table in the right-hand pane. This can assist greatly with fixing any issues prior to migration of the database. Just to remind you, all of these features are available for use *before* you actually convert a single table, giving you plenty of scope for fixes and improvements before converting the objects for use on SQL Server 2005. At the moment, you have simply loaded your Access metadata into a new project; you have not as yet done anything to physically move the schema to SQL Server.

Connecting to SQL Server Express

The next step in the migration process is to connect to SQL Server Express: on the main toolbar, click Connect to SQL Server, complete or accept the values in the Connection dialog box, and click OK.

Figure 7-13 shows the SQL Server Metadata Explorer with the Northwind Access database open and a connection to SQL Server Express available. Note that I have enabled the Migrate SQL Server database check box option, as this is the target database for the migration on SQL Server 2005.

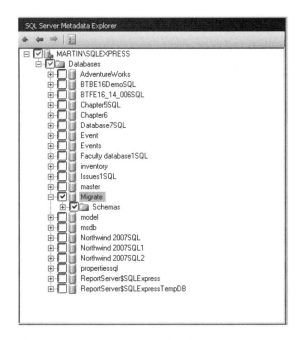

Figure 7-13. *SQL Server Metadata Explorer*

■**Note** For the migration project, it's worthwhile to create a database on SQL Server 2005 to which you will migrate. In my case, I created an empty database called Migrate, as you see in Figure 7-13. It is not possible to create a new database with Migration Assistant for Access.

Converting Your Access Objects to SQL Server Syntax

At this point, you can convert the Access objects to SQL Server. Note the objects are not being moved to SQL Server, rather they are being converted to the appropriate SQL Server syntax to ready them for the move. At this point, you can convert all tables or select individual tables, right-click, and select Convert Schema. All converted objects appear in bold in the interface.

In this case, also note that your tables are visible in the SQL Server Object Explorer but as yet do not physically exist there. Clicking the SQL table in the SQL Server Metadata Explorer while a table is selected on the server will show you the SQL script that will be used to create the table. Listing 7-28 shows the script for the Customers table (this is also another good example of a stored procedure). Note that all Access constraints on the table have been included within the SQL script. (These items are shown in bold.)

Listing 7-28. *Migration Assistant SQL Script*

```
IF  EXISTS (SELECT * FROM sys.objects WHERE object_id = ➥
OBJECT_ID(N'[dbo].[Orders]') AND type in (N'U'))
BEGIN

  DECLARE @drop_statement varchar(500)

  DECLARE drop_cursor CURSOR FOR
      SELECT 'alter table '+quotename(schema_name(ob.schema_id))+
      '.'+quotename(object_name(ob.object_id))+ ' drop constraint '➥
 + quotename(fk.name)
      FROM sys.objects ob INNER JOIN sys.foreign_keys fk ON ➥
fk.parent_object_id = ob.object_id
      WHERE fk.referenced_object_id = OBJECT_ID(N'[dbo].[Orders]')

  OPEN drop_cursor

  FETCH NEXT FROM drop_cursor
  INTO @drop_statement

  WHILE @@FETCH_STATUS = 0
  BEGIN
    EXEC (@drop_statement)

    FETCH NEXT FROM drop_cursor
    INTO @drop_statement
  END

  CLOSE drop_cursor
  DEALLOCATE drop_cursor
```

```
  DROP TABLE [dbo].[Orders]
END
GO


SET ANSI_NULLS ON
GO
SET QUOTED_IDENTIFIER ON
GO

CREATE TABLE
[dbo].[Orders]
(
   [OrderID] int IDENTITY(1, 1)  NOT NULL,
   [CustomerID] varchar(5)  NULL,
   [EmployeeID] int  NULL,
   [OrderDate] datetime  NULL,
   [RequiredDate] datetime  NULL,
   [ShippedDate] datetime  NULL,
   [ShipVia] int  NULL,
   [Freight] money DEFAULT 0  NULL,
   [ShipName] varchar(40)  NULL,
   [ShipAddress] varchar(60)  NULL,
   [ShipCity] varchar(15)  NULL,
   [ShipRegion] varchar(15)  NULL,
   [ShipPostalCode] varchar(10)  NULL,
   [ShipCountry] varchar(15)  NULL
)
GO

ALTER TABLE [dbo].[Orders]
 ADD CONSTRAINT [Orders$PrimaryKey]
 PRIMARY KEY
   NONCLUSTERED ([OrderID] ASC)
GO

ALTER TABLE [dbo].[Orders]
 ADD CONSTRAINT [SSMA_CC$Orders$CustomerID$disallow_zero_length]
 CHECK (len([CustomerID]) > 0)
GO

ALTER TABLE [dbo].[Orders]
 ADD CONSTRAINT [SSMA_CC$Orders$ShipName$disallow_zero_length]
 CHECK (len([ShipName]) > 0)
GO
```

```
ALTER TABLE [dbo].[Orders]
 ADD CONSTRAINT [SSMA_CC$Orders$ShipAddress$disallow_zero_length]
 CHECK (len([ShipAddress]) > 0)
GO


ALTER TABLE [dbo].[Orders]
 ADD CONSTRAINT [SSMA_CC$Orders$ShipCity$disallow_zero_length]
 CHECK (len([ShipCity]) > 0)
GO


ALTER TABLE [dbo].[Orders]
 ADD CONSTRAINT [SSMA_CC$Orders$ShipRegion$disallow_zero_length]
 CHECK (len([ShipRegion]) > 0)
GO


ALTER TABLE [dbo].[Orders]
 ADD CONSTRAINT [SSMA_CC$Orders$ShipPostalCode$disallow_zero_length]
 CHECK (len([ShipPostalCode]) > 0)
GO


ALTER TABLE [dbo].[Orders]
 ADD CONSTRAINT [SSMA_CC$Orders$ShipCountry$disallow_zero_length]
 CHECK (len([ShipCountry]) > 0)
GO



ALTER TABLE [dbo].[Orders]
 ADD CONSTRAINT [Orders$CustomersOrders]
 FOREIGN KEY
   ([CustomerID])
 REFERENCES
   [master].[dbo].[Customers]      ([CustomerID])
     ON DELETE NO ACTION
     ON UPDATE CASCADE
GO


ALTER TABLE [dbo].[Orders]
 ADD CONSTRAINT [Orders$EmployeesOrders]
 FOREIGN KEY
   ([EmployeeID])
 REFERENCES
   [master].[dbo].[Employees]      ([EmployeeID])
     ON DELETE NO ACTION
     ON UPDATE NO ACTION
GO
```

```
ALTER TABLE [dbo].[Orders]
 ADD CONSTRAINT [Orders$ShippersOrders]
 FOREIGN KEY
   ([ShipVia])
 REFERENCES
   [master].[dbo].[Shippers]  ([ShipperID])
     ON DELETE NO ACTION
     ON UPDATE NO ACTION
GO
```

Right-clicking in the SQL pane allows you to save the SQL as a script for later execution. You can also right-click over the Tables folder and create an SQL script of the entire database for execution later or as a backup in case something goes wrong.

Of course, when you move objects to SQL Server 2005, the syntax of SQL can change, and some of your standard Access functions will also need to be redone. For the impatient developer, there is also a one-click migration button that will cut out all the intermediate steps and simply migrate the database to SQL Server. Once the conversion has been completed, Migration Assistant will report back on what has happened. Again, this is a useful aid in tracing and fixing any potential problems that may occur. Figure 7-14 shows the Conversion – Error List dialog box. Double-click an error in the dialog box to open Migration Assistant's Table Design dialog box, where changes can be made directly within Migration Assistant.

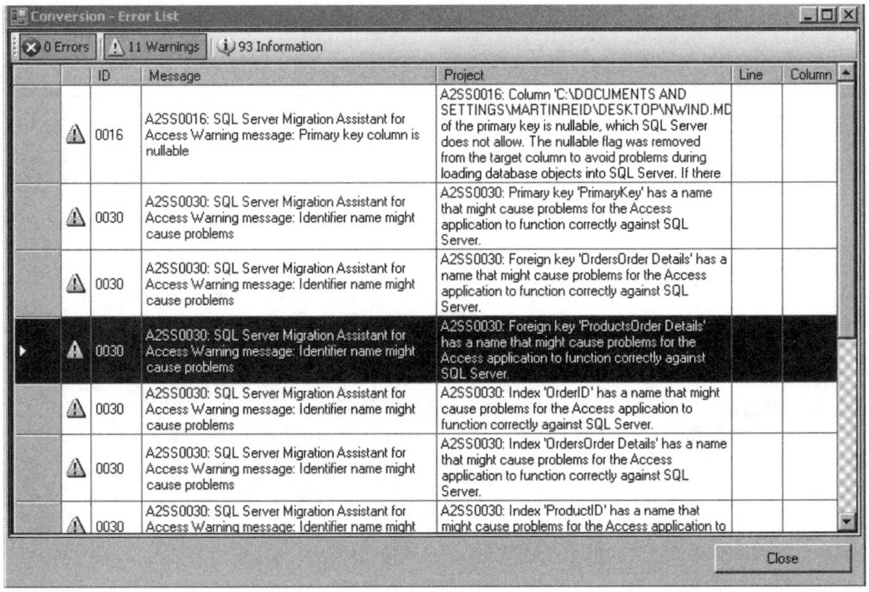

Figure 7-14. *Conversion Error report*

The next sections provide a comprehensive list of JET Versus SQL Server statements and their equivalent SQL Server 2005–suggested syntax. This is a very comprehensive list, and I feel it is of sufficient value to be included here.

Miscellaneous Statements

This section compares various forms of SQL SELECT statements generally used with Access and their SQL Server equivalents.

JET	SQL
Select Distinctrow <FieldsList> from Table	Select <FieldsList> From (Select distinct * From Table) Table
SELECT Suppliers.* INTO Suppliers IN 'Backup.mdb' FROM Suppliers;	SELECT Suppliers.* INTO BackupDB..Suppliers FROM Suppliers;
SELECT (Price * discount) as saving, (Price - saving) as NewPrice FROM Products	SELECT (Price * discount) as saving, (Price - Price * discount) as NewPrice FROM Products
SELECT Sum(discount = 0.8) FROM Products	SELECT Sum(Case discount when 0.8 then -1 Else 0) FROM Products
SELECT top 3 * FROM Products	SELECT top 3 With Ties * FROM Products
SELECT x.a.AAAA, x.b.AAAA FROM [SELECT a.AAAA, b.AAAA FROM table1 a Inner Join Table2 b On a.ID = b.ID]. AS x	SELECT x.Field1, x.Field2 FROM [SELECT a.AAAA as Field1, b.AAAA as Field2 FROM table1 a Inner Join Table2 b On a.ID = b.ID]. AS x

Update Statements

Following is a comparison of JET and SQL Server SQL UPDATE statements:

JET	SQL

Update AAA Inner Join BBB On AAA.ID = BBB.ID
    Set AAA.value = 'A', BBB.value = 'B'
    Where <SomeCondition>
	Update AAA
	        Set value = 'A'
	            From AAA Inner Join BBB On
	AAA.ID = BBB.ID
	            Where <SomeCondition>
	            Update BBB
	            Set value = 'B'
	            From AAA Inner Join BBB On
	AAA.ID = BBB.ID
	                Where <SomeCondition>

UPDATE Table2 RIGHT JOIN Table1
ON Table2.ID = Table1.ID
    SET Table2.AAAA = Day(Table1.AAAA),
Table2.ID = Table1.ID
        WHERE Table1.ID > 2;
	INSERT INTO Table2 (ID) -- List of
	Joined fields here
	        Select ID From Table1 -- List of
	Joined fields here
	            Where Not exists (Select 1 From
	Table2 where ID = Table1.ID)
	            UPDATE Table2
	            SET Table2.AAAA = Day(Table1.AAAA),
	Table2.ID = Table1.ID
	            From Table2 Inner Join Table1 ON
	Table2.ID = Table1.ID
	                WHERE Table1.ID > 2

Delete Statements

Following is a comparison of JET and SQL Server DELETE statements:

JET	SQL
Delete * From Table	Delete From Table
DELETE DISTINCTROW a.* FROM a some JOIN b ON ...	DELETE FROM a FROM a some JOIN b ON ...

Commonly Used Statements

Here is a comparison of other commonly used statements in JET and SQL Server:

JET	SQL
Select * from foo where c1 = 'a' & 'b'	Select * from foo where c1 = 'a' + 'b'
a \ b	Cast(Round(@a, 0) as int) / Cast(Round(@b, 0) as int)
a mod b	Cast(Round(@a, 0) as int) % Cast(Round(@b, 0) as int)
a ^ b	Power(@a, @b)
#03-22-2006#	'03-22-2006'

Functions

This section shows some common JET functions with their SQL Server T-SQL counterparts.

JET	SQL
ASC('A')	ASCII('A')
CHR[$](65)	CHAR(65)
LCASE[$]('ABCDEFG')	LOWER('ABCDEFG')
UCASE[$]('abcdefg')	UPPER('abcdefg')
LEFT[$]('String', Number)	LEFT('String', Number)
RIGHT[$]('String', Number)	RIGHT('String', Number)
LTRIM[$]('String')	LTRIM('String')
RTRIM[$]('String')	RTRIM('String')
FORMAT("12345.678", "#, ##0.00")	No equivalent
INSTR(String, subString)	CHARINDEX(String, substring)
INSTR(startposition, String, subString)	CHARINDEX(String, substring, startposition)
INSTR(startposition, String, subString, ComparisionType)	No equivalent
INSTR(String, subString, ComparisionType)	No equivalent
MID[$](String, StartPosition, numberOfChararcters)	SUBSTRING(String, StartPosition, numberOfChararcters)

Continued

JET	SQL
MID[$](String, StartPosition)	SUBSTRING(String, StartPosition, Len('String') - StartPosition + 1)
REPLACE(String, Find, Replacement)	REPLACE (String, Find, Replacement)
REPLACE(String, Find, Replacement, Start)	SubString(String, 1, start - 1) + Replace(SubString(String, Start, Len(String) - start + 1), Find, Replacement)
REPLACE(String, Find, Replacement, Start, Count)	No equivalent (emulated as UDF Replace5)
REPLACE(String, Find, Replacement, Start, Count, ComparisionType)	No equivalent
STRCONV(Text, ConversionType[, LCID])	No equivalent
ISDATE(expression)	ISDATE(expression) = 1
ISNULL(expression)	Expression is null
ISNUMERIC(expression)	IS NUMERIC(expression) = 1
NZ(expression1, expression2)	ISNULL(expression1, expression2)
IIF(condition, statement_if_true, statement_if_false)	CASE WHEN condition THEN statement_if_true ELSE statement_if_false END
SWITCH(condition1, statement1 … [,conditionN, statementN])	CASE WHEN condition1 THEN statement1 ... [WHEN conditionN THEN statementN] ELSE null END
Choose(position, value1, value2, ... value_n)	No equivalent
CURRENTUSER()	CURRENT_USER()

Domain Functions

Following is a comparison of JET and TSQL domain functions:

JET	SQL
DAvg()	Avg()
DCount()	Count()
DFirst()	No equivalent
DLast()	No equivalent
DLookup()	Skipped (use only expression in SELECT clause)
DMin()	Min()
DMax()	Max()
DSum()	Sum()

Mathematical Functions

Here is a comparison of JET and T-SQL mathematical functions:

JET	SQL
ABS(ABC)	ABS(@ABC)
ATN(ABC)	ATAN(@ABC)
COS(ABC)	COS(@ABC)
EXP(ABC)	EXP(@ABC)
FIX(123.456)	CAST(123.456 as integer)
INT(123.456)	FLOOR(123.456)
LOG(ABC)	LOG(@ABC)
RND	RAND()
ROUND(ABC, 2)	ROUND(@ABC, 2)
VAL (" 34 10 Main Street ")	No equivalent

Date Functions

The following compares the date functions used by Access against those used by SQL Server:

Access Definition	Explanation	SQL Server Possible Equivalents
yyyy	Year	year, yyyy, yy
q	Quarter	quarter, q, qq
m	Month	month, mm, mm
y	Day of the year	dayofyear, dy, y
d	Day	day, dd, D
w	Weekday	weekday, dw
ww	Week	week, wk, ww
h	Hour	hour, hh
n	Minute	minute, mi, n
s	Second	second, ss, s

Date/Time Functions

Following is a comparison of JET and T-SQL date/time functions:

JET	SQL
DATEADD('interval', Number, date)	DATEADD(interval, Number, date)
DATEDIFF('interval', date1, date2)	DATEDIFF(interval, date1, date2)
DATEPART('interval', date)	DATEPART(interval, date)
DAY(date)	DAY(date)
MONTH(date)	MONTH(date)
YEAR(date)	YEAR(date)
NOW()	GETDATE()
DateSerial(2005, 11, 22)	CAST('2005'+'11'+'22' as DateTime)
HOUR(NOW())	DATEPART(hour, GETDATE())
MINUTE(NOW())	DATEPART(minute, GETDATE())
MONTHNAME(NOW())	DATENAME(month, GETDATE())
SECOND (NOW())	DATEPART(second, GETDATE())
DATE()	CONVERT(datetime,CONVERT(varchar,GETDATE(),1))
DATEVALUE("Jun 30")	No equivalent
TIME()	No equivalent
TIMESERIAL(hoursexpression, minuteexpression, secondexpression)	No equivalent
TIMEVALUE("3:12:54 PM")	No equivalent
WEEKDAY(NOW())	DATEPART(weekday, GETDATE())
WEEKDAY(NOW(), firstdayofweek)	No equivalent

Data Type Conversion

Following is a comparison of JET and SQL Server data type conversions:

JET	SQL
CByte(expression)	CAST (ROUND(expression) as tinyint)
CCur(expression)	CAST (expression as money)
CDate(expression)	CAST (expression as datetime)
CDbl(expression)	CAST (expression asfloat)
CDec(expression)	CAST (expression as decimal())
CInt(expression)	CAST (ROUND(expression) as smallint)
CLng(expression)	CAST (ROUND(expression) as integer)
CSng(expression)	CAST (expression as real)
CStr(expression)	CAST (expression as varchar)
CVar(expression)	CAST (expression as sql_variant)
CVDate(expression)	CAST (CAST (expression as datetime) as sql_variant)

Aggregate Functions

The following table compares JET and SQL Server aggregate functions:

JET	SQL
AVG(expression)	AVG(expression)
COUNT(expression)	COUNT(expression)
MIN(expression)	MIN(expression)
MAX(expression)	MAX(expression)
SUM(expression)	SUM(expression)
SELECT FIRST(expression), Min(Field1) from SomeTable	SELECT (SELECT Top 1 expression From SomeTable) as first, Min(Field1) From SomeTable
SELECT LAST(expression), Max(Field1) From SomeTable	SELECT (SELECT Top 1 expression From SomeTable Order by IdentityField Desc) as first, Min(Field1) From SomeTa.ble

Moving Objects into SQL Server Using Migration Assistant for Access

Once you are happy with the schema changes, you can then move the tables into SQL Server. At this point, you again have total control over what is moved. You can move the entire database or take it in table by table. You can exclude an index by unchecking the check box next to it in the Indexes folder and do the same with primary keys. Unchecked items are excluded from the process. Moving the structure of your database to SQL Server is as simple a clicking the Load to Database button on the main menu. It is also possible to link the tables to the Access application by right-clicking a table name and choosing Link Table. The process can be reversed by selecting Unlink Table. As of this writing, query migration is not yet complete in Migration Assistant, and information for this section of the book can be downloaded as an additional free chapter from http://www.apress.com once this feature is available.

Wrapping Up Migration

As you can see, using Migration Assistant is a slightly more sophisticated process than using the Upsizing Wizard, and it could reduce the market for some third-party tools already mentioned in this book. Personally, I feel the more tools available for migration, the better, and all continue to have a role to play in the process. The more you plan and build for possible migration, the better the end result will be. Just remember, the last step in the process, whatever migration tools you use, should be the actual moving of tables and data to SQL Server. The less redesign you have to do to get your back-end applications into SQL Server, the better. Therefore, the same old rule applies irrespective of new tools on the market: plan and design the database professionally from the start.

Summary

SQL Server Express offers Access developers a way to improve the speed and performance of their applications. Although it is free, it does have its limitations—you can't have everything. However, it provides a fine back-end database engine for work group databases, integration with Windows Security when required, and many server-side objects for use in your applications. Microsoft is touting this as a database for hobbyists; in my opinion, this is wide of the mark, and this tool should be in the day-to-day workbox of almost all Access developers.

Later in the book, you will see how you can take the back end for an Access application and create a basic .NET web-based application, making use of the same back-end objects as your Access front end does.

■**Note** If this chapter has interested you in learning more about SQL Server 2005 Express, I recommend you pick up a copy of *Beginning SQL Server 2005 Express Database Applications with Visual Basic Express and Visual Web Developer Express: From Novice to Professional* by Rick Dobson (Apress, 2005).

CHAPTER 8

■■■

DAO, Complex Data Types, and Macros

This chapter, devoted to the power user, provides a solid introduction to working with Microsoft Access 2007 via DAO. It also covers the new features introduced in Access 2007. Why power users? In my view, most professional developers reading this book will be well up to speed with DAO, and there is little that I can teach them here. In addition, many published titles, including the *Access Developers Handbook* series (Sybex), cover DAO in a much more detailed fashion than I can in one chapter. For the professional developer, Chapter 13, which presents code you can steal, should more than make up for anything that may be missing here!

Power users, on the other hand, are different. Many power users do not use code in Access, at least those I have contact with, and this chapter is aimed mostly at that market. The chapter starts off with demonstrating DAO and the various commands available to you, followed by a look at opening tables and queries in code, adding new records, editing records, and of course deleting records, all using DAO and Access 2007. Even if you are a professional developer, you'll find the information and examples on the new features of DOA and Access toward the end of the chapter useful. When you are developing applications with Access, DAO is the way to go in terms of programming, particularly if the application you are developing is a pure Access database solution. DAO still provides you with the best tool set and ease of use of virtually any language when you are developing MDB files, and that still holds true for ACCDB files in Access 2007. Access 2007's default library is DAO 3.6.

Also included here is a discussion on macros. You might be wondering why this appears in a chapter on DAO; I decided to include the macro coverage here for two reasons: macros have received substantial focus in Access 2007, including some changes that allow you to use them from DAO, and (being honest) there is not enough material on this topic for developers to fill a complete chapter.

■**Note** At the time of writing, it has been announced that the Developer Extensions for Access 2007 will be available free of charge. This includes the runtime and the tools required to create template databases. The files can be downloaded from `http://www.microsoft.com` where you will be able to search for the downloads once the software is released.

Getting Started with DAO

The examples in this chapter will use unbound Access forms to illustrate many of the features of DAO. *Unbound forms* are forms populated via code rather than by being assigned a record-set directly from a table or stored query. In this way, we can look at several techniques used to manipulate databases and their records via code. Given the nature of this chapter, I am likely to repeat some of the code you have already seen, and for that I apologize in advance. For the example code, you will be working with a copy of the Northwind example file available with Access 2007, and this will be used to demonstrate many of the features of DAO. To follow the examples, simply make a copy of Northwind and save it as NorthwindCopy. To get started, the first example will simply populate a form with some data from the Customers table in Northwind. First of all, let's have a look at the DAO Object Model.

DAO Object Model

Right at the top of the tree in Access is the DBEngine object, which serves as the interface to the actual ACE engine itself. Next up, we have the Workspaces objects, which contain two collections, Users and Groups. Both of these are used occasionally; for example, Workspaces would be used mainly when you are working in multiuser systems. However, the next object, the Database object, you will meet every day and in every application you are writing DAO for. The Database object contains the following collections:

- Containers
- QueryDefs
- Recordsets
- Relations
- TableDefs

Of the preceding collections, again, in terms of programming and DAO, you will tend to spend most of your time manipulating the recordset to get data to and from your application. However, an appreciation of QueryDefs and TableDefs will also prove useful. So let's take a closer at these three most popular and necessary collections and how you can use them in your access database, starting with TableDefs.

TableDefs

One table definition exists for every table within the database including system tables. Listing 8-1 loops through the TableDefs in Northwind, printing each table name to the Intermediate window, including the Access system tables.

Listing 8-1. *Using TableDefs*

```
Public Sub ex1()
On Error GoTo Err_ex1
Dim db As DAO.Database
Dim tdf As DAO.TableDef
```

```
Set db = CurrentDb

For Each tdf In db.TableDefs
Debug.Print tdf.Name
Next tdf
End

Exit_ex1:
On Error Resume Next
    If Not (db Is Nothing) Then db.Close: Set db = Nothing
Exit Sub
Err_ex1:
        MsgBox Err.Description, , "Error in Sub Module1.ex1"
        Resume Exit_ex1
    Resume 0    '.FOR TROUBLESHOOTING
End Sub
```

Changing the `Debug.Print` line to the following example will show additional information about the table. In this case, you can see whether the table is updatable, the date the table was created, and the `RecordCount` (that is, the number of records in the table).

```
Debug.Print tdf.Name & " " & tdf.Updatable & " " & tdf.DateCreated & ➥
" " & tdf.RecordCount
```

In a standard linked application, you can also use `TableDefs` to output the current back-end paths of your application. It can be quite difficult to read the paths using the linked table manager, and one solution is to create your own form providing this information. The next example creates an Access `Form Load()` procedure, which will show the paths to any linked tables in the database. Listing 8-2 shows the code required. In this case, you amend the earlier procedure and pass the values to a string. The string is displayed using a basic text box located on a form. In this code, you use additional properties of the `TableDef` object, `Connect` and `SourceTableName`.

Listing 8-2. *Listing Linked Tables*

```
Private Sub Form_Load()
On Error GoTo Err_Form_Load

Dim strConnect As String
Dim db As DAO.Database
Dim tdf As DAO.TableDef


On Error Resume Next

Set db = CurrentDb

DoCmd.Hourglass True
```

```
For Each tdf In db.TableDefs
        If Len(tdf.Connect) > 0 Then
            strConnect = tdf.Name & "   " & tdf.Connect & "   " & ➡
tdf.SourceTableName & vbCrLf
        End If

Next

DoCmd.Hourglass False

' Display the linked paths in the text box.
Me.lstLink = strConnect

Set db = Nothing

Exit Sub
Exit_Form_Load:
On Error Resume Next
    If Not (db Is Nothing) Then db.Close: Set db = Nothing
Exit Sub
Err_Form_Load:
        MsgBox Err.Description, , "Error in Sub Form_frmLinkedTables.Form_Load"
        Resume Exit_Form_Load
    Resume 0    '.FOR TROUBLESHOOTING
End Sub
```

To run the example, create a new blank Access form containing a single text box. Add the code in Listing 8-2 to the form's On Load event. Open the form to preview the information. You may find you have to extend the size of the text box in order to display the full path to your linked tables.

■**Note** This technique will also display other linked objects—for example, Excel 2007 spreadsheets.

You could also use TableDefs to actually create a table within the database. Listing 8-3, written by John Colby of Colby Consulting, does just that using a function.

Listing 8-3. *Creating a Table*

```
Function tblBld(strTblName As String, ParamArray strFields()) As Boolean
On Error GoTo Err_tblBld
Dim db As Database
Dim tdf As TableDef
Dim intI As Integer

    Set db = CurrentDb
```

```
    ' IF THE TABLE ALREADY EXISTS, JUST OPEN THE TABLE
    If ccObjectExists("Tables", strTblName) Then
        Set tdf = db.TableDefs(strTblName)
    Else    ' ELSE Create a new TableDef object.
        Set tdf = db.CreateTableDef(strTblName)
    End If
    With tdf
        ' Create fields and append them to the new TableDef object. This must
        ' be done before appending the TableDef object to the TableDefs collection
        ' of the db.
        For intI = 0 To UBound(strFields())
            .Fields.Append .CreateField(strFields(intI), dbText)
        Next intI

        ' IF THE TABLE ALREADY EXISTS, JUST ERROR AND CONTINUE
        db.TableDefs.Append tdf
    End With
    db.TableDefs.Refresh
    tblBld = True
Exit_tblBld:
On Error Resume Next
    Set tdf = Nothing
    Set db = Nothing
Exit Function
Err_tblBld:
    Select Case Err
    Case 0      '.insert Errors you wish to ignore here
        Resume Next
    Case 3191   ' THE FIELD ALREADY EXISTS
        Resume Next
    Case 3367   ' THE TABLE ALREADY EXISTS
        Resume Next
    Case Else   '.All other errors will trap
        Beep
        MsgBox Err.Description, , "Error in Function C2DbTableBuilder.tblBld"
        Resume Exit_tblBld
    End Select
    Resume 0    '.FOR TROUBLESHOOTING
End Function
```

You call the function in Listing 8-3 as follows:

```
 tblBld "tblMyTableName", "Field", "Field", "Field", "LineCnt", "Field"
```

Recordsets

You will use the recordsets collection almost every day when working with VBA and Access 2007. Basically, a recordset is a set of records. Simply open an Access table in datasheet view, and you are looking at a recordset. To get you started with recordsets, execute the code shown in Listing 8-4, which will simply print the Company record from the Northwind Customers table to the Intermediate window.

Listing 8-4. *Printing Out the Company Name*

```
Public Sub ListCompany()
On Error GoTo Err_ListCompany
Dim rstCoName As DAO.Recordset
Dim strSQL As String
Dim db As Database

Set db = CurrentDb
strSQL = "SELECT Company from Customers"

Set rstCoName = db.OpenRecordset("strSQL")

Do While Not rstCoName.EOF
Debug.Print Company
rstCoName.MoveNext
Loop
rstCoName.Close


Exit_ListCompany:
On Error Resume Next
    If Not (rstCoName Is Nothing) Then rstCoName.Close: Set rstCoName = Nothing
    If Not (db Is Nothing) Then db.Close: Set db = Nothing
Exit Sub
Err_ListCompany:
        MsgBox Err.Description, , "Error in Sub Form_frmLinkedTables.ListCompany"
        Resume Exit_ListCompany
    Resume 0     '.FOR TROUBLESHOOTING
End Sub
```

Let's take Listing 8-4 apart and look at each section. First, you set rstCoName as the DAO recordset. Note that you use the DAO object library reference. You could have omitted it, but using the DAO reference explicitly tells you which library you are using for the recordset. Next, you set strSQL to the SQL statement that you use to populate the recordset, and then set rstCoName as the open recordset. After this, you use a While loop to move through the record-set. The loop continues until you have reached the end of file (EOF). During the loop, the value of EOF is set internally to the value of true. The loop ends when you have reached the end of the records. When this happens, the value of EOF internally changes from true to false.

The most important statement in the listing is OpenRecordset. In this example, you pass in an SQL string to OpenRecordset. However, you could just as easily have used the actual table name (for example, db.OpenRecordset("Customers")), and the end result of the code would have been the same. Using an SQL string can be useful. When you use the table name, all the records are returned; but if you only need a subset of fields, you can use another SQL string method, such as a prebuilt query. The full syntax of the `OpenRecordset` method is

```
OpenRecordset,Name,Type,Options,LockEdit)As Recordset
```

You have already seen the name passed to a recordset can be a table, a saved query, or an SQL string. The following section explains the remainder of the options using recordsets.

Types of Recordset

Of course, different types of recordset are available to you depending on what you want to do with the resulting data:

Table: Returns a table of editable records. This can only be used with a table name, and the table must be local. Example: `db.OpenRecordset("tableName")`.

Dynaset: Represents a set of pointers to a table or tables. The returned recordset may not be editable. Example: `db.OpenRecordset("name",dbOpenDynaset)`.

SnapShot: Serves as a copy of the data created at the time the statement is executed. Recordsets of this type cannot be updated. Example: `db.Openrecordset("Name",dbOpenSnapShot)`.

In addition to the different recordset types you can use, several options are also available to you when working with recordsets. Table 8-1 shows some of the options available.

Table 8-1. *Recordset Options*

Options	Comment
dbAppendOnly	Allows new records only to be appended to dynasets.
dbSQLPassThrough	Executes the SQL on another database engine (for example, SQL Server 2005).
dbSeeChanges	Ensures that any records added to the recordset are available to you. You will find that you must use this when working with DAO and SQL Server recordsets that contain an Identity column.
dbDenyWrite	Prohibits anyone else from changing records while you have them open.
dbDenyRead	Prohibits other users from viewing the data while you have the recordset open.
dbForwardOnly	Limits users to only moving forward within the recordset.
dbReadOnly	Defines the recordset as read-only. However, other users of the application can edit the records.
dbInconsistent	Records can be changed even if they break relationship rules.
dbConsistent	Records can be changed only if they don't break relationship rules.
LockEdits	Used when you may have multiple users in the application and offers the following: dbReadOnly: Records can be viewed by you, but other users can change them. dbPessimistic: A data page will be locked as soon as editing begins and remains locked until the editing is finished. This is known as *pessimistic locking*. dbOptimistic: The data page is locked only when you update the changes. This is known as optimistic locking.

Moving in a Recordset

As you are starting to see, there is a great deal of flexibility available to you when working with DAO and recordsets, and we have only looked at the recordset object. Once you have a recordset open, you will, of course, need to move through it. DAO enables you to do this with MoveNext, MovePrevious, MoveFirst, and MoveLast. Each of the statements will do exactly as you might guess based on the name. The next example puts this all together and creates a form with a fully editable recordset, command buttons to permit you to move around in the recordset, and some functions to deal with other issues. The form will display the values from the Customers table. When the form opens, the data will be locked. Users will be able to navigate the recordset but unable to add, edit, or delete records until they click the appropriate command button. This is achieved by simply looping over all the form objects and setting the enabled property to false and the locked property to true. So let's get started and create a new Access form to demonstrate working with the recordset and its methods. To begin, create a new blank Access form.

Create the text boxes shown in Table 8-2, if you would like to run the example code in this section; otherwise, remember to change the form object references to those you will be using. You will not be using all of the Customers table fields, but enough so that you get the general idea of creating the procedure and an overview of how this works. Once you have created the form, save it as frmCompany.

Table 8-2. *Unbound Customer Form Objects*

Object Type	Object Name
Text box	txtCompanyName
Text box	txtFirstName
Text box	txtLastName
Text box	txtJobTitle
Text box	txtBusinessPhone
Command button	cmdEdit
Command button	cmdDelete
Command button	cmdAdd
Command button	cmdSave
Command button	cmdNext
Command button	cmdPrevious
Command button	cmdLast
Command button	cmdFirst

Listing 8-5 shows the initial code required to populate the text boxes on the form. The code is created within the form's On Open event. Note the position of the Dimension statement for the recordset. Because you may reuse this recordset, you can dimension the recordset outside the procedure to enable its reuse in other procedures and functions within the form's module. At the end of the module, remember to close the recordset and set it to nothing (for example, rst.Company.close, set rstCompany = nothing).

Listing 8-5. *Initial Form Open Code*

```
Option Compare Database
Dim db As Database
Dim rstCompany As DAO.Recordset

Private Sub Form_Open(Cancel As Integer)
Set db = CurrentDb
Set rstCompany = db.OpenRecordset("SELECT Company,[First Name],[Last Name],➥
[Job Title],[Business Phone] FROM Customers")

getCustomers
Call Lockform

End Sub
```

Note that you have two calls within the form's open event: getCustomers and Lockform. getCustomers is shown in Listing 8-6, and it simply supplies the initial records for the form. Lockform, shown in Listing 8-7, loops over all of the form controls, locking them and setting the enabled property to false.

■**Note** If your field names contain spaces, you must surround them with square brackets. However, standard practice is not to have spaces in field names. The only reason spaces are used here is because if you are trying this example out, this is how the field names appear in the Northwind demo database.

Listing 8-6. *getCustomers*

```
Public Sub getCustomers()
On Error GoTo Err_getCustomers
With rstCompany
txtCompanyName = !Company
txtFirstName = ![First Name]
txtLastName = ![Last Name]
txtBusinessPhone = ![Business Phone]
txtJobTitle = ![Job Title]
End With

Exit_getCustomers:
Exit Sub
Err_getCustomers:
        MsgBox Err.Description, , "Error in Sub Form_frmCompany.getCustomers"
        Resume Exit_getCustomers
    Resume 0    '.FOR TROUBLESHOOTING
End Sub
```

Listing 8-7. *Lockform*

```
Public Sub Lockform()
On Error GoTo Err_Lockform
' Lock Controls
Dim ctl As Control

    For Each ctl In Me.Controls
        If ctl.Tag = "Lock" Then
            ctl.Enabled = False
            ctl.Locked = True
        End If
    Next

Exit_Lockform:
Exit Sub
Err_Lockform:
        MsgBox Err.Description, , "Error in Sub Form_frmCompany.Lockform"
        Resume Exit_lockform
    Resume 0    '.FOR TROUBLESHOOTING
End Sub
```

Listing 8-7 contains an added feature. The test "Lock" has been added to each form control tag that should be locked. The procedure then simply loops over each form control and locks a control when it reads this value in the control's tag property. When the form opens, the values that are displayed by the user cannot interact with any of the controls shown. As you have already seen in other examples in this book, this will display a single record on the form. For example, if you click the Move Next button, nothing happens. You need to add in the code to make the record move. Listing 8-8 shows the MoveNext code. If you do not have any records (that is, BOF and EOF are true), you exit the procedure. If you do have records, you move to the next record.

Listing 8-8. *MoveNext*

```
Private Sub cmdNext_Click()
' Call CheckForSave

    If rstCompany.BOF = True And rstCompany.EOF = True Then Exit Sub

    If rstCompany.EOF = False Then rstCompany.MoveNext
    If rstCompany.EOF = True Then rstCompany.MoveLast

    Call getCustomers

End Sub
```

The code required to move back within the recordset is shown in Listing 8-9 and is very similar to the code used for MoveNext. On this occasion, you are using MovePrevious to return to the previous record in the customer recordset.

Listing 8-9. *MovePrevious*

```
Private Sub cmdPrevious_Click()
On Error GoTo Err_cmdPrevious_Click
 If rstCompany.BOF = True And rstCompany.EOF = True Then Exit Sub

    If rstCompany.BOF = False Then rstCompany.MovePrevious
    If rstCompany.BOF = True Then rstCompany.MoveFirst

    Call getCustomers

Exit_cmdPrevious_Click:
Exit Sub
Err_cmdPrevious_Click:
        MsgBox Err.Description, , "Error in Sub Form_frmCompany.cmdPrevious_Click"
        Resume Exit_cmdPrevious_Click
    Resume 0     '.FOR TROUBLESHOOTING
End Sub
```

So let's just pause here for a recap. At the moment, you have an Access form that is provided with data by a recordset created using VBA, as opposed to simply binding the form directly to the Customers table, which I agree would have been real easy to do. You have two functioning buttons that move the user one record at a time through the recordset, again using some simple VBA code. I am sure you may already be beginning to see the amount of work required from you in coding this approach.

Basic Record Editing

Now let's move on and add some code to the Edit button so you can actually see how much more work is required to manage a recordset and its interaction with a form and a form's objects. Listing 8-10 shows the code to be added to the On Click event of cmdEdit. Initially, all you are doing is unlocking the controls previously locked. As you can see, the code is much the same as that used to perform the lock. This time, however, you simply unlock the controls again based on their tag. But as you will see, this actually isn't sufficient when dealing with an unbound recordset.

Listing 8-10. *cmdEdit On Click Event*

```
Private Sub cmdEdit_Click()
On Error GoTo Err_cmdEdit_Click
UnlockForm
Exit_cmdEdit_Click:
Exit Sub
Err_cmdEdit_Click:
        MsgBox Err.Description, , "Error in Sub Form_frmCompany.cmdEdit_Click"
        Resume Exit_cmdEdit_Click
    Resume 0     '.FOR TROUBLESHOOTING
End Sub
```

Once you have added the preceding code to cmdEdit's On Click event, return to the form and click the Edit button. The text boxes are now available for edit, but the rest of the form's buttons (those that you have coded thus far, Next and Previous) are also available. What you really want to do is lock users into the record they are going to edit until they are either ready to save the edits or cancel the edit. That being the case, in addition to opening the text boxes for edit, you should also disable the navigation buttons when editing a record—bearing in mind that once the edit has been saved or cancelled, you will need to relock the form and enable the command buttons again. You can take care of this by writing a couple of functions to turn the buttons off and on at will.

Editing a Record in the Real World

DAO also provides you with a method to edit existing records. Again, for this example, you will be using an unbound form. When you use a bound form, Access deals with the edit under the covers, and you don't need to worry about it. However, when going the unbound route, the edit is completely in your control. Listing 8-11 shows the basic syntax used to edit a single record in a table. The recordset is populated using an SQL SELECT statement that restricts the recordset to a single record based on its primary key value. Once the recordset is available, you use the Edit method to actually carry out the record edit required. Visually on the form you change the caption of the Edit command button to Save. This syntax is simply meant to show the process, not serve as an example of working code. It is worth stating that there are occasions when you will not be able to update a record (for example, if you are using a crosstab or Union query to populate the form).

Listing 8-11. *Editing the Current Customer Record*

```
    .FindFirst "fldAssetBarCode = '" & txtAssetBarCode & "'"
    If .NoMatch = True Then
    Else
        MsgBox "The Company Already Exists.", vbExclamation
        Exit Sub
    End If
End If
' Add or Edit
        .AddNew
    Else
        .Edit
    End If
```

To implement this for a real-world database, however, requires a few more lines of code and a little more thinking. In general, what you want to do is to call a dedicated save function; the edit button will unlock the records for edit, the caption will change to Save, and the save routine will test the record to see whether anything has changed or indeed whether the user has added a new record. In effect, you are killing two birds with one stone. Listing 8-12 shows the basic approach when editing a record. (Listing 8-14, which you shall see shortly in the "Adding a New Record" section, takes this whole process one step further using a number of DAO methods.) A discussion of each of the new methods follows the listing. Note that you don't even bother to check which particular field has been changed. Given the speed at which DAO works, this isn't really required and, being honest, isn't worth the coding effort to implement. Just simply save the whole record!

Listing 8-12. *Edit Syntax*

```
rstCompany.Edit
rstCompany.Field = Value
rstCompany.Update
```

In this case, because you are updating all the records, this process is fairly easy. All you need do is to call a DAO Update method on the recordset and save the changes. It is also possible to actually test the recordset for changes using its Dirty property.

One of the major issues with the unbound recordset approach is highlighted in the following quote:

> *One problem with unbound is the whole locking issue, which the bound method handles for you. Unless you place a lock on the record you are editing, then how do you know that the underlying record wasn't updated by another user while this user was eating lunch? Thus for simple unbound, probably only updating fields changed is the safest. If your form is going to lock the record being edited, then you can safely update the entire record. Or you could refetch the original, compare the field values of the original to the "old values" of the unbound form, and warn the user if there were changes to the original.*

> John Colby, Colby Consulting

Being a great believer in not reinventing the wheel, I refer you to Chapter 2 of *Access 2002 Enterprise Developers Handbook* by Ken Getz, Mike Gunderloy, and Paul Litwin (Sybex, 2001), which contains an excellent example of handling record locking in a multiuser environment.

Deleting a Record

Using DAO to delete a record is about as easy as this stuff gets; all that is required is that you delete the current record and repopulate the form. Of course, it is always useful to allow users to confirm that they actually want to delete the record before removing it from the table. Note the use of the word "removing." Many developers do not actually delete records. In many cases, they add an additional field to the table that describes the state of the record as either Active or Inactive. When "deleting" a record, this state field is simply updated to Inactive, and the record no longer appears in the form. This approach requires that the SQL statements used to create the recordset always contain a WHERE clause (for example, WHERE Active = True). In this way, inactive records are never displayed. Listing 8-13 demonstrates deleting a record. In this case, you do not need to reopen the recordset, as it is currently open. Remember from earlier that you dimensioned the recordset at the top of the module to enable its use anywhere? Note also the use of the WITH statement, which saves you having to explicitly refer to every method of the recordset object.

Listing 8-13. *Deleting a Record*

```
intRpy = MsgBox("Are you sure you want to delete this Company?", vbYesNo)
    If intRpy <> 6 Then Exit Sub
With rstCompany
    .Delete
    .Requery
    If .BOF = False And .EOF = False Then getCustomers
End With
```

Adding a New Record

Adding a new record via the unbound form is again basically a straightforward process. In this case, the Add button will clear the form, unlocking the controls and allowing the user to enter new data. However, here it is important that before you actually carry out the INSERT operation, you check the record does not already exist within the table being added to.

Listing 8-14, which appears toward the end of this section, shows the procedure that is run in response to the On Click event of an Add button. The save procedure (available in the Chapter8 example database, frmCustomer, of the book's source downloads) demonstrates one approach to using the DAO FindFirst method to make sure a record doesn't already exist. If the record doesn't exist, you know you are working with a new set of data. If the record already exists, you know this must be an edit (or nothing has changed). The procedure in Listing 8-14, taken from a real working application, combines all of the methods already discussed, checks whether this is a new record, if it is, adds it to the table; if it is an existing record, .Edit is called to edit the record.

On this occasion, to demonstrate the ability to work with more than one recordset at a time, the example database will also write the changes into a history table. Writing records to a history table is one way you can audit database changes. I should say that because this is from a working application, some of the references to control objects will be different from those you will have used in the preceding examples.

For this example, I am interested in showing you the technique involved in the real world as opposed to explaining the theory behind the code. There are several steps involved in this process. If the user clicks the Add command button, the check for whether the record is a new record or an already existing record is done in a novel way, by testing the color of the command button caption text. When the user clicks a command button to carry out an action, the caption of the button is changed, and the fore color is set to red. For example, clicking Add changes the caption displayed on cmdAdd to the text Cancel Add, and the fore color is changed from blue to red. In the same way, when a user clicks cmdEdit, the caption is changed to read Cancel Edit, which the user can click if he or she changes his or her mind, and the fore color changes from blue to red. We can use these color changes to our advantage during the save operations. Following is the process required when the user clicks the Add command button. The variables gconRed and gconBlue are global variables set in a public module.

1. Empty the form of existing records by blanking out the text boxes. Simply use a function to set the value of each text box on the form equal to "".

2. Turn off and on the appropriate command buttons. In this case, make sure that the Save button is enabled.

3. Change the caption of the Add command Button to Cancel Add and set its ForeColor to red. This is actually carried out in the function required to clear the form.

4. Enable the Save button.

Listing 8-4 demonstrates only the code behind cmdAdd. The full working routine can be downloaded from the Source Code/Download page on the Apress web site (http://www.apress.com).

Listing 8-14. *cmdAdd Routine*

```
Private Sub cmdAdd_Click()
If cmdAdd.ForeColor <> gconRed Then
' Add a new record
      Call EmptyBoxes
    cmdAdd.Caption = "Cancel &Add"
    cmdAdd.ForeColor = gconRed
    cmdSave.Enabled = True
    cmdSave.ForeColor = gconRed
    cmdUndo.ForeColor = gconRed
    cmdUndo.Enabled = True
    cmdEdit.Enabled = False
       Call UnLockForm
    'txtCompany.SetFocus
Else
' Cancel adding a new record
    cmdSave.ForeColor = gconBlue
    cmdUndo.ForeColor = gconBlue
    cmdAdd.ForeColor = gconBlue
    cmdAdd.Caption = "&Add"
      cmdAdd.Caption = "&Add"
    cmdAdd.ForeColor = gconBlue
    cmdSave.Enabled = False
    cmdSave.ForeColor = gconBlue
    cmdUndo.ForeColor = gconBlue
    cmdUndo.Enabled = False
    cmdEdit.Enabled = True
    If rstCompany.BOF = True And rstCompany.EOF = True Then
        Call EmptyBoxes
        Exit Sub
    End If
   rstCompany.MoveFirst
    Call getCustomers
    cmdExit.SetFocus
End If
Exit_cmdAdd_Click:
Exit Sub
```

```
Err_cmdAdd_Click:
    Select Case Err
    Case 0      '.insert Errors you wish to ignore here
        Resume Next
    Case Else   '.All other errors will trap
        Beep
        DoCmd.OpenForm "frmErrorMessage ", , , , , , "Error: " & Err.Number & ➥
" - " & Err.Description & vbCrLf & "In: frmAsset.cmdAdd_Click"
        Resume Exit_cmdAdd_Click
    End Select
    Resume 0    '.FOR TROUBLESHOOTING
End Sub
```

■**Note** Check out this example in the demonstration database available with the book to see how you can fit the whole mechanism together and create a fully updatable form without actually binding anything directly to a table.

BOOKMARKS

The Bookmark property allows you to set the current record in the form to the matching record in the recordset. In this case, you are saving a reference to the Bookmark property in a variable to ensure you can return to the same record in the form when you have finished a process.

QueryDefs

QueryDefs (the saved definition of an Access query) allow you to create and manipulate Access queries via DAO. For example, to execute a preexisting action query, you could use the code shown in Listing 8-15, which updates a single company record. The criteria in this case is actually dealt with inside the query definition.

Listing 8-15. *Executing a Query*

```
Public Sub execquery()
On Error GoTo Err_execquery
Dim db As Database
Set db = CurrentDb
Dim qdf As DAO.QueryDef
Set qdf = db.QueryDef("qryupdatecompany")
qdf.Execute
```

```
Exit_execquery:
On Error Resume Next
    If Not (qdf Is Nothing) Then qdf.Close: Set qdf = Nothing
    If Not (db Is Nothing) Then db.Close: Set db = Nothing
Exit Sub
Err_execquery:
        MsgBox Err.Description, , "Error in Sub Module1.execquery"
        Resume Exit_execquery
    Resume 0    '.FOR TROUBLESHOOTING
End Sub
```

This code could be made to execute any action query by simply changing a few lines and passing the query required into a function. Listing 8-16 shows a slight modification to the code to use this approach.

Listing 8-16. *Generic Query Execution*

```
Public Sub genericQry(qryName as string)
Dim db As Database
Set db = CurrentDb
Dim qdf As DAO.QueryDef
Set qdf=db.QueryDef(qryName)
```

This type of process is useful when, following a set of actions, for example, you need to export, append, or remove data from a table once processing is complete. In addition to executing an action query, you can actually use QueryDefs to create new queries within VBA. Listing 8-17 shows one approach to how you can create queries.

Listing 8-17. *Creating a Query in Code*

```
Public Sub CreateQuery()
On Error GoTo Err_CreateQuery
With CurrentDb
        .CreateQueryDef ➥
            Name:="qrytest", ➥
            strSQL:="Select CustomerID, CompanyName, Country" ➥
                & " From Customers"
        .QueryDefs.Refresh
End With
Exit_CreateQuery:
Exit Sub
Err_CreateQuery:
        MsgBox Err.Description, , "Error in Sub Module1.CreateQuery"
        Resume Exit_CreateQuery
    Resume 0    '.FOR TROUBLESHOOTING
End Sub
```

Of course, you could always run a bit of SQL within the VBA to do the same thing as shown in Listing 8-18.

Listing 8-18. *Using SQL to INSERT a Record*

```
strSQL = "INSERT INTO COMPANY( VALUES] )" ➡
        & " SELECT Fields from some TABLE"
DoCmd.RunSQL (strSQL)
```

If required, you can also change the SQL used to define a query using a similar technique, in this case changing the SQL property of the QueryDef object (for example, qdf.SQL = "Your SQL String"). The SQL statement will replace the existing SQL statement used by the saved query.

Up to this point, in order to demonstrate some of the features of DAO, you have been working with unbound recordsets. During the writing of this chapter, I had a discussion with some developers on the AccessD list, and almost all of them agreed that when working in a strictly Access environment, it is in many cases better to work with bound record sources (that is, the form or report is bound directly to its data source, either a table or saved query). One of the main reasons for this is the topic I touched on briefly earlier: locking of records in a multiuser environment, which is not an easy task even for experienced programmers. The consensus is to leave that to Access. Unbound sources really come into play when working with external data sources—for example, SQL Server 2000 or 2005. The article "From DAO to ADO" by Marc Israel (*Database Journal*, 2000, http://www.databasejournal.com/features/msaccess/article.php/1490571) provides a useful overview of moving from DAO when working with server-side data. Previous chapters in this book also cover some of this topic, and you can find out more in another title I cowrote with Susan Sales Harkins, *SQL: Access to SQL Server* (Apress, 2002).

Building SQL Statements with DAO

DAO and VBA also allow you to construct SQL statements within your code; for example, using VBA, you can create SQL INSERT statements. Listing 8-19 creates one such statement that adds records to a local table. In this case, you are using the local table to populate an Access report. This is sometimes useful for performance reasons and removes the need to, say, work with complex JOINs when populating a report. Listing 8-19 simply shows a code fragment demonstrating how the SQL statement is put together. Note that the first step in the process is to execute a DELETE statement in order to ensure that only the records you require are included in the table.

Listing 8-19. *Using SQL Within VBA*

```
Set db = CurrentDb
db.Execute "DELETE * FROM tblLocalReportData"
strSQL = "INSERT INTO tblLocalReportData ➡
( fldRequired1, fldRequired2,fldRequired3,fldRequired3 )" ➡
&"SELECT tblCustomer.fldRequired1, tblOrder.fldRequired2,➡
tblOrder.fldRequired3 FROM tblCustomer
```

The SQL statement being constructed can be almost any valid Access SQL, ranging from as simple as the fragment shown to very complex. Either way, it is always useful to use the Query Editor to ensure you have valid SQL before actually adding it to the code. Once the SQL is valid, most other errors are mainly as a result of incorrect line breaks within the VBA IDE when you paste the SQL into your code. A good example of the use of SQL in this way is shown in Listing 8-20; here you use the fields from a DAO recordset to create a dynamic SQL statement, which in turn provides a new recordset for further manipulation. In this case, you are passing the value of txtCustomerID to the code in order to restrict the records returned to the recordset. This is useful if you need to populate a recordset with specific data.

Listing 8-20. *Dynamic SQL*

```
Set rsttest = db.OpenRecordset("SELECT* FROM tblCustomer WHERE ➥
fldCustomerID = " & Val(txtCustomerID) ➥
&" ORDER BY fldOrderDate DESC")
```

Again, the example shown is basic, but as before, the SQL statement being created can be as complex as required using any and all form control objects, for example.

Access 2007 and DAO

There have been several additions to DAO in Access 2007, mostly to deal with the new data types available and to enable integration with MOSS 2007. A good friend of mine, Shamil S., has posted a list on his web site showing over 300 new properties available with Access 2007 (http://smsconsulting.spb.ru/info/acc2007/newPrpsInAccess2007.htm). As you will see, a large number of the new properties are used for embedded macros—in fact over 157 of them! A shortened version of Shamil's list of new properties appears in Table 8-3. In general, you will now find that a report has much the same functionality as a standard Access form in terms of controls and their events. However, in the majority of cases, the property relates to the use of embedded macros as opposed to VBA.

Table 8-3. *New Access 2007 Properties*

Property	Property Type
AfterDelConfirmEmMacro	Embedded macro
AfterFinalRenderEmMacro	Embedded macro
AfterInsertEmMacro	Embedded macro
AfterLayoutEmMacro	Embedded macro
AfterRenderEmMacro	Embedded macro
AllowDesignChanges	Yes/No
AllowFilters	Yes/No
AllowLayoutView	Yes/No
AllowReportView	Yes/No
BeforeDelConfirmEmMacro	Embedded macro

Continued

Table 8-3. *Continued*

Property	Property Type
BeforeInsertEmMacro	Embedded macro
BeforeQueryEmMacro	Embedded macro
BeforeRenderEmMacro	Embedded macro
BeforeScreenTipEmMacro	Embedded macro
CommandBeforeExecuteEmMacro	Embedded macro
CommandCheckedEmMacro	Embedded macro
CommandEnabledEmMacro	Embedded macro
CommandExecuteEmMacro	Embedded macro

For a quick example of using On Click with a report field, open the Northwind Contacts report and click the Customer Name field to view the selected customer's details. In this case, a form opens allowing you to work directly with the underlying records. The form will open filtered at the appropriate customer record.

Note If you edit the record while the form is open, the changes do not automatically appear within the report.

This is achieved using the On Click event of the report control to execute an embedded macro. In terms of DAO and VBA, generally the programming model remains much as it was with the exception of manipulation of the new data types such as the attachment data type and Allow Multiple Values property columns, which will only be available when working with the new Access 2007 database file type, ACCDB. For standard MDBs, they are not available.

Note Many developers have stated their intention not to use the new data types and properties in applications, because from a developer's point of view, they break some of the rules of database design and normalization. However, I would expect these new data types, particularly the attachment data type, to be very popular with end users, and it is important that developers do have an understanding of how they work.

Complex Data Types

Access 2007 introduces *complex data types*, which visually appear to store more than one data item in a field. Under the covers (which you cannot get at by the way), Access implements a fully relational model for these data types using hidden system tables. During the beta, many developers requested access to these system tables. At each occasion, Microsoft appeared to say that it would give some consideration to this. At the time of writing, Microsoft was still considering the request.

Attachments

The attachment data type allows you to associate many different files with a database record. What you end up with is two recordsets where the attachment data is actually a recordset in itself in addition to the main recordset containing the table data. In order to manipulate attachment data, you must use two recordsets. The field with the attachments is a child recordset of the main recordset. For example, in a Company table, you would create a recordset returning the company data. If you then wanted to manipulate the attachment field in that table, you would open a second child recordset to access the attachment data.

As stated before, the primary purpose of these new data types is to provide integration with SharePoint Server lists, which already provide this functionality. Internally, the Access database will create one or more system tables for the attachments. This is an effort by Microsoft to retain relational design. However, one of the major drawbacks to this is the system tables are not visible to developers, so there is no way to interact with them directly. However, the system table MSysComplexColumns contains information on each of the complex types you have defined. Table 8-4 shows the columns that are exposed in the system table.

Table 8-4. *MSysComplexColumns*

Column	Comment
ColumnName	Name of the complex column in the database table.
ComplexID	AutoNumber primary key for the system table.
ComplexTypeObjectID	Attachments have an ID of 39; multivalue fields an ID value of 27.
ConceptualTableID and FlatTableID	Columns that refer to the hidden system table used to maintain this data type. You do not have access to these system tables at this time.

The other major drawback is database bloat. Try it out by adding a few attachments to an Access 2007 database, and note how the database file size increases as you add each attachment. For example, an empty database containing a single table (with no date) is approximately 280KB. If you add a single short Word 2007 document to the file, it will increase in size to 380KB, and the file size will continually grow as attachments are added. However, in terms of storage, this is still a major improvement on OLEB, which increases the actual file size itself. Of course, this would apply if you were storing the graphic within the database application to begin with. Just like everything else, there are several issues surrounding attachments, and the following list provides a summary of the major ones:

- The individual attachment file size is 256MB.
- The data type is only available in the new ACCDB format.
- The maximum attachment size is the Access file size 2GB.
- Files are stored in the database, leading to database bloat.
- There is no Access to the system tables for attachments.
- Once created in the table, an attachment field cannot be changed.

In addition, many files are automatically blocked by Access 2007. Table 8-5 shows the blocked file types that at this time cannot be amended (that is, you cannot unblock them).

Table 8-5. *Blocked Attachment File Types*

ADE	INS	MDA	SCR
ADP	ISP	MDB	SCT
APP	ITS	MDE	SHB
ASP	JS	MDT	SHS
BAS	JSE	MDW	TMP
BAT	KSH	MDZ	URL
CER	LNK	MSC	VB
CHM	MAD	MSI	VBE
CMD	MAF	MSP	VBS
COM	MAG	MST	VSMACROS
CPL	MAM	OPS	VSS
CRT	MAQ	PCD	VST
CSH	MAR	PIF	VSW
EXE	MAS	PRF	WS
FXP	MAT	PRG	WSC
HLP	MAU	PST	WSF
HTA	MAV	REG	WSH

The easiest way to work with attachments is via the user interface using the GUI tools provided. However, as usual, you can also manipulate the attachment via DAO. Listing 8-21 shows a simple procedure that loads up an image file to a record in the attachment field of the Northwind Customers table. In order to do this, you need two recordsets: the first gets the customer data, and the second deals with the attachment field. Two new methods have been added to DAO to deal with this: LoadFromFile and SaveToFile. The demo code provided by Microsoft had one major problem: you need to already have an existing record for the example to work. Listing 8-21 adds a new attachment to a Tasks table. The attachment field is called Attachments. This example includes the "testing" debug statements to let you see the procedure as a working example. Remember to change the path to your image file for this example.

Listing 8-21. *Loading an Attachment*

```
Private Sub cmdAdd_Click()
On Error GoTo Err_cmdAdd_Click
Dim rstTasks As Recordset2
Dim rstAttach As Recordset2
Dim fld As Field2
MsgBox "start"
Set rstTasks = Me.Recordset
Set rstAttach = rstTasks.Fields("Attachments").Value
```

```
' The basic idea is of a recordset within a recordset, i.e., the multivalue
' attachment field is exposed as a recordset within each record of
' the main recordset.
' Parent child recordsets, I guess?
Set fld = rstAttach.Fields("FileData")
rstTasks.Edit
rstAttach.AddNew
fld.LoadFromFile "C:\Documents and Settings\marty\My Documents➡
\polar bear penguin.jpg"
Debug.Print fld.Name
Debug.Print fld.Value
Debug.Print rstAttach.Fields("FileType")
Debug.Print rstAttach.Fields("FileName")
Debug.Print rstAttach.Fields("FileTimeStamp")
Debug.Print rstAttach.Fields("FileURL")
  rstAttach.MoveFirst
    Do While Not rstAttach.EOF
        Debug.Print rstAttach!FileName, rstAttach!FileType, ➡
rstAttach!FileTimeStamp, rstAttach!Fileflags, rstAttach!FileURL
        rstAttach.MoveNext
    Loop
rstAttach.Update
MsgBox "File added"
rstTasks.Update
Me.Refresh ' Otherwise picture may not be updated
MsgBox "update" & rstTasks.Updatable
Exit_cmdAdd_Click:
On Error Resume Next
    If Not (fld Is Nothing) Then Set fld = Nothing  ' fld.close remove
    If Not (rstAttach Is Nothing) Then rstAttach.Close: ➡
Set rstAttach = Nothing 'rstAttach.Close:
    If Not (rstTasks Is Nothing) Then Set rstTasks = Nothing  'rstTasks.Close:
Exit Sub
Err_cmdAdd_Click:
        MsgBox Err.Description, , "Error in Sub Form_Tasks.cmdAdd_Click"
        If (Err.Number = 3820) Then
        MsgBox " A duplicate of a file name " & ➡
            vbCrLf & "has already been added to this record."
        End If
        Resume Exit_cmdAdd_Click
    Resume 0    '.FOR TROUBLESHOOTING
End Sub
```

One of the issues you will have when adding attachments is the possibility that the file already exists. Error handling in Listing 8-21 takes care of this in terms of the Error section. Of course, as in everything to do with DAO, there is more than one way to check this. If the file already exists, the user may want to replace it with a new copy. If the file does not already exist, you can simply add it to the recordset. The code fragment shown in Listing 8-22 also deals with this issue, and it checks using a simple recordset count before editing or adding the new attachment to the recordset. If the count is less than 1, you are adding a new record, and if it is greater than 1, it is an edit. This fragment can be added to the code in Listing 8-21. Remember that you will need to update both the parent (rstTasks) and the child (rstAttach) recordsets, and you need to move through the recordset to get an accurate record count before doing anything. If you don't do this, the record count will be for the number of records returned to date as opposed to the count of the entire recordset.

Listing 8-22. *Checking for Attachments*

```
rstAttach.Movelast
rstAttach.MoveFirst
If rstAttach.Recordcount >= 1 then
        rstAttach.Edit
Else
        rstAttach.AddNew
End If
        rstAttach.Update
        rstTasks.Update
```

You could also make the procedure a little more generic by passing the file location into the procedure. It is also possible to view attachment data via standard SQL statements as shown in Listing 8-23. As you may be able to tell, this SQL statement was generated by the Access query builder and returns data in the standard Access way.

Listing 8-23. *Using SQL to Select Attachment Data*

```
SELECT Customers.Company, Customers.Attachments.FileData,➡
 Customers.Attachments.FileName,
Customers.Attachments.FileType, Customers.Attachments
FROM Customers
WHERE (((Customers.Attachments.FileName) Is Not Null));
```

■Note You cannot run an UPDATE or a DELETE statement on a multivalued field such as Attachments using the query builder.

Traditionally, almost all Access developers do not store associated files, for example, Word documents and image files, within the database. They simply store the path to the document or image within a field. This avoids the issue of database bloat arising. One very simple approach to this is to store, for example, an image file name within the table. The actual image file can be stored in the same folder as the database. To view the file on an Access form, simply concatenate the path of the database file to the image name, producing a fully qualified file name. It would also be possible to store the full path and use this as the control source of an Access image control. This would also solve the problem of a database bloat. The main consideration with this approach is that the files required must be available in the same folder as the Access file itself. To get the current database path in Access 2007, you can use the function shown in Listing 8-24, which will return the full path for the currently open database.

Listing 8-24. *Getting the Current Database Path*

```
Public Function GetPath() As String
    GetPath = CurrentProject.Path & "\"
End Function
```

Then simply append the image file name, located in a text box control on the form, to the path returned by the function and load the image control. Listing 8-25 demonstrates this.

Listing 8-25. *Concatenating a Path and File Name*

```
Private Sub Form_Current()
Picture = GetPath & Me.txtImage
Me.image1.Picture = Picture
End Sub
```

The following short exercise brings this approach together using a form, an image control, and a small amount of VBA to load the required image into the control.

1. Create a new table called tblImages containing two fields, an AutoNumber primary key and a text field called ImageName.

2. Save an image file into the same folder as the database.

3. Enter the name of the saved image file into tblImages.

4. Create a new blank Access form based on tblImages.

5. Add an image control by dragging it from the Design Ribbon onto the form.

6. Name the image control Image1.

7. Add a text box to the form bound to the ImageName field named txtImage.

8. Add the following code to the form's On Current event:

   ```
   Private Sub Form_Current()
   Picture = GetPath & Me.txtImage
   Me.image1.Picture = Picture
   End Sub
   ```

9. View the form to see the loaded image file.

As you can see, using two very basic functions allows you to place images onto a form with little effort. While this does not have the flexibility of the new attachment data type in that it only works for image files, with a few lines of code it does solve the issue of database bloat.

Multivalued Fields

You will either love or hate multivalued fields. I will be totally up front here and tell you that I think it's an awful invention from the Access application side. However, when you work with SharePoint Server, it maps directly to the ability in lists to store multiple values; like the attachment data type, the main purpose in life for this feature is to work with SharePoint. Speaking as someone who will be moving into SharePoint projects real soon, this will prove useful in some areas. As you know, this isn't what multivalued fields will be used for. You will on many occasions be required to fix up databases containing this structure, as discussed in Chapter 7. Just like the attachment data type, multivalued fields are nonfunctional with SQL Server, in any edition.

Figures 8-1 and 8-2 show a multivalued field, Givento, first in the Tasks table and then on a form displaying the tasks. Visually, within the table level, this feature again breaks every rule of relational design, and under the covers the relational model is supported in hidden system tables, just as with the attachment data type. Within the database, a many-to-many structure is maintained; you just can't see it or get at it in any real meaningful shape or form. However, I would guess that users are going to love this, particularly the multiple-selection list box shown on the form, and will make a lot of use of such list boxes.

Figure 8-1. *Multivalued field data*

Figure 8-2. *Multivalued field displayed on an Access form*

The multivalued type is very similar to the attachment type and has a similar `.Value` property. In this case, `.Value` will hold the number value of the record being referred to; for example, it will display an employee name but actually store the employee ID number within the hidden system tables. This is the standard behavior of lookup lists and one of the reasons many developers don't encourage their use. The idea behind this is to make life easier for end users. Following is a quote from the Microsoft web site (`http://www.microsoft.com`) on using a multivalued field in a query:

> *In this example, the contact name field does not reside in a table. Instead, it resides in the source query that provides data for the multivalued AssignedTo field. You can join the source table or query for the multivalued field with the table that contains the multivalued field in order to include a field (contact name in this example) from the source table or query in the query result. You can then search that field instead of the multivalued field.*

I don't know about your end users, but that one will give some of mine a bit of trouble! Personally, I would find it much easier to explain and demonstrate how to work with and create a proper many-to-many relationship in the first place. No point moaning on about this feature; it is in Access, and there it will stay. From an SQL point of view, you can work directly with the `.Value` property in multivalued fields as shown in the following SQL fragments, which assumes there are two tables, Tasks and Employees. Tasks contains a multivalued field, Givento, which contains the ID primary key field in the Employee table. Listing 8-26 shows the UPDATE statement, while Listing 8-27 shows the DELETE statement.

Listing 8-26. *Update Statement*

```
UPDATE Tasks
SET Tasks.Givento.[Value] = 1
WHERE Tasks.Givento.Value)=2
```

Listing 8-27. *DELETE Statement*

```
DELETE Tasks.Givento.Value
FROM Tasks
WHERE Tasks.Givento.Value =2
```

As you will see when you run a SELECT query, you have two fields to work with. In my case, the Givento field will display all data items in a single cell, and the Givento.Value field, which is a child of Givento, will display each individual data item (in my case, each name assigned to the Givento field). If you want to delete the entire record, you use the Givento field. Individual items are dealt with by using the `.Value` item.

New Macro Features

There have been substantial changes to Access macros including error control, temporary variables, single-stepping in macros, and the ability to embed macros in form objects. One of the basic reasons for the changes that have taken place with macros is Microsoft's expanded view on security. Code should only be executed from and on trusted sources and locations. If your database is heavily VBA driven and is not in a trusted location on the PC, the VBA code will be disabled. In this case, all you have to execute will be macros. It is recommended that you use macros (which are available on the Create Ribbon) for simple processes; for example, when opening a database in an untrusted location, simply pop up a more descriptive message telling the user how to solve the issue.

You can determine whether your application is trusted by checking the new CurrentProject IsTrusted property and fork your application to either macro control or VBA as required. Of course, you would need to do this in an AutoExec macro, because if the application is not trusted, the code would never run anyway! Listing 8-28 shows the required VBA to do this. Yes, I know it has to be a macro, but it is worth using VBA to show the syntax of the new commands. You can view the macro in the Northwind 2007 database. Just open the AutoExec macro to view the design. Also note the new Arguments column available with macros in Access 2007.

Listing 8-28. *CurrentProject.IsTrusted*

```
If (Not .CurrentProject.IsTrusted) Then
        DoCmd.OpenForm "Startup Screen", acNormal, "", "", , acNormal
    End If
    If (.CurrentProject.IsTrusted) Then
        DoCmd.OpenForm "Login Dialog", acNormal, "", "", , acNormal
    End If
```

Why Access doesn't just open a form automatically with the relevant user action information already in place is beyond me!

Perhaps the biggest change in terms of experienced Access developers are TempVars and the ability to embed a macro as part of the form object itself. We'll take a look at these next.

TempVars

TempVars are essentially global variables that are available to both macros and VBA code, although they are more likely to be used with macros. They exist for the lifetime of the database; that is, when you close the database, you lose whatever values they contain. You can define up to 255 TempVars in the application. There are three new macro actions available: SetTempVar(name,expression) allows you to set the variable, RemoveTempVar(name) removes an individual variable from the store, and RemoveAllTempVars removes all variables from the TempVar store. It is good practice to remove all variables once you have finished with them.

TempVars are also available to VBA because there is a single TempVar store per application enabling this sharing. In my opinion, TempVars are not tools aimed at professional developers but rather at the power user who may need some data available in several places (for example, a company name or other generic application detail). However, unlike global variables, TempVars are not wiped if there is an error in the application.

For example, to assign the current database path to a TempVar, you could use the following code:

```
TempVars ("DBPath").Value = CurrentProject.Path
```

You can return a listing of all TempVars currently in use by creating a small procedure to loop through the collection, returning the TempVar names and values. Listing 8-29 shows how this works, printing the name and value of the TempVar to the Intermediate window using the .Name and .Value property of the TempVar. In the case of Listing 8-29, this will print out the name and value of DBPath if you have tried out the preceding example. You could also have carried out the same procedure using a macro and used the variable within VBA if required.

Listing 8-29. *Listing TempVars*

```
Public Sub DisplayTempVars()
On Error GoTo Err_DisplayTempVars
    Dim tempV As Variant
    For Each tempV In TempVars
        Debug.Print tempV.Name & " = " & tempV.Value
    Next tempV
End


Exit_DisplayTempVars:
Exit Sub
```

Listing 8-30 demonstrates the use of a TempVar to populate a text box with the current database path.

Listing 8-30. *Using a TempVar*

```
Private Sub Form_Current()
On Error GoTo Err_Form_Current
Me.txtPath = TempVars("DBPath").Value
Exit_Form_Current:
Exit Sub
Err_Form_Current:
        MsgBox Err.Description, , "Error in Sub Form_Customer List.Form_Current"
        Resume Exit_Form_Current
    Resume 0    '.FOR TROUBLESHOOTING
End Sub
```

Embedded Macros

Just like the name suggests, an embedded macro belongs to the object in which it is created, just like a control's event procedure. When you copy an object, the macro is copied with it. An example of an embedded macro can be seen in the Northwind database CustomerList form. If the form is in Design view, click the CollectDataViaEmail button and look at its On Click property. You will see that this is a very simple macro that executes a `RunCommand`, specifically `CollectDataViaEmail`. The actual macro steps are as follows: open the query, execute a `RunCommand` to start the Collect Data Through Email Wizard, and close the query.

The actual macro is not visible in the normal Macro view in the Navigation Pane; you have to click the build button within the On Click property in Design view to see it. The Command Button Wizard, when working in form design view, will also generate embedded macros when adding buttons to the form, as opposed to VBA code.

Macro Error Control

Microsoft has added a new error control action to macros, OnError, which is functionally the same as its cousin, the VBA OnError statement. Three statement arguments are available: Next, Macro Name, and Fail.

If the Next argument is selected, the error is recorded in the MacroError object. Execution continues to the next statement. If the Macro Name argument is selected, execution is passed to the named macro that will handle the error. If the Fail argument is selected, it stops the execution of the named macro. It will revert the macro behavior of handling errors back to the "old" way in the previous version of Access. When creating and using macro error control, you can use the MacroError object to help create meaningful messages to the user, replacing the standard Access error messages. For example, placing the following in the Argument Macro column will replace the default error message with one more accurately reflecting the error that has occurred.

```
="Error # " & [MacroError].[Number] & " on " & ➥
[MacroError].[ActionName] & " action."
```

Once this has been done, you can call ClearMacroError to remove the error number from the MacroError object. It is worth noting that the MacroError object will be cleared at the end of macro execution anyway. You can also use Docmd.ClearmacroError to achieve the same thing.

Summary

This chapter discussed DAO, complex data types, and some of the new features in macros in Access 2007. In all honesty, DAO is much the same in this release as in all other releases, and there are few if any major changes other than those related to the new data types. Complex data types designed to fit in with the SharePoint list model will find their way into standard Access applications, and you will see them being used in almost all user-created Access 2007 applications. Many developers will refrain from using them, but the functionality, particularly the multiple-selection lists, may actually mean you have little choice in the face of user demand. Macros will continue to be the preserve of power users and other high-end users of Access, with most if not all professional developers sticking to the power of VBA, including its excellent error trapping capability. However, again, there will be an increase in the use of embedded macros if only due to the fact that the wizards will be using them to provide functionality in, for example, command buttons. Many users will also take advantage of the ease in which they can be created and copied between objects.

CHAPTER 9

■■■

Introduction to SharePoint Server

Microsoft Access 2007 will bring many changes to the developer and power user. One of the major focuses of this version is its interaction with Microsoft Windows SharePoint Services (WSS). It appears SharePoint will be receiving tremendous focus from Microsoft as it becomes the main data store for the information worker. In case you missed it, Access is aimed directly at this market—those individuals who process, add value to, and work with information as part of their day-to-day roles. It is my opinion that interaction with SharePoint will see increased functionality with each progressive release of Access from here on in, and it is worthwhile for Access developers to make themselves aware of the capabilities this software offers.

On the other hand, many developers have asked how the small to middle-size businesses they deal with will use this software or indeed afford it. Affording it is easy; it's a free download and is part of the Windows Server 2003 operating system. Will a small business use it? Other developers have asked what use is it and why Microsoft has appeared to shift focus within MS Access from SQL Server migration to SharePoint. To be honest, I think SQL Server is still the way many developers will go, specifically to SQL Server 2005 Express, and as such the ability to link to SQL Server tables will also see increased focus from the Access team. From my own personal experience, I have yet to meet users or members of a particular business area within my own organization who, once they have seen how WSS operates and the feature set it offers, have not asked for it to be introduced as a major feature when managing business collaboration.

This chapter lays the groundwork for the following chapters by showing you what Windows SharePoint Services is and what it is capable of. We will look at working directly within SharePoint to create sites, lists, and workspaces. In the next chapter, you will use the new copy of Northwind to migrate a database to SharePoint and see how to link to WSS lists. In doing so, you will see why Microsoft has added in the new attachment data type and the Allow Multiple Values property.

We will look at SharePoint and how it interacts with the Office 2007 applications during the next three chapters; it is my belief that although Access developers might be tempted to dismiss this out of hand, they need a good overview of what SharePoint is and what it is capable of. The next three chapters will, I believe, prove my point. So I ask you to suspend judgment until you have actually tried out the examples in these three chapters as we look at Windows SharePoint Services before you decide it's not for you.

What Is Windows SharePoint Services?

WSS is a collaborative environment supplied by Microsoft as a downloadable component for the Windows Server 2003 operating system. It provides a complex environment for sharing different types of information and can be tightly integrated with Active Directory. SharePoint is a web application that is available internally as an intranet solution or can be configured to act as an extranet, thus allowing external access to internal company resources. Out of the box SharePoint provides superb features, and when used with Office 2007, it can fundamentally change the way in which you work with data and the sharing of information. Figure 9-1 shows the interface to Windows SharePoint Services once a site has been created.

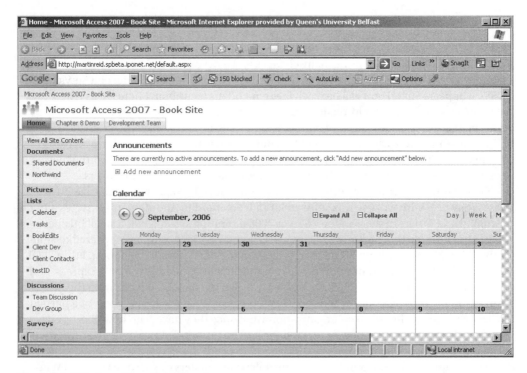

Figure 9-1. *Windows SharePoint Services*

As you may have guessed, I would be classed as a SharePoint convert, as the potential of this software to provide an environment that brings data and documents to life is excellent. By "bringing to life," I'm referring to the interactivity SharePoint provides. Each component in Office 2007 has been changed to enable increased interaction with WSS, and Access is no different. New features include the ability to take SharePoint data offline, migrate your application to a WSS server, and link directly to WSS. Additional interaction has been added to Word and Excel in respect to WSS.

For many Access developers, the biggest drawback will be actually getting the software to run this on. WSS itself is free, so that is not much of a problem; however, you need to install it on Windows Server 2003, which can be a problem given the cost of the software and indeed the hardware to run it on. One solution, at least to the software problem, is to install Windows Server 2003 on a Virtual Machine, either Microsoft Virtual Server 2005 or some other VMware solution. Virtual Server 2005 is another free download from Microsoft, and for testing purposes an evaluation copy of Windows Server 2003 can be downloaded. In addition, a 30-day trial site for SharePoint is available by registering at `http://www.sharepointtrial.com/welcome.aspx`.

■**Note** The example sites in this chapter have been created on a demonstration site provided by Microsoft during the beta for Office 2007.

I would hope that this trial site will be upgraded to version 3 by publication date. One of the major changes in WSS with this new version is that it is based totally on .NET Framework 2.

Microsoft Office SharePoint Server 2007

It's impossible to talk about WSS without mentioning Microsoft Office SharePoint Server (MOSS) 2007. WSS does one thing for you; behind all the hype it's a bit of software that allows you to create web sites, also called web applications. Using WSS, you (and your users) can create many sites to assist in the day-to-day operations of a business. SharePoint Server provides the means to aggregate content from multiple WSS sites and presents it in a common interface. I will primarily discuss WSS in this and the succeeding chapters, but some areas of MOSS will also be covered for completeness. Unlike WSS, MOSS 2007 is not free and must be licensed, but it does provide some great features over and above those of WSS—for example, the ability to create audiences to whom content can be targeted, full site searching and indexing capability, and the ability of users to create a personal view of the SharePoint application using a "my site" feature. MOSS 2007 is highly recommended for wide-scale deployment needs in the enterprise.

Data within an organization exists in many places: as Word documents, Excel spreadsheets, and PowerPoint presentations; in e-mail folders (local and remote); in HTML on the Web; in network shares and other applications; and, of course, the bit where you tend to be involved, within many small to medium-sized Access databases. Given the IT world is not the whole preserve of Microsoft, data also exists in other applications and software ranging from Oracle to, in my case, Ingres databases. The focus of Microsoft has been to make this data available to the user no matter what the source—of course, if it's in a Microsoft product, all the better and all the easier to get at!

People within business also interact with each other and with information. Many developers create Access databases that fit into a particular area within a business process; they tend not to see how that area fits in the business as a whole, how the information is shared within an office or indeed an organization. What happens to that report you spent weeks programming? Who has it? What will that person do with it? Who else needs it? Does anyone even know it exists outside the user you created it for? And does that matter? Many ad hoc Access databases are also created for one-off tasks and projects, and this information may need to be shared in a secure manner. SharePoint is an attempt to answer these questions and make information much more active and available no matter where it is stored. SharePoint also provides a focus on team work, supplying out-of-the box sharing features for documents and other information.

Behind the Scenes of WSS

WSS is almost completely database driven using either SQL Server 2005 or SQL Server 2005 Express. All content that appears on the site is actually stored within an SQL Server database. Each WSS installation will use several SQL Server databases for management and application content. It is recommended that you leave these databases alone and work with SharePoint via the management interface provided or via the object model, which is very extensive. On the front end, SharePoint provides web applications for the user to work with, a web application being a web site created by the user and based on the .NET Framework. A page within a WSS site contains .NET Web Parts. *Web Parts* are .NET controls that provide a degree of functionality for the user; for example, a Web Part can display the user's Outlook inbox or perhaps a dataset from Access or SQL Server. WSS comes with many Web Parts already available to you, and developers can create their own using any of the MS .NET languages. Each page may contain a number of Web Part zones, each containing in turn a number of Web Parts. Almost everything you will see within a WSS web page will be contained within a Web Part zone of some share or form, and this will apply to your Access data as well. We will be looking at using such Web Parts in Chapter 11 to work with Access tables.

WSS will contain at the least two databases: a content database and a configuration database. Of course, based on the database names, you can guess that one contains all site content and the other configuration data for the installation.

What Can You Do with WSS?

WSS provides the ability to create collaborative web sites, which is best explained by briefly looking at one of the sites that I have managed for a particular organization. As part of a training program, staff can undertake exams, and in order to support each course, resources and other training materials are made available on this site. The way this was historically done was to simply place documents onto an Apache web server and create a standard web page. Users could then download the documents to their PCs. This process worked very well, and no issues arose. However, in order to provide a little more interactivity and to make the actual upload process as easy as possible, it was decided to create a WSS site to store the materials. In this site, I created a folder structure reflecting the courses being held and a subfolder structure for the materials stored by file type. All of the training resources could then be placed into the appropriate folder system on WSS. This alone probably doesn't sound very impressive, but out of the box, WSS provided the following capabilities not available on the site originally:

- Automatically e-mail users when materials have been updated or added.

- Direct File ➤ Save As from MS Word to the WSS folder structure.

- Create an interactive discussion forum per course.

- Have full access to Active Directory Security.

- Use interactive Outlook calendars for training events.

- Perform internal task management for document production.

- Distribute interactive training surveys.

And not one line of code had to be written. Now, that's a vast improvement over a simple file share download of some training materials. Again, you may be asking what this has got to do with Access, but just think, if I then tied in the training course booking system with WSS, taking the best of both worlds, the organization I work for would have client-side database management and interactive web sites without too much effort. But, being honest, it's highly likely that WSS would provide everything you need either out of the box or with a little .NET coding.

Granted, I work in a large organization with lots of servers and can do this sort of thing with minimal cost. But the average developer may not have the resources for this sort of development; however, the average power user may well have access to a similar range of software, and one of the great things about WSS is that a WSS site, once created, can be passed over to the user for management when appropriate. From the user's point of view, one of the other features available is interaction with other individuals while on the web site via text-based chat. Once logged in, users can interact with other members of staff interested in the same training area, hopefully leading to a degree of peer support between those involved in the training sessions.

From the desktop side of things and standard business processes, WSS provides many useful features—for example, the ability to build ad hoc web sites for specific tasks or the development of meeting materials.

■Caution Because of this ability of users to create ad hoc business sites, there is a certain amount of work required to manage the server and its web site. It is easy to forget that users may be creating single-purpose sites that may not be reused. Such sites may contain links to your Access tables but will not be reused. From the other direction, it is possible that your Access applications can be linked into nonused sites. It is therefore important that sites or subsites that are no longer used are removed from the structure by SharePoint administrators.

WSS provides several built-in templates for things such as project management and meeting organization: with a couple of mouse clicks, the user has a complete meeting management web site up and running using all the features for which that user has permissions, including Active Directory for security and user management. The following site/workspace templates are available with WSS version 3:

- Team Site

- Blank Site

- Blog Site

- Wiki Site

In addition, the following workspaces are available:

- Basic Meeting

- Blank Meeting

- Decision Meeting

- Social Meeting

- Multiple Page Meeting

One other interesting feature about SharePoint that I have so far neglected to mention is the ability to set each site up for mobile access (that is, connect to your site via a mobile device such as a PDA). For many developers, this could be useful for giving full access to documents, lists, events—in fact all the features of SharePoint. This has proven to be a useful project management tool while "out and about" in my own employment. All you need is a mobile device and a connection to the Internet. No other work is required, as mobile pages are created by WSS once the feature has been enabled. Not only that, but you could, if required, permit your clients to have access to the site again for project-related materials. This does, however, require a little bit of work on your part to enable forms-based authentication using .NET and SQL Server. We will be looking at this in Chapter 11 when we explore some .NET coding issues. Of course, unlike the systems in many large organizations, it is also possible to add clients directly into the Active Directory of the Windows Server hosting the WSS server. Much easier!

The rest of this chapter provides you with the background information you may need if you are going to take things forward using WSS and the Web. We will be looking at many of the areas you will require knowledge of in order to use WSS as a back-end data store and as a migration point for your Access databases.

Permissions

All users within a WSS site must have specific permissions to carry out site actions. Permissions can be either granted to an individual user or assigned to a group to which your users are added. The following permissions are available:

- *Full control*: Administration permissions on your WSS site

- *Design*: Ability to edit lists, document libraries, and pages within the site

- *Contribute*: Access to the site and ability to edit lists and documents

- *Read*: Read-only access to the site

WSS groups are recommended, as it is easier to manage security if it is group based, as opposed to managing several hundred users when using user-level security. To assign permissions, click People and Groups on Quick Launch. It is also possible within lists themselves to further refine the security to individual items.

Lists

Almost everything in WSS is regarded as a list containing information; for example, a Document Library list contains a list of documents, and a Tasks list contains a list of events. A list is similar to a table within a database; each item in the list would correspond to a single record about a specific event, task, or document.

The great thing about lists is they are accessible from within Access and other Microsoft applications. For example, a document in a list can be opened, edited, and saved from within

Word 2007. A Tasks list can be opened within Access; in fact, an Access table can be linked to a SharePoint list or indeed migrated from Access to SharePoint. Later, you will see how to migrate the entire Northwind application to SharePoint and look at the objects that result from the migration and how you interact with them. Do not be misled by the word "list"; a list in SharePoint is not a static object—for example, in a Document Library list, it is possible to check a document out, edit the document with Word, and resave back into the SharePoint list.

Another useful feature is the ability to retain history of documents within WSS. Almost all of the new template databases supplied with Access 2007 are geared for use on Share-Point. In fact, any database using the new data types cannot be migrated out of the box to anything other than SharePoint. They are all list-based applications or applications that can easily be converted over to the SharePoint list type. For example, the attachment data type permits you to associate several documents with a particular Access field. The same feature is available in SharePoint: a list item can have several attachments associated with it. The new Allow Multiple Values property is again designed to allow the migration of tables to WSS and have them fit in with the way WSS uses such data.

WSS provides the following lists:

- Document Library

- Form Library

- Wiki Page Library

- Announcements

- Contacts

- Discussion Board

- Links

- Calendar

- Tasks

- Project Tasks

- Issue Tracking

- Survey

You can also create your own individual custom lists should the templates not meet your requirements. Lists can be further customized via the creation of views, which can be used to create highly personal information systems by restricting list information to data added or of interest only to the current user.

Perhaps the best way to understand WSS is to create a site and look at the functionality provided from both the server and the client before looking at interaction with Access 2007. It is worth having a sound understanding of the capabilities of WSS before moving on to look at interaction with Access 2007. As is the case with many Access developers and power users, this may be the first opportunity you have had to play with such collaboration software.

Creating a Team Site

For this example, you will create a functioning team site using one of the WSS templates. This site will be used to manage project development for a fictitious client. For this example, you must use the following software installed on a single machine:

- Windows Server 2003 SP1

- Windows SharePoint Services version 2005

- SQL Server 2005 Express Edition

- Access 2007

If you don't have access to WSS, you can get a 30-day trial account from `http://www.sharepointtrial.com/welcome.aspx` that can be used to test out the features I will be discussing. However, bear in mind that some of the administrative features of the software may not be available to you.

To create a new team site with WSS open, follow these steps:

1. Click Site Actions.

2. Select Create.

3. Select Sites and Workspaces in the Create Page screen.

4. Complete the following details in the new SharePoint site form:

   - *Title*: Client Development

   - *Description*: SharePoint Site for Access Project Development

   - *URL Name*: Type Client Development

   - *User Permissions*: Accept the default

   - *Display on Quick Launch*: Enter Yes

   - *Team Site*: Select or accept this option

10. When done, click Create.

WSS will create the site for you, opening the default home (Default.aspx) page shown in Figure 9-2.

This site will form the basis for the interactive client site used for the development project in this chapter.

The site will also contain the following features:

- A document library used to store specifications, project notes, and other client documents

- A calendar that will show any events related to projects (for example, meeting dates)

- Tasks associated with a particular project

- A discussion forum to be used by a team of developers or by indeed the client

- Integration with Active Directory for security

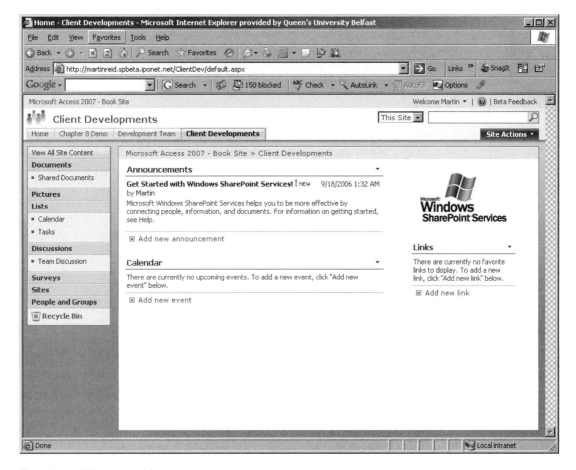

Figure 9-2. *WSS team site home*

We will also look at customization and how you can set the site up so that each developer or group of developers can personalize the site for themselves.

Once the site has been created, the Quick Launch menu on the left of the screen shows some of the default items already added to this site for you: document library, pictures, lists, discussions, surveys, sites, people, and groups. The first thing you will do is to simply change the name of the web site. In this case, you will replace the default site name with your own. In doing this, you will see how easy it is at a lower level to begin personalization of a web site using WSS as opposed to something like SharePoint Designer. (However, for full branding of a WSS site, SharePoint Designer would be the tool of choice.) To change the site name, follow these steps:

1. Click Site Settings.

2. Click Title ➤ Description ➤ Icon.

3. Enter Access Client Site in the Title and Description text box.

4. Click OK to save the changes.

The following list outlines the site settings available to you depending on the permissions you have on the WSS site:

People and Groups

Advanced Permissions

Title, Description, and Icon

Navigation Options

Site Theme

Top Link Bar

Quick Launch

Reset to Site Definition

Master Pages

Site Content Types

Site Columns

Regional Settings

Site Libraries and Lists

Site Usage Data

User Alerts

Web Discussion

RSS

Sites and Workspaces

Site Features

Delete This Site

Go to Top-Level Site Settings

As you can see, there are a wide range of items you can work with at the site level. For the site you are creating, we will only be looking at the following: People and Groups, Site Theme, Quick Launch, Site Content Types, Site Columns, User Alerts, Web Discussions, and Sites and Workspaces.

People and Groups: People and groups provide you with the ability to secure your web site/application. Only those users you grant permissions to will be able to access the information. It is worth noting that you can set up anonymous access for a site if required.

Site Theme: You can select from a set of prebuilt themes that affect the layout and color scheme of your web site. New themes can also be created within SharePoint Designer and added to the collection.

Quick Launch: This is the WSS-side menu system. Items (links to lists) can be added or removed from the Quick Launch menu. The Quick Launch menu can also be customized using SharePoint Designer.

Site Content Types: You can customize each of the content types associated with a WSS site (for example, documents, lists, and folders). The easiest way to explain this feature is to use a document as an example. Say you need to capture metadata for a particular document. Using content types, you can define the metadata required, and this information is stored with the file.

Site Columns: Available is an editable list of all columns used throughout the WSS sites. Columns can be changed or added to the global set of columns available. Once columns have been created, they can then be reused across all sites on the WSS server.

User Alerts: User alerts permit those using a list to request e-mail notification when an item is added or changed. E-mails can be interactive (that is, sent as soon as a change happens or rolled up on a weekly basis, depending on the frequency of change). For example, if a developer places a new working document onto a list, an e-mail can be issued to the rest of the team advising of its location.

Web Discussions: We will be looking at Discussion Board lists later in this chapter in the section "Creating a Developer Discussion Group," but most developers will already be familiar with browser-based discussion groups.

Sites and Workspaces: Each WSS site will have one top-level web site and any number of sub sites and workspaces. Workspaces are increasingly used to manage the day-to-day activities of many organizations; for example, if the development team needs to organize a meeting, all the administrative planning and notification could be carried out via a WSS Meeting Workspace. Once the meeting has taken place, the site can be deleted or archived. It is worth pointing out that workspaces could be one of those things that you actually need to manage closely when using WSS. Users are free to create workspaces virtually at will, and before long their growth can be uncontrolled, and you can end up with sites several levels deep. Workspace creation and site creation in general should be carefully managed to maintain the integrity of the web site.

Libraries, Lists, and Workspaces

At the heart of WSS lie its sites, libraries, lists, and workspaces. It is within these objects that the majority of work will take place. From lists and Web Parts, data will be displayed, enabling you to share data with users from a single interface tied tightly to Office 2007 and Access. Using tools like SharePoint Designer, you will quickly be able to develop basic Web Parts containing data from a number of sources, including Access and SQL Server. From within Access, you will be able to migrate to WSS, link to WSS lists, and take data offline for updating later. This next section of the chapter takes you over some of the more important lists and libraries and services you are likely to need when you first start off working with WSS.

■**Note** A *WSS list* is a single record or group of records much like an Access table containing columns and rows. A *library* is a collection of items, for example, Word Documents, PowerPoint files, or Excel Workbooks.

Document Library

The Document Library is used to store and share documents required by the team site members—for example, working papers, specifications, meeting agendas, and any permitted file type required to be shared by the team. (File types are set by the system administrator and can include Access database files.) Click the menu item Document Library to open the library interface. Figure 9-3 shows the library. To upload a document, click the Upload button. Note you can upload single or multiple files in a Windows Explorer–type interface.

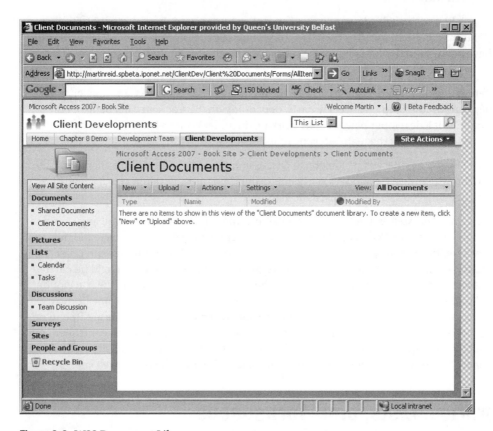

Figure 9-3. *WSS Document Library*

Table 9-1 lists the menu options and the choices available in the Document Library.

Table 9-1. *WSS Document Library Menu Options*

Menu	Options	Comment
New	Document	Create a new document in Word.
	Folder	Create a new folder in the library. Useful for file organization.
Upload	Document	Upload a single document.

Menu	Options	Comment
	Multiple	Upload multiple documents at the one time.
Actions	Edit in Datasheet	Edit list in an Access table look-alike sheet.
	Open with Windows Explorer	Open file in Windows Explorer.
	Connect to Outlook	Connect to Outlook. Great for Calendar-type lists.
	Export to Spreadsheet	Export to Excel.
	View RSS Feed	Associate with an RSS Feed.
	Alert Me	Set up an e-mail alert for this list.
Settings	Create Column	Add a new column to the list.
	Add from Existing	Add a new column from existing columns.
	Create View	Create a new view on the list.
	Settings	Manage the setting for this list.

As you can see, there is a lot you can do to customize a list and its objects, and to make items widely available to staff from linking to Excel to providing data via RSS feeds. One of the more impressive areas of configuration is the ability to create custom views of list items (for example, only showing those items a particular user has contributed).

In the next example, you will open a Word document and look at some of the client-side features available when working in WSS. For this example, you will need to upload several documents into the library. Simply click Upload ➤ Multiple Files and select a range of MS Word documents to load into the site. Note, however, that you are not restricted to only uploading Word documents; you can upload many different file types depending on the file type permissions set for the particular server. In my case, I have uploaded several Word, PowerPoint, and Excel documents into the library.

Once you have a document within the library, you can then begin to see how WSS interacts with client programs. For example, you can hover the mouse over a Word document and click the downward arrow (located on the right) to reveal a submenu. From here, you can view and edit the document properties, manage permissions, edit the document in Word, send it via e-mail to another Document Library, and download a copy. A Check Out feature is also provided (and can be enforced at the server level) to notify other users that the document is out for edit. WSS version 3 also contains comprehensive versioning for documents.

Once you've uploaded some Word documents, follow these steps:

1. Select a Word document in the library and click Edit in Word. The document will open in Word 2007.

2. Using the Office button, select Server ➤ Document Management Information. (Figure 9-4 shows the Document Management Task Pane open in Word 2007.)

From within the client application (in this case Word), the following items are available: status, the members online, associated tasks, documents within the list, and web links available from the WSS site. If other members of the site happen to be online, true document collaboration will be available via the client program. Saving a document back up to the WSS site is as simple as selecting File Save As, entering the address of the site, and saving. Your new document will be placed into the WSS area chosen. You may also view version history for the current document if version history has been enabled for the Document Library.

Figure 9-4. *Word 2007 Document Management Task Pane*

Calendar Lists

On the front page of your WSS site, you will see a Calendar Web Part. This is a fully functional Web Part that will allow you to record appointments with clients and any other date- or time-related information. Click the Calendar link to bring up the Calendar Web Part. To add an item to the Calendar, follow these steps:

1. Click the Calendar from the home page of your site.

2. Click a date within the Calendar.

3. Click a time (for example, for an 8 a.m. meeting, click 8).

4. Complete the details in the Add Item Listing page.

When you return to the home page of your site, you should see the meeting listed within the Calendar Web Part. You can take this one step further and customize the listing. To the right of the Calendar title, you should see a small downward-pointing arrow. Click the arrow to reveal the Web Part menu, shown in Figure 9-5.

The menu is used to customize the look and feel of the Web Part. All Web Parts within WSS sites have this built-in customization feature available. Clicking the menu reveals several choices: Minimize, Close, Modify Shared Web Part, and Help. For this example, click Modify Shared Web Part. Once selected, your web page should change into edit mode, and all Web Parts within the page should now be visible. You will now edit the Calendar Web Part.

The Calendar Task Pane should be available to the right of the screen as shown in Figure 9-6.

Figure 9-5. *Calendar Web Part menu*

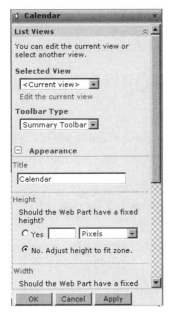

Figure 9-6. *Calendar Task Pane*

If you expand all the options within the Navigation Pane, you'll see the Add item form contains several useful capabilities:

- Add recurring events.

- Create a new workspace to deal with a meeting.

- Add attachments to the specific list item.

- View by day, week, or month.

The Actions item also provides some nice capabilities:

- Connect to Outlook.

- Export to spreadsheet.

- Open with Access.

- View with RSS feed.

- Set up e-mail alerts.

The ability to connect your Calendar to Outlook is useful, as you can work in either direction, updated directly from within Outlook or by logging into the WSS site and adding items. You could also give the client access to the Calendar or, better yet, create a private workspace below the main client site and provide the clients with access to that area. If you look at the built-in functionality of the Calendar in WSS, you can begin to see the power available using this software without any coding required. The amount of code you would need to write, debug, and test to give you the same functionality would be enormous, but with WSS, it is part of a free software download. Just like all other Web Parts in WSS, the Calendar can be customized and different views presented. To customize the Calendar, follow these steps:

1. Click the downward-pointing arrow to the right of the Calendar.

2. Select Modify Shared Web Part.

3. In the Calendar Task Pane, select Current View. You'll see that several options are available as follows:

   - *All Events*: Show all events recorded in the list.

   - *Calendar*: Show an interactive Calendar Web Part as opposed to a list view.

   - *Current Events*: Show events for today.

   For this example, just leave the defaults.

4. Click Apply to exit edit mode.

When working with WSS lists, several customization options are available to you. In list view, access these options by clicking Settings ➤ Select List Settings. The best way to learn the options is to simply play with them and look at how the Calendar changes. One of the interesting options available is the ability to enable version history on the listing. This can prove very useful for those projects that require an audit trail. In addition, almost every list in WSS has the same customization features for you to set. In any list, simply click Settings ➤ Select List Setting to open the customization screen.

Tasks List

The Tasks list allows you to enter details about upcoming work schedules and any other task-related information. Task information can be updated directly within WSS, Access, or Outlook. Information in the list can be shared with those who have access to the site or can be customized on an individual basis, showing each site member only assigned items. In the following example, you will be doing all three. To create a new Tasks list:

1. Click Site Actions.

2. Select Create.

3. From the Tracking category, select Tasks.

4. Enter Client Updates as the name for this new Tasks list.

5. Click Create.

This will give you the basic task listing facility, which like all other lists can be customized. Of particular interest is the ability to create views of lists. In this next example, you will add a Gantt chart to the Tasks list.

Creating a Gantt Chart

Once you have a basic Tasks list created, you can go another step further and display the data as a Gantt chart. Figure 9-7 shows the results of creating a view on the Tasks list created previously as a Gantt chart.

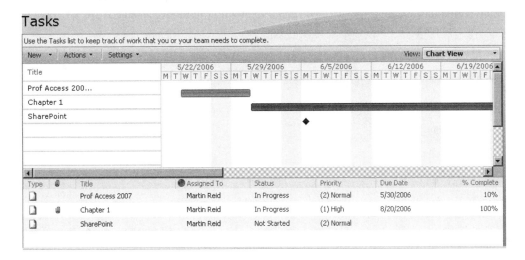

Figure 9-7. *Gantt chart view*

The basic ideas behind creating this view of the Tasks list can be applied to all of the lists within WSS. Of course, what you can do with a view depends ultimately on the data and information it contains. But the general techniques used here can be applied. To create the Gantt chart view of your Tasks list, follow these steps:

1. Open the Tasks page.

2. Select Settings ➤ Create View.

3. Select Gantt View.

4. Enter a name for the view.

5. Create a public view.

■Note You can also create a private view, which will be restricted to yourself.

6. Accept the default columns.

7. In the Gantt Columns section, select the following using the drop-down lists:

- Title

- Start Date

- Due Date

- % Complete

8. Scroll to the bottom of the page and click OK.

Enter a new task into the list, remembering to include a start and end date for the item. The Gantt chart should be updated to reflect the changes. Using the drop-down Project Tasks menu (located to the right of the list), you can also create "interactive" views of the data using one of the following options:

- Active Tasks

- All Tasks

- By Assigned To

- Due Today

- My Tasks

- Modify the View

- Create a New View

The Gantt chart is only one type of view that can be created within WSS lists. As I am sure you have noticed, within the Create View form there are several additional options that can be used to create very complex views of list data, including the ability to create the view using Access 2007. We will be looking at interactive Access features in Chapter 11. A Project Tasks list is also available, which is a standard WSS list type and includes the features of the Gantt chart without having to create a view of an existing listing.

Creating a Developer Discussion Group

Out of the box, WSS provides a somewhat limited, but still useful, discussion group, which can provide additional features to your development team. The Discussion Board list can be used by ten members and clients, if authorized, to discuss issues related to projects both onsite and offsite. To create a discussion, follow these steps:

1. From the Quick Launch menu, select Discussions.

2. Click Create.

3. Select Discussion Board from the Communication category.

4. Name the discussion Client Discussion and accept the default as shown in Quick Launch.

5. Click Create.

You will now be taken to the blank Discussion Board list. To add a new discussion topic:

1. Click New.

2. Select Discussion (topic).

3. Enter a description.

4. Enter some content.

5. Click OK.

Figure 9-8 shows the screen at this point.

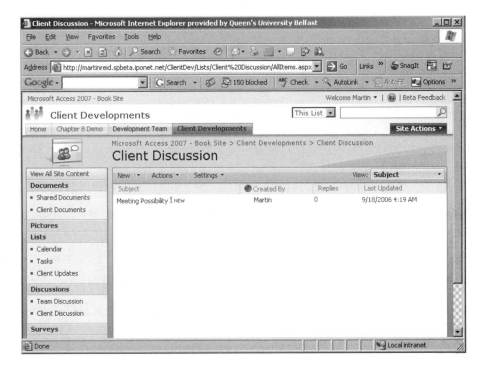

Figure 9-8. *Discussion group in WSS 3*

As with other lists within WSS, the Discussion Board list can also be customized. Generally, one of the first things many people do is to change the look of the list from Flat to Threaded. Simply click the View drop-down list and select Threaded to do so.

The Actions drop-down list provides similar customization options as other lists. The following sections discuss some of the options available with Discussion Board lists.

Connecting to Outlook

Connecting to Outlook is an interesting option when you are using Outlook 2007, because once you are linked, it is then possible to access and interact with the discussion via the mail client. Figure 9-9 shows the same discussion you first saw in Figure 9-8, but this time within Outlook 2007.

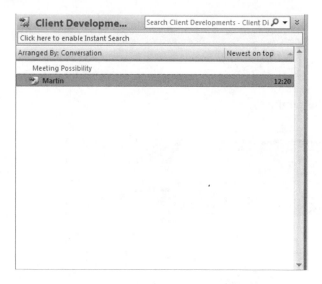

Figure 9-9. *Discussion list in Outlook 2007*

The following options are available to allow you to export and interact with the discussion in other ways:

- *Export to Spreadsheet*: Export the selected list to Excel 2007.

- *Open with Office Access*: Limited in usefulness as the discussion is linked as a flat table.

- *View RSS Feed*: Create an RSS feed of the discussion for use by members or clients. The RSS can be made available within Outlook 2007.

- *Alert Me*: Create an e-mail alert when an item is added to the discussion.

■**Note** It is also possible to attach files when posting a reply. Attachments will also be available in a client application; for example, Access will use the new attachment data type to make attachments available in a table or form based on a link to the list.

While limited in functionality compared to many online discussion forums, WSS provides a basic, usable discussion form for ad hoc project items and could be a useful tool when for project and client communication. Note that fully featured discussion forum applications can also be purchased from third-party suppliers.

Surveys

Surveys provide you with the basic ability to create an online questionnaire. This could prove useful when dealing with clients and gathering project requirements. To create a survey, follow these steps:

1. Click Surveys in Quick Launch.

2. Click Create.

3. Select Survey on the Create Page screen.

4. Enter a name and description for the survey and accept the remaining defaults.

WSS will create the Survey list and open the Create Questions form. There are several options available to you when creating answers to the survey questions:

- Single line of text

- Multiple lines of text

- Choice (list box–type menu that allows you to select an answer)

This can be configured as radio buttons, combo boxes, or check boxes if you need to permit the user to record more than one response to a single question. The following question types are available to you when building the survey:

Rating Scale: Sliding scale of options from which the user can select, for example, High, Low, Wonderful.

Number: Numeric response. A maximum and minimum value can be set.

Currency: Currency types. These can be sent using a drop-down list of values.

Date and Time: Standard date/time data type.

Lookup Information: Option for allowing you to add information that is already on this site for example a specific user or existing list.

■**Note** Lookups are particularly useful, as they let you populate responses from information already contained with the site. Once the Lookup type is selected, another drop-down list is provided, called Get Information From, which makes available information from existing lists on the site. Selecting a list results in another combo box from which you can select the column of interest from the selected WSS list.

Yes/No: Simple Yes/No question response.

Person or Group: Drop-down list of WSS individuals or groups of users for the respondent to select from.

Page Separator: Page break, which the user can insert into the survey. Useful for longer surveys.

Surveys also support *branching*. Once you have created a survey, return to the Survey settings page to create the branching logic. For example, if a client responds to question 1, you may require further information. Using conditional branching, you can immediately present additional questions on response. This is particularly useful when you are using an answer of type Choice. The user is presented with a range of answers, and, based on his or her response, can be directed to additional relevant questions. To set up branching, click the Survey settings link to return to the Customize the Survey page and click a question to open it for editing. Branching options will be available toward the bottom of the edit form. Select the question you would like to branch to follow a user response.

At the moment on the example developer web site (Internet or intranet), you have, with minimal effort, the following features:

- An Active Directory–secured web site

- Interface document library with check-in/check-out capability and versioning

- An event calendar

- A Tasks list and Gantt chart for projects

- A client survey questionnaire

■**Caution** Not a bad start, and we have barely scratched the surface of WSS. As I have said on several occasions in this chapter, WSS is free. However, this is a slight distortion. It is free in that the software itself doesn't cost any money, but as you may be beginning to see, it does require management, which does come at a cost. Such costs will rise as customization is required (for example, developing specific Web Parts).

WSS Workspaces

I have already touched on WSS workspaces in this chapter. In this section, we will look at them in some more detail, particularly the Meeting Workspace. Workspaces generally are created to serve a particular need; for example, the Meeting Workspace is used to organize meetings and provides a central location for agendas, invitations and confirmations, documents, and calendars. For this next example, you will create a totally blank Meeting Workspace and manually add functionally using WSS built-in Web Parts. To create a Team Meeting Workspace, follow these steps:

1. Click the Site Actions drop-down list.

2. Select Create.

3. Select Sites and Workspaces.

4. Enter the following information:

   - *Title and Description*: Development Team

   - *Description*: Meeting site for the Access Dev Group Meeting

   - *URL Name*: devgroup

- *User Permissions*: Same permissions as parent
- *Display on Quick Launch*: Yes
- *Use Top Link from parent*: Yes
- *Language*: English or whatever is required from the list

5. Click the Meeting tab.

6. Select Blank Meeting Workspace.

7. Click Create.

WSS will create the blank meeting space for you. At this point, you need to decide what Web Parts are required for this subsite. In this case, you want to add the following features:

- Agenda
- Attendees
- Objectives
- Decisions
- Tasks

To begin adding the required Web Parts, follow these steps:

1. Select Site Actions ➤ Edit Page to switch the page into edit mode. Note that once in edit mode, placeholders for Web Parts are already in place and the Add Web Part Task Pane should be open on the right side of your screen.

2. Select the following Web Parts from the task pane and drag them into the appropriate placeholder:
   - *Agenda*: Left placeholder
   - *Attendees*: Right placeholder
   - *Objectives*: Center placeholder

3. Exit edit mode. Figure 9-10 shows the new screen once the Web Parts have been added.

4. Return to edit mode and add the following Web Parts to the placeholders:
   - *Decisions*: Right placeholder
   - *Tasks*: Left placeholder

You have now created an almost fully functional Meeting Workspace. But WSS has another trick up its sleeve: the ability to connect and filter Web Parts. For example, you can create a connection from the Agenda Web Part to the Task Web Part and show tasks related to agenda item owners. We will be looking more closely at this topic in Chapter 11 when we examine creating Web Parts populated from Access tables. For now, here are the general steps to take to create such a connection. Make sure your page is in edit mode and select a Web Part. Click the Edit drop-down list and select Connections. Using the submenu, select one of these options: Provide row to, Provide data to, or Get row/filter from. Once an option has been selected, a short wizard-based form interface opens requesting details of the data to be used for the connection.

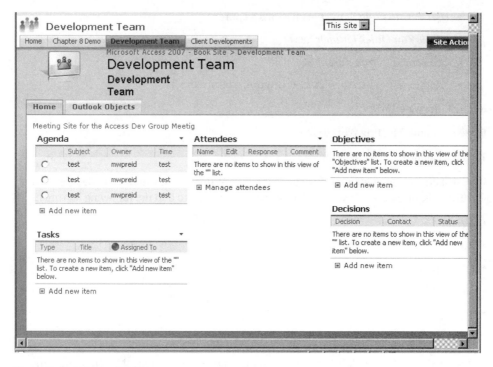

Figure 9-10. *Meeting Workspace*

Personalization with Microsoft Office SharePoint Server 2007

As you have seen, there are many things you can do to personalize objects such as lists and document libraries within WSS. However, personalization can be taken to another level by adding objects like personal e-mail folders, Outlook tasks, and calendars to the web site. The only drawback here, and it is a significant one, is that you will need to use the full version of Microsoft Office SharePoint Server 2007. Again, like many of the objects you have seen in this chapter, this is an out-of-the-box experience with MOSS 2007. In addition to the Web Parts you have already seen, MOSS 2007 includes the following personalization parts (in addition to many others):

- Colleague Tracker
- My Calendar
- My Contacts
- My Inbox
- My Links
- My Mail Folder
- My SharePoint rollups
- My Workspace Sites

The ability to display a personal Exchange inbox with no coding is a useful tool and one that has been greatly admired by the team of developers I work with. MOSS 2007 also allows users to create fully personalized views of the entire web application, showing only the information they require for a specific business need. Figure 9-11 shows the My Site feature displaying my own inbox and calendar using MOSS 2207 and Exchange 2003.

Figure 9-11. *MOSS 2007 My Site feature*

Of course, both the inbox and calendar are fully functional. The main drawback is if you are not using Outlook 2007, updating is in a single direction only, from SharePoint to Outlook. Outlook 2007 provides two-way communication with SharePoint, allowing you to update information from within Outlook or SharePoint. Interaction with WSS and MOSS 2007 is also fully available within each of the Office 2007 applications.

Summary

In this chapter, you have learned how to put together a fully functioning interactive web site, out of the box. No .NET programming was required, and for me that is a superb bonus. I hope that by reading this chapter and trying out the examples, you will begin to have an appreciation for what this product can offer the modern information worker without too much work from you. In the next chapters, we will be taking this basic experience forward by looking at some of the more advanced WSS features. We begin in Chapter 10 by looking at interaction with Access 2007 and finish in Chapter 11 seeing how with Web Parts, Access 2007, and SQL Server work together to demonstrate some of the data-handling capabilities of this collaboration software.

CHAPTER 10

■■■

Access and SharePoint Applications

Chapter 9 provided an overview of Windows SharePoint Services (WSS). In this chapter, we will again be looking at WSS, but this time concentrating on its interaction with Microsoft Access. From my own contact with developers, I believe many are still confused as to how WSS is designed to fit into the Access development world, and this chapter should help in answering that question. We will kick off by looking at linking to WSS lists and working with them in Access. Then we will move on to migrating an Access database (Northwind 2007) to WSS and look at working with WSS objects in code. However, most Access developers will not be working in code with WSS data; instead, they will be using built-in features of Access, queries, forms, and reports to build rich applications containing WSS list data.

More and more large organizations are moving into the WSS area by either using the full portal product SharePoint Portal Server 2003 or upgrading to the new Microsoft Office SharePoint Server (MOSS) 2007. However, many smaller businesses will only be running WSS, a downloadable component for Windows Server 2003. This chapter concentrates on working with WSS, but for completeness, you will see some examples of interaction with MOSS 2007. For the current WSS or MOSS user or developer, Access can serve as another tool to get richer views of data to the client by providing many new built-in features to expand WSS sites into new applications.

Using WSS Lists with Access

As the growth of WSS increases, you can expect more data to be held within WSS lists (for example, contacts, document libraries, image banks, and tasks). In the previous chapter, you saw how to create a WSS web application to serve as a simple project management site. What if you need to reuse some of that information—for example, pull in a set of project tasks for reporting purposes? As you may have noticed, WSS has no reporting tools available within the software, and one option is to use Access reports for this purpose. Access provides three main means of communication with WSS data: linking to lists, importing from WSS into Access, and migration of the whole show to WSS applications. It may also be required that individuals have access to WSS data offline, and therefore Access could be a suitable tool for this use (taking lists offline and then updating back to the WSS application on return to the office, for example).

The new Access file type, ACCDB, takes full advantage of WSS, including the ability to make use of the new attachment data type and multivalued fields. Creating a link to a WSS list is similar in many ways to linking to any other object from Access. You can also work in both directions from Access 2007 or from within many WSS lists. Of course, there are some subtle differences, which we will explore as we go along. However, applications based on Access and WSS have one huge drawback: Referential Integrity is not currently supported by WSS. This is of course an important restriction, and one I am sure Microsoft has considered for future releases. However, if you migrate Northwind to a WSS list, for example, you will find that relationships' primary key/foreign key pairs are maintained as links between the WSS lists.

In terms of security and WSS, the security model you are using on your WSS server will be reflected in the Access application. For example, if you require an Active Directory username and password, they will also be required when working with data linked into Access. WSS security information is not stored with the Access application, and that includes within the linked table connection string. Once you are authenticated to the server, the authentication lasts for the life of the Access application.

■**Caution** What you do need to be careful of is saving the username and password combination on your PC. Speaking from personal experience, it can be a little embarrassing when your Active Directory security is bypassed because of a simple error that you forgot about.

Connecting to WSS Lists from Access

From within WSS, it is possible to open a WSS list within Access. Figure 10-1 shows the Actions menu with the Open with Microsoft Office Access option highlighted.

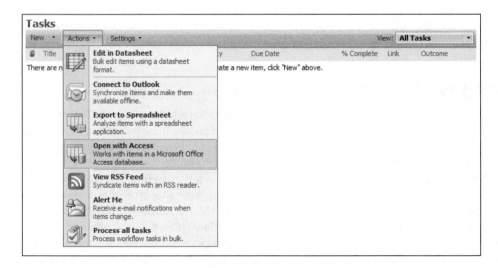

Figure 10-1. *Opening a WSS list through Access 2007*

■**Note** At the time of this writing, Access must be running on the local PC for the Open with Microsoft Office Access command to work.

WSS will begin the process by offering a location and name for a new Access database based on the new Access database file type. You can also link or import the list to the new database. Figure 10-2 shows the WSS Open in Microsoft Office Access dialog box. In this case, I am going to link to the WSS list from Access.

Figure 10-2. *Open in Microsoft Office Access dialog box*

To continue, click OK and log in to the WSS site if prompted. Access will create a new database containing a link to the WSS list. Once the database opens, note that Access has created additional objects for you, in this case several objects related to contacts, reports, forms, and an Access query. Figure 10-3 shows the results viewed in the Access 2007 Navigation Pane. This again is an attempt by Microsoft to get users up and running with a basic functioning application that they can then build upon.

Within Access, the linked table functions as any other linked data source. You can add, edit, and delete records, provided you have the appropriate permissions. If you have created a link to the WSS list, changes made via the Access interface will immediately become available on the list. To view the changes in WSS, simply refresh the page in the browser. If the WSS list contains "new" data types (for example, an attachment), they will be copied over into the new Access 2007 application. This is where the new attachment data type really comes into play. Once a table has been migrated to WSS, the attached documents then become active, meaning that table can then take advantage of WSS features (for example, version history and check-in/check-out).

Another interesting feature when linking via the Access interface is the Open Default View button located at the top right of the generated Contact List form. Clicking this button will open the original list on the WSS site.

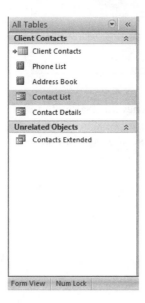

Figure 10-3. *Access database objects created when linking from WSS*

When linking to WSS, it is also possible to take the data offline—for example, if you require access to WSS data from home and perhaps have no connection to the WSS server. Using the features of Access, you can make changes to the data offline, and then go back online when you can to update your WSS list with the changes. On the main Ribbon, when you are working with a linked list, a SharePoint Lists group becomes available. Initially, there are three options, including Work Offline. When you click this option, Access will take your WSS list data offline. Once offline, the contextual group buttons change to appropriate buttons that give you the ability to take the list back online, change management, and synchronize data. We will be looking at an example of this next.

Working with Lists in Access 2007

Once you hit the Synchronize button, all changes made to the offline Access list will be copied to the WSS version, but your Access linked list will remain offline until you click Reconnect All. This is a great feature when working with linked lists, as only data changes are passed to the server rather than full tables or lists. In offline mode, data can be cached within the Access database file and only updated when required. Caching can be activated via the SharePoint Lists group on the Access Ribbon.

Caution This can lead to an increase in database size as large lists are cached within the file. In addition, any data cached within the database will be available to anyone with access to the database file, even if they do not have permissions to view the data on SharePoint.

In order to improve cache performance, data will be refreshed and/or updated in the following circumstances:

- The first time data is taken from the server

- When the user deliberately refreshes the data via the Ribbon options

- Explicitly via code when taking data offline

Once you have a linked SharePoint list in the application, you will then have access to the SharePoint Lists contextual menu. Simply click the External Data tab to view the SharePoint Lists group. The button to cache data in the current database will then be available. Several contextual options are available, of course, depending on what you happen to be doing with the linked list and the operations you are carrying out. Figure 10-4 shows the SharePoint Lists group in the External Data Ribbon. In this case, note that some options are grayed out, as they do not apply at this point.

Figure 10-4. *SharePoint Lists group*

This group offers you the following options:

- Cache List Data

- Refresh All Lists

- Discard All Changes and Refresh

- Discard All Changes

- Synchronize

- Work Offline (check box control type)

One of the drawbacks when using the interface to create links is that you will be linking to the entire list and accessing all its data. In order to reduce the data being pulled from WSS, a new macro action has been added, TransferSharePointList, that will allow you to link to WSS views in addition to standard lists, resulting in less, yet more meaningful, data being pulled from the WSS sites. This is an important improvement when working with WSS from Access, as it is always critical in terms of performance to try and reduce the data being pulled from the server whenever possible. It is also the case that for the majority of users, a full list is not actually what they want to see. When accessing a list, many individuals are only concerned with tasks assigned to them. Using the WSS view creation feature, you can create a view of a list restricted to the current user or for a specific time period. Previously, it has been difficult to work via VBA with SharePoint data, and while this is still the case, this new option does simplify the process somewhat. Table 10-1 shows the arguments available to you using TransferSharePointList.

Table 10-1. *TransferSharePointList Arguments*

Argument	Comment
Transfer Type	Import or link. Importing moves a copy of the list into Access. Changes made to the list will not be reflected in the database. Linking to the list will reflect changes made on the WSS site.
Site Address	URL of the WSS site you want to use.
List ID	GUID of the required list. This is a required item.
View ID	GUID of the view you want to use. Leave this blank if you want all items.
Table Name	WSS object name once imported or linked to in Access.
Get Lookup Display Values	Retrieves a lookup that displays text rather than the ID.

■**Note** In order to use the TransferSharePointList action, the database must be in a trusted location.

This all appears nice and straightforward, but there's a real kicker in here. Note the required value List ID. This is a GUID (that is, a unique ID for the list of interest). The GUID provides a unique identity for each list on a WSS site. The recommended way to get this value is to copy it from the URL displayed in the browser address bar. However, you can't simply copy and paste the GUID into your code—you have to carry out some replacements first. The following instruction is taken from the Access 2007 help file:

*The address in the browser's address bar contains the GUIDs for both the list and the view. The GUID for the list follows **List**=, and the GUID for the view follows **View**=. However, in the address, each { (left brace) character is represented by the string **%7B**, each - (hyphen) character is represented by the string **%2D**, and each } (right brace) character is represented by the string **%7D**.*

Listing 10-1 shows one example of how to sort out the GUID using the Access Replace function.

Listing 10-1. *Using Replace to Fix a SharePoint GUID*

```
Function fixGUID()
Dim site As String
site = "%7B357B4FE6%2D44CF%2D4275%2DB91F%2D46558301579B%7D"
site = Replace(site, "%7B", "{")
site = Replace(site, "%2D", "-")
site = Replace(site, "%7D&", "%7D")
site = Replace(site, "%7D", "}")
Debug.Print site
End Function
```

This outputs a correctly formatted GUID to the Intermediate window structured as follows:

```
{357B4FE6-44CF-4275-B91F-46558301579B}
```

From within Access, when you have a list already linked, the easy way to find out the GUID is to do a SELECT from MSysObjects where Name = Linked Object Name. The Database field contains the following data:

```
{7E154024-643C-4F3F-BA87-B02676296647}
```

which is the GUID for the list. The actual SQL statement is shown in Listing 10-2.

Listing 10-2. *Returning a GUID Using SQL*

```
SELECT MSysObjects.Name, MSysObjects.Database
FROM MSysObjects
WHERE (((MSysObjects.Name)="Customers1"));
```

■**Note** You could also use WHERE Type = 6, which will return a SharePoint linked list.

This statement will return the full HTTP string for the linked table, and you then simply extract the GUID without having to worry about replacing tokens as in the previous example. However, from the WSS side, or to access a list via code (if you have not already linked to the list), getting the GUID is the only way to proceed.

To demonstrate the process, I have created a view of the Northwind Orders list on WSS. The view only retrieves records for Orders where the order date is within the current month. I named the view simply ThisMonthsOrders. Because I have not linked this view to Access, I will have to rip the GUID from the address bar in Internet Explorer. The partial URL is as follows (I have clipped the string, as it is fairly long and not of particular interest here):

```
View=%7B3C648DC4%2DF1D3%2D4365%2D9B5A%2DB4217605E1A8%7D
```

Passing this string into the function created in Listing 10-1 will retrieve the GUID to use for this example. The correctly structured string for this example is {3C648DC4-F1D3-4365-9B5A-B4217605E1A8}. The function to transfer this view to Access 2007 is shown in Listing 10-3.

Listing 10-3. *Using TransferSharePointList*

```
DoCmd.TransferSharePointList (acLinkSharePointList), ➥
"http://martinreid.spbeta.iponet.net", ➥
ListID = "Orders", ViewID = "{3C648DC4-F1D3-4365-9B5A-B4217605E1A8}"
```

Of course, this is just the same as using the SharePoint menu items to run the wizard to actually do the linking for you. It is important to note that a typo in the view or list name site will not result in an error message from the server.

Menu Commands from VBA

In addition to the interface changes, the following RunCommands are available when working with SharePoint data programmability, and they allow you to carry out Access menu commands without recourse to actually clicking the menu item. Each menu item in Microsoft Access will have a corresponding RunCommand available for you to use. For example, within VBA or embedded macros, you have the following SharePoint RunCommands available:

- acCmdBrowseSharePointList: Opens the SharePoint list on the server, which in the following example is named "Contacts":

```
DoCmd.SelectObject acTable, "Contacts"
DoCmd.RunCommand acCmdBrowseSharePointList
```

- acCmdShareOnSharePoint: Starts up the move to SharePoint Wizard.

- acCmdRefreshSharePointList: Refreshes the linked SharePoint list.

- acCmdDeleteSharePointList: Deletes the currently open SharePoint list. The following fragment will delete a linked list called Contacts:

```
DoCmd.SelectObject acTable, "Contacts"
DoCmd.RunCommand acCmdDeleteSharePointList
```

  This will not only break the link to the Contacts table in the Access database, but also delete the list from the SharePoint site. Make sure this is what you really want to do before running the command.

- acCmdDiscardChangesAll or acCmdDiscardChangesRefreshAll: The former allows you to discard all changes you made to a WSS listing, and the latter will discard the changes and refresh the linked SharePoint list. Start the Export to WSS Wizard to move the currently open table onto the WSS server. Listing 10-4 shows a basic example of this process. In this case, the table must be open for the process to work. The function simply starts up the wizard, which enables you to select the server for the transfer and actually move the data to a WSS list.

Listing 10-4. *Moving a Table to WSS*

```
Function CopytoWss()
On Error GoTo Err_CopytoWss

    DoCmd.SelectObject acTable, "Customers"
    DoCmd.RunCommand acCmdExportSharePointList


Exit_CopytoWss:
Exit Function
Err_CopytoWss:
        MsgBox Err.Description, , "Error in Function CopytoWss"
        Resume Exit_CopytoWss
    Resume 0    '.FOR TROUBLESHOOTING
End Function
```

- `acCmdImportAttachSharePointList`: Starts the SharePoint Attach to List Wizard to walk you through the process of attaching a SharePoint list within Access.

- `acCmdModifySharePoint`: Changes the structure of an existing WSS list.

- `acCmdRelinkSharePointLists`: Forces a relinking to take place to the SharePoint lists.

- `acCmdSharePointSiteRecycleBin`: Simply opens the SharePoint recycle bin if it has been activated by the server administrator. This allows you to retrieve deleted lists and is a useful feature to turn on when you first start modifying lists and other server objects.

One of the chief reasons for moving to SharePoint is to connect to data you may otherwise have to duplicate (for example, stored documents that may not otherwise be available to you within the Access interface) or to which you would have to code to get the same level of access. That said, many Access developers may need to just bite the bullet when it comes to the use of WSS and its widespread adoption within many organizations. This can be particularly true of databases created using the new Access data types. As I have said before, you cannot move these databases to SQL Server and retain the out-of-the-box functionality of data types such as attachment and multivalued fields. However, if it is a linked application, you could move particular tables to WSS lists and the rest of the database to SQL Server. This gives you the best of both worlds: the use of SQL Server for the majority of your data-processing tasks and the use of the new functionality retained by using WSS lists. The new local caching of SharePoint list data makes this a possibility.

Moving WSS Data Between Servers

Another new feature in Access 2007 is the ability to move WSS lists between servers. This process is designed to assist developers in the move from a test server environment to a production server environment. However, it must be stressed that this is a list-based option, and if you need to move an entire WSS application between servers, other tools are available to assist you in using the management features of WSS. This built-in feature of Access is, however, particularly useful if you need to move lists between a production server and the development server.

Migrating an Access Database to WSS

In addition to the more common approach of migrating an Access database to SQL Server, you will now be able to migrate an Access database to a WSS server via the user interface. This could be a useful alternative to SQL Server, particularly if some of the new data types have been used in the Access application. As mentioned in Chapters 6 and 7, SQL Server will not understand the new data types, and considerable manual work is required by you should you take this route to duplicate the functionality of, for example, an attachment data type. In this section of the chapter, I will walk you through migrating Northwind 2007 to a WSS server.

■Note You can also migrate to a WSS version 2 web site.

Before actually migrating a database, it is worth pointing out some of the major issues that can slow down the process. After the migration of a database, a new table will be created in the original database containing migration errors reported during the process. The major issues reported with the Northwind application are as follows:

- SharePoint does not support Referential Integrity.

- Only indexes with unique IDs are supported.

- Cascade updates are not enforced.

- Cascade deletes are not enforced.

- The decimal data type is not supported.

You can expect similar issues to arise when working with your own applications, particularly the core problems related to Referential Integrity and cascade updates and deletes. At the end of the day, WSS is not a relational database, but an application that contains lists of data, though these lists are not related in the same sense as those in a database like Access 2007. However, it does bring new features to the game and should not be ignored because of these obvious limitations for relational purists.

Migrating Northwind

I have created a document library specifically for this migration. The document library is called Northwind—just to keep things obvious during the process. Figure 10-5 shows the newly created document library on WSS. (It may be easier to follow the example if you create a similar library.)

Enter the name for the WSS site you would like to connect to. For the moment, leave the Linked check box unchecked. You will return to this option shortly.

Once you click Next, the Move to SharePoint Site Wizard will immediately begin the migration process. Figure 10-6 shows this stage in the process.

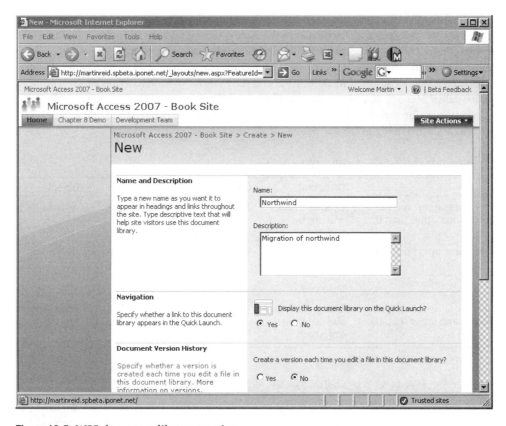

Figure 10-5. *WSS document library creation*

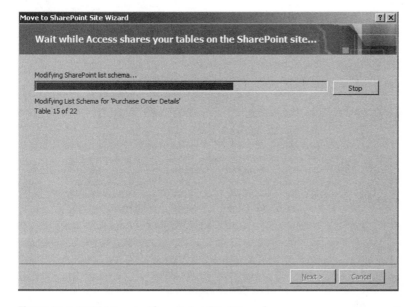

Figure 10-6. *WSS Move to SharePoint Site Wizard*

During the migration process, each table in Northwind will be migrated to a correspon-ding WSS list and a link created to the list in the Access database. Migration can take some time, as each Access table is adjusted for WSS. Table 10-2 shows some of the errors resulting from the migration. The error list is very extensive, covering 71 issues. However, generally they are the same issues as outlined in Table 10-2, and they will be written to a new table in your database called Move to SharePoint Issues. The table is very comprehensive and provides detailed information down to the property level. An abbreviated copy of the table created by the wizard is shown in Figure 10-7.

Table 10-2. *Employee Table Migrated to a WSS List*

Issue	Comment	Object	Table	Object
SharePoint does not support unique indexes on any column other than ID.	Unique index will not be enforced.	Table	Customers	Attachments
SharePoint does not support referential integrity.	Referential integrity will not be enforced.	Relationship	Customers-Orders	ID
SharePoint does not support unique indexes on any column other than ID.	Unique index will not be enforced.	Table	Employees	Attachments

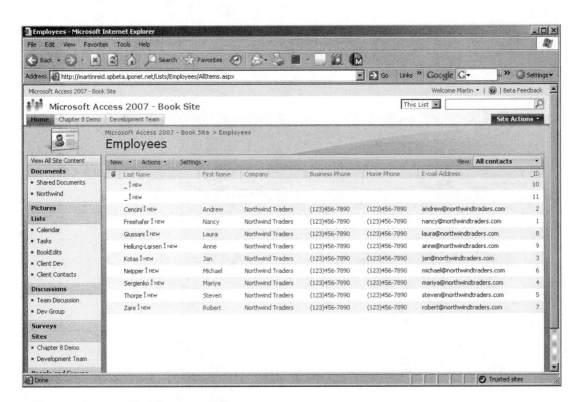

Figure 10-7. *Access table migrated to WSS*

In terms of data types, Table 10-3 shows the results on WSS of Access tables exported as a list to the server. There will also be additional fields available in the data taken directly from the WSS listing: ID, which contains a unique reference number; Modified By, which contains the user name of the user who changed a record; and Created By, which contains the name of the user who created the item. These three items provide you with a useful audit trail in terms of the list data.

Table 10-3. *Access and WSS Data Type Comparison*

Access Data Type	WSS Data Type
Text	Single line of text
Memo	Multiple lines of text
Number	Number
Date/Time	Date/Time
Currency	Currency
AutoNumber	Number
Yes/No	Yes/No
OLE Object	Not exported
Hyperlink	Hyperlink
Attachment	Attachment
Multivalue	Choice

Note When viewed within Access, the linked list will show standard Access data types as opposed to those from the WSS list definition.

As part of the migration process, the database will be backed up. For a large database, the process can be time consuming.

At the end of the process, you will receive a confirmation message. In this dialog box, click the Show Details check box to view a brief summary of the process, which should look similar to the following information that appeared on my system:

```
Microsoft Office Access has created a backup copy of your database.
C:\Documents and Settings\mwpreid\My Documents\Northwind 2007_Backup.accdb
The following URL takes you to the published copy of your database where it can ➥
be downloaded!
http://martinreid.spbeta.iponet.net/Northwind/Northwind 2007.accdb
WARNING:
Some issues were encountered while moving your tables. Access has created ➥
a log table called 'Move to SharePoint Site Issues' listing these issues.
```

■**Note** The following lists have been created on the SharePoint site `http://martinreid.spbeta.iponet.`
`net`, which is a private beta list hosted by Microsoft and therefore will not be available to you. I have simply
used it for demonstration purposes.

Customers, Employee Privileges, Employees, Inventory Transaction Types, Inventory Transactions,
Invoices, Order Details, Order Details Status, Orders, Orders Status, Orders Tax Status, Privileges, Products,
Purchase Order Details, Purchase Order Status, Purchase Orders, Sales Reports, Shippers, Strings, Suppliers

Your first stop following the migration should be the error table generated by the migration process. The error table, discussed earlier, will contain information on each issue that resulted from the migration to WSS.

Table 10-4 shows the results in terms of data types for the Northwind customer table when converted to a list. Unlike a standard linked front end, there will be no local tables in the migrated database application—hence the backup copy created during the process. It is probably worthwhile creating your own backup as well before starting the process, just in case. Table 10-4 shows the customer table definition on WSS and the new data types associated with the linked list. From Design view in Access, however, the data types will remain as they were before the migration.

Table 10-4. *Northwind Customer Table Migrated*

Column (Click to Edit)	Type Required
Last Name	Single line of text
First Name	Single line of text
Full Name	Single line of text
E-mail Address	Single line of text
Company	Single line of text
Job Title	Single line of text
Business Phone	Single line of text
Home Phone	Single line of text
Mobile Phone	Single line of text
Fax Number	Single line of text
Address	Multiple lines of text
City	Single line of text
State/Province	Single line of text
ZIP/Postal Code	Single line of text
Country/Region	Single line of text
Web Page	Hyperlink or picture
Notes	Multiple lines of text
_ID	Number
Created By	Person or group
Modified By	Person or group

From the WSS side of things, Chapter 9 covered some of the basic interaction you can carry out; however, it is worth knowing about some of the additional functionality available to you once the tables have been migrated:

- Adding additional indexes to the columns on the WSS server. This should help improve speed when working with the list via the Internet.

- Adding new columns to the list. However, this will mean that the list is now out of synch with the original database.

- Creating sophisticated views of the list and relinking these views back to Access. This can also help in the reduction of network traffic, as by default in Access you will have access to the entire list data, which in some cases can result in large amounts of data being cached in the database.

- Turning off list versioning for all lists or specific lists, removing the need to code VBA history data when data is manipulated by end users.

- Caching data from the server within the Access application.

Features Available After Migration

Linking the tables is sort of part one in the process of migration.

A new property, Display on SharePoint, has been added to forms and reports. Forms and reports with this property set to Follow Table Links will be added to the views created by the Move to SharePoint Site Wizard on the WSS server.

If you look at a list definition on the WSS server after a migration and select Settings ➤ List Settings, the Customize List screen will open. Scroll to the bottom of the screen and check out the views. This particular property, Follow Table Links, should form part of the premigration process, deciding which forms, reports, and queries you would like to migrate to the WSS server in addition to your tables.

Table 10-5 shows the views created for the Northwind Customers table during the migration process and equates them back to the original Access object.

Table 10-5. *Customer Views on WSS*

View Name	Access Object
All Contacts	Default view for this list
Customer List	Access form
Customer Details	Access form
Customer Address Book	Access report
Customer Phone Book	Access report
Order Details	Access report
Monthly Sales Report	Access report
Quarterly Sales Report	Access report
Yearly Sales Report	Access report

Clicking the view opens a read-only copy of the full database if you have Access 2007 installed on the calling machine. The read-only copy of the database will contain links back to the WSS lists on the server. However, both the form and report definitions still reside in your Access database. One of the main uses for this approach is to permit access to the lists and thus the database while "on the road." If required, you can save a local copy of the database for additional offline work.

Creating an Access View from WSS

Up to this point, we have been looking at interaction from the Access side of the fence. However, you can also interact with Access directly from within SharePoint lists, and in particular when working with list views. List views are very similar to other views in Access, and they are useful tools not only to Access developers, but also for WSS users and developers who would like to add some rich interface design to their WSS applications and sites. WSS views give you a powerful feature to restrict the data being made available via Access.

From within WSS, you can also create an Access-based view of any list to which you have permissions. Clicking Create View opens a WSS form that gives you a range of options, one of which is Access View. This option will create a linked Access database (as has already been discussed in Chapter 9). Of course, the primary means of view creation for Access developers will continue to be using queries and VBA to restrict the data being displayed. However, server-based views have the advantage, as they restrict the amount of data pulled down into the WSS cache within the database and, of course, along the network.

Linked Lists and VBA

Once you have linked your WSS lists to Access, you can treat them like any other table and manipulate the data via VBA code. For example, to get a list of all the fields in an Employees list, execute the code in Listing 10-5, which will print each field in the recordset to the Intermediate window.

Listing 10-5. *Printing WSS Lists via VBA*

```
Public Sub WSSData()
On Error GoTo Err_WSSData
Dim rstEmp As Recordset
Set db = CurrentDb
Set rstEmp = db.OpenRecordset("SELECT * FROM Employees")
For Each fld In rstEmp.Fields
        Debug.Print fld.Name
Next fld
Exit_WSSData:
On Error Resume Next
    If Not (rstEmp Is Nothing) Then rstEmp.Close: Set rstEmp = Nothing
Exit Sub
```

```
Err_WSSData:
      MsgBox Err.Description, , "Error in Sub Module1.WSSData"
      Resume Exit_WSSData
   Resume 0    '.FOR TROUBLESHOOTING
End Sub
```

As you can see, this is just the same as working with any other linked table within Access and VBA. The only difference this time is that the data is actually held on a Windows 2003 SharePoint Server. Data held on WSS can be used with forms and reports again just like any other linked table. This makes it very easy to include WSS list data within the Access application. Once you have got the data, you can then carry out many of the basic day-to-day data management tasks. You then also have the added advantage of using Access to build typical rich Access interfaces to the list data, which allows you to extend the desktop database directly out to the Internet with little effort. The next example will look at an asset record recorded as having been sighted and logged on a WSS asset list. Listing 10-6 demonstrates the features. I have included only the first section of the procedure merely to illustrate the use of VBA to grab WSS list data. In this case, rstWSSImport refers to a WSS linked list. rstAsset here would be a local Access table into which you would be placing the WSS asset records.

Listing 10-6. *Processing Linked WSS Records Using VBA*

```
Private Sub cmdImportWSS_Click()
If boolTrapErrors = True Then On Error GoTo Err_cmdImport_Click
fAssetTypeNotFound = False
Set db = CurrentDb
' Open recordsets
Set rstAsset = db.OpenRecordset("Select * FROM tblAsset")
Set rstIWSSImport = db.OpenRecordset("Select * FROM WSSAssetList")
'Set rstRoom = db.OpenRecordset("Select * FROM tblLab")
Set rstRoom = db.OpenRecordset("qryGetRooms")
Set rstCondition = db.OpenRecordset("Select * FROM tblCondition")
Set rstHistory = db.OpenRecordset("Select * FROM tblHistory")
Set rstAssetType = db.OpenRecordset("Select * FROM tblAssetType")
Set rstFundingType = db.OpenRecordset("Select * FROM tblFundingType")
Set rstConfig = db.OpenRecordset("Select * FROM tblConfig")
With rstWSSImport
If rstWSSImport.BOF = True And rstWSSImport.EOF = True Then GoTo EndIt:

' Loop through the Linked ASSETlist and process all records with a date.
.MoveFirst
Do While Not .EOF

' If !AssetCode = "10101010101010" Then MsgBox "Stop"

' Is it an added asset?
   If rstAsset.BOF = True And rstAsset.EOF = True Then GoTo AddAnAsset:
```

```
    rstAsset.MoveFirst
    rstAsset.FindFirst "fldAssetBarCode = '" & !AssetRef & "'"
    If rstAsset.NoMatch = True Then GoTo AddAnAsset:
    'If !assetid = 0 Then GoTo AddAnAsset:

' Is It Still in the Asset Table?
    'rstasset.FindFirst "fldAssetID = " & !assetid
    '    If rstasset.NoMatch = True Then
    '        MsgBox "Warning!! Asset Logged with Reference " & ! AssetRef & ➥
" does not appear in the database!!", vbExclamation
    '        GoTo NextImport:
    '    End If


' Add History Record of WSS log
        rstHistory.AddNew
            rstHistory!fldAssetID = rstAsset!fldAssetID
            rstHistory!fldXactTypeID = 1 ' Record 1 in the ttype Table is ➥
'Logged on WSS'!
            rstHistory!fldUSerID = !CreatedBy
            rstHistory!fldHistoryDate = !SIGNTEDDATE
            rstRoom.FindFirst "fldRoomID = " & !SCNDRMID
            rstHistory!fldHistoryNote = "Sighted in Building " ➥
                & rstRoom!Bldg & " Rm/Loc" & rstRoom![Rm/Loc]


        rstHistory.Update
' Did condition change?
    If Nz(!NEWCOND) <> "" Then
```

As you can see, this code opens and manipulates several VBA recordsets including data drawn in from WSS. The advantage in using the WSS list to capture the asset logging data is that you can make the list available directly on a secured web site, but only to those users you grant permissions to. The rest of the data lives in Access but could just as easily be linked-in SQL Server 2005 or Oracle data. Could you do the same with Access and put a table on the Web to capture this information? Of course, but that would mean writing all the code and the user interface to deal with the system, including the security system. Using WSS is a totally out-of-the-box solution to this particular problem.

From a front-end point of view, you can again treat the linked list as if it were a local table, but doing this will negate some of the benefits of actually using WSS. For example, take the customer table; if you where to simply create a form within Access, any user who needs to update a customer record would be required to have a local copy of the database. Using WSS, all the user requires is access to the list on the server, and you have immediate two-way communication between your WSS customer list and the linked Access table. "Well, so what?" I hear you say. Now that the data is on the WSS server, you can take full advantage of WSS features, including version history for individual list items (for example, who changed a customer record and when did he or she change it), and if required, you have the ability to roll back to a previous version. All of this, of course, is secured using Active Directory permissions to your WSS list. None of this is available in a standard Access application without a considerable amount of programming from developers.

Working with WSS Data Offline

As mentioned earlier in this chapter, when there is a requirement to have access to WSS data offline, this can also be achieved using Access. Simply take the linked table offline, take the database on the road with you, and upload any changes to the lists when you return to the office. For example, when visiting customers, it is an easy matter to take the customer database with you on a laptop, make any revisions (for example, adding customer details or creating new orders), return to the office, and synch the database back to the WSS lists. To demonstrate this process using a linked customer list from Northwind, create a new form based on the customer linked list. Open the customer form and notice the status bar information. Figure 10-8 shows the online SharePoint information.

Figure 10-8. *Online with SharePoint status bar indicator*

To take the list offline, click the text Online with SharePoint to open the context menu. Click Work Offline to break the link between your linked list and Access. A dialog box will inform you that the data is being taken offline, and you will need to reopen the customer form, which will now be in offline mode. Changes made to the Access version will not at this point be reflected in the WSS version and vice versa. To try out the process, make some changes to the offline linked list in Access.

To return to online mode, simply click the Offline with SharePoint text on the status bar and click Work Online. To simply synchronize your changes, click Synchronize in the context menu. If you choose to synchronize, you will remain offline, but your data from WSS will be refreshed. You will again have to reopen the customer form to view the changes. Selecting Online will return the live link into the WSS list for the linked table. The context menu also offers you the opportunity to disregard all changes and to refresh the list. In the case of this example, I have had versioning history turned on for the WSS side. This enables me to maintain a history of all changes made to the data on the WSS server, and again this information is also available to me should I need to roll back a particular change.

List Management from Access

Access also provides you with the ability to carry out basic list management on individual linked lists via the GUI. Right-click a linked WSS list and select SharePoint List Options. From the context menu, you can make a selection of the following options on the WSS server:

Open Default View. This opens the linked list on the WSS server. This gives you direct access to the features of WSS. This is an interactive view, and any changes made to the list will be reflected in the linked Access list.

Modify Columns and Settings: This opens the Customize web page for the selected WSS list. From here, you can manage the column settings for the list, and add indexing, version history, and other management features available to you on WSS. If you need to create a custom view of the list (for example, for display as an Access form), you can set this up in this area. One interesting feature with views is the ability to create a new Access application complete with forms and reports for the view. If you need to do this, simply click Create View ➤ Access View. If you are creating a standard view, you will need to create a new link within your current Access application, as linking in this case will not be an automatic process.

Alert Me: This is one of my favorite features in Windows SharePoint Services, as it notifies you if something of interest on a list is added to or changed. This removes the need to constantly check for changes personally via the Web. In the case of alerts, I can have the system monitor the list on my behalf and e-mail me if something is changed. For example, sales staff could be e-mailed when you have updated the Access product table with new pricing, and accounts can be notified once the overdue invoices table is updated. Of course, all of this is automatic once the user subscribes to the alert. A system administrator can subscribe the user as well.

Modify Work Flow: A workflow is basically a set of business processes. For example, you e-mail a document ready for review to your boss, and your boss reviews it and passes it to the next in line. This process would form a simple workflow, each stage of which would be incorporated into WSS. In this simple example, the workflow could simply move the document once approved into your personal WSS document library for further work. We will look at authoring this simple workflow in Chapter 11 when we explore how Access, SharePoint, and SharePoint Designer interrelate.

More complex workflows are created using Visual Studio 2005, but for our purposes SharePoint Designer will meet the requirements. Workflows are defined on the WSS list and not within Access, although from within Access you can carry out basic workflow processes.

Change Permissions for This List: This allows you to set up new permissions for the WSS list. However, this only applies server side and has no impact on the Access database security. The linked list is, however, covered by the security model used on the WSS server.

SharePoint Site Recycle Bin: This gives you access to the WSS recycle bin, which is really useful if you happen to delete a file in error.

Relink Lists: When building a WSS site, it is common to do so on a development server. Relinking the Access lists to the production server is a useful feature in this release. This is a wizard-driven interface that allows you to select one or more lists you have linked to on the development server and relink them to the live production versions.

Refresh List: This allows you to update the current WSS link in your application.

Delete List: This allows you to delete the currently selected list from the WSS server. This does not break the link between Access and WSS; it actually deletes the list from the server, so be careful. From within Access, you have limited management features, and the majority of WSS management tasks will actually take place on the Windows 2003 server on which WSS is running.

Data Conflict Errors

When working in multiuser applications, there is always the possibility of data conflict errors. If such an error occurs, particularly when working offline, the Conflict Resolution dialog box is available. Using this dialog box, you can cancel your changes or try to apply them once more. The dialog box can also be used to see further information about each conflict and take appropriate action.

Reporting

One of the features obviously lacking in WSS is the ability to actually report on the data. You can create complex views via the interface, but there is no built-in reporting tool available. Access provides the perfect environment to permit you to build complex reports against WSS list and list view data. For Access developers, everything works as before in terms of report creation; as for end users, they now have an ad hoc reporting tool that can be used to enhance list data. The ability to cache data within the Access application should provide a solution to some of the issues that have been reported, in terms of performance when using Access as an ad hoc WSS reporting tool.

Summary

There have been many advances in Access 2007 and WSS integration. Personally, I don't see any reason why Access developers cannot make use of both products to further extend the reach of Access databases. Indeed, many Access developers are often asked to make data available via the web browser, and WSS provides the perfect platform to do so. Many organizations are moving into WSS as the product of choice for collaborative work, and it would be unwise to ignore the shift in emphasis placed by Microsoft on this product. Data Access Pages are no longer available, and WSS is a more than worthy replacement. The collaboration features available not only via the Internet, but also from the entire range of Office 2007 applications, make this a compelling piece of software for Access developers and power users to become familiar with.

CHAPTER 11

■ ■ ■

Access, SharePoint, and SharePoint Designer

Microsoft Access 2007 is missing support for two technologies used by developers who want to get data onto the Internet: Active Server Pages (ASP) and Data Access Pages (DAPs). Never being a great fan of DAPs, I will not miss them. When I first started out with Access and the Web, I made great use of the Save As ASP feature in Access to make simple datasets available. In this chapter, we will be looking specifically at what more you can do once you have your Access application on Windows SharePoint Services (WSS) and how you can use the replacement to FrontPage 2003, SharePoint Designer (SPD), to make your data available via the Internet. SPD is designed to work directly with SharePoint and can be used as a design and development tool when communicating with WSS sites. However, you can also use SPD to create standard web pages displaying data from Access 2007. In this chapter, you will learn about both options.

■**Note** In order to use an MDB or ACCDB file with SPD and WSS, it must be located on the front-end web server so that it is visible to the .NET controls.

The interaction between the Access GIU and WSS, while good from a data point of view, is restricted when it comes to building database applications that do not conform to the WSS list-based model. This is where SPD comes in, allowing you to create database sites using both Access and WSS data. In addition, SPD can also be used to bring other data into the web site (for example, XML data, SQL Server data, and other data from multiple sources). This gives you a very powerful tool you can use to combine data from many different sources into a single interface or application available via the web browser. Many of the techniques and .NET objects will be the same as those used when working with Visual Studio Express tools, the main difference being how you interact with them using SPD.

In this chapter, we will look at the features of SPD used to

- Customize a WSS site.

- Create a WSS Workflow.

- Design a Workflow from Access 2007.

It's also important to state that most Access developers are not web developers or design-ers, both of which require a different skill set than they might have. However, the requirement to make your data available via an Internet browser is becoming increasingly popular, particu-larly if we do indeed see a huge takeoff in the use of WSS. It is therefore important to have some understanding of the technology used to work with and extend WSS.

Are other tools available? Of course, one of which is the Visual Web Developer 2005 Express environment also provided by Microsoft, only free of charge (see Chapter 12 for more on this environment). So why use SharePoint Designer? Well, it's a full professional develop-ment environment containing many of the features of Visual Studio 2005. In addition, it is designed to be used with WSS sites and provides a seamless experience when working with such sites.

Note I have stated several times in the last three chapters that SharePoint will be the future of Access, and this is becoming more apparent. A recent blog post by Clint Covington, Access program manager, con-tained a couple of job postings for the Access team that will be working on Office 14. I quote a line from one of the Access team job specifications:

The next version of Access will embrace Web 2.0 technologies, while continuing to build on our push toward ease of use for the consumer and deeper SharePoint integration.

I think that sort of sums up the future of Access and Windows SharePoint as one that is tightly coupled—a future most Access developers cannot ignore.

Getting Started: SharePoint Designer

In the example in this section, you will be working with the Northwind demonstration data-base that has been migrated to WSS. Later, you will create a site from scratch and build some data interfaces. Before getting started, let's have a look at the Data Source Library. In order to keep things simple for the first example, I have created a new copy of Northwind and only upsized the Customers and Orders tables. This is sufficient to demonstrate some of the tech-niques you will be learning.

Data Source Library When Connected to WSS

The Data Source Library allows you to use many different sources of data available within the web site. You can add XML files, Access MDB and ACCDB files, web services, SQL Server files, Oracle files, and of course WSS list data to the library. Once added to the library, the data retrieved by the various library items (connections) is available for use within your web site. This library reflects the real world where data can be held in a number of different systems and formats. The use of the library allows you to bring this data together inside your applications. For the example web site, the first thing you will do is add a connection to the Northwind 2007 demonstration database and a connection to a WSS list. Figure 11-1 shows the existing Data Source Library when the site is first opened.

Figure 11-1. *Data Source Library*

An existing item in the library can be expanded by clicking the plus (+) symbol beside its name; for example, clicking the plus beside SharePoint Lists reveals the initial eight lists available on the server I am using, as you can see in Figure 11-1. Note that the following categories of library items are available to you within the Data Source Library:

- SharePoint lists

- SharePoint libraries

- Database connections

- XML files

- Server-side scripts

- XML web services

- Business data catalog

- Linked sources

As you can see, there is a great deal of flexibility when it comes to working with data, including the availability of all the SharePoint lists and, as you will see, your recently upsized Access database. One of the interesting options available is the linked sources items, which allow you to combine different related data sources into a single view or indeed a linked view on the web page—for example, this feature lets you combine a staff table with a SharePoint

Tasks list. In this way, you could show information from the staff table, which is not held on SharePoint, with information for the Tasks list, which is held on SharePoint. We will return to linked sources later in the chapter.

Creating a Data View Web Part

To begin the process of working with data and SPD, you will create a special set of Web Parts for the Customers and Orders lists that have been upsized from Northwind 2007 to a Microsoft Office SharePoint Server (MOSS) 2007 site. In this web page, you will display a list of customers. When a customer name is clicked, you will open a corresponding listing of customer records on the page. There is one main issue you need to consider, however: once you move the data to WSS, you lose the relationships you created in Access, and you also lose the ability to enforce the relationships on WSS. However, for this example, remember you will have migrated the primary key of the Customers table and the corresponding foreign key in the Orders table and can therefore make use of this feature when you create the .NET page as part of the next example. In order to follow this example, you will need to be logged in to a WSS site and have a migrated copy of the Northwind 2007 Customers and Orders tables available. To begin, follow these steps:

1. From the main menu, select File ➤ New.

2. On the New dialog box's Page tab, select General, select ASPX as the file type, and specify VB as the programming language.

3. Click OK to close the New dialog box, leaving you in the new ASPX web form page.

4. From the main menu, select Data View ➤ Insert Data View to insert a placeholder for the data into the blank ASPX page you have just created.

It's worth looking at the code behind the page before and after this insertion. Before you insert the Data View control, the HTML in the ASPX file is shown in Listing 11-1.

Listing 11-1. *HTML Before Inserting Data View Control*

```
<%@ Page Language="VB" %>
<html dir="ltr">

<head runat="server">
<meta http-equiv="Content-Type" content="text/html; charset=utf-8">
<title>Untitled 1</title>
<meta name="Microsoft Theme" content="Belltown 1011, default">
</head>

<body>

<form id="form1" runat="server">
</form>

</body>

</html>
```

Listing 11-2 shows the same fragment once you have inserted the Data View control. The new code has been highlighted in Listing 11-2 for clarity.

Listing 11-2. *After Inserting a Data View*

```
<%@ Page Language="VB" inherits="Microsoft.SharePoint.WebPartPages.WebPartPage, ➡
Microsoft.SharePoint, Version=12.0.0.0, Culture=neutral, PublicKeyToken=➡
71e9bce111e9429c" %>
<%@ Register tagprefix="WebPartPages" namespace="Microsoft.SharePoint.➡
WebPartPages" assembly="Microsoft.SharePoint, Version=12.0.0.0, ➡
Culture=neutral, PublicKeyToken=71e9bce111e9429c" %>
<html dir="ltr">
<head runat="server">
<meta name="ProgId" content="SharePoint.WebPartPage.Document">
<meta name="WebPartPageExpansion" content="full">
<meta http-equiv="Content-Type" content="text/html; charset=utf-8">
<title>Untitled 1</title>
<meta name="Microsoft Theme" content="Belltown 1011, default">
</head>

<body>

<form id="form1" runat="server">
<WebPartPages:DataFormWebPart runat="server" IsIncluded="True" FrameType="None" ➡
NoDefaultStyle="TRUE" ViewFlag="0" Title="DataView 1" __markuptype=➡
"vsattributemarkup" __WebPartId="{E51F2A8C-1FFE-4DE5-8634-1028DE9F9E72}" ➡
id="g_e51f2a8c_1ffe_4de5_8634_1028de9f9e72">
<DataSources>

</DataSources>

<datafields/>
        <XSL>
</XSL>
</WebPartPages:DataFormWebPart>
</form>

</body>
</html>
```

■**Note** The Data View Web Part is a special Web Part that acts as a client to the data retrieval service, as it can retrieve and manipulate data from any data source supported by data retrieval services. The data retrieval service is a web service, thus it returns data in the form of XML. The Data View uses Extensible Stylesheet Language Transformations (XSLT) on this XML to format the data.

What you are doing here is inserting a Web Part, a component that you can reuse within your web site. If you have been playing with WSS, you will see that there are many Web Parts available to you, and you can also create your own. Later in this chapter, you will in fact be creating a simple Web Part for reuse on a WSS site. For more information on Web Parts, please see the "Web Parts and Workflow" section later in this chapter.

To continue with this example, hover the mouse over the Customers list in the Data Source Library, click the drop-down list arrow, and select Show Data to view the data within the WSS Customers list. Notice that the tab title changes to Data Source Details. To drag a field onto the ASPX page, hold down Ctrl and drag the Company and ID fields onto the Data View region. Once the mouse is released, the data should be immediately available on the screen

If you return to the code view of your page, you should see a huge difference in the code generated by SPD. Reading the code, you may now begin to see that you are using XML to display the data from the Customers list on WSS. This is one of the things that make this approach so popular. You can take any XML-based data and create objects like this within your WSS site (for example, Oracle or SQL Server XML exports). Figure 11-2 shows the SDP at this point.

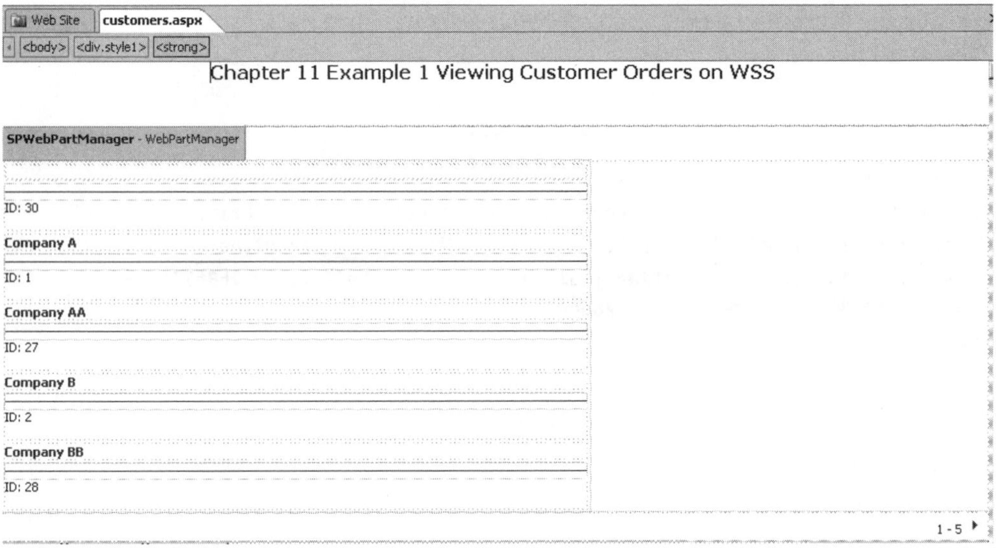

Figure 11-2. *Displaying the customer data*

Next you need to add another Data View control to the page, this time displaying data from the Orders list. Follow the procedure outlined previously to add this control, only this time choose the following fields from the Orders list: Order Date, Shipped Date, Shipped Address, Shipped City, and CustomerID. Add the fields to the Orders Data View control.

At the moment, you have two totally unconnected Data View controls on the page. The next step is to create the relationship between the parts. In fact, what you will do is pass a filter to the Orders Data View based on the currently selected customer's name in the Customer Data View. To continue:

1. Within the Customer Data View, select the customer name.

2. Right-click and select Web Part Connections.

   Web Part connections allow you to pass values between different Web Parts to build and interact with Data Views on the web page.

3. Accept the default, Send Row of Data To.

4. Click Next.

5. Accept the default, Connect to a Web Part on This Page.

6. Click Next.

7. Accept the default target Web Part, in this case, Orders, and the default target action, Get Filter Values From.

8. Click Next

9. The next screen allows you to select those data items that you want to use to create a relationship between the Web Parts. Scroll down the Inputs to Orders column until you reach CustomerID.

10. Click in the cell in the Customers column directly opposite CustomerID.

11. Select Company from the drop-down list within the cell.

12. Click Next.

13. Accept the default, Create a Hyperlink on Company, in the next screen.

14. Click Next.

15. Click Finish.

This completes the setup of the connection between the Customers Web Part and the Orders Web Part for the moment. You will return to the connection shortly. To continue:

16. Save the file as Customers.aspx on the WSS site.

17. From the File menu, choose File Preview in Browser and then select the browser you would like to use from the list. Figure 11-3 shows the resulting page previewed in IE 7. You may be required to log in to the WSS site at this point.

Try out the Web Parts by clicking a customer's name to view the associated order information. This could be a useful technique when data (for example, contact information) is stored within a WSS list and the customer information is held in another system, which could be an Oracle, SQL Server, or indeed Access system.

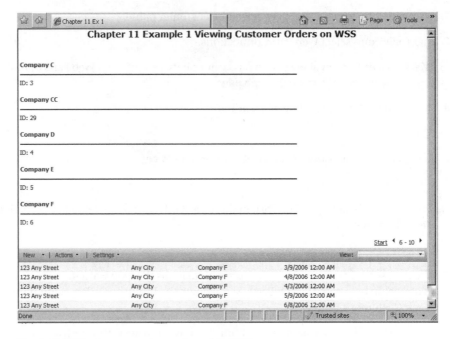

Figure 11-3. *Customers.aspx previewed in IE 7*

Formatting the Data View Web Part

Up to this point, you have two plain Data Views. However, using SPD, you customize the Web Parts to improve the overall look and feel and to deal with those situations when the Web Part does not return data. In order to work with the formatting options, follow these steps:

1. Select the Customers Data View.

2. Click the small right arrow located at the upper-right corner of the Web Part to open the Common Data View Tasks list.

3. From the list, click Change layout.

4. In the Data View Properties dialog box, under HTML view styles on the Layout tab, select the style that you want.

■**Tip** Click a view style to read a brief description of it. If you select and apply a layout that displays fewer fields than your original Data View, those fields are removed from your Data View. For example, if you create a Data View that displays four fields, and then you apply a layout that displays one of those fields, the other three fields are removed from your Data View. If you change the layout, any custom formatting or provider Web Part connections are removed.

---

5. Click OK.

One of the problems you will face at this point (and in fact the reason why I have presented this exercise in this order) is that once you change the style of the Customers Web Part, you will lose the Web Part connection, which is not what you want. The general idea is that, when using SPD and Web Part connections, you will want to format the style for your Web Parts before creating any connections. However, this is a minor issue, as all you need do in this case is select the Orders Web Part, right-click, and step through the Web Parts connections process again to re-create the connection for your Customers Web Part.

Setting Data View Properties

If you are familiar with WSS Web Parts, you may have noticed that the Customers and Orders Web Parts do not have the usual WSS drop-down list options. However, using the properties of the Data View, you can add these menu items to the Web Parts. Remember, you want the Web Parts you create to behave as the default Web Parts supplied with WSS. To add the WSS menu items to the Orders Web Part, follow these steps:

1. Open the Data View Properties dialog box.

2. On the General tab, select SharePoint List Toolbar.

3. Go to the Show toolbar with check box options for filter, sort, and group and enable all three items. Grouping is a nice feature and will create a tree view–type grouping structure within the Data View, which can be expanded to view data items within the group.

4. Save the changes and preview the results in your browser. Figure 11-4 shows the results of the changes you have made.

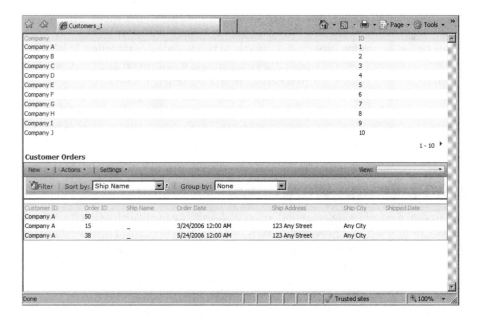

Figure 11-4. *Data View in the initial format*

The following WSS menu items will be fully functional. This will allow your user to work with the Web Parts using standard WSS features (for example, the ability to minimize the Web Part).

- Add a new item to the Orders WSS list

- Export to a spreadsheet

- Open in Access

- Set up to use with RSS

- Set up e-mail alerts for changes to the order data

- Create views of the order data

- Sort and group the data

- Apply filters to the order data

There are additional properties you can set for the Data View. On the General tab, you can choose Header and Footer – View, or Display text if no matching records are found to allow you to add your own message such as "Data is not found here." On the Layout tab, choose a layout for the Data View Web Part. On the Source tab, define and link to your own XSLT style sheet, which you can then apply to the Data View. On the Paging tab, set the paging options for the Data View. On the Editing tab, set the options for editing if you would like the user to be able to change or delete items in the Data View via this Web Part.

The Web Part itself has another set of properties that duplicate those you will see on all Web Parts on a WSS page. To view the properties, right-click the Orders Web Part and select Web Part Properties. Within the Web Part Properties dialog box, you can edit the XSL files and set other properties that affect how the Web Part behaves once inside WSS.

One of the interesting properties available to you is audience targeting. In WSS, you can create an audience of users to whom this Web Part is available or targeted at. Only the users within the audience will see the Web Part on WSS. The audience is created from the group of your Active Directory users. For example, your Customers and Orders Web Parts may only be available to staff in the Order department or sales staff. Using the audience option allows you to restrict the Web Parts to only those staff who need to see it by simply making it available to an Active Directory or SharePoint user group of that staff.

Web Parts and Workflows

Web Parts are the technology that underpins WSS and provides much of the functionality on the WSS site. As described previously, a Web Part is a discrete block of functionality that can be reused. For example, a Web Part is available that can be configured to display your Microsoft Exchange inbox or calendar. This Web Part can be placed on any number of WSS ASPX pages, though it is commonly placed on the MySite personalization site. Web Parts can also be used to expose data to the end user, and like most other Web Parts on WSS, it can target a specific user or group of users. In the previous example, you created two Web Parts embedded within a Customers.aspx page used to display customer records.

Workflows allow you to create structured processes that follow a set of business rules, for example, routing a document for approval before publication. In the following text, we take a look at how Workflows and Web Parts work together.

Linked Lists and Workflows

From the Access 2007 side, as you have seen, you can also link to WSS lists from a database application. This is not limited to a single WSS site, but you could if required link into listings from several sites. The great thing about this is the option to take the Access application offline, work on the data, and then synch the changes back to the WSS list concerned.

This next example features a MOSS site called Training Admin; on the site is a Tasks list to which you assign specific tasks to members of staff. The Staff table is stored on a small Access personnel database as opposed to the WSS site. Even though each person's tasks are visible on WSS, the staff requests the option to work with the Tasks list in offline mode. The obvious answer to this is to link to the MOSS list from Access 2007 and permit staff to take the data offline for updating.

On the WSS site it is possible to assign more than one member of staff to a particular task, and this fits in with the new multivalue fields capability in Access 2007. Integration with the WSS data types and list features is where the new feature set in Access comes into play. For the user, the experience is seamless. From the SPD side, you also have another toolbox option available to allow you to build a Workflow on a particular WSS list.

Creating a WSS Workflow Using SPD and Access

In order to use Workflows with WSS, you will need to download and install .NET Framework 3.0. However, it is highly likely that this is already available on the server running WSS, as it is embedded within the SharePoint software.

A Workflow can be something as simple as routing a document from a WSS list through an approval process to something completely customized to your organization's business process. As this is a WSS process, it will also be triggered from Access 2007 when you are linking to a WSS list or object. You can author Workflows directly using SPD or code them using Visual Studio 2005. There are major differences in the Workflows designed by each of these software tools, however; for example, VS 2005 Workflows can contain your own code using code-behind files, whereas SPD Workflows cannot. With SPD, you create a Workflow for a single WSS list; however, a VS 2005 Workflow can be used with many different lists. One of the other major differences is that VS 2005 workflows can be modified by the user at run-time, while those created using SPD cannot be modified by the user and will execute until completion.

In the example that follows, you will be using SPD to create a Workflow that will route a document through a checking process. Workflows, even out-of-the-box stuff that can be designed using SPD, are very powerful tools that allow you to specify how a process is managed and additional information collected for the user during the process. In this Workflow example, you will set up an authorization to approve a purchase requisition. One of the conditions is that only a purchase order with a value in excess of $200 needs to be approved. The idea here is to demonstrate the process and features of the Workflow designer tools, and you can then apply the process to other more complex Workflows.

To get started, follow these steps:

1. Log in to a WSS site using SPD.

■**Note** From the WSS side, the Purchase Order list (which I have created on my WSS server for this example) has also had document versioning turned on. This also enables a history or log of changes to individual documents to be maintained by the WSS server.

---

2. From the main menu, select File ➤ New.

3. Click the SharePoint Content tab.

4. Select Workflow.

5. Click OK.

6. Enter a name for the Workflow (in my case, I entered CustomerWF).

7. Select a list you want the Workflow to be attached to. I selected Purchase Orders, a WSS list created for this purpose.

8. You can then choose from three selections as follows:

   - Allow this Workflow to be manually started from an item

   - Automatically start this Workflow when a new item is created

   - Automatically start this Workflow when an item is changed

   In my case I have left the selection with the default value, Automatically start this Workflow when a new item is created.

Before proceeding, we should also look at the command button options on this screen. The following two options are available to you:

Check Workflow: You can click this button at any point in the process to have SPD check the Workflow for errors.

Initiation: This one will open a dialog box that permits you to create a .NET form, which will be available to the user as soon as the Workflow begins. For example, in the case of a user entering a company name to the list, you could open the .NET form and allow the user to enter any special comments he or she might have.

To return to the example, click Next. In the next screen, you can begin to create the conditions for the Workflow. Here you can create a simple Workflow; for example, you can e-mail an administrator or use branching logic to route a document through an approval process. For this Workflow, you want to enforce a couple of rules for the purchase order:

- All purchase orders with a value over $200 must be approved.

- Each purchase order approver will receive an e-mail notifying him or her of the request, and a task will be added to WSS directed at each approver.

Let's create the condition:

1. Click the Conditions button and select Compare PurchaseOrder field.

2. Click the first hyperlink in the word field and select Total Amount from the drop-down list.

3. Click the default equal hyperlink and select Greater Than from the list.

4. Click the second hyperlink and enter 200 as the value. The screen should now show the following text as the condition: If Total Amount is greater than 200.

Note You can build a very sophisticated AND/OR condition by clicking the condition again and building up your statements.

---

5. Next click the Actions button and choose Send an Email.

6. Click the hyperlink text "This message," and complete the e-mail screen with a valid e-mail address and message.

Note The address book is to the right of the To text box. This allows you to look up site users or site groups.

At this point, the screen should look as shown in Figure 11-5, with the Actions step containing the following text:

Assign Purchase Order to USERNAME

Then Email USERAME

7. Click Finish.

Any errors in the Workflow will be flagged using yellow exclamation marks beside the step containing the errors. You can correct the errors and continue to complete the Workflow design. Test out this first stage in the Workflow and ensure it is working (that is, check that you get an e-mail if a purchase order meeting the conditions is added to the list via Access 2007 or directly in WSS) before continuing with adding additional functionality to the Workflow.

At this point, when the user enters a new purchase order with a value greater than $200, the nominated user will receive an e-mail asking him or her to go to the WSS list and approve the item. At the same time, the purchase order will be added to the specific Tasks list for the user specified in the action step.

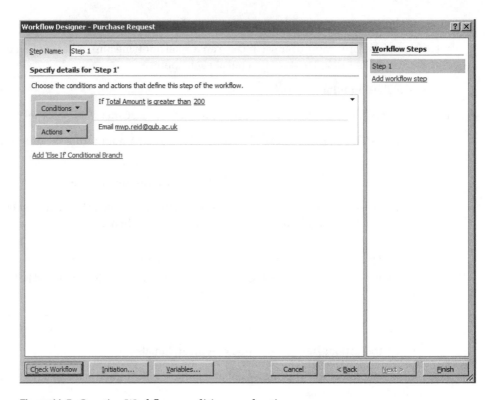

Figure 11-5. *Creating Workflow conditions and actions*

Within SPD, a new folder containing the Workflow code and any forms defined for the process will be created within the WSS site structure. In order to edit the Workflow, you need to double-click the Workflow file with the .xoml extension. To view the files associated with the Workflow, follow these steps:

1. Expand the Workflow folder.

2. Select and expand the folder named as your Workflow.

3. Double-click the XMOL file to reopen the Workflow designer.

Once you have created the basic Workflow, you can edit it using the designer to add additional steps. For example, you could add an action that deals with purchase orders over $500, routing them to a more senior member of staff for approval, or indeed you could have the purchase order immediately rejected using the Workflow.

From the Access 2007 side, you can also interact with Workflows set for specific lists. For example, you could right-click over the linked Purchase Order list in Access and select Share-Point List Options ➤ Modify Workflow. This will take you to the Workflow screen in Windows SharePoint Server. However, you cannot modify a Workflow created in SPD using WSS directly. The Workflow must be amended using SPD. What you can do from the Access interface is create a Workflow. For example, if you right-click the Purchase Order list and select Modify

Workflow, you will be taken to WSS with a Change Workflow Settings screen. From this screen, you can add Workflows to a list, but you are restricted to those defined by WSS, which aren't as flexible as the Workflows you can author yourself. Within WSS, you can define four out-of-the-box Workflow options:

Approval: Routes a document for approval to a member or members of the WSS site. Assigns the approval to a WSS Tasks list for the users concerned. Records details of the actions taken into a Workflow history list. The approval Workflow does contain some flexibility; for example, a user involved in the process can be given permission to reroute the document if required to another user for approval.

Collect feedback: Routes a document for approval and permits users to provide feedback.

Collect signatures: This Workflow cannot be started within WSS and must be started from an Office application.

Disposition approval: Allows users to decide when a document expires from the site.

At this point, it has to be said that the real power of SharePoint Workflows lies in .NET and Visual Studio 2005, where very complex Workflows can be authored using any of the .NET languages. This topic is well outside the scope of this chapter, but if you are seriously interested in Workflows, this is a topic you should investigate further. Workflows provide excellent functionality, and SPD allows you to create sophisticated Workflows without too much effort. WSS itself also permits Workflow creation without too much effort. Of course, you could duplicate this functionality directly via Access and VBA, but the Workflow (even one as basic as that shown) is created with no programming and provides the user with an interactive experience. Even if you excluded the e-mails, users would still be informed that a task was outstanding via their SharePoint Tasks list. Also note that the Workflow function is available in other Office 2007 applications; for example, a document approval Workflow is available from Word 2007 when you are using SharePoint as your document store. This Workflow will route a document to different staff members for approval and edit.

In addition to creating and designing Workflows, SPD also allows you to create objects on the SharePoint site and to design existing layouts and other objects. From the SPD design interface, you can create new WSS lists, libraries, and surveys. In terms of working with the style of your SharePoint site, one of the main design tools at your disposal is the .NET master page. Think of a master page as the design template for your web site and any subsites it contains. Design and structure in the master page will be replicated on any page it is associated with using the master page directive. In terms of presentation of your page and its content, Cascading Style Sheets (CSS) are used. Now you may not have a great deal of experience when it comes to working with master pages and CSS and web design in general. Master pages are one of those things you will need to at least understand in order to begin the process of site customization. The "Master Pages" sidebar provides a high-level introduction to the concept of .NET master pages. If you are already familiar with .NET 2.0 master pages, you will find little difference when it comes to working with master pages in SharePoint.

MASTER PAGES

A master page looks after the structure and layout of your web page and will typically contain content place-holders. Master pages are merged with the content at runtime. You can view the SharePoint master pages by expanding the Catalogs folder and the Master Page subfolder. In the subfolder, you will find the default master page, default.master. Figure 11-6 shows the default master page for a site I am working on.

Figure 11-6. *default.master page in SPD*

The only safe way to work with the default master page is to make a copy of it. Do not mess with the original copy unless you really know what you are doing. You can use the copy to try out the various editing features when working with master pages. To view an associated CSS style for an item on a master page, simply click the item; the style will be highlighted in the Apply Styles pane within SPD. SPD Help contains a brief introduction to master pages, and more information is available by performing a quick web search on the subject.

Summary

In this admittedly brief overview of SPD, Access, and SharePoint, I have touched on the major areas for further investigation: Web Parts, master pages, and .NET. All of these areas will see increased focus from Microsoft in future releases of Office including Access, and it is perhaps time for many Access developers like myself to begin making moves into these areas. Share-Point will figure highly in my own future work, as I have a great deal of faith in its ability to solve business process problems. However, this does not exclude Access and the power we all know Access has to build the best desktop applications in the world.

CHAPTER 12

■■■

Getting Started with .NET Tools

Many Access developers and power users occasionally need to use Microsoft Access data without actually using Access as the front end. For example, you may have a requirement to make data available on the Internet or for a web-based data collection form. Often, the time you have to complete such small-scale applications is usually short, while the learning curve required to develop them could be long, given the languages and development environments involved.

The Microsoft Express set of free software applications can be used to meet your needs for small one-off projects without requiring you to learn languages such as VB .NET, ASP, or formal VB to any great depth. Express Editions are advertised by Microsoft as tools for the student or hobby programmer, but this is misleading. Many Access developers work within tight budgets and cannot afford products such as Visual Studio 2005. The Express Editions offer a way around these budget limits, as all of the software is free, albeit somewhat restricted. For example, Express Editions offer only a single-language development environment, usually either Visual Basic or C#. However, it's been my experience that many developers work in a single language anyway and have no requirement for a multilanguage-capable tool.

In this chapter, we will look at using some of the Microsoft Express Editions to solve simple data projects using Access 2007. The examples outlined in this chapter are real-world basic data problems I have been requested to solve. None of the applications can be classified as "rocket science." They provided solutions to basic data requirements that covered specific business requirements.

Several Express Editions of the software are available, and we will be using two of them in this chapter: Visual Web Developer 2005 Express (Web Dev Express) and Visual Basic 2005 Express (VB Express). Microsoft has also provided a huge resource of learning materials available at `http://msdn.microsoft.com/vstudio/express/vb/` for each of the Express Editions. This resource should be your first port of call for anything related to these tools. Another resource I have used for many years is `http://4guysfromrolla.com`, one of the oldest sites, and in my view the best, on ASP and now ASP.NET development on the Web. Microsoft also provides starter kits to get you up and running in each development environment with sample applications.

EXPRESS STARTER KITS

Microsoft provides prebuilt development kits for both Web Dev Express and VS Express that get you up and running with each of the development environments. Starter kits are a great learning tool, particularly for those who have never worked in the language or indeed interface before, and it is well worth your time to see what kits are provided, read the documentation, and download the extra kits available online at `http://msdn2.microsoft.com/en-us/vstudio/aa718342.aspx`.

   VB Express comes with two starter kits, with additional kits available for download. (Most kits are available in either VB or C#.) For database developers, the My Movie Starter Kit is the more useful of the two, as this application interacts with an SQL Server database file. The other starter kit is the Screen Saver Starter Kit. You can access these starter kits by selecting File ➤ New Project.

   Several starter kits are also available for Web Dev Express, and again it is worthwhile downloading them and trying them out. The Time Tracker application would be a useful place to start for many Access developers.

Creating Web Applications with Visual Web Developer 2005 Express

Visual Web Developer 2005 Express is a cut-down .NET developer's environment that is provided for free by Microsoft. You can download a copy from the Microsoft Express web site at `http://msdn.microsoft.com/vstudio/express/vwd/`. Notice that there is a Reporting Services add-in also available on the download page. It really is worthwhile to download this application if you are considering moving into some form of web development environment. It can be used to build basic web applications and even fairly complex SQL Server 2005-driven web applications.

Creating a Basic Web Application in Web Dev Express

First we'll look at a simple application that makes data available on the Web for training sessions and other events. This application was requested by the people in my unit. I was required to take existing data, build a small Access back-end database, and make the information available online. The only other side issue was that it had to be dynamically displayed on a large LCD screen. Visitors to the building would then see a listing of training and other events to be held that day, and another scrolling page showing events due to take place the next day. The data was stored in a MySQL database on a UNIX box. So rather than try to learn PHP fairly quickly, I opted to write the system using Web Dev Express. The Access database eventually consisted of three tables: a table for events (tblEvent) and two lookup tables (tblEventCategory and tblLocations). As I said earlier, this was nothing complex, just a basic data requirement that had to be met, but it proves useful here to illustrate the features of the software.

Running Web Dev Express

Upon starting Web Dev Express, you will see the very professional interface to this software. If judged purely on the interface, it's hard to see the difference between this edition and a professional development environment. Figure 12-1 shows the initial screen for the administrative interface.

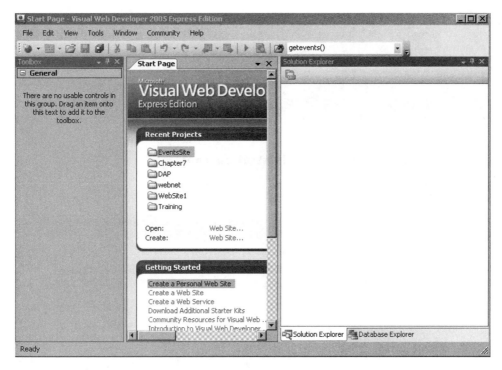

Figure 12-1. *Web Dev Express interface*

As shown in Figure 12-1, the main working area of the screen is divided into a toolbox, a work area, and Solution and Object Explorers. As you work over a project, other windows become available (for example, error listings and a Properties Explorer).

Jumping right in, the first thing you need to do is to create a new project. Click File ➤ New Web Site and select ASP.NET Web Site from the dialog box. Either accept or change the default project location and click OK. You will arrive in the new project window containing a blank default.aspx page. In the Solution Explorer, you should see some new items: App_Data, which is a new folder, and Web.Config.

Web.Config is an XML file that is vital to the operation of your web application. It contains information on authentication, error handling, and other configuration options for the application. It is generated automatically by the software when you create a new web project. It can be edited by hand, but if this is your first time out, you should consider using the web interface for this file, available by selecting Web Site ➤ ASP.NET Configuration from the main menu. Figure 12-2 shows the web-based interface used to manage the Web.Config file for this project. In this case, I have the Home tab selected, which presents the main menu system for this application. This administration tool is available by selecting Application Configuration on the Web Site Administration Tool dialog box. As you try out these examples, check back with the Web.Config file, as this is where you will be placing the connection strings for the database.

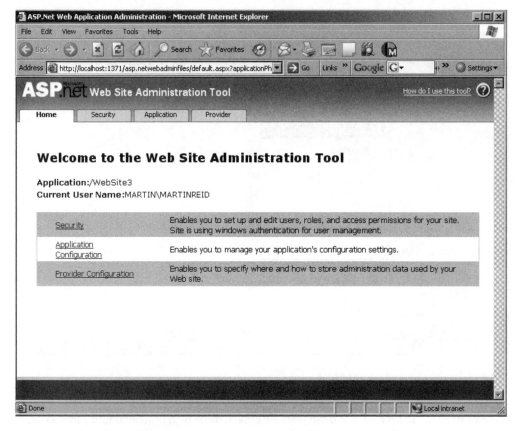

Figure 12-2. *Web.Config management using the Web Site Administration Tool*

You now need to add a database connection to the project. Web Dev Express provides several connectors for you to use as follows:

- `ObjectDataSource`, for connecting to a middle tier object that can return data

- `SqlDataSource`, for working with SQL Server, Oracle, or other .NET managed providers including OLEDB and ODBC

- `AccessDataSource`, for working with Access databases

- `XMLDataSource`, for working with XML files

- `SiteMapDataSource`, for working with .NET site maps

■**Note** It is worth pointing out that this software almost always defaults to SQL Server when adding data connections. Here, you will be using Access, but the process is more or less the same when working with SQL Server. Of course, your connection string will be different. Personally, I have noticed no difference when using either `SqlDataSource` or `AccessDataSource` when creating a connection to Access, and I simply treat them as the same connection object.

To add a connection to a project, follow these steps:

1. Click Tools on the main menu.

2. Select Connect to Database.

3. At the Data Source drop-down list, click the Change button.

4. Select <other>.

5. Select .NET Framework Provider for OLEDB.

■**Caution** Do not select Access if you are using the new Access database file type (ACCDB). In order to connect to the new file type, you need to select the Microsoft Office 12 Access Database Engine OLEDB Provider.

---

6. Click OK.

7. Select Microsoft Office 12 Access Database Engine OLEDB Provider from the OLEDB provider drop-down list.

8. Navigate to the Access database file required and select it.

9. Click OK.

The database will be added to the Database Explorer. Using its tree view, you can navigate the database objects, tables, views, stored procedures, and functions. As you may now see, all are fairly specific SQL Server objects, even though you are using an MDB file.

Creating Data Grids with ASP.NET

ASP.NET allows you to build highly interactive web applications using a common set of tools and languages. Any of the supported languages—VB, C#, or J#—may be used. In this sample application, you are interested in using this technology to get some data from a database and make it available via the browser. ASP.NET will allow you to do this by using the graphical tool set to add server objects to the web page. In order to display data on the page, you can use built-in .NET objects (controls) that will "hold" and display the data, allowing a user to navigate, add, delete, and edit records. All of these features are available out of the box, and as is often the case, if you need advanced or additional functionality, you do need to code it yourself. The easiest way to get data to the page is to simply drag a table or query from the Database Explorer into the document window.

■**Note** For the example that follows, you will need a new project and a connection to the Events database. Detailed instructions follow in the "Getting More Interactive" section of this chapter. For now, I just want to give you an overview of the process and the features of the software.

This will create a fully functional data grid on the page. Once on the page, you can set the properties of the grid using a GridView Tasks menu. Figure 12-3 shows the default grid with the GridView Tasks menu showing.

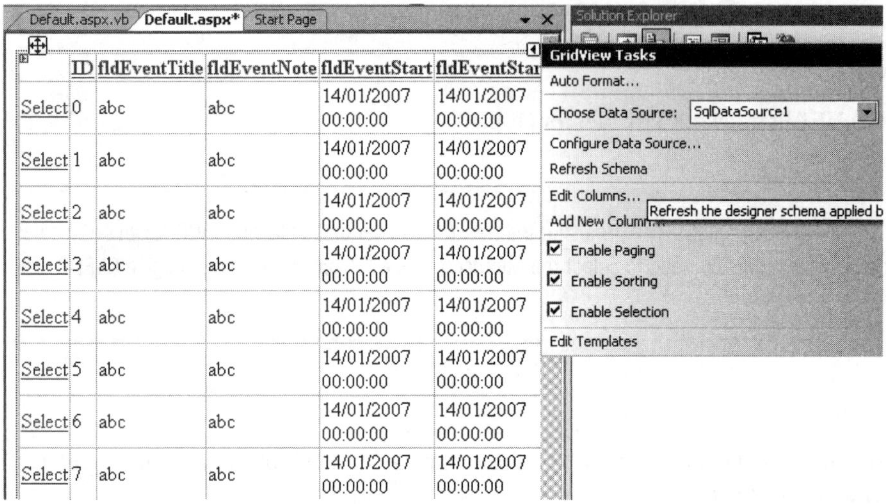

Figure 12-3. *Data grid and GridView Tasks menu*

Using the menu, you can enable the following features depending on the requirements:

* *Enable Paging*: Allows you to display restricted groupings of records—for example, 10 records at a time out of a possible 100 available. The user can then click a button or link to view the next set of 10 records. This is very useful when you have a large recordset to display.

* *Enable Sorting*: Sorts the recordset using a hyperlink within the header of the form. Useful for recordsets containing dates or times.

* *Enable Editing*: Allows the user to edit the records being displayed.

* *Enable Deleting*: Permits the user to delete a record or records from those displayed.

* *Enable Selection*: Permits selection of the data item when clicked.

Enabling each feature will add the appropriate hyperlink to the grid.

There are many other data-centric controls that you can add to the page from the Data section of the toolbox as follows:

* DataView

* DataList

* DetailsView

* FormView

* Repeater

The data grid can also be customized using the built-in features of the control and the GridView Tasks Smart Tag. To customize a data grid:

1. Right-click and select Show Smart Tag.

2. Click AutoFormat.

This will open the AutoFormat Smart Tag from which you can select one of many prebuilt designs. Column headers can also be changed from the field names used by default. To change column headers, click Edit Columns in the Smart Tag. In the Selected fields section of the screen, simply click a field name to select it. In the BoundField properties area, click in the HeaderText property and change the text. Figure 12-4 shows the Fields dialog box.

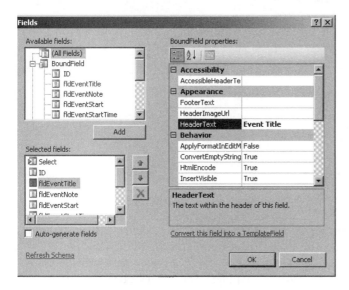

Figure 12-4. *Changing a field header in the Fields dialog box*

Once you have selected a format for the grid and changed the field names, you can then save the page and preview it in a web browser. Figure 12-5 shows the Events table in a browser. In this case, I have applied some basic formatting to the control. Note that in the first record, the Edit link has been clicked. The data can now be edited. What was once static text has been "converted" on the fly into an interactive text box that permits editing of the data once the user clicks the Edit hyperlink.

You can also review the code produced by the editor by looking at the source of the page. Listing 12-1 shows a partial block of code produced by the interface for the data grid. It is interesting to look at the placeholder question marks created by the development environment and the number of lines generated and compare this code with the code you will create manually (shown later in this chapter in Listings 12-4 and 12-5).

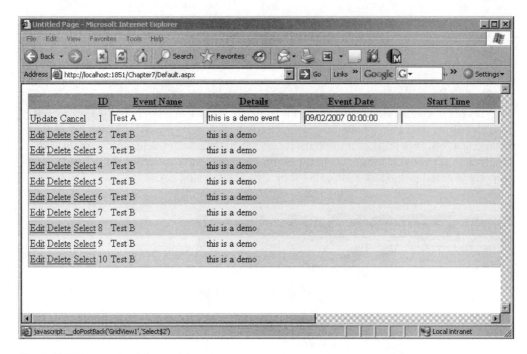

Figure 12-5. *Customized data grid*

Listing 12-1. *Data Grid Code*

```
<asp:GridView ID="GridView1" runat="server" AllowPaging="True" AllowSorting="True"
AutoGenerateColumns="False" BackColor="LightGoldenrodYellow" BorderColor="Tan"
BorderWidth="1px" CellPadding="2" DataKeyNames="ID" DataSourceID="AccessDataSource1"
EmptyDataText="There are no data records to display." ForeColor="Black" ➥
GridLines="None"
 Height="279px" Width="770px">
<FooterStyle BackColor="Tan" />
<Columns>
 <asp:AccessDataSource ID="AccessDataSource1" runat="server" ➥
DataFile="C:\AccessBook\Chapter7\Events.mdb"
DeleteCommand="DELETE FROM `tblEvent` WHERE `ID` = ?" ➥
InsertCommand="INSERT INTO `tblEvent` (`ID`, `fldEventTitle`, ➥
`fldEventNote`, `fldEventStart`, `fldEventStartTime`, `fldEventEndTime`, ➥
`fldEventLocation`, `fldEventCategory`) VALUES (?, ?, ?, ?, ?, ?, ?, ?)"
SelectCommand="SELECT `ID`, `fldEventTitle`, `fldEventNote`, `fldEventStart`, ➥
`fldEventStartTime`, `fldEventEndTime`, `fldEventLocation`, `fldEventCategory` ➥
FROM `tblEvent`"
 UpdateCommand="UPDATE `tblEvent` SET `fldEventTitle` = ?, `fldEventNote` = ?, ➥
`fldEventStart` = ?, `fldEventStartTime` = ?, `fldEventEndTime` = ?, ➥
`fldEventLocation` = ?, `fldEventCategory` = ? WHERE `ID` = ?">
```

> **■Note** I have removed the central block of generated code to save space.

Like most wizard-generated code, you can see the choices made during the design process—for example, `AllowPaging="True" AllowSorting="True"`.

You can also see the set of commands required to allow you to delete, select, and update records within the grid, which you'll recognize as your basic SQL statements required for this purpose.

Creating the What's On Web Site

For this example, you will be using an Access 2007 database containing a single query. As stated previously, the database contains three tables, named and structured as follows:

tblEvent:

ID, primary key, AutoNumber

fldEventTitle, text

fldEventNote, memo

fldEventStart, Date/Time

fldEventStartTime, text

fldEventEndtime, Date/Time

flsEventLocation, lookup to tblLocation

fldEventCategory, lookup to tblCategory

tblLocation:

ID, primary key, AutoNumber

fldLocation, text

tblEventCategory:

ID, primary key, AutoNumber

fldCategory, text

> **■Note** For speed, you will use tblLocation and tblEventCategory as lookups to the main table.

You can create and save the database anywhere on the PC, as you will copy it into your new web project environment once created. To get started, follow the instructions earlier to create a new web site in Web Dev Express. Once created, you will add your database to the application. To add the database, right-click the App_Data folder in the Solution Explorer and select Add Existing Item. Using the Add Existing dialog box, navigate to the database file and add it to the project. You can use the App_Data folder to save any data or information required by your project (for example, XML or image files). However, now that you have done this, realize that it is virtually useless because Web Dev Express does not support the new Access file type in this manner. You cannot even simply drag an AccessDataSource onto the page and configure it if you are using the new file type. In the normal course of things, this is the preferred approach to working with the database: place it in the App_Data folder.

If you would like to view the structure of the database, add it to the Database Explorer. To add the connection, click the Database Explorer, right-click Data Connections, and select Add Connection. Remember to change the connection type to <other> and choose the Microsoft Office 12 Access Database Engine OLEDB Provider for this connection. Once you have created a valid connection, you can use the Database Explorer to examine and review the structure of the database. Figure 12-6 shows the Database Explorer for this project with the Events database expanded.

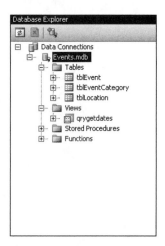

Figure 12-6. *Current Database Explorer view for this project*

Now back to the problem at hand. This is simply a list of events taking place today and another list of events taking place tomorrow. A query would solve the data problem and has been created directly within Access. However, Web Dev Express also permits you to create queries directly via its interface, which does save a little time. The Query Designer is almost identical to that in SQL Server Express, so it should be familiar to many developers and power users. To create a query, follow these steps:

1. Right-click anywhere within the Database Explorer and select New Query.

2. Select a table (in the case of this example, Events) from the Add Table dialog box.

3. Click Close.

Accessing Data Using Queries

You may find that the SQL statement in the Query Designer is not what you expect when it first opens. For example, the query type available to you when you first open the Query Designer may default to a DELETE query. To change the query type on the main menu, follow these steps:

1. Click Query Designer.

2. Select Change Type.

3. Choose the appropriate query type from the submenu.

The query I required was very basic. I just needed to select those events taking place today. Listing 12-2 shows the SQL statement required in this case within the Access database. I have saved this as qryTodaysEvents.

Listing 12-2. *SQL Statement*

```
SELECT     fldEventTitle, fldEventNote, fldEventStart,
fldEventStartTime, fldEventEndTime, fldEventLocation, fldEventCategory
FROM        tblEvent
WHERE      (fldEventStart = NOW())
```

■**Note** Always select the fields required and do not be tempted to write a SELECT * statement even if you do actually require all the fields. It is considered bad practice to retrieve fields you are not actually going to use, as it can have an impact on performance.

To place the data onto the page using a .NET web control, follow these steps:

1. Add a new blank ASPX file to the project, and from the toolbox drag a DataList control onto the web page.

2. Open the DataList control Smart Tag.

3. Select Configure <New Data Source>.

4. In the Configuration Wizard, click Database (do not select the Access option that is available to you in the dialog box).

5. Rename the Data Source ID to EventsAccess.

6. Click OK.

7. Click New Connection.

8. Click Change (beside the Data Source drop-down list).

9. Select Other.

10. Click OK.

11. In the OLEDB Provider drop-down list, select Microsoft Office 12 Access Database Engine OLEDB Provider.

12. Enter the full path to the ACCDB file in the Server or file name text box.

13. Click OK.

14. Click Next.

15. Accept the default connect string name and click Next.

16. Make sure the query you created earlier is selected, and select the field returned by the query you would like to appear on the form.

17. Click Next.

18. Click Finish.

The bare data list appears within the Design view window. Figure 12-7 shows the list provided by Events.aspx.

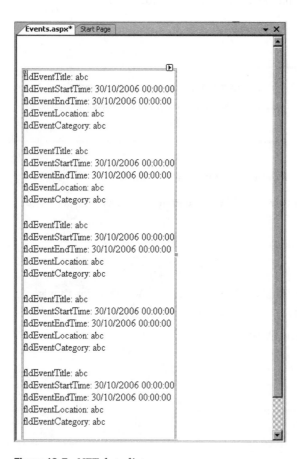

Figure 12-7. *.NET data list*

As you can see, there's nothing too exciting at this point. Next, you will add some customization to the listing, which is little more than an HTML table containing some data. First, let's look at a data list.

List Templates

The data list web server control is really a set of templates that are used to define the layout of the data. The data list has the following templates available, each of which performs a specific task:

ItemTemplate: Displays the data being returned to the list. This template looks after each individual item returned to the browser. Listing 12-3 shows the ItemTemplate used in this example. As you can see, each field within the template is treated as a distinct item. You can use any valid HTML within the ItemTemplate (for example, you could add in table tags, changing the way the code in Listing 12-3 appears to a standard HTML table).

Listing 12-3. *ItemTemplate*

```
<ItemTemplate>
                fldEventTitle:
                <asp:Label ID="fldEventTitleLabel" runat="server" ➥
Text='<%# Eval("fldEventTitle") %>' >
                </asp:Label><br />
                fldEventStartTime:
                <asp:Label ID="fldEventStartTimeLabel" runat="server" ➥
Text='<%# Eval("fldEventStartTime") %>'>
                </asp:Label><br />
                fldEventEndTime:
                <asp:Label ID="fldEventEndTimeLabel" runat="server" ➥
Text='<%# Eval("fldEventEndTime") %>'>
                </asp:Label><br />
                fldEventLocation:
                <asp:Label ID="fldEventLocationLabel" runat="server" ➥
Text='<%# Eval("fldEventLocation") %>'>
                </asp:Label><br />
                fldEventCategory:
                <asp:Label ID="fldEventCategoryLabel" runat="server" ➥
Text='<%# Eval("fldEventCategory") %>'>
                </asp:Label><br />
                <br />
            </ItemTemplate>
```

■**Note** The `Eval` function is a read-only method and is used to return the value of the data as a string.

AlternatingItemTemplate: Used to format the display of the list in alternating row colors.

SelectedItemTemplate: Controls the layout and appearance of the item selected (for example, the behavior of a data item in a grid or the background color of the selected item).

EditItemTemplate: Enables editing of a data item. A common example is to use a text box control to permit editing of a record field.

HeaderTemplate: Defines the content and layout of the list header.

FooterTemplate: Defines the content and layout of the list footer.

SeparatorTemplate: Places a separator between list items.

You can edit each of the templates used via the interface by clicking the object's Smart Tag and selecting Edit Templates. Pick the appropriate template to edit using the drop-down list and make your changes. When finished with the edit, click the Smart Tag and select End Template Edit. Using templates gives you a great deal of flexibility over how your .NET control is rendered in the browser.

Customizing the Data List

Customization of the data list is straightforward and is achieved by either using the object Smart Tag or going directly to the control's properties. To add a heading to the data list, follow these steps:

1. Select the control object (the data list) by clicking it.

2. Click the object Smart Tag.

3. Click Edit Templates.

4. Select Header Template from the Display drop-down list.

5. Enter the text you would like to use into the header cell.

6. Click End Template Editing.

If you check out the source of the page, you will now find a HeaderTemplate has been added at the bottom of the document.

```
<HeaderTemplate>
Chapter 7 List Demo
</HeaderTemplate>
```

Of course, you could have simply entered this yourself manually into the source of the page. The heading can be further customized by clicking Property Builder in the object's Smart Tag. In the resulting dialog box, you can set font, font color, and alignment of the header object.

Amending the ItemTemplate

To change the default field names used by the list, again, using the object Smart Tag, select Edit ItemTemplate and simply change the default labels to something more meaningful. As you can see, amending the various templates is a fairly straightforward process. But what if you would like to do something more meaningful with the list—for example, adding a button to allow the user to delete or add a record? You can do this, but you'll have to make do without a wizard.

Getting More Interactive

In this next example, you will use the same database, but this time you will make the web page fully interactive. In this case, you will be using a data grid that is another .NET server-side control. To get started, follow these steps:

1. Create a new blank ASPX page.

2. Drag an SQLDataSource onto the page.

3. Click Configure Data Source.

4. Select the existing Events connection for this example.

5. Click Next.

6. Select tblEvents from the Name drop-down list.

7. Select all the records from tblEvent.

8. Click the Advanced button.

9. Click Generate INSERT, UPDATE, and DELETE statements.

10. Click OK to close the Advanced dialog box.

11. Click Next.

12. Click Finish.

What you have done is to create the connection and, using the Connection dialog box, set up the required structures to enable the user to edit the grid. If you check out the source code now, you will see that you have generated the required SQL statements to perform the insert, update, and delete tasks. To continue:

13. Drag a GridView onto the page.

14. Using the Smart Tag, set the data source to the connection created previously.

15. Click the grid's Smart Tag icon and select the following properties:

   - Enable Paging

   - Enable Sorting

- Enable Editing

- Enable Deleting

- Enable Selection

You should now have a fully interactive data grid on the page. You can check out the functionality by clicking File ➤ View in your browser.

Creating a Search Page

For this example, you will create a basic search page using a drop-down list to select an event location and display the associated events in the page dynamically. To begin, follow these steps:

1. Create a new ASPX page.

2. Add an SQLDataSource to the page. Create a new connection to the event location table, tblLocations. Select the primary key and the location description field.

3. Drag and drop a DropDownList control onto the page and click Choose Data Source in the drop-down Smart Tag.

4. Using the Choosing a Data Source dialog box, select the data source you created earlier using the drop-down list; select the field to display, fldLocation, in the second drop-down list; and select the primary key value, ID, in the third drop-down list.

5. Check the Enable AutoPostBack check box in the Smart Tag menu.

6. Click OK to finish configuring the drop-down list.

You will be using the primary key value shortly as part of the WHERE clause used to populate a data grid also on the page. The data grid will be used to display the associated events for the location chosen. The location primary key value will be passed to the SQL statement for the connection in the data grid. To continue:

7. Drag a new data grid onto the same web page. Create another data source and point the new source at the Events table in the Access database.

8. Click the WHERE button when asked to configure the SELECT statement.

9. In the resulting screen, you can build your clause, passing in the selected value from the drop-down list created earlier to the SQL statement used by the data grid. To do this:

   a. Select ID from the Column drop-down list.

   b. Select = as the operator using the drop-down list.

   c. Select control from the Source drop-down list.

   d. In the Parameter Properties section of the dialog box, select the drop-down list created previously as the ControlID.

   e. Enter a default value of 1.

   f. Click Add.

Figure 12-8 shows the dialog box when you have completed this initial WHERE clause setup.

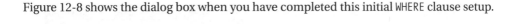

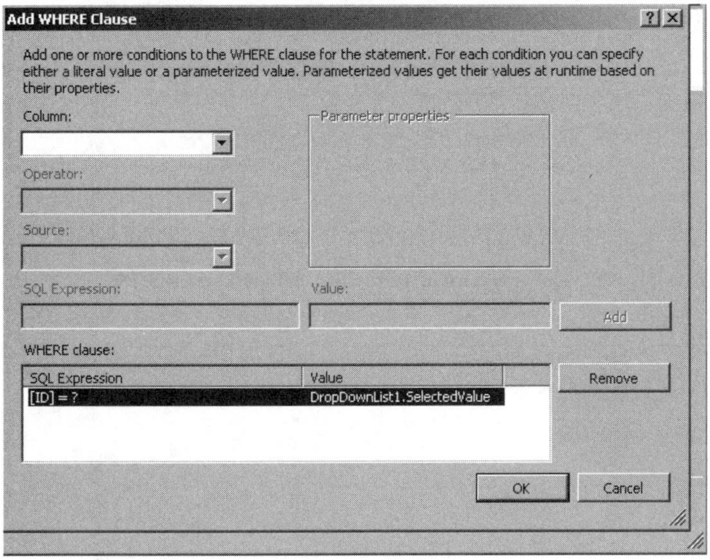

Figure 12-8. *Setting up the WHERE clause*

To preview the page in the browser, press Ctrl+F5, which will open the page in your default web browser. Figure 12-9 shows the results in Internet Explorer.

Try out the form by selecting a value in the drop-down list and watch how only those values matching the ID value from the drop-down list are returned in the data grid. What if there are no matching records? You can cover that possibility by amending the EmptyDataTemplate of the data grid. To do this, follow these steps:

1. Select the data grid's Smart Tag.

2. Select Edit Templates.

3. Select the EmptyDataTemplate.

4. Enter the text "There are No Records matching your search" into the template.

5. Click End Template Editing.

Now if there are no matching records, the text you entered will be displayed. Try it out selecting a value in the drop-down list that you know will have no matching records in the template table.

You could also replace the drop-down list with a text box, allowing the user to type values into the box and returning matching records. Your query would need to change slightly to make use of the LIKE comparison operator instead of the = sign when setting up the WHERE clause.

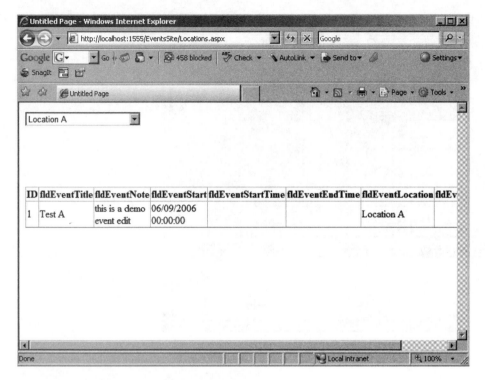

Figure 12-9. *Browser preview of the search form*

It would also be possible to combine both dialog box controls (the drop-down list and the text box) to create a more complex query restriction. For example, you can add ANDs and ORs to the SQL statement used by the data grid based on the user selecting a value from the drop-down list and entering a search string in the text box. Remember, all you are doing via the interface is referencing controls as parameters, which in turn are added to the SQL statement used by the grid. Think of a standard Access query-by-form interface, and you will immediately see the possibilities here!

If you would like to add a command button to the .NET page, simply drag one from the toolbox. No code is required, and, when clicked, the button will send the data to the server for processing.

Before ending this section, let's look at one more area: the use of a TableAdapter. This control will allow you to get data onto the page and bind it to the full range of .NET server controls with a very small amount of code. It is also used to begin the process of breaking apart your applications into their respective layers. So far in this chapter, you have been using the built-in features of the software to basically drag and drop controls onto the page and bind them to their respective data stores. In the following example, you will again use the interface, but you'll begin to open the door to the powerful combination of .NET and the Web.

Moving into Application Tiers

So far in this chapter's examples, you have embedded the data and code within your web pages. This example takes this a step further and builds a data access layer accessible from anywhere within your web project file.

■**Note** In order to follow this example, you will need a database located in the App_Data folder of your web project. This example uses the Events database, so remember, if you are using another database, follow the instructions, renaming objects as appropriate.

■**Note** When I first worked with web sites, I usually created applications by embedding code within the ASP file itself. Then I found http://www.4guysfromrolla.com, Scott Mitchell's web site. This is one of the oldest and best ASP and .NET web sites around. Scott's set of articles on http://www.asp.net are a must read for those who are new to .NET and working with databases. I recommend them highly. I picked up the techniques shown here from the set of tutorials on this Microsoft web site, and I would like to thank Scott and Brian Goldfarb for permission to outline the thinking and functionality presented there.

In this section, I will discuss how you can design and build your web application using a three-tiered approach involving data, presentation, and business logic layers. All the code required to access and manipulate data will exist in the data access layer, and the front-end pages will simply make calls into and out of the layer. So let's have a look at a small example to illustrate the principles of classes and tiered application building. To get started, follow these steps:

1. Create a new web site project.

2. Add the Events Access database to the project's App_Data folder.

■**Note** If you select New Item Web Dev Express and then SQL Database in the Add New Item dialog box, you can create a new SQL Server database for use by the project.

Once you have the database connection set up, you will add a dataset to the project. To add the dataset, continue with these steps:

3. Right-click the project name in the Solution Explorer and select Add New Item.

4. Click the Dataset icon in the New Item dialog box.

■Note A dataset returns a collection of data in the form of data table instances for use in the application.

---

5. Name the dataset EventsDS.XSD.

6. Click Add.

■Note You may receive a warning message that the dataset should be placed in the App_Code folder. Web Dev Express will offer to do this for you. Click Yes in response to this message.

---

7. If you wait a second, the TableAdapter Configuration Wizard will start up to allow you to add a TableAdapter to the dataset. Any database in the App_Data folder will be available using the drop-down list, or you can go ahead and create a new connection if required. Click Next.

8. Accept the default selection by clicking Next.

9. In the next dialog box, select all records from tblEvent or enter the correct SQL statement if you are not using the Events database.

10. Click the Advanced Options button on the dialog box.

11. Accept the default selection, Generate INSERT, UPDATE, and DELETE Statements.

12. Click OK.

13. Click Next.

14. Change the method name to GetEvents (the default will be GetData).

15. Click Finish.

Figure 12-10 shows the TableAdapter at this point. What you have created is a dataset with one data table, tblEvent, and a DataAdapter class called `EventTableAdapters. tblEventTableAdapter`, which contains a `GetEvents()` method. The `GetEvents()` method returns your tblEvents data.

Figure 12-10. *Selecting tblEventTableAdapter*

Now that the TableAdapter is set up and ready to use, create a new web form (ASPX file) called Events.aspx. When creating the file, make sure you check the Place Code in Separate File box. In this case, you are going to have two files: a .NET web page (think Access form) and a code page (think Access class module). Your "form" page will make use of the code page in a way similar to how Access uses a form's code module to carry out an action. In this example, what's going to happen is similar in theory to using an unbound form and populating it using VBA in the form's open event. Here, you are going to use the .NET PageLoad event to populate a data grid. Enter the code shown in Listing 12-4 into Events.aspx.

Listing 12-4. *Events.aspx Code*

```
<%@ Page Language="VB" AutoEventWireup="true" ➥
CodeFile="Events.aspx.vb" Inherits="Events" %>

<!DOCTYPE html PUBLIC "-//W3C//DTD XHTML 1.0 Transitional//EN" ➥
"http://www.w3.org/TR/xhtml1/DTD/xhtml1-transitional.dtd">

<html xmlns="http://www.w3.org/1999/xhtml" >
<head id="Head1" runat="server">
    <title>View All Events in a GridView</title>

</head>
<body>
    <form id="form1" runat="server">
    <div>
        <h1>
            Our Events</h1>
        <p>
            <asp:GridView ID="GridView1" runat="server"
             CssClass="DataWebControlStyle">
                <HeaderStyle CssClass="HeaderStyle" />
                <AlternatingRowStyle CssClass="AlternatingRowStyle" />
            </asp:GridView>
             </p>

    </div>
    </form>
</body>
</html>
```

The next step is to add the code to actually load up the data grid created in Listing 12-4. In the code-behind file, which should be named Events.aspx.vb, enter the code shown in Listing 12-5. Note the availability of IntelliSense when building the code up.

Listing 12-5. *Events Code Behind*

```
Imports EventDSTableAdapters

Partial Class Events
    Inherits System.Web.UI.Page

    Protected Sub Page_Load(ByVal sender As Object, ByVal e As ➥
System.EventArgs) Handles Me.Load
        Dim EventsAdapter As New tblEventTableAdapter
        GridView1.DataSource = EventsAdapter.GetEvents()
        GridView1.DataBind()
    End Sub
End Class
```

Notice the difference between this example and the previous examples—in particular, the small amount of code required to actually do this. In addition, there is no code, data connection, or anything else related to the actual database in the Events.aspx page.

■**Note** A .NET page goes through a series of stages, each of which can cause events to take place, and just like an Access form, you can code for the events. In this case, you are looking at the Page_Load event and adding some code to be executed. Another basic example is the button event, ButtonClick(), similar to a command button in Access. You can add code to execute in response to the button being clicked.

To test out the page, press Ctrl+F5 to preview in the default browser. Figure 12-11 shows this example, and I have also used the GUI tools to lay out and format the grid. (Click the grid's Smart Tag in Events.aspx to edit the control.)

This really only covers the basics of the tiered approach to web applications; a full and extensive tutorial is available at http://www.aspnet.com, and I highly recommend it. I do hope in this basic example you have begun to see the possibility for rapid development of simple .NET web sites.

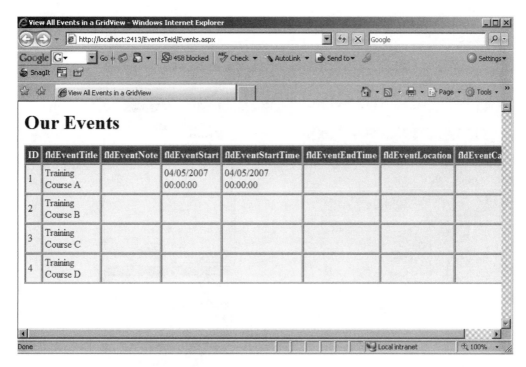

Figure 12-11. *Training events preview*

Creating Windows Applications with Visual Basic 2005 Express

In this section, you are going to use VB Express (which you can download from http:// msdn.microsoft.com/vstudio/express/vb/download/default.aspx) to create the same application you just created for the Web using ASP.NET, only this time you will build the structure using a Windows Form and reuse some of the objects you have already seen when working on the Web. You are going to create a Windows Form application that will display data from the Events database. If you are using your own example database, remember to change references and code as appropriate.

To get started, follow these steps:

1. Use VB Express to create a new project, selecting Windows Application in the New Project dialog box and naming your project Events.

2. Click OK to create the initial project files.

Figure 12-12 shows the design interface at this point.

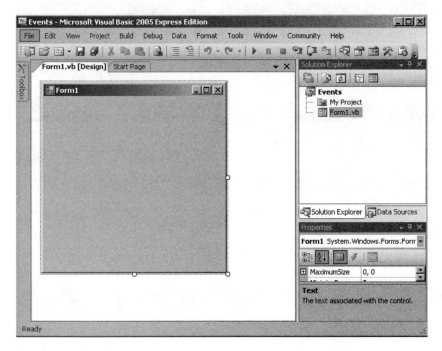

Figure 12-12. *VB Express Interface*

Next, you need to add a connection to the database. To do this from the main menu, follow these steps:

1. Click Data.

2. Select Add New Data Source.

3. Click Next to accept the default database.

4. Click Next.

5. Click New Connection.

6. Click the Change button beside the Data Source text box.

7. Select Access Database file.

8. Browse to the database file to select it.

9. Click OK once you have selected the database file.

10. Click Next. Accept the offer to copy the local database file into the project if you are asked to.

That's basically the first stage, configuring the connection. The Connection dialog box will then continue to permit you to create a dataset. To do so:

1. Click the Tables check box in the next page of the dialog box.

2. Select all the tables in the database for this example.

3. Name the dataset dsEvent.

4. Click Finish.

The dialog box will have added your database connection and dsEvent to the Solution Explorer. If you click the Database Explorer tab, you will also have access to tblEvents from the database. Your screen should resemble Figure 12-13.

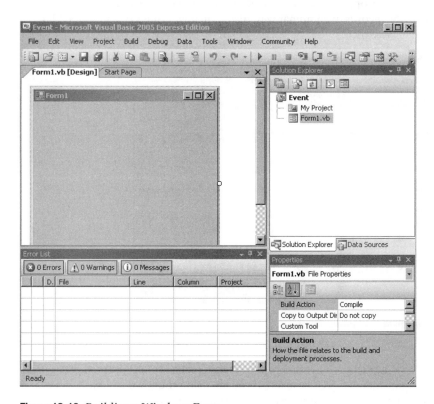

Figure 12-13. *Building a Windows Form*

The easy way to add to the Windows Form is to simply drag and drop tblEvents onto the form. To do this:

1. Click the Data Sources tab.

2. Expand the database.

3. Drag tblEvents onto the blank form.

Note that several objects are created for you within the project as follows:

- A data set (EventsDataSet).

- A TableAdapter (tblEventsTableAdapter).

- A binding source (tblEventBindingSource), which acts as the data source for the controls on the Windows Form.

- An EventBinding navigator (tblEventBindingNavigator), which resembles the Access navigation bar at the bottom of a form. Within VB Express, it's comprised of a tool strip containing objects, allowing you to navigate and manipulate the bound records.

Preview the new form by pressing Ctrl+F5. Figure 12-14 shows the form in debug mode. Note that by dragging and dropping, you have created a fully interactive data grid that will allow you to navigate the records in a familiar way. Also note how similar the navigation bar is to that used on an Access form.

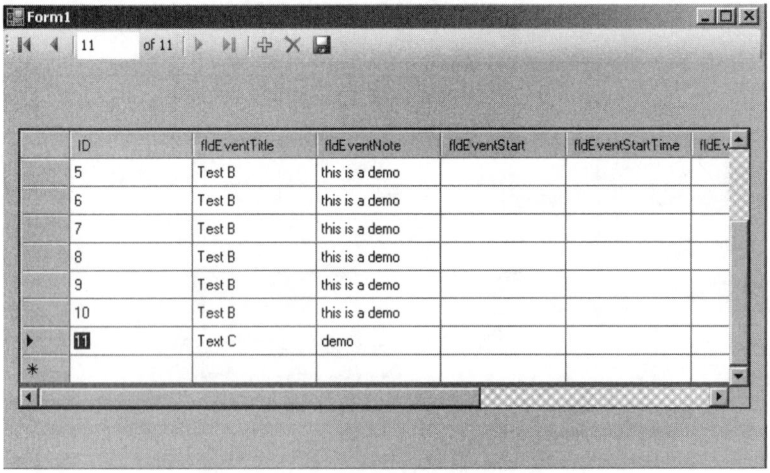

Figure 12-14. *The completed Windows Form*

To demonstrate the power of VB Express, you will next create a small Windows Form application for the Events database. Once again, if you are using your own database, remember to change field and connection references as appropriate. To get started:

1. Create a new project.

2. Add a connection to the project.

3. Select Data from the main menu.

4. From the toolbox, drag a tab control onto the blank form.

5. Resize the tab as appropriate.

6. Click the Data Sources tab.

7. Drag tblEvents onto Tab1 in the tab control.

8. Move the navigation bar to the bottom of the form by clicking its Smart Tag and selecting the Bottom Placement option.

9. Click the text Insert Standard Items to add additional features to the navigation strip.

Figure 12-15 shows the designer window at this point.

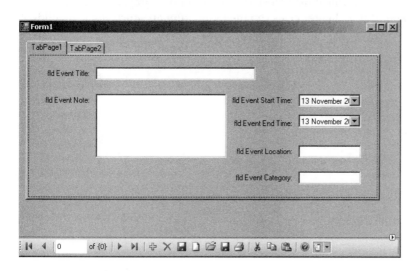

Figure 12-15. *Creating a Windows Form for the Events database*

Press Ctrl+F5 to see the form running. Notice the built-in Date Picker control used for the Date/Time data type. Figure 12-16 shows the control on your tabbed form.

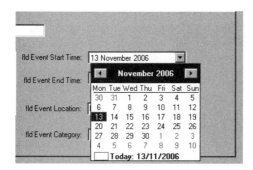

Figure 12-16. *Date Picker control*

At this point, you could go ahead and actually build this into a Windows application by selecting Build ➤ Publish from the main menu. The Publish Wizard will kick in, allowing you to create a small Windows application that can be installed on the PC. Try it out and see how it goes.

Summary

In this chapter, you have seen how you can use the free .NET tools, both web and Windows-based, to quickly generate basic applications using Access databases. Both Web Dev Express and VB Express offer you much more functionality than previously discussed features of Access, for example, using Data Access Pages and exporting as an ASP file. Both products get you started on the road to .NET development and provide at least a launching point for its huge range of features. By exploring mostly the GUI features of the software to generate basic working applications, this chapter gives you the foundation on which you can build your .NET skills.

CHAPTER 13

■■■

Code You Can Steal!

In this chapter, thanks to many of the members of AccessD who gave permission, I will be providing several examples of Access VBA using DAO, ADO, and some Windows API calls. The code comes from working Access developers and is free for you to use in any application. Where copyright is included in the code headers, I request that you retain it. The code is not categorized into specific functional areas. Where appropriate, I have also added the question that resulted in the code example in an attempt to place it into some context. However, feel free to sign up to AccessD (http://databaseadvisors.com/mailman/listinfo/accessd) and ask questions about specific code yourself! The code examples are available for download with the book's demonstration databases and within the archives of AccessD.

■**Note** Some examples are basic, some intermediate, and some highly complex. Some contain a few lines of code, others classes and modules. All are available, as stated, in the book's source code (which you can download from http://www.apress.com), where many are placed into context (for example, hooked up to forms, command buttons, and events).

We all stand on the shoulders of giants, and here for you is the code from the giants of AccessD! In no particular order of merit, the "giants" in question are

- Marty Connelly

- John W Colby

- Drew Wutka

- A. D. Tejpal

- Rocky Smolin

- Charlotte Foust

- Darren Dick

- Gustav Brock

- Jim De Marco

- Mark A. Matte

- Robert L. Stewart

- Stuart McLaughlin

- Susan Sales Harkins

- William Hindman

- Gary Klos

- Andy Lacey

Question: How can I return the exchange rate from a web page?

Answer: Place the code in Listing 13-1 into a new module.

Listing 13-1. *Returning an Exchange Rate, Example 1*

```
Option Compare Database
Private Declare Function URLDownloadToFile Lib "urlmon" Alias ➥
        "URLDownloadToFileA" (ByVal pCaller As Long, ByVal szURL ➥
        As String, ByVal szFileName As String, ByVal dwReserved As Long, ➥
        ByVal lpfnCB As Long) As Long


Function CurrencyConversion(strOriginal As String, strFinal As String, intValue ➥
As Currency) As Currency
Dim strPath As String
Dim strURL As String
Dim strSearch As String
Dim f As Long
Dim strData As String
Dim strFirstData As String
Dim strEndData As String
strSearch = "<span style=""font-size:14pt; font-weight:bold;"" "
strPath = Application.CurrentProject.Path & "\CurrencyTestData.tmp"
If Dir(strPath) <  "" Then Kill strPath
strURL = "http://www.xe.com/ucc/convert.cgi?From=" & strOriginal & "&To=" & ➥
strFinal & "&Amount=" & intValue
URLDownloadToFile 0, strURL, strPath, 0, 0
f = FreeFile
Open strPath For Binary Access Read As f
strData = Space(LOF(f))
Get f, , strData
Close f
Kill strPath
strData = Mid(strData, InStr(1, strData, strSearch, vbTextCompare) + Len(strSearch))
strFirstData = Left(strData, InStr(1, strData, "</span ") - 1)
strData = Mid(strData, InStr(1, strData, strSearch, vbTextCompare) + Len(strSearch))
strEndData = Left(strData, InStr(1, strData, "</span ") - 1)
CurrencyConversion = Left(strEndData, Len(strEndData) - 4)
End Function
```

In order to try out the preceding example, you will need to create an Access form. The following instructions outline the process and the names for the form controls:

1. To the form, add an unbound text box named txtStartingValue.

2. Add a combo box bound to a currency table (fields named Currency, Abbreviation) and name it cbmStart.

3. Add a combo box named cbmNew, also bound to the currency table.

4. Add an unbound text box and name it txtNewValue.

5. Add a command button and place the following code in the click event:

    ```
    me.txtNewValue = CurrencyConversion(Me.cmbStart, Me.cmbNew,
    Me.txtStartingValue)
    ```

6. Enter a value into the Starting Value text box and click the command button to return the exchange rate.

Just to prove there's more than one way to skin a cat, Listing 13-2 contains code that shows a different way of returning an exchange rate.

Listing 13-2. *Returning an Exchange Rate, Example 2*

```
Option Compare Database
Option Explicit
 Dim mcolRate As Collection
Sub testxml()
  Set mcolRate = New Collection
GrabXMLFile ("http://www.ecb.int/stats/eurofxref/eurofxref-daily.xml")
  Debug.Print mcolRate("USD")
  MsgBox "US dollar  Euro Rate ECB " & mcolRate("USD")
End Sub

Public Function GrabXMLFile(ByRef AdviserXML As String)
  ' http://www.ecb.int/stats/exchange/eurofxref/html/index.en.html

' Base currency is Euro so you will have to do a conversion for USD.
' Note the link for other pages with sources for XML, etc.
  ' http://www.ecb.int/stats/eurofxref/eurofxref-daily.xml

  ' On Error GoTo ErrorHandler
  ' needs reference set to XML 4.0 and maybe ADO 2.8
  Dim oDOMDocument As MSXML2.DOMDocument40
  Dim oNodeList As IXMLDOMNodeList
  Dim oAdviserDetailsNode As IXMLDOMNode
  Dim oLowestLevelNode As IXMLDOMElement
  Dim oNode As IXMLDOMNode
```

```
   Dim objXMLDOMNamedNodeMap As IXMLDOMNamedNodeMap
    Dim xPError As IXMLDOMParseError
   Dim Mydb As Database
  ' Dim myrs As ADODB.Recordset
   Dim sTempValue As String

   Set oDOMDocument = New MSXML2.DOMDocument40

   oDOMDocument.async = False
   oDOMDocument.validateOnParse = True ' You may want to parse for errors
   oDOMDocument.resolveExternals = False
   oDOMDocument.preserveWhiteSpace = True

   ' Use if XML disk file
     If Not oDOMDocument.Load(AdviserXML) Then
       MsgBox ("XML File error")
           Set xPError = oDOMDocument.parseError
       DOMParseError xPError

     End If
 Set oAdviserDetailsNode = oDOMDocument.documentElement
   Debug.Print oDOMDocument.XML

 ' Use appropriate XPath expression to select nodes

 ' Set oNodeList = oAdviserDetailsNode.selectNodes("Envelope/Cube/Cube/@*")
 Set oNodeList = oAdviserDetailsNode.selectNodes("//@*")

   Debug.Print oNodeList.length

   For Each oNode In oNodeList

     '  Debug.Print "*" & oNode.Text; oNode.nodeName & "*"

       Select Case oNode.nodeName
           Case "currency"
               sTempValue = oNode.Text

           Case "rate"
             ' This path is used to store a variable on the collection
               On Error Resume Next
                mcolRate.Remove sTempValue
                mcolRate.Add oNode.Text, sTempValue
                  Debug.Print sTempValue & " rate " & oNode.Text
               On Error GoTo ErrorHandler
```

```vb
            End Select
        Next
    Set oNodeList = Nothing
    Set oDOMDocument = Nothing
    Set oAdviserDetailsNode = Nothing
    Set objXMLDOMNamedNodeMap = Nothing
    Exit Function
ErrorHandler:
  '  Call NewError.Raise(Err.Number, Err.Source, Err.Description)
End Function


Sub DOMParseError(xPE As IXMLDOMParseError)
    ' The document failed to load.
    Dim strErrText As String
    ' Obtain the ParseError object
    With xPE
    strErrText = "Your XML Document failed to load" & ➡
        "due the following error." & vbCrLf & ➡
        "Error #: " & .errorCode & ": " & xPE.reason & ➡
        "Line #: " & .Line & vbCrLf & ➡
        "Line Position: " & .linepos & vbCrLf & ➡
        "Position In File: " & .filepos & vbCrLf & ➡
        "Source Text: " & .srcText & vbCrLf & ➡
        "Document URL: " & .url
    End With
    Debug.Print strErrText
  Dim s As String
  Dim r As String
  Dim i As Long
   s = ""
  For i = 1 To xPE.linepos - 1
    s = s & " "
  Next
  r = "XML Error loading " & xPE.url & " * " & xPE.reason
  Debug.Print r
    ' Show character postion of error; tired of counting chars in XML file
  If (xPE.Line    0) Then
    r = "at line " & xPE.Line & ", character " & xPE.linepos & vbCrLf & ➡
        xPE.srcText & vbCrLf & s & "^"
  End If
  Debug.Print r
    MsgBox strErrText, vbExclamation
End Sub
```

As you can see, this one question has two excellent solutions.

Question: I want to output a sequence number as a field in a query result. Each time the query runs, it should restart the sequence number from 1.

Answer: The code shown in Listing 13-3 performs this function.

Listing 13-3. *Adding a Sequence Number to a Query*

```
Public Function SequentialID( ➡
  ByVal booReset As Boolean, ➡
  Optional ByVal varDummy, ➡
  Optional ByVal intIncrement As Integer = 1, ➡
  Optional ByVal lngInitialID As Long) ➡
  As Long

  ' Increments static variable lngCurrentID with intIncrement.
  ' Returns the new value of lngCurrentID.
  ' Parameter varDummy is used to force repeated calls of
  ' this function when used in a query.
  ' Reset to start counting from zero incrementing by one:
  '   Call SequentialID(True)
  ' Reset to start counting from 1000:
  '   Call SequentialID(True, Null, 1, 1000)
  ' Reset to start counting from zero incrementing by 2:
  '   Call SequentialID(True, Null, 2)
  ' Reset to start counting from -2000 incrementing by -8
  ' and returning initial ID:
  '   lngID = SequentialID(True, Null, -8, -2000)  '
  ' Retrieve the current ID:
  '   lngID = SequentialID(False)
  ' Do a count by one and retrieve the current ID:
  '   lngID = SequentialID(False, Null, 1)
  ' Do a count by one in a query and retrieve the current ID:
  '   lngID = SequentialID(False, [fldAnyField], 1)
  ' Do a count by minus two and retrieve the current ID:
  '   lngID = SequentialID(False, varAny, -2)

  Static lngCurrentID As Long
  Dim intSgn        As Integer

  If booReset = True Then
    ' Reset ID.
    lngCurrentID = lngInitialID
  ElseIf Not intIncrement = 0 Then
    intSgn = Sgn(intIncrement)
    If intSgn * lngCurrentID < intSgn * lngInitialID Then
      ' Reset ID.
```

```
      lngCurrentID = lngInitialID
    Else
      ' Increment ID.
      lngCurrentID = lngCurrentID + intIncrement
    End If
  End If
  SequentialID = lngCurrentID
End Function
```

Alternative Answer: Again, to demonstrate that developers will often come up with different solutions to the same problem, Listing 13-4 shows another approach to this issue.

Listing 13-4. *Sequential Row Numbers*

```
Fn_RowNum() - User defined function

Function Fn_RowNum(ByVal QueryName As String, ➡
                   ByVal PrimaryKeyName As String, ➡
                   ByVal PrimaryKeyValue As Long) As Long
' Returns Row number for the record having primary key field
' named PrimaryKeyName with a value = PrimaryKeyValue,
' in source query named QueryName
    Dim Rct As Long
    Dim rst As DAO.Recordset

    Rct = 0
    Set rst = CurrentDb.OpenRecordset(QueryName)
    rst.FindFirst PrimaryKeyName & " = " & PrimaryKeyValue
    If Not rst.NoMatch Then
        Rct = rst.AbsolutePosition + 1
    End If

    Fn_RowNum = Rct
    rst.Close
    Set rst = Nothing
End Function
======================================
```

So long as the source table has a primary key field, simplified function Fn_RowNum() gets sequential row numbers, starting from 1, as the sample query in Listing 13-4 demonstrates. This function has an additional advantage in that the output is stable compared to alternatives using increments to static or global variables, where the results are volatile and prone to change with repeat navigation (up and down) through the column concerned. Q_Source is the source query (where the content of source table(s) is duly collected and sorted as desired), while ID is the name of primary key field in source table. If you want to use raw data in a single source table directly, without any sorting, the name of this table can be used (in lieu of Q_Source) in the following sample query:

```
SELECT Q_Source.*,
Fn_RowNum("Q_Source","ID",[ID]) AS RowNum
FROM Q_Source;
```

The next example is a lovely bit of code written by A. D. Tejpal, one of the most talented and original Access programmers I know. The issue this time is how to create a complete duplicate of a currently running application, including multiple back-end Access databases, and switch the user into this duplicate application. Once the user is finished testing in the duplicate application, a means must be provided for that user to return to the original database. I will not display all of the code here, as you will be able to download a fully working version as part of the code downloads for this book. The function in Listing 13-5 is used to create and link your original front-end application to the new back end.

Listing 13-5. *Duplicating an Application*

```
Private Sub P_CreateAndLinkTempBE()
    On Error Resume Next              ' Reqd for (A), which follows
    Dim db As DAO.Database, tdf As TableDef
    Dim fso As FileSystemObject
    Dim Cnc As String, CncMaster As String, CncTemp As String
    Dim Qst As String, BeFolderPath As String, BeFileName As String
    Dim BePathOriginal As String, BePathTemp As String

    Set db = CurrentDb
    Set fso = New FileSystemObject

    ' Clear table T_Link
    Qst = "Delete * From T_Link;"
    db.Execute Qst, dbFailOnError

    CncMaster = ""                              ' (See note that follows)
    For Each tdf In db.TableDefs
        ' Get value of Connect string for the linked table
        ' and create temp copy of BE if the new connect
        ' string (Cnc) is not zero length string (i.e., BE exists)
        ' and it is not a repetition of any previous one (i.e., it is not
        ' found in CncMaster)
        Cnc = tdf.Connect
        ' Ignore nonlinked and tables with Deleted status
        If Len(Cnc)    0 And Left(tdf.Name, 1) <   "~" Then
            BePathOriginal = Fn_GetBeFullPath(Cnc)
            BeFolderPath = Left(BePathOriginal, ➥
                                InStrRev(BePathOriginal, "\") - 1)
            BeFileName = Mid(BePathOriginal, ➥
                                InStrRev(BePathOriginal, "\") + 1)
```

```
            If fso.FileExists(BePathOriginal) = True Then
                BePathTemp = BeFolderPath & "\" & ➥
                                        TempPreFix & BeFileName
                CncTemp = Replace(Cnc, BePathOriginal, BePathTemp)

                If InStr(CncMaster, Cnc) = 0 Then
                    ' Delete temp BE if existing
                    Kill BePathTemp                              ' (A)
                    ' Make temp copy of this BE
                    fso.CopyFile BePathOriginal, BePathTemp, True
                    ' Update value of CncMaster
                    CncMaster = CncMaster & "< " & Cnc
                End If

                ' Relink the table
                tdf.Connect = CncTemp
                tdf.RefreshLink
            Else
                BePathTemp = "<< Original BE Path Is Not Valid    "
                CncTemp = Cnc
            End If

            ' Append data to table T_Link
            Qst = "INSERT INTO T_Link (T_Name, Link_Original, " & ➥
                    "Link_Current, BE_Original, BE_Current) " & ➥
                    "VALUES ('" & tdf.Name & "', '" & ➥
                    Cnc & "', '" & CncTemp & "', '" & BePathOriginal & ➥
                    "', '" & BePathTemp & "');"
            db.Execute Qst, dbFailOnError
        End If
    Next

ExitPoint:
    Set tdf = Nothing
    Set fso = Nothing
    Set db = Nothing
    On Error GoTo 0
End Sub
```

Question: How can I select multiple records on a subform?

Answer: Once again, the answer has been provided by A. D. Tejpal. Listing 13-6 will ensure that all records selected by the user are highlighted.

Listing 13-6. *Selecting Multiple Records on a Subform*

```
Private Sub Form_Click()
    P_SetFormat_A
End Sub
Private Sub Form_Current()
    P_SetFormat_A
End Sub


Private Function Fn_SelectedBlock(ByVal PkNumber ➥
                                              As Long) As Long
    ' Returns 1 if the record with this PkNumber
    ' falls in selected block, otherwise 0
    Dim rst As DAO.Recordset
    Dim RecNum As Long, InSelection As Long

    InSelection = 0   ' Default
    Set rst = Me.RecordsetClone
    rst.FindFirst "ID = " & PkNumber
    If Not rst.NoMatch Then
        RecNum = rst.AbsolutePosition + 1
        If RecNum  = Me.SelTop And ➥
                         RecNum <= Me.SelTop + ➥
                         (Me.SelHeight - 1) Then
            InSelection = 1
        End If
    End If

    Fn_SelectedBlock = InSelection

    rst.Close
    Set rst = Nothing
End Function

Public Sub P_SetFormat_A()
    ' Sets fresh Conditional Formatting in Detail section
    Dim ct As Control

    For Each ct In Me.Detail.Controls
        P_SetFormat_B ct.Name
    Next

    Me.Repaint
End Sub
```

```
Private Sub P_SetFormat_B(ByVal ControlName As String)
' Sets fresh Conditional Formatting
' (in text box named ControlName)
    Dim Cdn As String

    On Error Resume Next    ' For controls not suited to
                                ' conditional formatting
    With Me(ControlName).FormatConditions
        .Delete

        Cdn = "Fn_SelectedBlock(ID) <  0"
        With .Add(acExpression, , Cdn)
            .BackColor = 16777164
            .FontBold = True
        End With
    End With
    On Error GoTo 0
End Sub
```

Question: Is it possible to check the visible property of a control on a form in another database that is an MDE?

Answer: The function in Listing 13-7 will retrieve the visible status of a control in an external database file. It opens the target form, but this process is invisible to the end user.

Listing 13-7. *Retrieving the Visible Status of a Control in an MDE*

```
Function Fn_IsControlVisibleInExternalDb( ➡
ByVal FilePath As String, ➡
ByVal FormName As String, ➡
ByVal ControlName As String) As Boolean
 ' Returns True if the control is visible.
 ' Otherwise False    On Error GoTo ErrTrap
    Dim acp As Access.Application

    Fn_IsControlVisibleInExternalDb = False     ' Default

    Set acp = New Access.Application
    acp.OpenCurrentDatabase FilePath

    acp.DoCmd.OpenForm FormName

    If acp.Forms(FormName)(ControlName).Visible ➡
                                                = True Then
        Fn_IsControlVisibleInExternalDb = True
    End If
    acp.DoCmd.Close acForm, FormName
```

```
ExitPoint:
    On Error Resume Next
    acp.Quit
    Set acp = Nothing
    On Error GoTo 0
    Exit Function

ErrTrap:
    MsgBox "Err " & Err.Number & " - " & Err.Description
    Resume ExitPoint
End Function
```

Question: How can I inform users if they have added too much text to a text box?

Answer: Listing 13-8 will restrict users to inputting less than 255 characters in a text box.

Listing 13-8. *Restricting Text Entered into a Text Box*

```
Private Sub txtRegarding_Change()
    ' Comment: prevents users from adding too much text to the Regarding line
        On Error GoTo Form_Open_ERR
        If Len(Me.txtRegarding.Text) > 255 Then
        MsgBox "The Regarding line can only contain 255 characters, " & ➥
        "please use the message box for longer text."
        Me.txtRegarding.Text = Left(Me.txtRegarding.Text, 255)
    End If

Form_Open_EXIT:
    Exit Sub

Form_Open_ERR:
    MsgBox Err.Description
    Resume Form_Open_EXIT

End Sub
```

Question: How can I clear a missing reference check box using VBA?

Answer: The procedure in Listing 13-9 can be called from a form's command button.

Listing 13-9. *Clearing Missing References via VBA*

```
Private Sub CmdTest_Click()
    Dim ref As Reference

    For Each ref In Application.References
        If ref.IsBroken = True Then
```

```
            MsgBox "Missing Reference: " & ref.Name & ➡
                        vbCrLf & "Path: " & ref.FullPath & ➡
                        vbCrLf & "(This Reference has now been removed)"
            Application.References.Remove ref
        End If
    Next
En Sub
```

Question: How can I change the existing criteria in a query via VBA?

Answer: You could consider the simple alternative of setting up a wrapper saved query whose WHERE clause could be modified as required from time to time. The original query would be a standard SELECT query, without the WHERE clause. This approach should suit most situations unless it is a case of a Totals query, where the criteria needs to be applied before the Group By clause. Function Fn_PutQueryFilter(), shown in Listing 13-10, will create the required wrapper query (or modify the query if it already exists). It takes the name of original query and the criteria string as its arguments. For example, if the original query is named Q_A, a new query called Q_A_Filtered will be created, incorporating the desired criteria in its WHERE clause (where query Q_A is the plain query with no WHERE clause). If Q_A_Filtered already exists, it will be modified.

Listing 13-10. *Changing Query Criteria via VBA*

```
Function Fn_PutQueryFilter(ByVal QueryName As String, ➡
            Optional ByVal CriteriaString As Variant) As Long
    ' Creates new saved query named QueryName_Filtered
    ' based upon saved query named QueryName and returns
    ' 1 if successful, otherwise 0
    On Error GoTo ExitPoint
    Dim Status As Long, Qst As String
    Dim NewQueryName As String, Rtv As Variant
    Dim db As DAO.Database

    Status = 0    ' Default
    NewQueryName = QueryName & "_Filtered"
    If IsMissing(CriteriaString) Or ➡
                        Len(Nz(CriteriaString, "")) = 0 Then
        Qst = "Select * From " & QueryName & ";"
    Else
        Qst = "Select * From " & QueryName & ➡
            " Where " & CriteriaString & ";"
    End If

    Set db = CurrentDb
    On Error Resume Next
    Rtv = db.QueryDefs(NewQueryName).Name
```

```
    If Err.Number = 0 Then
        db.QueryDefs(NewQueryName).SQL = Qst
    Else
        db.CreateQueryDef NewQueryName, Qst
    End If
    Err.Clear

    db.QueryDefs.Refresh

    Status = 1

ExitPoint:
    Fn_PutQueryFilter = Status
    On Error GoTo 0
End Function
```

Question: Given the following data:

```
1234,Name,Address
1234,Name,Address
1234,Name,Address
1234,Name,Address
2345, Name Address
2345,Name Address
```

How can I get a mailing label structured as follows?

```
1234, Name1, Name2,Name3,Name4
Address

2345,Name1,Name2
```

Answer: The sample query in Listing 13-11 should get you the desired label strings for each distinct four-digit identifier prefix. It makes use of function Fn_GetLabel(). DataString is the name of the field holding comma-separated raw data in table T_Data.

Listing 13-11. *Creating Label Strings*

```
SELECT Query
======================================
SELECT Left([DataString],4) AS PreFix, Fn_GetLabel(Left([DataString],4)) ➡
AS LabelString  FROM T_Data
GROUP BY Left([DataString],4);
======================================
```

```
Function Fn_GetLabel(ByVal IdString As String) As String
    On Error Resume Next
    Dim rst As DAO.Recordset
    Dim Txt As String, Qst As String, Rtv As Variant

    Txt = ""          ' Default
    Qst = "SELECT * FROM T_Data " & ➥
                "Where Left(DataString, 4) = '" & ➥
                IdString & "';"
    Set rst = CurrentDb.OpenRecordset(Qst)

    Do While Not rst.EOF
        Rtv = Split(rst.Fields("DataString"), ",")
        Txt = Txt & IIf(Len(Txt) > 0, ",", "") & Rtv(1)
        rst.MoveNext
    Loop

    Txt = IdString & "," & Txt & "," & Rtv(2)
    Fn_GetLabel = Txt

    rst.Close
    Set rst = Nothing
    On Error GoTo 0
End Function
```

Question: Using a continuous form, I want to type in the text box and have the form go to the first record that matches what I typed. How can I do this without filtering?

Answer: If the form is used independently, the sample code in the form's module in Listing 13-12 will perform the required action. If the form is used as a subform and the desired search value is contained in a text box on the parent form, sample code in the parent form's module in Listing 13-13 would apply. MyNumberField and MyTextField are names of pertinent bound controls on the continuous form.

■**Note** The value of ControlSource is used in VBA statements in order to provide situations where the name of the bound control is different from its control source.

■**Note** In Listing 13-12, TxtSearch is a text box in the header or footer of the form.

Listing 13-12. *Code in Module of Independent Continuous Form*

```
' For locating number type field
Me.Recordset.FindFirst ➡
            Me.MyNumberField.ControlSource & ➡
            " = " & Me.TxtSearch
' For locating text type field
Me.Recordset.FindFirst ➡
            Me.MyTextField.ControlSource & ➡
            " = '" & Me.TxtSearch & "'"
```

■**Note** In Listing 13-13, TxtSearch is a text box on parent form. SF_SearchSub is the name of control on the parent form, acting as container for the subform.

Listing 13-13. *Code in Module of Parent Form*

```
' For locating number type field on subform
Me.SF_SearchSub.Form.Recordset.FindFirst ➡
        Me.SF_SearchSub("MyNumberField").ControlSource & ➡
        " = " & Me.TxtSearch
' For locating text type field on subform
Me.SF_SearchSub.Form.Recordset.FindFirst ➡
        Me.SF_SearchSub("MyTextField").ControlSource & ➡
        " = '" & Me.TxtSearch & "'"
```

Question: How can I check whether a particular field exists using VBA?

Answer: The code in Listing 13-14 will search for an existing field in the specified table.

Listing 13-14. *Checking for Field Existence*

```
Function Fn_FieldExists(ByVal FieldName As String, ➡
ByVal TableName As String) As Boolean
    On Error Resume Next
    Fn_FieldExists = Not IsError(DLookup(FieldName, TableName))
End Function
```

Question: How can I filter a report using the values in a multiple-selection list box?

Answer: Listing 13-15 shows how to check the values in a list box and filter a report using the results.

Listing 13-15. *Filtering a Report Using a List Box*

```
Dim frm As Form, ctl As Control
Dim varItem As Variant
Dim strSQL As String
    Set frm = Me
    Set ctl = frm!lstBusType
    strSQL = "[BusTypeID]="
    For Each varItem In ctl.ItemsSelected

        strSQL = strSQL & ctl.ItemData(varItem) & " OR [BusTypeID]="
    Next varItem
strSQL = Left$(strSQL, Len(strSQL) - 16)
DoCmd.OpenReport "rptBusinessType", acViewPreview, , strSQL
```

Question: How can I delete a table using VBA?

Answer: On this occasion, the response is based on using ADO as opposed to DAO, which illustrates the need to be reasonably flexible in your coding approach. Listing 13-16 demonstrates how to delete a table using VBA.

Listing 13-16. *Deleting a Table Using VBA*

```
Dim cnn as ADODB.Connection
Dim rs as ADODB.Recordset
Set cnn=new ADODB.Connection
Cnn.Provider="Microsoft.Jet.OLEDB.4.0"
Cnn.Open "D:\Test.mdb" ' Change this to the path of the database you want to
                        ' use this for
Set rs = Cnn.OpenSchema(adSchemaTables)
If rs.EOF = False Then rs.MoveFirst
Do Until rs.EOF = True
    If rs.Fields("TABLE_NAME").Value = "schednew" Then
      Cnn.Execute "DROP TABLE schednew"
    End if
Rs.movenext
Loop
Rs.close
Set rs=nothing
Cnn.close
Set cnn=nothing
```

This will work from outside the database. To use this inside, change it to the code used in Listing 13-17.

Listing 13-17. *Deleting a Table from an External Source*

```
Dim cnn as ADODB.Connection
Dim rs as ADODB.Recordset
Set cnn=CurrentProject.Connection
Set rs = Cnn.OpenSchema(adSchemaTables)
If rs.EOF = False Then rs.MoveFirst
Do Until rs.EOF = True
    If rs.Fields("TABLE_NAME").Value = "schednew" Then
Cnn.Execute "DROP TABLE schednew"
End if
Rs.movenext
Loop
Rs.close
Set rs=nothing
Set cnn=nothing
```

Question: How can I print out the fields for each table within a database?

Answer: The code in Listing 13-18 uses ADO to accomplish this task. Please ensure you have set the appropriate references in Access 2007.

Listing 13-18. *Printing Out Table Fields*

```
Public Sub GetTablesFields()
  Dim cnn    As ADODB.Connection
  Dim rstTbl As ADODB.Recordset
  Dim rstCol As ADODB.Recordset
  Set cnn = CurrentProject.Connection
  Set rstTbl = cnn.OpenSchema(adSchemaTables, Array(Empty, Empty, Empty, "Table"))
  ' List tables.
  With rstTbl
    Do While Not .EOF = True
      Debug.Print .Fields(2).Value
      Set rstCol = cnn.OpenSchema(adSchemaColumns, ➥
Array(Empty, Empty, CStr(.Fields(2).Value)))
      ' List fields of table.
      With rstCol
        Do While Not .EOF = True
          Debug.Print vbTab & .Fields(3).Value
          .MoveNext
        Loop
        .Close
      End With
      .MoveNext
    Loop
    .Close
  End With
```

```
If rstCol.State = adStateOpen Then
  rstCol.Close
End If
If rstTbl.State = adStateOpen Then
  rstTbl.Close
End If
If cnn.State = adStateOpen Then
  cnn.Close
End If
Set rstCol = Nothing
Set rstTbl = Nothing
Set cnn = Nothing

End Sub
```

Question: I have got a user running a database in Access. A list of names have been input into a single "name" field, rather than using both a "last name" field and a "first name" field. How would I split these names up, taking into account the fact that there are some "double" first names—for example, Jr. and Sr. suffixes?

Answer: The function shown in Listing 13-19 will solve this issue including the suffixes.

Listing 13-19. *Splitting Names Including Suffixes*

```
Function Fn_FirstName(ByVal FullName As  String) As String
    ' Returns first name
    Dim Txt As String, Cnt As Long
    Dim SuffixList As String, Rtv As Variant
    SuffixList = "Sr-Jr-Dr-Esq-Rev-Hon-Sir-Lord"
    Txt = FullName
    Rtv = Split(SuffixList, "-")
    For Cnt = 0 To UBound(Rtv)
        Txt = Trim(Replace(Txt, " " & Rtv(Cnt), ""))
    Next
    Fn_FirstName = Trim(Left(Txt, InStrRev(Txt, " ") - 1))
End Function

Function Fn_LastName(ByVal FullName As String) As String
    ' Returns last name
    Dim Txt As String

    Txt = Fn_FirstName(FullName)
    Fn_LastName = Trim(Mid(FullName, Len(Txt) + 1))

End Function
```

Question: How can I set the color of a text box based on its value?

Answer: Listing 13-20 will do this for you.

Listing 13-20. *Changing a Text Box Color Based on Its Value*

```
Private Function SetTest(ByVal varValue As Variant) As Variant

  Dim lngForeColor  As Long

  With Me!txtTest
    ' Specify default ForeColor value.
    lngForeColor = vbBlack
    If IsNumeric(varValue) Then
      If Val(varValue) > 500 Then
        lngForeColor = vbBlue
      Else
        lngForeColor = vbRed
      End If
    End If
    ' Make other tests.
    ' ...
    ' Set ForeColor
    .ForeColor = lngForeColor
  End With

  SetTest = varValue

End Function
```

The function is then called by setting the `ControlSource` of text box txtTest to

```
=SetTest([txtInput])
```

Question: How can I prevent users from entering data into a subform before they enter data into the main form?

Answer: Assume SF_01 is the name of a control on main form, acting as container for the subform in question. Adding the code shown in Listing 13-21 to the control's Enter event will ensure that if a user tries to go into it while it happens to be in a locked state, there will be a message followed by a transfer of focus to the required control on the main form.

Listing 13-21. *Locking Subform Controls*

```
Private Sub SF_01_Enter()
    If SF_01.Locked = True Then
        MsgBox "Please Make Entry In ... First"
        ControlOnParentForm.SetFocus
    End If
End Sub
```

Question: I have a custom toolbar for reports that gets displayed in report preview if the database is an MDE. It has only a printer icon, close button, and zoom control. The paging navigation is, of course, at the lower left of the screen in preview mode. Can I add navigation buttons to the custom toolbar where an inexperienced user might be more likely to see them?

Answer: The code in Listing 13-22, when added to the module of a pop-up form, enables page navigation of report named R_Test. A command button named CmdNext allows users to step forward through the pages, while the button named CmdPrev does the reverse. You might like to adapt it suitably for your specific situation.

■**Note** For the SendKeys command (up or down arrow) to be effective, it is necessary that the report be in FitToWindow mode and that the report's window is the active one.

Listing 13-22. *Report Page Navigation*

```
Code module for Pop Up Form
' Declarations Section
Private RepHdw As Long, FrmHdw As Long

Private Declare Function BringWindowToTop Lib "user32" ➥
                                (ByVal hwnd As Long) As Long
Private Sub CmdNext_Click()
    DoCmd.Echo False
    Me.Visible = False
    BringWindowToTop RepHdw
    DoCmd.RunCommand acCmdFitToWindow
    SendKeys "{DOWN}", True
    DoCmd.RunCommand acCmdZoom100
    Me.Visible = True
    BringWindowToTop FrmHdw
    DoCmd.Echo True
End Sub

Private Sub CmdPrev_Click()
    DoCmd.Echo False
    Me.Visible = False
    BringWindowToTop RepHdw
    DoCmd.RunCommand acCmdFitToWindow
    SendKeys "{UP}", True
    DoCmd.RunCommand acCmdZoom100
    Me.Visible = True
    BringWindowToTop FrmHdw
    DoCmd.Echo True
End Sub
```

```
Private Sub Form_Activate()
    DoCmd.Restore
End Sub

Private Sub Form_Load()
    RepHdw = Reports("R_Test").hwnd
    FrmHdw = Me.hwnd
End Sub
```

Question: Is it possible to set the cursor at the beginning of a field when it receives the focus?

Answer: The following line of code sets the cursor to the last position of a piece of data in a field:

```
txtMyFormField.SelStart = txtMyFormField.SelLength
```

Question: How can I deselect all items in a multiple-selection list box?

Answer: Attach the code in Listing 13-23 to a command button. Remember to change the list box reference (lstCompany) to your own reference.

Listing 13-23. *Deselecting All Items in a List Box*

```
Private Sub CmdClearList_Click()
Dim lcv As Integer

For lcv = 0 To lstCompany.ListCount - 1
    lstCompany.Selected(lcv) = False
Next lcv
End Sub
```

Question: Is there a SQL syntax or method for identifying duplicate records and automatically removing (or marking) the second and subsequent instances of that record?

Answer: The sample query in Listing 13-24 will remove all duplicates (other than the first occurrence for each case). T_Data is the name of table, while F1, F2, and F3 are the names of fields whose combined value determines whether a record is a duplicate or not. ID is the primary key.

Listing 13-24. *Removing Duplicate Records*

```
DELETE * FROM T_Data
WHERE (SELECT Count(*) FROM T_Data As T1
WHERE (T1.F1 & T1.F2 & T1.F3 = T_Data.F1 & T_Data.F2 & T_Data.F3)
 AND (T1.ID <= T_Data.ID)) > 1;
```

To finish off the book, here is something just for fun: the code to create a route using Microsoft Virtual Earth to Area 51! Listing 13-25 is an example of just playing with Access and seeing what you can see. However, it shows what's possible, and it does have a serious side, too (it shows the use of XML and the Internet within an application). Please be very careful with the wrapping in the code, as it is fairly complicated and easy to make a mistake.

This is not something every developer will do or indeed want to do, but it is a fine example of pushing VBA and Access to the limit and demonstrates what can be done with skill and imagination. The code is here to make it fairly easy for you to read through it. A working example is available in the code download for this book. Personally, I found it very instructive. For those who would like to explore the possibilities of this a little further, the following web sites will be useful:

- http://dev.live.com/virtualearth/sdk/

- http://www.ftponline.com/special/web20/pvarholasp/default.aspx

Also note that some of the functions within the following code module are useful in their own right—for example, the creation of HTML strings and output to an HTML file in the current database directory. To try out the function, run the following in the intermediate window:

```
testVirtualEarthMap
testVirtualEarthMapRoute
```

Also note the HTML file output to the Intermediate window once the procedure has been executed.

Listing 13-25. *Going to Area 51*

```
' MashUp Using Virtual Earth

Function testVirtualEarthMap()
'------------------
' Display Virtual Earth at a fixed latitutude and longitude
' then click the map to display lat/long position of cursor.
' For info see
' http://dev.live.com/virtualearth/sdk/
' http://www.ftponline.com/special/web20/pvarholasp/default.aspx

Dim objExplorer As Object
Dim objDocument As Object
Dim strHTML As String

Set objExplorer = CreateObject("InternetExplorer.Application")

objExplorer.Navigate "about:blank"
objExplorer.Toolbar = 1 ' 0= off
objExplorer.StatusBar = 1 ' 0 =off
objExplorer.Width = 800
objExplorer.Height = 870
objExplorer.Left = 0
objExplorer.Top = 0
objExplorer.Visible = 1

Do While (objExplorer.Busy)
Loop
```

```
Set objDocument = objExplorer.Document
objDocument.Open
' Create HTML string and dump to a test file
 strHTML = ""
 strHTML = strHTML & createhtml
' Output HTML file to same directory as MDB.
' Use HTML for debugging or later viewing in IE.

WriteFile CurrentDBDir & "test.html", strHTML

objDocument.Write strHTML
objExplorer.Refresh ' ??This has to be done because
                    ' of http://local.live.com/veapi.ashx
'objDocument.Close 'stall here
Do While (objExplorer.Busy)
Loop
'MsgBox "finished"
'Set objExplorer = Nothing
'Set objDocument = Nothing

End Function

Function testVirtualEarthMapRoute()
'------------------
' Display Virtual Earth at a fixed lat/long
' then click the map to display lat/long position of cursor.
' This then displays a route map from Microsoft.
' There will be a 5-10 second pause while route map comes up.
' For info see
' http://dev.live.com/virtualearth/sdk/
' http://www.ftponline.com/special/web20/pvarholasp/default.aspx

Dim objExplorer As Object
Dim objDocument As Object
Dim strHTML As String
Dim strFileHTML As String
Set objExplorer = CreateObject("InternetExplorer.Application")

objExplorer.Navigate "about:blank"
objExplorer.Toolbar = 1 ' 0= off
objExplorer.StatusBar = 1 '0 =off
objExplorer.Width = 800
objExplorer.Height = 870
objExplorer.Left = 0
objExplorer.Top = 0
objExplorer.Visible = 1
```

```
Do While (objExplorer.Busy)
Loop


Set objDocument = objExplorer.Document
objDocument.Open
' Create HTML string and dump to a test file
' strHTML = ""
' strHTML = strHTML & createhtml

'WriteFile "c:\gis\test.html", strHTML
strFileHTML = CurrentDBDir

strHTML = createhtmlroute


' Output HTML file to same directory as MDB.
' Use HTML for debugging or later viewing in IE.

WriteFile CurrentDBDir & "route.html", strHTML

objDocument.Write strHTML
objExplorer.Refresh ' ??This has to be done
                    ' because of http://local.live.com/veapi.ashx
'objDocument.Close 'stall here
Do While (objExplorer.Busy)
Loop
objExplorer.Refresh
' Might be able to retrieve text route directions
' via this method.
'Dim strHTMLout As String
'strHTMLout = objExplorer.Document.BODY.parentElement.outerHTML
 Debug.Print strHTML
'Set objExplorer = Nothing
'Set objDocument = Nothing
End Function

Private Sub WriteFile(ByVal sFileName As String, ByVal sContents As String)
' Dump XML or HTML string to file for debugging
    Dim fhFile As Integer
    fhFile = FreeFile
   ' Debug.Print "Length of string=" & Len(sContents)
    Open sFileName For Output As #fhFile
    Print #fhFile, sContents;
    Close #fhFile
    Debug.Print "Out File" & sFileName
End Sub
```

```
Public Sub ReadFile(ByVal sFileName As String, ByRef sContents As String)
' Dump XML string to file for debugging
Dim strLine As String
Dim intLine As Long
Dim fhFile As Integer
    intLine = 0
    sContents = ""
    fhFile = FreeFile
    ' Debug.Print "Length of string=" & Len(sContents)
    Open sFileName For Input As #fhFile
Do While Not EOF(1) ' Loop until end of file.
    Input #1, strLine    ' Read data
    intLine = intLine + 1
    sContents = sContents & strLine
    'Debug.Print sContents  ' Print data to Debug window.
Loop
Close #fhFile    ' Close file.
    Debug.Print "Input File" & sFileName & " lines=" & intLine
End Sub


Function createhtml() As String
Dim strHTML As String
 strHTML = ""
 strHTML = strHTML & "<html><head><title>Virtual Earth Map</title></head>"
  strHTML = strHTML & "<meta http-equiv=""Content-Type"" ➥
content=""text/html; charset=utf-8"">"
' When your page has referenced the map control, set up the call to display
' a default map by completing a LoadMap ( ) method call:
 strHTML = strHTML & vbCrLf & "<script ➥
src='http://dev.virtualearth.net/mapcontrol/v3/mapcontrol.js'></script> "
'  strHTML = strHTML & vbCrLf & "<script type='text/javascript' ➥
src='http://local.live.com/veapi.ashx'></script>"
 strHTML = strHTML & vbCrLf & "<script language=""javascript"" ➥
type=""text/javascript"">"
'  strhtml = strhtml & vbCrLf & "<!-- "
 strHTML = strHTML & vbCrLf & "     var map=null;"
 strHTML = strHTML & vbCrLf & " function ShowLatLon(e)"
 strHTML = strHTML & vbCrLf & "         {"
 strHTML = strHTML & vbCrLf & "alert('Latitude = ' + e.view.LatLong.Latitude + ➥
' Longitude = ' + e.view.LatLong.Longitude);"
 strHTML = strHTML & vbCrLf & "         }"
 strHTML = strHTML & vbCrLf & " function GetMap()"
 strHTML = strHTML & vbCrLf & " { "
 strHTML = strHTML & vbCrLf & "          map = new VEMap(""myMap"");"
 strHTML = strHTML & vbCrLf & "map.onLoadMap = function(){ alert➥
('The map has loaded.') };"
```

```
 strHTML = strHTML & vbCrLf & "          map.LoadMap(new VELatLong➡
(48.51, -123.36), 10 ,""h"" ,false);"
 strHTML = strHTML & vbCrLf & "    map.AttachEvent(""onclick"", ShowLatLon);"
 strHTML = strHTML & vbCrLf & " }"
 strHTML = strHTML & vbCrLf & "</script>"
' strhtml = strhtml & vbCrLf & "// -->"
' Last, you display the map:
 strHTML = strHTML & vbCrLf & "<body onload='GetMap();'>"
 strHTML = strHTML & vbCrLf & "<div id='myMap' ➡
style='position:relative; width:600px; height:600px;'></div>"
 strHTML = strHTML & vbCrLf & "<td> right or left click map for ➡
latitude longitude position </td>"
 strHTML = strHTML & vbCrLf & "</body>"
 strHTML = strHTML & vbCrLf & "</html>"
'WriteFile CurrentDBDir & "test.html", strHTML
createhtml = strHTML
End Function
Function CurrentDBDir() As String
Dim strDBPath As String
Dim strDBFile As String
    strDBPath = CurrentDb.Name
    ' May need to call Win API apiFindFirstFile
    ' to get true name, otherwise DOS contracted form.
    strDBFile = Dir(strDBPath)
    CurrentDBDir = Left$(strDBPath, Len(strDBPath) - Len(strDBFile))
End Function

Function GetDirPath() As String
Dim db As Database
Set db = CurrentDb
GetDirPath = db.Name
GetDirPath = fGetLongName(GetDirPath)
End Function
Function CurrentDBDirLong() As String
Dim strDBPath As String
Dim strDBFile As String
    strDBPath = CurrentDb.Name
   ' strDBPath = fGetLongName(strDBPath) 'removes "~" in path
    strDBFile = Dir(strDBPath)
    CurrentDBDirLong = Left$(strDBPath, Len(strDBPath) - Len(strDBFile))
End Function

Function createhtmlroute() As String
Dim strHTML As String
 strHTML = ""
 strHTML = strHTML & "<html><head><title>Route Microsoft ➡
To Area 51 Virtual Earth Map</title></head>"
```

```
'   strHTML = strHTML & "<meta http-equiv=""Content-Type"" content=""text/html; ➥
charset=utf-8"">"
' When your page has referenced the map control, set up the call to display
' a default map by completing a LoadMap ( ) method call:
 strHTML = strHTML & vbCrLf & "<script src=➥
'http://dev.virtualearth.net/mapcontrol/v3/mapcontrol.js'></script> "
'   strHTML = strHTML & vbCrLf & "<script type='text/javascript'➥
 src='http://local.live.com/veapi.ashx'></script>"
 strHTML = strHTML & vbCrLf & "<script language="➥
"javascript"" type=""text/javascript"">"
'   strhtml = strhtml & vbCrLf & "<!-- "
 strHTML = strHTML & vbCrLf & "      var map;"
 strHTML = strHTML & vbCrLf & "    function GetMap ()"
 strHTML = strHTML & vbCrLf & " {"
 strHTML = strHTML & vbCrLf & "          map = new VEMap (""myMap"")"
 strHTML = strHTML & vbCrLf & "  alert (""1"");"
 strHTML = strHTML & vbCrLf & "          map.LoadMap(new VELatLong➥
(48.51, -123.36), 10 ,""h"" ,false)"
 strHTML = strHTML & vbCrLf & "  alert (""12"");"
 strHTML = strHTML & vbCrLf & "          map.GetRoute(""microsoft"", ➥
""area 51"",null,null,onGotRoute)"
'   strHTML = strHTML & vbCrLf & "  alert (""13"");"
 strHTML = strHTML & vbCrLf & " }"
 strHTML = strHTML & vbCrLf & " function onGotRoute(route)"
 strHTML = strHTML & vbCrLf & " {"
 strHTML = strHTML & vbCrLf & "   var routeinfo=""Route info:\n\n"";"
 strHTML = strHTML & vbCrLf & "  routeinfo += ""Total distance: "";"
 strHTML = strHTML & vbCrLf & " routeinfo += route.Itinerary.Distance+"" "";"
 strHTML = strHTML & vbCrLf & "   routeinfo += route.Itinerary.DistanceUnit+""\n"";"
 strHTML = strHTML & vbCrLf & "    var steps="""";"
 strHTML = strHTML & vbCrLf & "   var len = route.Itinerary.Segments.length;"
 strHTML = strHTML & vbCrLf & "   for(var i = 0; i<len ;i++)"
 strHTML = strHTML & vbCrLf & "  {"
 strHTML = strHTML & vbCrLf & "      steps+=➥
route.Itinerary.Segments[i].Instruction+"" -- ("";"
 strHTML = strHTML & vbCrLf & "      steps+=➥
route.Itinerary.Segments[i].Distance+"") "";"
 strHTML = strHTML & vbCrLf & "      steps+=route.Itinerary.DistanceUnit+""\n"";"
 strHTML = strHTML & vbCrLf & "   }"
 strHTML = strHTML & vbCrLf & "   routeinfo += ""Steps:\n""+steps;"
 strHTML = strHTML & vbCrLf & "   alert(routeinfo);"
 strHTML = strHTML & vbCrLf & " }"
strHTML = strHTML & vbCrLf & "</script>"
' strhtml = strhtml & vbCrLf & "// -->"
' Last, you display the map:
strHTML = strHTML & vbCrLf & "<body onload='GetMap();'>"
```

```
 strHTML = strHTML & vbCrLf & "<div id='myMap' ➥
style='position:relative; width:600px; height:600px;'></div>"
 strHTML = strHTML & vbCrLf & "<td> right or left click map for ➥
latitude longitude position </td>"
 strHTML = strHTML & vbCrLf & "</body>"
 strHTML = strHTML & vbCrLf & "</html>"
'WriteFile CurrentDBDir & "test.html", strHTML
createhtmlroute = strHTML
End Function
```

Summary

In this chapter, I have provided many examples of real-world Access programming issues, some minor, some more complex—but all should prove useful. The examples here come from real working developers who give freely of their time and experience to help other developers. The Internet is full of communities like AccessD, but AccessD is different in many ways from most other lists. It is a community of peers and professional developers, but mostly friends, and it is an honor to be a part of it and to learn from some of the best Access developers around.

So that's about it: we started looking at what's new in Access 2007, took a tour of SQL Server and Windows SharePoint Services, and ended up at Area 51—sounds about right for a day in the life of an Access developer!

■ ■ ■

RibbonX and Custom Add-Ins

This text is reproduced with the permission of Patrick Schmid, who maintains one of the most informative RibbonX web sites on the Internet (http://pschmid.net).

RibbonX lets you do a lot of things, but which actions are the right ones? How should your add-in behave and integrate itself into the Office UI? Where should you place your add-in? Which modifications are OK, and which are not? This appendix provides some guidance on these topics. In a more generic sense, I am going to talk about user interface style guidelines. When you take RibbonX into your hands, the deciding factor on what you should do is whether you control (directly or indirectly) the Office application. You control the Office application if any of the following applies:

- You are writing a full-fledged application based on it. The two most notable examples are Access 2007 applications and Excel dictator applications. In both situations, your code completely takes over the Office application, frequently to the point where the user does not even recognize anymore that there is an underlying Office application.

- You are modifying the Ribbon of your own personal copy of Office 2007.

- You are designing the corporate "look" of an Office application. Many corporations choose to roll out Office applications with a set of add-ins and with a UI that is customized to the needs of their corporate users.

- You are developing a template or document that is rather unique and offered in a corporate environment. A good example for a rather unique template is Word's blogging feature, which displays very different tabs. However, the blogging template does not fit into the controlled category per se, because a user could install add-ins that modify those tabs. If the blogging template were to be used in a corporate environment with IT preventing users from installing any add-ins themselves, it would be considered controlled.

- You are developing an add-in for a corporate environment. Generally, corporate IT controls which add-ins can be installed, and hence you have some control about which other add-ins are changing the user interface.

You do not control the Office application if

- You don't know and/or can't influence what other add-ins, documents, and/or templates might be installed.

- You are not developing for one particular client. That means you are developing a commercial add-in that is available for anyone who wants to have it (via a free download, purchase, and so on). If you are developing a customized solution for one particular client, you might be dealing with a controlled situation, but not necessarily.

The distinction between controlled and uncontrolled is crucial, because in an uncontrolled situation, you do not know (and have no way of finding out) what other add-ins, documents, or templates (which Microsoft collectively refers to as "solutions," but here will be referred to by the umbrella term "add-ins") might be doing to the user interface. You also do not have any way of figuring in changes to the basic user interface by Microsoft. Office 14 might seem far away (Microsoft is skipping version 13), but your program might be around a lot longer than 2 or 3 years on a machine. In addition, you cannot control which locale (user interface language) a user is running your add-in with. With Office 2007, changing the UI language is as simple as a few mouse clicks, given that appropriate language packs are installed.

If two add-ins modify the same element on the Ribbon, the last one to load wins. As you cannot control nor predict whether your add-in will be the last one to load, this is an extremely indeterministic situation—one you should avoid at all cost. Therefore, whether you are working in a controlled or uncontrolled situation, keep your UI modifications to a minimum. Let's now discuss the implications of both situations and then talk about modifying the Ribbon UI in general.

Controlled Situation

In a controlled situation, you could do whatever you want. I say "could," because you should restrain yourself and follow these guidelines:

- Do not use RibbonX to restore an Office 2003–like UI. This might be tempting to avoid the training costs associated with upgrading, but it is not a forward-looking investment. Future upgrades from Microsoft will probably require additional work. Most importantly, though, you are not reaping any benefits from the new UI design. If you want an Office 2003–like UI, stick with Office 2003 and do not upgrade.

- You will want to make sure that your UI is similar in behavior to the Office UI, so that users can transfer their knowledge of how to use Microsoft components to your own components. Users might have no familiarity with the Office 2007 UI experience currently, but they will definitely have some one year from now, and they will expect identical behavior from your program. Follow the general UI guidelines to ensure this.

- Do not use the `startFromScratch` attribute for the Ribbon tag unless you are developing an application based on an Office application. `startFromScratch` truly means that the Ribbon starts from scratch. This is a killer approach when you have to deal with more than one add-in, even in a controlled scenario. Avoid it, avoid it, avoid it! If you have to use it, remember that you should ensure that only one add-in, namely yours, contains

RibbonX. If you use `startFromScratch` in a scenario with two or more add-ins modifying the Ribbon UI, you are setting yourself up for a disaster. You should also know that `startFromScratch` does not reset the contextual tabs. Even with `startFromScratch`, all contextual tabs will still be there and look as they were created by Microsoft. The only way to deal with them in this case is to individually alter or hide them.

- Decide carefully about what you place in the Quick Access Toolbar. There are only 40 spots, and every one you use is one less your user has available. Users can place any Ribbon control on the Quick Access Toolbar and might want to make good use of this, even in a strictly controlled corporate environment. In contrast to previous Office versions, your users will not be able to mess up most of the user interface, and so won't generate lots of support requests as a result. You should therefore leave them some freedom to do with their Quick Access Toolbar what they like. Microsoft preloads the Quick Access Toolbar with three to five controls. I suggest that you keep the number of preloaded Quick Access Toolbar items to less than 15 (including the Microsoft ones). Note that you can only modify the Quick Access Toolbar if you are using `startFromScratch`.

- "Everything starts from the Ribbon." Microsoft didn't follow this mantra 100% of the time. (There are commands not in the Ribbon that can be added to the Quick Access Toolbar. Some exist by default only in the Quick Access Toolbar, namely Undo and Redo.) However, you should try to follow it as best as you can. That means do not put a control only in the Quick Access Toolbar. All your controls should be either in the Office button menu or on the tabs, and only added to the Quick Access Toolbar as an additional means to find it. So do not use the Quick Access Toolbar as the primary and only location for a functionality. Remember that a user can remove any item on the Quick Access Toolbar with a right-click followed by a left-click; if that is the only place where a user can access some functionality and the user removes it, he or she will probably need support to get it back.

Uncontrolled Situation

In this kind of situation, you really have to be a good Office citizen. The most important guidelines to follow are these:

- Do not use `startFromScratch`.

- Do not put anything in the Quick Access Toolbar. The Quick Access Toolbar is for the user to use, not for you to advertise your add-in. If the user wants to put any of your functionality in the Quick Access Toolbar, he or she can do so manually. You, however, should never touch the Quick Access Toolbar with RibbonX. Note that you can modify the Quick Access Toolbar only if you are using `startFromScratch`, which you should *never* do in this situation.

- Remember, your add-in is not the most important thing in the Office user interface. Do not make it prominently available just because you can.

- "Everything starts from the Ribbon" applies as well to uncontrolled situations, obviously.

- Follow the general UI guidelines outlined in the next section.

- Make your add-in fit in with the rest of Office 2007.

- Mark your add-in clearly as such in the UI. If your add-in blends seamlessly with Microsoft features and there is no way to distinguish your add-in from any Microsoft component, your users will first go to Microsoft for help. Microsoft's web site already gets more traffic than your web site, so why increase it even more? To mark your add-in, include the words "add-in" somewhere where the user can see it. For example, include it as part of the group label. Or add a labeled menu separator to the top of a menu like I did for my own add-in:

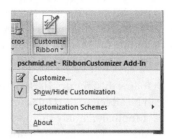

- Tell your users how to get in touch with you. For example, I include an About button that shows a dialog box with the URL for my web site on it.

General UI Guidelines

After discussing the general implications of each situation, we will now turn our attention to more generic guidelines that apply in both situations.

Repurposing Commands

RibbonX lets you "hijack" any MS command and redirect it to your own add-in. As with any RibbonX conflicts, if two add-ins repurpose the same command, the last add-in to load wins. Except for a controlled situation, you should never repurpose a command. Even in a controlled situation, repurpose only when there is a very good reason (doing so in your own application based on an Office application is the only one that comes to my mind). Whenever you repurpose a command, the original functionality of the command is no longer accessible to the user or any other add-in at all. There is no workaround; the access to the Microsoft functionality is gone while your add-in is loaded. Repurposing is tempting, but following are two examples why you should not use it.

Word 2007 has built-in functionality for creating citations and bibliographies. However, that functionality is inferior compared to a full-fledged citation manager like EndNote. End-Note comes with an add-in for Word to easily insert citations into documents. It would be tempting for the creators of EndNote to repurpose the Word 2007 controls for the Citations & Bibliography group on the References tab with a new version of the EndNote add-in to provide seamless integration into Word 2007. What happens though if the user gets a document that was created using the built-in feature? If EndNote repurposed all the built-in commands, the user would not have any way of editing those citations, because access to the MS functionality would be gone. Repurposing in this situation proves even more problematic if another citation manager, RefWorks, decides to do the same. If a user installs both, the user might one day have access to EndNote via the built-in UI items and another day have access to RefWorks, simply depending on which add-in managed to load first on a given day. A much better solution would be for EndNote and RefWorks to each add its own group to the References tab and leave the MS commands alone.

As another example of the pitfalls of repurposing, take the control for labels that appears in the Create group on the Mailings tab. As you might know, label manufacturers provide add-ins for Word that are designed to work specifically with their labels. What if two label manufacturers, say Avery and Herma, both decide to repurpose that particular control to provide access to their custom label wizards? If a user installed both, which is quite plausible, he or she would have access to only one of the two wizards, again depending on the load order of the add-ins. The user would also lose access to the MS label functionality.

Adding to the Home Tab

If you want your add-in to be visible immediately when a user opens a Ribbon application, where do you put it? On the Home tab, of course. Are the commands of your add-in among the 80% most used commands when you count all MS and add-in commands? No? Does your add-in provide functionality that is similar to the functionality of the MS commands on the Home tab (or expands on it, for example, by providing a button for Paste Special as Image)? No? If you answered no to both, what is your add-in doing on the Home tab?

Do not put your add-in on the Home tab simply because you want users to be able to find it. Advertising your add-in is not a good reason to clutter the Home tab. Be a good Office citizen and remember that the Home tab is for the functionality that a user accesses 80% of the time.

Creating Your Own Tab

It is tempting to create your own tab, but do you really need it, or do you just want to advertise your add-in (as it would be prominently displayed with the other tabs at all times)? The rule for creating your own tab is simple: if you can fill the tab, make one; otherwise do not. If your add-in can be logically categorized to fit into any of the existing tabs, put it there, except if you really need the space of a full tab. A full tab generally has at least three groups (a tab that is full but has only one group is a sign of a poor layout). "Full" means that when viewed with a 1024×768 resolution (the MS target resolution for the Ribbon UI), you cover at least 70% of the tab space (estimate based on the least-full MS tabs).

Creating Your Own Group

Your own group is the only way you are able to add controls to tabs. The question is mainly where to put your group. If your functionality fits into any of the existing tabs logically, put it there. Otherwise, use the Add-Ins tab. Remember that your functionality might fit best into a contextual tab, because it is only relevant when a picture, chart, table, and so on is selected. If your add-in is limited in functionality to any of the built-in objects that have contextual tabs, you should definitely place it there.

Modifying Microsoft Groups and Controls

You cannot modify any MS groups directly. For example, if you wanted to add a Paste Special as Image button next to the Paste button in the Clipboard group on the Home tab, you would have to make your own group and put it next to the Clipboard group, as you cannot modify the Microsoft group. What you could do is hide the MS group and create a new group that contains all the MS controls plus your own. While this would conserve space, you should never do this in an uncontrolled situation. If you do, you rob any other add-in from access to that particular group, and you really do not know what other add-ins might do. It is feasible that another add-in will display the Clipboard group again if it loads after yours. In that case, the user would now suddenly have two Clipboard groups.

Avoid hiding or disabling MS controls and groups in an uncontrolled situation. Again, you do not know what other add-ins will do and what the overall effect for the user will be.

Using Microsoft Groups and Controls

You can use any Microsoft group, control, or tab in your own Ribbon by specifying it via RibbonX. Unfortunately, there are several limitations. You can only use core tabs, for example Home, as core tabs. That means a core tab cannot be used within a contextual tab set. Vice versa, a contextual tab cannot be used outside its tab set. Also, the groups on the Add-Ins tab displaying legacy add-ins can only be on that tab or in the Quick Access Toolbar.

You are also not able to change the order of Microsoft tabs and groups in their default location. That means, for example, that you cannot place the Create tab before the Home tab. It also means that you cannot change the order of the groups originally placed on the Home tab by Microsoft. Hence Views will always be before Clipboard. You can, however, place a group not originally on a tab anywhere on that tab. For example, the Tables group of the Create tab can be placed anywhere you choose on the Home tab.

Using As Little Space As Possible

Space is at a premium on a tab. Microsoft groups will shrink in size and make space available for your groups (to see this effect, just slowly make a window narrower and watch what happens to the Ribbon). You cannot shrink your own groups automatically, though. If your group uses a lot of space, this means that one or more MS groups shrink if the screen resolution is 1024×768, which is the screen resolution you should target in a noncontrolled situation. As MS groups shrink, however, the user has to click twice to get to the same functionality that he or she could get to with one click before your add-in was added. If your add-in uses space too freely and forces the user to click too much, the user might just get annoyed with your add-in and uninstall it. Remember that space is at a premium, and it is your job to use it wisely. Also, remember that yours might not be the only add-in on any particular tab using space. You should consider using a `menuButton`, `splitButton`, or `dynamicMenu` for all your functionality to consume as little space as possible.

Adding Your Functionality Only Once

There really is no need to put your functionality in more than one place, except if you are working with some contextual tabs. For example, the Format contextual tab is repeated almost identically for SmartArt graphics, charts, and shapes. If your add-in extends the functionality offered on a particular tab, you should add it to all similar tabs.

However, there is no reason to put your functionality on two regular tabs. Put it only in one.

Changing Visibility

You can change the visibility of tabs, groups, and controls dynamically. Don't. If you go through the Office UI, you should notice that no group, tab, or control ever disappears or appears magically. If something is not available, it is visible but not enabled. The rule is this: from the time you open a particular Ribbon to the time you close it, the visibility of your items should not change (although there are some exceptions, which I mention toward the end of this section). Do not change the visibility of your controls ever during runtime. You should determine the visibility once and then leave it at that. As an example, the Ink group on the Review tab is only visible if you have a Tablet PC, but this visibility is never altered during runtime. Office determines at startup whether you have a Tablet PC or not and sets the visibility accordingly.

Why should you not change the visibility? The Ribbon UI is all about the user finding features. If your UI elements are visible, but not enabled, the user knows that the functionality is there, but that he or she cannot use it currently. If your UI elements are not visible, the user will go searching for them and become frustrated. Your user will even be more frustrated if one time the elements are suddenly there and another time they are not. Remember that whether something is visible or not might be logical to you (as it is context dependent and you know what the context is), but to your user this might be totally random and serve as a source of frustration.

There are exceptions to the rule, of course. It could be that a certain user action triggers a fundamental change. For example, you might require the user to log in somewhere, and after a successful login, a lot more functionality is available to the user. This is a situation you should try to avoid, but it would be a case where you might be able to get away with changing the visibility during runtime. Creating your own "fake" custom contextual tab set is also an example. You cannot create an actual contextual tab set, but you can fake it by changing the visibility of a core tab based on the context, and potentially switching to that tab.

If you decide to hide certain elements of your add-in's UI via RibbonX, you should also disable all those elements. In the case of a group or tab, you should also disable every single control in the group or tab. The reason is that invisible controls are still accessible to the user via the Quick Access Toolbar and its customization dialog box. That means a user could add a control of yours to the Quick Access Toolbar, and it would be available to him or her even when you explicitly hide it. The only way to prevent the user from using a hidden control therefore is to ensure that it is also disabled.

Changing UI Elements Dynamically

You might want to change UI elements dynamically in a rather drastic manner. Again, don't. Look at the Office UI itself and you will see that no group (including all controls, labels, and icons) ever changes during runtime. The reason is the same as with the visibility issue.

If you have to change your UI dynamically, do what Office does: change a menu. You might notice that the menus that you can open from the Ribbon buttons change their content frequently, yet the buttons themselves stay. You can do the same by using a `dynamicMenu`.

To sum up: leave your groups and controls visible and unchanged during runtime. Use a `dynamicMenu` to deal with dynamic UI modifications.

Adding to the Office Button Menu

Again, the Office button menu is no place to simply advertise your add-in. Add commands to it if your add-in affects the entire database. As you can see from the built-in menu, commands for sharing, printing, sending, saving, and opening are there instead of in the tabs.

Using Custom Task Panes

According to the Office UI style guide (`http://www.microsoft.com/downloads/details.aspx?FamilyID=19e3bf38-434b-4ddd-9592-3749f6647105`), if "your solution needs to present data about a document that is required to be visible, in a nonmodal fashion, use a custom task pane. However, only display this task pane based on user actions. Also use one if you need to use custom controls that are outside of the Ribbon control set."

No Surprises

The Office UI style guide summarizes this one best: "Task panes or dialogs do not appear automatically on document open. Only user actions should open and close task panes or dialogs. Ideally, all task panes are opened using a button in the Ribbon. For example, clicking the launcher button on the Clipboard group opens and closes the Clipboard task pane."

Switching a Tab

You should only trigger a tab switch if you are creating your own fake contextual tab set. Triggering a tab switch requires you to send the KeyTip as keyboard input for it to Access. This is rather problematic, as different locales provide different KeyTips, and other add-ins might request the same KeyTip as yours. Avoid doing this except in a controlled situation.

Making Your Tab the First Tab

Office does not necessarily treat the Microsoft Home tab as the Home tab (that is, the one it shows at startup and returns to by default). Rather, the first tab is treated as such. That means you could create your own tab and put it in order before the Home tab using `insertBeforeIdMso="Home"`. The answer to when you should do this should be rather clear by now: never, except in a controlled situation, and even then very sparingly (such as the situation where your application is based on an Office application).

Summary

The Ribbon gives you a very flexible way to create a navigation structure for your Access (and Office) 2007 applications, and the guidelines are really there to assist you and your users to make best use of the interface and navigation tools. Following the "rules" means that in many cases Office 2007 users will already be familiar with Ribbons and should have little trouble taking advantage of any custom navigation you implement.

Index

■N

Find it faster at http://superindex.apress.com/

X

XML, brief overview, 21–24

XML configuration file, for recognizing data collection e-mails, 84

XML data, for a data collection task, 74–75

XML data collection file, table of tags and their meanings, 80–81

XML documents
structure of, 23–24
XML relationships in containers for, 25–26

XML field data, creating, 80–82

XML file
breaking down recipients section of, 78
contains data used for a table, 36
elements and attributes of, 75–76
structure of simple, 23–24

XML tutorial, website address for, 42

XMLDataSource connector, provided by Web Dev Express, 306

.xoml filename extension, for Workflow file to be edited, 298

XPath, website address for overview of, 77

XSD file
contains schema for a table, 36
defined, 36

Z

ZIP package, as parts container in Access XML structure, 25–26

You Need the Companion eBook

Your purchase of this book entitles you to buy the companion PDF-version eBook for only $10. Take the weightless companion with you anywhere.

We believe this Apress title will prove so indispensable that you'll want to carry it with you everywhere, which is why we are offering the companion eBook (in PDF format) for $10 to customers who purchase this book now. Convenient and fully searchable, the PDF version of any content-rich, page-heavy Apress book makes a valuable addition to your programming library. You can easily find and copy code—or perform examples by quickly toggling between instructions and the application. Even simultaneously tackling a donut, diet soda, and complex code becomes simplified with hands-free eBooks!

Once you purchase your book, getting the $10 companion eBook is simple:

❶ Visit **www.apress.com/promo/tendollars/**.

❷ Complete a basic registration form to receive a randomly generated question about this title.

❸ Answer the question correctly in 60 seconds, and you will receive a promotional code to redeem for the $10.00 eBook.

2560 Ninth Street • Suite 219 • Berkeley, CA 94710

eBookshop

ASP **Today**

Apress®
THE EXPERT'S VOICE™

Offer valid through 10/07.